Concise
American Composition
and Rhetoric

Donald Davidson

Professor of English
Vanderbilt University

Charles Scribner's Sons
New York

CONCISE
AMERICAN COMPOSITION
AND RHETORIC

PREFACE

This concise edition of *American Composition and Rhetoric* is intended for courses in which rhetoric, considered as the art of writing, is given positive emphasis. It is adapted for use either in courses where a separate textbook of rhetoric is desired to accompany and reinforce one of the standard handbooks or in those courses in which rhetoric is the major concern, and a handbook is used only for reference or not at all. I have therefore omitted from this shortened edition the "Concise Handbook" that has been a part of *American Composition and Rhetoric* in its previous editions. Also I have reduced the number of illustrative selections to the minimum needed for close study as models and have condensed the accompanying instructional text at various points. In this process I have used the opportunity to make some fairly extensive revisions, especially in Chapter 5, "The Sentence"; Chapter 6, "Words"; and Chapter 8, "The Research Paper." "The Review" and "The Critical Essay" are now combined as parts of "Project 5: Criticism" in Chapter 3, "Expository Writing." Descriptive and narrative writing are treated in a final chapter.

The book in which these changes are embodied does not, of course, propose to be a replacement for the regular comprehensive edition of *American Composition and Rhetoric*. It simply applies on a somewhat reduced scale the principles followed in the larger book. Within its dimensions it represents continued adherence to the views set forth in the Preface to the Fourth Edition of that book as to the general educational value of rhetoric as a cultural subject; the close alliance of rhetoric with the "grammar" of the written and not merely the spoken language; the need for prose models of enduring merit and of more than topical interest; and above all the supreme worth of the "positive" rather than the merely corrective approach to the study of rhetoric.

With these principles in mind, I have retained for this edition certain highly teachable selections that in a literary and rhetorical sense are still classics, even in an age when steamboats are obsolete, when the long scythe seldom whispers to the ground, and when the deafening snarl of the chain-saw is heard in the mountains far more often than the howl of the wolf. So, for example, the selections from Mark Twain, Belloc, Leopold, and Parkman once more appear in their old places; but many other selections, major and minor, long and short, are new to this edition. Varied and substantial exercise materials are provided throughout the book.

Again I owe expressions of gratitude to various friends who have made suggestions or given other valuable assistance during the preparation of earlier editions of *American Composition and Rhetoric*. For help in preparing this particular edition I am deeply grateful to my colleague, Professor Herschel Gower, director of freshman English at Vanderbilt University, by whose counsel and experience I have benefited immeasurably. For brilliant and expert assistance on the problems of the research paper I am indebted to Mr. Thomas Inge, of the Vanderbilt English Department. I wish to express my sincere thanks also to Professor James Tate Stewart, of Furman University, and other colleagues in various parts of the United States and Canada who have been kind enough to give me useful criticisms and suggestions.

D. D.

Vanderbilt University
Nashville, Tennessee

CONTENTS

*Contents*ix

- "The True Origin of Academic Freedom" by Russell Kirk 314
  [from *Academic Freedom*]
Freedom of Speech: Two Supreme Court Opinions   318

10. DESCRIPTIVE AND NARRATIVE WRITING   324

1. DESCRIPTIVE WRITING   325

"Overlooking Maggie" by Arnold Bennett   327
[from *The Old Wives' Tale*]

"Manhattan from the Bay" by Walt Whitman   329
[from *Specimen Days in America*]

"The Valley of the Great Dairies" by Thomas Hardy   330
[from *Tess of the D'Urbervilles*]

"Peggotty's House" by Charles Dickens   332
[from *David Copperfield*]

"In the Misses Morkan's Drawing-Room" by James Joyce   333
[from *Dubliners*]

"The House of Usher" by Edgar Allan Poe   334
[from "The Fall of the House of Usher"]

"Army Breaking Camp" by Robert Penn Warren   335
[from *Wilderness: A Tale of the Civil War*]

"Captain Ahab" by Herman Melville   337
[from *Moby Dick*]

"At the American Consulate" by Elizabeth Spencer   339
[from *The Light in the Piazza*]

"Hurricane" by Frances Woodward   342
[from *The Atlantic Monthly*]

"Lake Erie" by Harlan Hatcher   343
[from *Lake Erie*]

2. NARRATIVE WRITING   346

"The Run on the Cherokee Strip" by Marquis James   357
[from *The Cherokee Strip*]

"The Lieutenant Escapes" by Ernest Hemingway   362
[from *A Farewell to Arms*]

THE SHORT STORY   365

"The Last Day in the Field" by Caroline Gordon   374
[from *The Forest of the South*]

INDEX   385

CHAPTER 1

THE STUDY OF COMPOSITION
AND RHETORIC

THE colonists who landed at Jamestown in 1607 and at Plymouth in 1620 spoke and wrote the English of Shakespeare and Milton—that is, the language of their own age, the "Elizabethan English" of city or country, pulpit or university, palace or tavern. With the advent of these and later colonists the language of the North American continent began the series of changes that today differentiates "American" from "British" English. Noah Webster, maker of the first great American dictionary, went so far in 1789 as to argue that the people of the newly formed republic of the United States ought "to have a system of our own in language as well as in government." Thomas Jefferson, the studious third president of the United States, argued—though he was learned in the classical languages—for a deeper penetration into the Anglo-Saxon base of English. The study of Anglo-Saxon, Jefferson held, would not only enable us to "read Shakespeare and Milton with a superior degree of intelligence and delight"; it would also improve contemporary English.

Whatever weight one may give to such views, it is clear that the study of composition and rhetoric in twentieth-century America must deal with a language that, in a thoroughly realistic sense, is "American English." From Hudson Bay to the Gulf of Mexico, this English, in all its local varieties, is the highly flexible medium we use in American situations unlike any Webster or Jefferson knew.

It is equally clear that the instrument of language is very old and that the principles of good writing are universal. In some high sense the study of writing must be what it has always been—a study of the proper and persuasive use of

1

language and of the thought which uses language as its instrument.

In former times college students were likely to be concerned much more with spoken discourse than with written discourse. They studied rhetoric, in the old sense of the word, rather than writing. The word *rhetoric* comes from a Greek word meaning "orator," and the study of rhetoric was for many centuries mainly a study of oratory, or of a composition that imitated oratory. For better or worse, we have discarded the standards which, even as late as the time of Washington and Jefferson, put the emphasis on oral rather than on written performance. Today we study composition *and* rhetoric—or the principles of correct and effective writing.

Without laboring too much over definitions, we may say that *composition* refers chiefly to structural arrangement, organization, the putting together of parts to make a whole; and that *rhetoric* refers to the skill or artifice used in making the composition persuasive and effective. The study of these closely allied subjects rests upon a knowledge of grammar and usage; it must also make full use of the resources of logic.

The subject matter of composition and rhetoric is not as solid and precise as the subject matter of physical science, or history, or any other "content course." Nevertheless, the foundation is still knowledge—knowledge that must be acquired and mastered before the instrument of language can be used successfully in writing. Primarily, this means knowledge of language itself. The student must go beyond the uncritical knowledge of words that he has had ever since he began to talk. He must make his knowledge systematic and discriminating. To his earlier knowledge of grammar he is expected to add a comprehension of the part that grammar plays in fixing meaning and relationship. He should be in a position to realize that words do not change their forms or take certain prescribed groupings without reason, but that such changes and groupings are inherited conveniences which may serve, like traffic signs, to guide his thought. He should now learn that the correctness of this or that form depends not upon a grammarian's whim but upon a tradition of usage that grammar merely attempts to describe. The vocabulary of English, he should see, is a rich and varied store of words, his racial inheritance, a public treasury of language from which he can take according to his needs; and he can be sure that every conscious effort he makes to increase his private store is a step toward making his knowledge actually useful.

All this, however, is merely a knowledge of instruments. In the study of composition and rhetoric the emphasis will not be merely on *what* the student knows of grammar or language, but rather on *how* that knowledge may be used to express thought. A prose composition is language, grammar, mechanics brought to life and put into action by well-controlled thought and feeling. Only thus can writing have meaning and effect. Only thus can the student employ his knowledge intelligently and purposively. It is not enough to write a grammatical sentence, although that is the first requirement. A good writer must know *how* and *why* this correct grammatical expression is more or less useful than another one, equally correct. He must know *how* some words behave in a given passage and *why*, if put into another context, they change the meaning of what is said. In short, he must learn to command his resources rather than merely possess them.

TWO KINDS OF RESOURCES

Every student should possess and command two kinds of resources: first, the resources that belong to him as an individual—a person unique, peculiar, apart from other individuals; second, the resources that are common to all educated persons and that represent an inheritance stored up for everybody's use. The first kind may be called personal; the second, traditional.

The student's personal resources at a given moment are a compound of his native gifts and his education up to that point. Whether he can write well depends in part upon the talents he was born with and in part upon the use that he has made of his education, in school and out of school. No doubt he excels in some things and is weak in other things. He has had a good teacher one year, a poor or uninspiring teacher another year. He was born into a bookish family and found it the most natural thing in the world to write well; or perhaps he has had to struggle against a distaste for books and writing. Possibly he is weak in grammar, but he has a fine flow of words. Or he can write easily but never could spell. He has travelled much, or he has stayed at home. He has certain pronounced likes and dislikes, or is indifferent, or is bored. He is going to be an engineer, a lawyer, a doctor, a scholar; or he is just improving his mind.

Since the student is going to be required to use his full store of personal resources, this is a good time for him to take inventory of what he has. Where is he strong? Where is he weak? The instructor will find out in time. Perhaps the instructor will bring to light points of strength or weakness that he never dreamed of. That is part of the aim of a course in writing. The student should realize that, although he is a member of a class and will be asked to follow out a uniform system of instruction, it is not the purpose of the system to curb his individuality, but rather to bring it out. He is expected to remain an individual, to draw upon his own store of ideas and experiences, to look within himself, to reflect and ponder, indeed continually to explore himself and rediscover himself. If he does this, what he writes will be his, and his only.

But it would be a hardship if he were forced to rely altogether upon himself, with no help from without. It is true that power of self-expression is one of the objects of his study. It is true that he can teach himself a great deal— true even that in the end he will really learn only what, under guidance, he has taught himself. Yet self-expression might become a disaster, not a privilege, if we had to stand always alone and be forever original. He who rebels against grammar might think better of grammarians if he had to make up his own grammar from the beginning. The student may congratulate himself that most of the hardest work has already been done, and done for him. For instance, he does not have to invent a language. That has already been attended to, though perhaps not completely. The grammar is there, too, well enough established at all but a few doubtful points. The dictionaries are there, with more words than any single individual can ever command. The writings of all the world, the full resources of a library, the living world of periodicals and books—these are waiting to be taken and used. And one of the great rewards of a course in composition and rhetoric is that it increases a student's understanding and appreciation of books and ideas. Whether he learns to write brilliantly or just moderately well, he will have a keener eye for all sorts of writing than if he had never himself attempted to write at all.

Such are the resources of tradition. They belong to all humanity. In laying hold upon them, the student takes up his rightful inheritance. He is carried by the united strength of all civilization. Not in one year or in many years can he master all that tradition has stored up. But it is of great importance at the beginning of a composition course to understand the proper use of traditional resources. They are found in a convenient form in the dictionary, which the student must consult and ought to own; in the textbook, which is an ordered selection from the vast accumulated resources of tradition—a selection made in the light of contemporary needs; and in books of reference of all sorts.

Most important of all resources are the works of writers— British, American, classical—who form our literary tradition. It is not likely that a student who is unwilling to read will ever be able to make the best possible use of his powers as a writer, no matter whether his powers are large or small. It is advisable to lay out a course of reading over and above class requirements and to follow it up systematically.

Yet good reading alone does not make good writing. We learn by doing. The composition is the thought made into the deed. The student must begin to write before he knows all that there is to know about writing. The natural subject for him to begin with is a subject on which he is an authority— himself.

THE AUTOBIOGRAPHY

An autobiographical theme is likely to be one of the early assignments in a composition course. The instructor has his purpose in making such an assignment. He wishes to know the members of the class as persons, rather than as mere names on a roll. The writing of an autobiography is naturally a solitary task, and the reading of it by the instructor may be assumed to be private and sympathetic. The student is expected to introduce himself confidentially to his instructor, and the presumption is that he will wish to make the most of his opportunity, which will not come often in a lifetime.

Aside from that fairly exciting possibility, the assignment reminds the student that his own experience is probably the most important source of material for his themes. Later he will go to sources outside himself. Now he turns to what is most familiar—his personal experience.

As it exists in his mind, however, it may be vague and shapeless. His problem is to give that experience a significant shape. He cannot tell everything. He must select what will represent him as he would wish to be represented—those parts of his experience which actually go together to make a unified composition.

An aimless chronicle of events from birth to entrance into college will not have shape. An autobiography is not a dry collection of data: "Born at Stroudsburg, Kansas, 1947. Father's occupation, banking. Church, Presbyterian. Attended grade school and high school at Stroudsburg. Had an operation for appendicitis in my junior year at high school and so failed to make the basketball team. Made it in my senior year. Also edited school paper. Best grades, in history. Disliked mathematics and Latin. Expect to major in economics."

Even if expanded into a thousand words, such an account would be dull. From it, the writer would discover nothing new about writing or about himself. The first problem is to find significant events and put the insignificant ones aside. Look back, consider what has been decisive in your life history. What singular chain of events has brought you into a college composition class in this year and place? What facts, what experiences, what influences will you emphasize? What is it that the world has never understood in you? There are various ways of answering such questions effectively and honestly.

You may decide to make your autobiography a character study. If so, single out some dominant trait and arrange your autobiography around it. Or you may have a queer mixture of traits. Are you lazy, and yet well-meaning? Do you have a turn for music or painting or mechanics? Have you had to fight bashfulness, or are you a pre-eminently social creature? Whatever the trait that you select, centralize your autobiography about it. If you have been a bashful person, show how your bashfulness affected your life: perhaps it kept you in a corner with a book when others were at play; perhaps you overcame it when you decided to go out for the team or work in dramatics. If you have no exceptional traits, make that fact your story; explain what it means to be "just average."

You may prefer to dwell upon background and influences. Did you have to overcome certain obstacles in coming to college? If you had to fight poverty, show how, step by step, you won the fight. Has the life of some region or locality been the dominant fact in your life? Is it a Western ranch, a Southern farm, a Pennsylvania mining town, a great metropolis? Have you been influenced by some friend or relative? Have you modelled your life after some personal hero?

As a third choice, you may select some event that changed your life—a fire, a flood, a long illness, a trip, a friendship, a sudden removal of your family to some new place, a revelation, at some critical moment, of what you could and would do.

The second problem is how to arrange your sketch: where to begin, where to end, what to do in between. If your autobiography is a character sketch, you may begin with some early incident that illustrates your dominant trait (stubbornness, resourcefulness, bookishness, or the like), and then show how this trait has affected your career. The order of time will give you a good arrangement if you wish to show the influence of some friend; up to the time of your meeting with him, your life was thus and so, and afterwards it was —whatever it was. If you concentrate on some event, you may begin with it, relate it in some detail, and then explain how it has affected your life. Or you may reverse this order: show yourself, in a snapshot, as you are now, and then give the events or analyze the causes that explain the portrait. The easiest plan is to give a brief sketch that "places" you as a person and then to deal with experiences that you deem important. If you follow this plan, you must not ramble. Make your selected material lead to some clearly defined estimate of yourself.

The third problem is language. Write as simply and directly as you can. Do not try to be pretentious. Do not be flippant. Be plain and straightforward.

The pronoun *I* will naturally appear in your personal history. Do not shrink from it. It is not an indelicate word. Autobiographies are generally written in the first person. Their chief value is often in their frankness, and frankness is not egotism.

On the other hand, you may assume the mask of the third person if you wish. You may gain a perspective by writing as if your story were the story of somebody else whom you are studying, for the moment, a little critically.

THE BOYS' AMBITION[1]   *by Samuel L. Clemens*

WHEN I was a boy, there was but one permanent ambition among
my comrades in our village on the west bank of the Mississippi
River. That was, to be a steamboatman. We had transient ambitions of other sorts, but they were only transient. When a circus
came and went, it left us all burning to become clowns; the first
negro minstrel show that ever came to our section left us all suffering to try that kind of life; now and then we had a hope that,
if we lived and were good, God would permit us to be pirates. These
ambitions faded out, each in its turn; but the ambition to be a
steamboatman always remained.

Once a day a cheap, gaudy packet arrived upward from St. Louis,
and another downward from Keokuk. Before these events, the
day was glorious with expectancy; after them, the day was a dead
and empty thing. Not only the boys, but the whole village, felt
this. After all these years I can picture that old time to myself now,
just as it was then: the white town drowsing in the sunshine of
a summer's morning; the streets empty, or pretty nearly so; one
or two clerks sitting in front of the Water Street stores, with their
splint-bottomed chairs tilted back against the walls, chins on
breasts, hats slouched over their faces, asleep—with shingle-shav-
ings enough around to show what broke them down; a sow and a
litter of pigs loafing along the sidewalk, doing a good business in
watermelon rinds and seeds; two or three lonely little freight piles
scattered about the "levee"; a pile of "skids" on the slope of the
stone-paved wharf, and the fragrant town drunkard asleep in the
shadow of them; two or three wood flats at the head of the wharf,
but nobody to listen to the peaceful lapping of the wavelets against
them; the great Mississippi, the majestic, the magnificent Mississippi, rolling its mile-wide tide along, shining in the sun; the
dense forest away on the other side; the "point" above the town,
and the "point" below, bounding the river-glimpse and turning it
into a sort of sea, and withal a very still and brilliant and lonely
one. Presently a film of dark smoke appears above one of those
remote "points"; instantly a negro drayman, famous for his quick
eye and prodigious voice, lifts up the cry, "S-t-e-a-m-boat a-comin'!"
and the scene changes! The town drunkard stirs, the clerks wake
up, a furious clatter of drays follows, every house and store pours
out a human contribution, and all in a twinkling the dead town
is alive and moving. Drays, carts, men, boys, all go hurrying from
many quarters to a common center, the wharf. Assembled there,
the people fasten their eyes upon the coming boat as upon a wonder they are seeing for the first time. And the boat *is* rather a
handsome sight, too. She is long and sharp and trim and pretty;
she has two tall, fancy-topped chimneys, with a gilded device of

---

[1] From *Life on the Mississippi*.

some kind swung between them; a fanciful pilot-house, all glass and "gingerbread," perched on top of the "texas" deck behind them; the paddle-boxes are gorgeous with a picture or with gilded rays above the boat's name; the boiler-deck, the hurricane-deck, and the texas deck are fenced and ornamented with clean white railings; there is a flag gallantly flying from the jack-staff; the furnace doors are open and the fires glaring bravely; the upper decks are black with passengers; the captain stands by the big bell, calm, imposing, the envy of all; great volumes of the blackest smoke are rolling and tumbling out of the chimneys—a husbanded grandeur created with a bit of pitch-pine just before arriving at a town; the crew are grouped on the forecastle; the broad stage is run far out over the port bow, and an envied deck-hand stands picturesquely on the end of it with a coil of rope in his hand; the pent steam is screaming through the gauge-cocks; the captain lifts his hand, a bell rings, the wheels stop; then they turn back, churning the water to foam, and the steamer is at rest. Then such a scramble as there is to get aboard, and to get ashore, and to take in freight and to discharge freight, all at one and the same time; and such a yelling and cursing as the mates facilitate it all with! Ten minutes later the steamer is under way again, with no flag on the jack-staff and no black smoke issuing from the chimneys. After ten more minutes the town is dead again, and the town drunkard asleep by the skids once more.

My father was a justice of the peace, and I supposed he possessed the power of life and death over all men, and could hang anybody that offended him. This was distinction enough for me as a general thing; but the desire to be a steamboatman kept intruding, nevertheless. I first wanted to be a cabinboy, so that I could come out with a white apron on and shake a tablecloth over the side, where all my old comrades could see me; later I thought I would rather be the deck-hand who stood on the end of the stage-plank with the coil or rope in his hand because he was particularly conspicuous. But these were only day-dreams—they were too heavenly to be contemplated as real possibilities. By and by one of our boys went away. He was not heard of for a long time. At last he turned up as apprentice engineer or "striker" on a steamboat. This thing shook the bottom out of all my Sunday-school teachings. That boy had been notoriously worldly, and I just the reverse; yet he was exalted to this eminence, and I left in obscurity and misery. There was nothing generous about this fellow in his greatness. He would always manage to have a rusty bolt to scrub while his boat tarried at our town, and he would sit on the inside guard and scrub it, where we all could see him and envy him and loathe him. And whenever his boat was laid up he would come home and swell around the town in his blackest and greasiest clothes, so that nobody could help remembering that he was a steamboatman; and he used all sorts of steamboat technicalities in his talk, as if he were so used to them that he forgot common people could not understand them. He would speak of the "labbord" side of a horse in an easy, natural way that would make one wish he was dead. And he was always talking about "St. Looy" like an old citizen; he would refer casually to occasions when he was "coming down Fourth Street," or when he was "passing by the Planter's House," or when there was a fire and he took a turn on the brakes of "the old Big Missouri"; and then he would go on and lie about how many towns the size of ours were burned down there that day. Two or three of the boys had long been persons of consideration among us because they had been to St. Louis once and had a vague general knowledge of its wonders, but the day of their glory was over now. They lapsed into a humble silence, and learned to disappear when the ruthless "cub"-engineer approached. This fellow had money, too, and hair-oil. Also an ignorant silver watch and a showy brass watch-chain. He wore a leather belt and used no suspenders. If ever a youth was cordially admired and hated by his comrades, this was one. No girl could withstand his charms. He "cut out" every boy in the village. When his boat blew up at last, it diffused a tranquil contentment among us such as we had not known for months. But when he came home the next week, alive, renowned, and appeared in church all battered up and bandaged, a shining hero, stared at and wondered over by everybody, it seemed to us that the partiality of Providence for an undeserving reptile had reached a point where it was open to criticism.

This creature's career could produce but one result, and it speedily followed. Boy after boy managed to get on the river. The minister's son became an engineer. The doctor's son and the postmaster's sons became "mud clerks"; the wholesale liquor dealer's son became a barkeeper on a boat; four sons of the chief merchant, and two sons of the county judge, became pilots. Pilot was the grandest position of all. The pilot, even in those days of trivial wages, had a princely salary—from a hundred and fifty to two hundred and fifty dollars a month, and no board to pay. Two months of his wages would pay a preacher's salary for a year. Now some of us were left disconsolate. We could not get on the river—at least our parents would not let us.

So, by and by, I ran away. I said I would never come home again till I was a pilot and could come in glory. But somehow I could not manage it. I went meekly aboard a few of the boats that lay packed together like sardines at the long St. Louis wharf, and humbly inquired for the pilots, but got only a cold shoulder and short words from mates and clerks. I had to make the best of this sort of treatment for the time being, but I had comforting daydreams of a future when I should be a great and honored pilot, with plenty of money, and could kill some of these mates and clerks and pay for them.

EXERCISES

1. What indications of time and place does Clemens make? Where do these indications appear? What is the importance of such indications in a reminiscence of this kind? Does the fact that steamboats are long out of date and that Samuel Langhorne Clemens ("Mark Twain") was born at Hannibal, Missouri, in 1835 diminish the validity and general effectiveness of this account?

2. Where is the theme, or central idea, of "The Boys' Ambition" first stated? Is it repeated or restated elsewhere?

3. What relation do the successive divisions of "The Boys' Ambition" have to the central idea? Is the elaborate description of the packet (beginning, "She is long and sharp . . .") a digression from the main theme or does it give the reminiscence an accent or enrichment that we find helpful and pleasant?

4. Is the word *packet* now in use in the meaning intended by Clemens? List other terms in this selection that apply to steamboating in some technical sense. Which are obsolete? Which are still in currency? Is the diction of this selection too technical for the general reader? To what extent does the effectiveness of the writing depend upon sharp visual images or other images that are sensory?

5. Why does Clemens dwell with humorous emphasis upon the career of the boy who "went away?" List some phrases or passages that derive their effectiveness from humorous exaggeration.

SUGGESTIONS FOR THEMES

The following titles are intended to suggest ways in which the assignment in autobiography may be treated. Use one of these titles or devise a similar one for your theme.

Then Father Was Sent Abroad	I Took the Advice
Up from Suburbia	Month of Decision
My New England (or Western or Southern) Slant	Now It's My Turn
	A Cadillac Farmer's Son
The Code of an Ex-Teen-Age Gangster	As the Twig Is Bent
	Father Is a Bureaucrat
My Lucky Star	A Wish Fulfilled

CHAPTER 2

THE COMPOSITION

1. THE PROBLEM

WRITING is a method of communicating thought. It is not the only method. There are situations in which a glance may mean more than words. Gestures and actions often communicate thought. The American Indians had a sign language which could be understood by all tribes. Many people believe that thought can be conveyed telepathically. Speech is the commonest means of communication. If, however, our conversations were reported stenographically or recorded by a dictaphone, we might be surprised to find out how fragmentary our actual spoken words are, when not accompanied by the smiles, nods, winks, finger-pointings, or shoulder-shrugs that we use in talking. It is a common saying that a Frenchman cannot carry on a conversation if his hands are tied.

That old joke will serve to illustrate the handicap under which we all suffer when we come to write our thoughts instead of speaking them. Our hands are tied—except as we use them to shape letters and words. We may write with a twinkle of the eye, or with an angry set of the jaw. We may, as we write, metaphorically saw the air with our hands. But the reader of the writing will see only the words on the page. The page will convey only what the words convey. If, therefore, you wish a reader to infer the twinkle in your eye, you must impart your good humor through the words that you write. This is the first thing to remember. You are limited by the written, typed, or printed page. Do not read into your writing an emotion or an idea which you have not actually put there, and do not expect anyone to read into your composition something that is not there.

But this limitation is not a disadvantage. Writing has a definiteness that other kinds of communication do not have. For this reason, contracts are put into written form, and the wisdom of generations, as well as yesterday's news, is not left to hearsay but is printed in books and periodicals. And writing can be definite, because both thought and words can be changed, restated, rewritten, until the writer has found a way to convey his thought exactly as he wishes. In short, writing can be controlled almost perfectly. And it can be controlled the more readily because it can be done in private, away from distraction and excitement, and because, through the device of the written word, a man can see his thought on the page before him, in a shape that he can handle, reconsider, criticize.

We may therefore state the general problem of the writer as a problem of control. The President addressing Congress and the freshman writing his first theme must both face this problem. And in order to gain control, all writers must ask two questions: (1) *What* do I wish to say? (2) *How* shall I say it?

To the beginner the problem generally comes as a task imposed upon him. He must write a theme, somehow or other, because the instructor says so. Then all at once a number of questions assail him. What subject shall I choose? How shall I begin? How much shall I write? What shall I put in? What shall I leave out? May I write in my own words—plainly? Or must I try to be literary? May I write to please myself, or must I write to please the instructor?

The answer to such questions is: That depends! Nothing can be decided until the aim of the writing is fixed. Until you are sure what game you are seeking, you will not know whether to take rifle, shotgun, steel trap, or rod and reel into the woods.

Suppose a friend invites you to attend a house party in a distant city and asks for an answer by telegraph. And suppose that your engagements prevent you from accepting. If you had time to write a letter, you could be expansive and intimate. You could say, "Charlie, my friend, you know how it is with me these days. I should like very much to come. I always enjoy your parties. But I am sorry to say that I have a previous engagement and can't get out of it." But the telegram allows you only fifteen words. Without much hesitation you write: VERY MUCH REGRET THAT ON

ACCOUNT OF A PREVIOUS ENGAGEMENT I AM NOT ABLE TO ACCEPT YOUR KIND INVITATION. You see that this first draft counts to nineteen words. You meet the emergency by striking out the article A and by substituting GREATLY for VERY MUCH, BECAUSE OF for ON ACCOUNT OF, UNABLE for NOT ABLE.

Your purpose here is to communicate a bare fact with a slight flavor of politeness. These factors guided your decisions: (1) a fifteen-word limit; (2) the necessity of being polite. All else is dismissed from consideration. You do not have to invent a formula of expression. Etiquette prescribes the formula: "greatly regret . . . previous engagement." You are governed by the principles of economy and politeness.

At the opposite extreme from the telegram is such a large prose work as Charles and Mary Beard's *The Rise of American Civilization*. In this task the authors had to accept certain limitations: (1) the objective content of the subject —actual events of American history from colonial times to our times, and (2) the order of presentation—which is the order of the events of American history. The authors were free to decide other questions: how much space to give to various events; whether to write in a plain style, or in an elaborate literary style, such as Edward Gibbon uses in *The Decline and Fall of the Roman Empire;* how far to go in making historical interpretations, and how far to depend on mere statement of facts; and above all, what interpretation to make.

In making such decisions, Charles and Mary Beard had a guiding purpose: to emphasize the role of social and economic forces in shaping the course of American civilization. Reading their version of American history, we find— possibly with some surprise—that they pass rather lightly over the battles and heroes of the Revolutionary period. Instead, they stress the economic causes behind great events and the social results of great men's thoughts and acts. Thus they differ from some older historians who dwell on Lexington, Concord, and Valley Forge and from later ones, like Frederick J. Turner, who may emphasize the role of the frontier. The organization of their "composition," their selection of material, their concern with interpretation rather than with mere facts, the tone of their writing, even to some extent their vocabulary—all are determined by their guiding purpose.

Some writing is as simple as the writing of a telegram. It follows a formula and requires a minimum of decision on the part of the writer. Much scientific and practical writing is of this baldly functional sort. A laboratory manual prescribes the form in which you record your experiment, provides the terms to be used, and enforces rigid economy of language. Technical reports, business letters, some kinds of written examinations, all have their own strict patterns, which have to be followed obediently. Such writing is said to be *conventionalized* or *stylized.*

Most writing is not strictly conventional. On the contrary, it puts upon the writer the responsibility of choosing the means to obtain a desired end. Whether long or short, simple or complex, the written composition takes the shape that the writer gives it. Although there are certain broad patterns and formulas (like those which distinguish prose from verse or the short story from the essay), the writer is not in general held down to prescriptions like those of the laboratory workbook or the business letter. But he will not really enjoy his freedom or be able to use it effectively if he does not master the principles of good writing. His concern is with principles rather than with formulas. The first study is, therefore, the study of organization and of how the guiding purpose influences organization.

EXERCISES

1. Using as a model the above discussion of *The Rise of American Civilization,* analyze one of the following to show how the guiding purpose of the author determines general organization, selection of material, emphasis, and tone:

(a) an editorial in a daily newspaper; (b) a column on public affairs by some well-known commentator; (c) an article of opinion in some weekly magazine, in comparison with a news report.

2. How will your guiding purpose affect the length, subject matter, and tone of the following letters that we shall assume you are writing:

(a) to a friend at another college with whom you are planning a holiday trip; (b) to your father or mother, explaining your holiday plans; (c) to a travel agency, requesting information.

3. What patterns of stylization are observed in the following:

(a) a drill manual of one of the armed services; (b) a recipe in a cook book; (c) a laboratory manual in one of the natural sciences; (d) the weather report; (e) an invitation to some formal social occasion.

2. THE GUIDING PURPOSE

The first step in composition is, then, for the writer to decide what is his purpose. We often say to some vague talker, "I can't see what you are driving at!" Because he has failed to centralize his thought around one definite idea or guiding purpose, we are confused when we try to follow him. Every good composition must have a central idea at which the writer "drives." Probably the well-established custom of calling freshman compositions "themes" grew out of this first necessity. A "theme" is, technically, a limited aspect of a subject, a precise topic, a thesis: George Washington as a Farmer; What Is Streamlining in Automobile Construction? A Defense of Costume Jewelry; The Spirit of Texas. When you were asked, in the assignment in autobiography, to concentrate upon some character trait or some incident in your life, you were asked to choose a "theme." By an easy extension of the term, an exercise in writing upon a limited aspect of a subject is called a "theme."

Often a beginner in writing is asked to choose a small subject rather than a large one, or to deal with a phase of a subject rather than attempt massive generalizations. This is good advice, but it is only another way of emphasizing the need of staying within chosen limits. In "The Boys' Ambition," Samuel Clemens concentrates on one overwhelmingly important fact: steamboats were so captivating that every boy wanted to follow steamboating as a career. Everything else is omitted or is subordinated to that "theme."

Your limitation of a subject should be of precisely this kind. If you are interested in machinery, you have a vast field of opinion and fact from which to draw material; but you will not write a good composition if you begin with the vague idea of saying "something about machinery." Instead, choose a definite topic: the effect of the invention of the cotton gin upon the South; the difference between a machine and a tool; the beauty (or ugliness) of machinery; the operation of a particular machine—cotton gin, internal combustion engine, lawn mower, automatic elevator.

If you are thus to limit your subject, you must decide, *before you begin to write,* exactly what your guiding purpose is. It is best to state it briefly in written form, so that it stands before your eyes. This statement of the guiding purpose is often called the *theme sentence.* It should be *one* sentence, as simple and compact as you can make it. It should answer the question: "What am I trying to say in this composition?"

The guiding purpose of Clemens' "The Boys' Ambition" is to depict the exaggerated, romantic importance that the life of the steamboatman had to boys of his generation who lived on the banks of the Mississippi. The theme sentence for "The Boys' Ambition" might be: "The one permanent ambition of every boy in my village was to be a steamboatman."

If you are writing about the duties of a counselor at a summer camp, your guiding purpose may be stated as follows: "A counselor at a summer camp is not so much a teacher as he is an older brother to the boys under his charge." If you are dealing with George Washington as a farmer, rather than George Washington as a military commander or as President, your guiding purpose might take this form: "Like most Virginia landowners of his day, George Washington was a practical farmer."

Often the guiding purpose is stated in the first paragraph or somewhere near the beginning of the composition. It would be clumsy, of course, to say, "My guiding purpose is to . . ." or "In the following pages I intend to discuss. . . ." Generally, if it is used thus, the wording of the theme sentence will be less obtrusive. The first two sentences of Clemens' "The Boys' Ambition" are: "When I was a boy, there was but one permanent ambition among my comrades in our village on the west bank of the Mississippi River. That was, to be a steamboatman." Even if a statement of the guiding purpose does not appear near the beginning, the reader must feel that it is implied. In your early themes, it may be helpful to write a *separate* statement of your guiding purpose and to put it at the head of your theme, between the title and the first paragraph. Put it at the head of an outline, when you make an outline.

The guiding purpose, we should always remember, is the conscious determination of the writer to make every part of his writing move in *one* direction and conform to *one* clear intention. It is like a counselor who stands at the writer's elbow and helps him when he is in trouble. Since it marks for him the limits of discussion, it can be consulted on the always bothersome problem of where to begin and where to stop. Suppose your guiding purpose is to explain the operating principle of hydraulic brakes. You do not need to begin with the invention of the wheel; the wheel must be taken for granted—your subject is hydraulic brakes. Probably you will want to begin by explaining briefly that the principle of hydraulic brakes is based upon use of the force exerted by a liquid under pressure. You will stop when your explanation of hydraulic brakes is completed; you do not need to add, and should not add, a sales talk on your favorite automobile.

The guiding purpose is especially important in determining the selection of material—that is, what to put in and what to leave out. If your guiding purpose is to emphasize the "older brother" relationship that a summer camp counselor has to the boys in his charge, you will not tell how to get a job as a counselor; you will not discuss the duties of the director, the value of a summer camp for city boys, or the quantity and quality of the food served at such a camp. On the other hand, you may draw upon your own experiences as counselor, if some incident from your experience illustrates a point that you wish to make. You may refer, by way of contrast, to an unpopular counselor who was ineffective in his work because he failed to be an "older brother" and tried instead to be a kind of gang boss or top sergeant.

To a certain extent the guiding purpose will influence even the vocabulary of the composition, its tone, its mood, its style. An explanation of hydraulic brakes cannot easily be written in the vocabulary of William Faulkner or of William Shakespeare. It is a technical subject and requires the use of technical terms and straightforward language. On the other hand, if Stephen Leacock, Clarence Day, or James Thurber should happen to write about automobiles, we know that the treatment would be informal and probably humorous. The knock in the engine or the rasp of the brakes might become a point in a joke or in some humorous comment on the difficulties men and women have with machinery.

Unity in the Composition

Above all, the guiding purpose gives unity to the composition. It enables the writer to see his work as a whole and to make the subordinate parts of his composition take their proper places in that unified whole. With a clearly stated guiding purpose, the writing is not left to chance. The writer will not go from one thing to another merely because one thing suggests another, but he will pause to consider the newly suggested item. He will ask himself whether it does actually help him to carry out his purpose, and if it does not, he will exclude it, no matter how interesting it is. In short, the guiding purpose enables a writer at every point to *control* his writing. His composition will not ramble; it will not be vague and disordered; and it will become *one* thing, a unit.

The guiding purpose means singleness of purpose, but it does not mean stark simplicity of purpose. Every paragraph and every sentence may be said to have a guiding purpose, too; and all these lesser purposes add up to make the general guiding purpose.

The result is unity. It is not the unity of monotony—a dull repeating of one idea or fact, without variation. It is not the unity of isolation—the single rock on the beach, the lone cipher on a bare page. Rather it is that organic unity which has been described as "the structural union of the parts." It is many things that, when written down together, or "composed," become one thing. A composition has organic unity when nothing can properly be added to or subtracted from it without injury to the sense of satisfaction that a reader may have from it.

How to Choose the Guiding Purpose

The choice of a guiding purpose depends upon (1) the personal taste of the writer, (2) his knowledge of the subject, (3) the nature of the subject itself, (4) the reader. Of these conditions, the first two are to some extent under the control of the writer. The latter two are not altogether under his control.

Personal Taste. Within reasonable limits, choose a subject that interests you as an individual, and present it in such a way as to bring out what seem to you its interesting or important aspects. The *originality* of your work will depend in great degree upon your ability to look at a subject with your own eyes rather than through borrowed spectacles. You are not expected merely to write glib reproductions of what other people say. You may very well make some original contribution, however small, to the subject; and that original contribution will inevitably come from the fact that you, as an individual, have a point of view of your own.

Machines, for example, affect different individuals in different ways. Individual *A*, looking at a bulldozer, thinks of it as a symbol of man's triumph over crude matter. His paper will emphasize the inventive genius that makes it possible for a weak midget of a creature to move tons of earth and rock by pressing buttons or pulling levers. But individual *B* may quite contrarily be moved to think of how many workers the great machine has displaced, and his paper may ask why man's ingenuity chooses to function in such a peculiarly self-destructive way.

The attitude of the writer may thus affect the treatment of any subject, but that attitude will naturally have freest play when the subject permits or invites an expression of opinion. Autobiographical themes, since they draw upon personal experience, naturally call for a good deal of personal expression. Informal essays—on such subjects as "Why I Like Cats," "On Raking Autumn Leaves," "The Pleasures of Sleeping Late"—are by definition an expression of personal taste, or even of prejudice.

But numerous occasions will arise when a writer's personal tastes must be suppressed or disregarded. If you are required to write an *explanation* of a machine—say, a bulldozer—your personal opinions and tastes in the matter of bulldozers are of no importance whatever. It is useless to attempt sprightly originality in explaining the manufacture of sulphuric acid or the origin of the United Nations.

Knowledge of the Subject.   Ordinarily you should write about a subject that is familiar to you; or, given a general subject with many possible aspects, choose a guiding purpose which permits you to treat some aspect familiar to you. Do not write about Tibetan yaks, if your sole acquaintance with those creatures is in books; write about horses, if you know horses; about dogs, if you are a dog-lover. If you are asked to write a character sketch, write about the news-vendor you see every morning, or your favorite uncle, or the historical character whom you know best. In such instances, your guiding purpose will be determined by the degree of your knowledge of the subject.

On the other hand, you may be led to consider an old and familiar subject in a new light. You may have thought, all your life, of earthworms as good only for fishing bait. But now the biology instructor asks you to study the anatomy of the earthworm, and suddenly you discover something of the marvelous in what you thought to be the dullest of earth's creatures. Or perhaps the agronomist asks you to study the relationship between the earthworm and the productivity of the soil. Then you may find yourself wondering whether there would be any vegetation at all, if there were no earthworms to perform their dark and obscure labors beneath the sod.

In other words, new knowledge may give you a new approach, and a new approach means a definite guiding purpose. Intellectual curiosity, which is the spirit of inquiry or the desire to explore new paths of knowledge, will lead you to new subjects and to new treatments of old subjects. Eventually you will be assigned research papers and critical essays. The object of such assignments, in your composition course as in other studies, is to tempt you to break through the limits of your previous knowledge. You may even be expected to write on subjects for which you have a positive distaste or to acquaint yourself with matters in which you have had no previous interest at all. If you can approach such tasks with a fair and open mind, you may be surprised to find your interest kindled in ways that you could not have anticipated; and at any rate you will have the reward that comes from self-mastery.

The Nature of the Subject Itself. For every writer one of the most important of all principles is attention to the subject and humility in the presence of the subject. In some themes the guiding purpose will be determined altogether by the nature of the subject itself. If your topic is "How to Give First Aid to a Drowning Person" or "How to Stop Arterial Bleeding," a life-and-death issue is involved, no nonsense about personal taste is permissible, your sole purpose must be to tell exactly what are the right steps to take in such emergencies. You must have no guiding purpose that will tempt you to color the facts.

But attention to the subject is of first importance in all written composition, and not merely in such special instances as those noted above. Until you find out what your subject really is, until you have looked at it closely and steadily and explored its various aspects, you will not be in a position to write about it intelligently. When people speak of ideas as "half-baked" or say that such-and-such a person "went off half-cocked," they mean that he had not really considered his subject; he wrote or spoke without taking the trouble to inquire into the matter under discussion. The rule is not always "Look in thy heart and write," as Sir Philip Sidney said in his sonnets to Stella, but far more often it is, "Look at the subject and write."

If you are poverty-stricken in ideas, if, like Sir Philip Sidney, you "bite your truant pen" and wonder what to say, remember that the ideas do not need to be "thought up." They are in the subject itself, very likely, and you have only to discover them and write them down.

The Reader.   The act of writing implies the act of reading, and therefore a writer must ordinarily consider who his reader or readers are to be. Samuel Pepys, it is true, wrote his famous diary in a cryptogram, presumably as a solitary amusement, never expecting that other human eyes than his would ever see it. But the exception proves the rule. We wish our writing to be understood and, if possible, to be liked by those who read what we have to say. The guiding purpose, and with it the composition, may therefore often be determined in part by the necessity of appealing to a certain kind of reader. Is the writer's audience expected to be large or small, friendly or hostile, ignorant or well-informed? Is he writing for a group with mixed opinions, or for a group with one opinion? Such questions undoubtedly have a large part in deciding the strategy of many kinds of writing.

If a housing expert is speaking on television on the subject of slum clearance, he will frame his speech to suit the mixed audience that he hopes to reach. He must get the attention and appeal to the understanding of the filling-station attendant, the ward politician, the rural voter who is jealous of urban expenditures, as well as the readers of Lewis Mumford's *The Culture of Cities*. He will therefore try to have enough solid substance in his speech to catch the attention of the most bookish of his hearers, but he will try also to put it in terms simple enough to reach the least educated. The same speaker, if he were writing an article for the *Atlantic Monthly,* might choose an entirely different approach, since he would then be writing for a smaller audience, of a more uniform culture.

You will not often be expected to make adaptations as wide as those mentioned above. Your instructor and your classmates are your audience, and you may generally suppose that this audience is prepared to respond to whatever you may have to say. But your guiding purpose will vary somewhat according to the kind of response that you wish to get. If you intend to please and entertain them with a light essay on the difference between plain dogs and dog aristocrats, your guiding purpose will certainly not be the same as if you were writing an informative article on what canned dog-food is. If you are writing an article of opinion on some controversial topic that touches politics, race, or religion, you had better consider the sensibilities of your readers; you cannot assume that they are all of your own opinion.

In general, it may be a considerable help to you in writing to keep in mind some particular person or group of persons for whom you are writing. Ask yourself, if you wish, what your Aunt Eustacia would say to this. Or write the kind of theme that your roommate will approve. It is better to write for somebody in particular than for nobody at all.

EXERCISES

Study at least one of the following groups of topics. Be able to demonstrate what differences in the treatment of the topic would result from the use of the various guiding purposes. Illustrate by composing brief outlines like those on pages 28 and 29.

1. Big-Time College Football (or Basketball).
    a. To account for its general popularity.
    b. To estimate its real value to an institution of higher education.
    c. To warn against the dangers of "professionalism."
    d. To set forth its historical background.
2. The American Senate.
    a. To explain its peculiarities to a European visiting the United States.
    b. To explain the action of the Constitutional Convention in allotting two senators to each state, regardless of the size of its population.
    c. To defend its often criticized indulgence in lengthy debates.
3. The Place of Television in Modern Society.
    a. To uphold television as home entertainment—"the rebirth of the family and of privacy."
    b. To compare television, as a social institution, with the regular theatre or the moving picture theatre.
    c. To deplore television as conditioning people to complete "passivity."
    d. To analyze its capacities as an art medium.

3. ADAPTING MEANS TO ENDS:
COHERENCE, OR HOW SHALL I SAY IT?

The guiding purpose answers the question: *What* do I intend to say? The next question is: *How* shall I say it?

One answer to such a question might be: Use appropriate language, and above all, clear language. Language is important beyond measure. Power of the word may even at times make up for serious faults in other respects. Thomas Carlyle is magnificent in his diction although his writing is so slovenly in organization as to be nearly unintelligible in some passages; he succeeds in spite of the defect, but we are nonetheless bothered by his disorderliness. Ralph Waldo Emerson used enchanting words and phrases; he was a master of the sentence, but he had little gift for organization; his famous essays are jumbles of fine sentences. The Elizabethans, drunk with the sheer novelty of words, were remarkably eloquent in poetry, but could not organize their prose. The frontiersmen of America had a natural gift of language which has left its mark upon American habits of speaking and writing; and yet they did not have the benefit of the elegant rhetoric taught in the Latin schools and academies of their time.

These, however, are special cases. Since we are dealing here with the whole composition, as a composition, it is necessary to postpone until a later chapter the study of sentence structure and diction. Through the action of the guiding purpose you have chosen the *material* that you will direct toward a certain end, and thus have assured *unity* to your composition. The next step is to secure *coherence:* that is, to *put the material together* so that all the parts of the composition come to the reader in an orderly sequence.

The organization of a composition is the order of its parts, in relation to one another and to the subject as a whole. The parts of a composition are the steps or stages of thought and expression, the "blocks" of thought, large and small, the related elements into which the subject may be broken up or into which it may be divided by its very nature.

In a book, the division into parts is indicated by the chapters and chapter headings; in a long composition there will be sections, with or without subtitles, and these sections in turn will divide into paragraphs; in a brief composition, the division will be indicated by paragraphs. All these parts, in turn, are in themselves units which subdivide into lesser units. The paragraph will have its subdivisions, which are frequently, though not always, indicated by transitional phrases. The smallest organized unit is the sentence, which has a grammatical organization of subject and predicate and their modifiers. The object of the general organization is to make all the parts work together as one.

The organization of a book is indicated, though sometimes rather briefly, by its table of contents. A glance at the table of contents of this textbook will reveal a systematic procedure, indicated by the numbers and titles of the various main divisions and subdivisions. In such a table of contents we have the equivalent of a topical outline. We are given the plan of the book, the framework for the detailed discussion of composition and rhetoric. Your composition, no matter how long or short it may be, should have an organization equally clear.

The difference between a composition that is not planned and one that is well planned is the difference between a pile of stones and a house made of stone. A pile of stones has no organization; it is a mere heap, a little chaos. A stone house has organization; the stones have been put into place according to a design; they are parts of a whole. A wild landscape may be said to be unorganized as compared with a farm. The aimless scribblings you make while talking over the telephone are unorganized as compared with a pencil drawing.

Good organization comes from keeping your guiding purpose in mind as you write and from seeing that your thoughts develop in an orderly sequences. But what is an orderly sequence? Or what is good order? There is room for choice; there are different ways of organizing a composition.

Two Kinds of Order

The structural organization of the composition generally depends upon the use of one or the other of two kinds of order:

(1) Natural order—the order inherent in the subject itself, as in a narrative, in which events are related in the order of their occurrence.

(2) Logical order—an order determined by the writer's own reason, as when, in the discussion of a character, we may begin by clearing away gossip, false interpretations,

popular misconceptions, and then go on to analyze the true man.

The distinction between these two kinds of order is largely a matter of the source from which they are derived. When a writer uses *natural order,* he is perceiving and following the order that he finds inherent in his subject: the phenomena of change from winter to spring; the successive details or stages of an event; the arrangement of furniture in a room. The order comes from the phenomena observed, and the writer adheres faithfully to it. On the other hand, when a writer uses *logical order,* he exercises his powers of reason to determine the order in which the subject is to be presented, in the interest of clarity and truth. His approach is active. He makes the subject yield to him.

Natural Order.   Use natural order when the subject requires an arrangement in time sequence (chronological order) or when it has a physical shape that must be described (order of space).

Most narratives, explanations with a narrative element, and descriptions containing a time element *require* a presentation in chronological order, and their organization depends upon careful observance of that requirement. The telephone company follows natural order in the instructions given for using a dial telephone: (1) Remove the receiver; (2) listen for the dial tone; (3) dial the number wanted. An explanation of how to use a dial telephone could not follow any other order. The agricultural expert who is explaining how to prepare a field for corn must follow natural order. All "how to do it" themes, such as explanations of processes, require natural order. It is the simplest of orders and gives an easy, straightforward movement to the composition.

Descriptions of places, houses, landscapes, and many other physical objects will generally require order of space. In describing a landscape, you will naturally proceed from right to left, from near to far, or from some notable landmark, such as a tree or house, to other parts of the landscape. A geographer may describe a range of mountains in terms of its location, its extension north and south, east and west, and of its relation to the coastal plains, river systems, or deserts that border it.

In all such instances, the subject imposes a certain order

of treatment upon the writer. He is not free to make changes. The order of the events or the arrangement of the landscape is the order of treatment for his composition and the source of his organization.

Less easily definable is the kind of natural order which may be called *associational*. The best example of associational order is found in the informal essay, where the writer makes a virtue of not controlling, or rather of seeming not to control, the flow of his ideas. He lets them run, and follows them; or apparently he does so.

Perhaps you recall finding a flint arrowhead in some meadow; or you have been looking at a collection of arrowheads and pots in a museum. The arrowhead suggests a picture of what the country was like when the Indians lived here before the coming of the white man. That picture suggests another—the contrasting picture of modern America, with its highways traversing the buffalo plains and its great cities towering where once was only a huddle of Indian tepees. Reflecting on the second picture, you suddenly recall the brutality of gangsters, the death rate from automobile accidents, and perhaps above all the great wars in which we have engaged in modern times. You may then be led to wonder whether the automobile age represents any real progress as compared with the stone age in which the Indian lived.

Such a composition would be an essay, in which the ideas had come together by a process of free association rather than of logic. It would have a design, rather than a logical plan; and the design would come from the series of contrasts into which your reverie had brought you. You would arrange your composition in a form that would effectively bring out the series of contrasts.

Logical Order. Logical order requires an act of analysis on the part of the writer. His subject exists in his mind only as an unwieldy lump, or it is merely a jumble of scattered material which makes no sense at all. He seeks to bring this lump or this jumble under the rule of reason. Either he must find a logical arrangement which will bring the subject into order, or he must continue studying it until he identifies in the subject itself some features or some principle that, when related to his own knowledge, will form the basis of organized discussion.

Let us suppose a subject consisting of scattered parts which cannot for the moment be seen in an orderly arrangement. It might be, for example, "Flood Control." Here is a great heap of information in periodicals and government reports—so much information that, the more we read, the more we are confused. There is talk about dams and levees; there are figures on soil erosion and reforestation; there are people who preach about little rivers and little dams, and other people who preach about big rivers and big dams; there are lectures on watersheds, terracing, dikes, spillways, dredges, cover crops. The subject evidently does not have a form of its own that a novice can easily follow. How can he be at all systematic in dealing with such a subject?

The first step toward being systematic is to choose a guiding purpose. Evidently there is some argument as to what is the *best* method of flood control. We are not experts, and we do not know what is the best method. We can, however, put all the suggested methods side by side and discuss them, one after the other. The guiding purpose then is to explain the most important methods of flood control.

What methods are important? We may dismiss from consideration any fantastic schemes for making water run uphill, or for retiring from cultivation all the arable land of the United States. Analyzing the other methods advocated by experts, we find that their suggestions fall into three main groups: there are advocates of levees and spillways, who propose to take care of danger points along the lower reaches of great rivers; there are advocates of flood control along entire river systems; and there are others who wish to stop or check the water before it reaches the rivers. These three groups can be treated in order, in the three main divisions of the composition. A preliminary topical outline will show the plan of procedure:

I. Flood control near river-mouths.
II. Flood control along river-systems.
III. Flood control of the entire countryside.

The problem of logical organization is to group the material under these main headings, which constitute the logical divisions of the subject. The next step is to expand the topical outline. We may decide that "at danger points" is a more inclusive heading for division I than "near river-mouths." The order of treatment is logical enough for our purposes, for we shall begin with the older methods (levees near river-mouths) and proceed to later devices. The expanded topical outline will read as follows:

I. Flood control at danger points, by means of
   A. Levees.
   B. Spillways.
II. Flood control along entire river-systems, by means of
   A. Multiple-purpose dams on important rivers.
   B. Storage dams on tributary rivers.
   C. Unified control systems for entire watersheds, as in Tennessee Valley.
III. Flood control of our complete natural terrain, by means of
   A. Reforestation.
   B. Control of agriculture through
      1. Terracing of slopes.
      2. Planting cover crops.
      3. Retirement of easily eroded land from commercial use.

In other kinds of subjects, it is best, before establishing the logical divisions of the subject, to find some central idea to serve as the principle of arrangement. In explaining the organization of the House of Representatives, Woodrow Wilson distinguishes this body from the Senate by noting that its function is to get business done rather than to deliberate and debate. This is the central principle of the organization that he seeks to explain; to set forth this principle, as applied to the House of Representatives, is his guiding purpose.[1]

A topical outline of the subject would therefore be constructed in part as follows:

I. The House as distinguished from the Senate.
II. Organization of committees to get business done.
   A. Numbers and names of committees.
   B. Powers of committees.
III. Powers of the Speaker.
   A. Appoints committees.
   B. Decides committee to which bills shall be referred.
   C. Regulates calendar of the House.
   D. Controls debate by power of recognizing members.
   E. Controls Committee on Rules.

Logical order can be obtained, then, either by analyzing the subject into its parts, and grouping facts and discussion

[1] Woodrow Wilson, *Constitutional Government in the United States*, 1908. (The powers of the Speaker have been greatly modified since Wilson discussed the subject of government, but Wilson's discourse is still a model of clear exposition.)

around the main divisions thus set up, or by following some central principle and noting the ways in which it makes itself manifest in the subject.

These, however, are not the only kinds of logical order. Your subject may suggest the advisability of reasoning from cause to effect, or from effect backward to the cause. For example, it would be logical to explain the systems of representation in the Senate and in the House of Representatives by starting with the debates at the Constitutional Convention. You would discover that our bicameral system—the two houses of Congress—is the result of a compromise between the large states, like New York and Pennsylvania, that wanted to be represented in proportion to their population, and the little states, like Rhode Island and Delaware, that wanted equal representation for all states. You would then be reasoning from cause to effect.

Or, if called upon to explain the presence of smog in some urban area, you could begin with a graphic picture of some morning when sunrise brings only a ghastly semidarkness, traffic gropes blindly, throats and eyes are irritated—and then work back to the causes: air-pollution by industrial plants, geographical location, special weather conditions, and the like.

It is also logical to proceed from less important to more important aspects of the subject. This arrangement builds toward a climax; the most important point is saved for the end of the composition.

For example, if you are explaining how a skillful trainer chooses, from various promising young bird dogs, the individual dog that he will prepare for field trials, in the hope of winning a grand championship, you may begin by discussing pedigree and may explain the importance of inherited characteristics. Next you may deal with the physical characteristics that a winner must have, whatever his pedigree, if he is to meet the severe test of a field trial. You may then go on to say that a fine pedigree and an ideal physique may make a "good" dog, but that they will not necessarily make a champion. A champion must have certain almost indefinable qualities, among which are an unusual amount of zest and a spirit of originality and enterprise that makes him somewhat independent of the trainer even while he is ultimately responsible to horn or whistle. Your discussion of this unique combination of qualities, which represents "genius" among bird dogs, will constitute the climax of your discourse. By the order of your discussion you will have emphasized the supreme importance of dog "genius," over and above other qualities, however desirable and necessary.

If the subject is treated very informally, the main divisions may be chosen rather selectively. You may show the important rather than all the possible features of the subject. A theme on college friendships may deal only with what interests the writer most: the natural good-fellowship in which college friendships originate; the romantic intensity of such friendships; their lasting quality. These three topics will constitute the three main divisions of the subject, and the effectiveness of the theme will depend upon how well the writer can expand them. If he has imagination and good sense, his writing will hold together even though he has chosen only a few out of many aspects of his subject—perhaps not any of those that a hard-headed sociologist, relentlessly engaged in studying human behavior, would want to use. Yet in this informal treatment, the writing must still have harmony and order. One part of the discussion must lead naturally to the next part. There must be no yawning gaps and no silly irrelevancies. The reader must be left with a sense of completeness and order.

To secure completeness and order, you must *plan* your composition before you begin to write. If it is not planned, it will not be a true composition, but an improvisation, which may or may not by sheer good luck fall into a sensible organization. Prepare an outline—either a topical outline or a complete sentence outline, like the model outlines given in Chapter 3. If your instructor does not require written outlines, use the outline anyway as a test of the organization of your theme. If your theme can be reduced to a logical outline, then it is logically arranged, and probably is a well-organized theme. Go over the first draft of your theme to see whether your thought is presented in logical sequence. Ask yourself whether you have chosen the right divisions of your subject and whether you have developed each division fully and clearly. If you have left out anything important, put it where it belongs. If you have put in the wrong thing, take it out and put in the right thing. If you have the right thing, but have put it in the wrong place, change it to another place.

EXERCISES

1. Which of the following topics require a treatment in natural order? Which in logical order?

> Why Winter Always Comes
> The Pageant of Autumn Colors
> Rewards and Punishments in Water-Skiing
> Why Congress Has Two Houses
> Vacant Periods on a College Campus
> Shell Collecting
> Learning to Ski: Principle and Practice
> The Barn Is Modern—But Not the Cow
> Fishing a Mountain Brook
> Why the United States Constitution Has a "Bill of Rights"
> Moods of the River
> What a Levee Is For
> The Origin of Christmas Carols
> Pro's and Con's of Functional Architecture

2. Could any of the above topics be discussed in a composition that combines natural and logical order?

3. Could any be developed by free association (see page 27)? Do any require an organization built upon a central idea (page 29)? Which should be developed by proceeding from cause to effect? From effect to cause? Make a brief outline of a theme that you might write on one of the above topics. Indicate the method of development that you have chosen.

4. THE MARKS OF GOOD ORDER: TRANSITION IN THE COMPOSITION

When the development of the subject is orderly, the reader will need little reminder of the steps by which the discussion is proceeding. If the steps are there, do not put labels on them. The reader may be bored by some tedious *firstly, secondly, thirdly* of the kind which in old-fashioned sermons too often suggested the distance between church and dinner rather than the progress of the soul toward salvation. Clumsy writers are forever throwing up enormous bridges of connection that connect nothing in particular. The good writer will take care to have the thoughts connected, and he will mark his connections only when marking is really needed.

Such connections are called *transitions*. A transition is, literally, a passing over. Transitional devices are the words, phrases, clauses, sentences, or paragraphs which serve to point out the steps of the thought, or the passing over from one thought to the next, or from one division to the next division.

When does the transition need to be marked, and how is the marking to be done?

Within the composition as a whole, marks of transition are needed mainly in the following places: (1) where major divisions of the thought, composed of groups of paragraphs, are joined; (2) where momentary digressions or sudden turns of thought are introduced; (3) at any other point where the reader needs to be specially prepared for what is to follow.

(1) Between major divisions of the thought, the *transitional paragraph* can be useful if it is skillfully managed. A transitional paragraph marks the end of one part of a discussion and the beginning of another. If the composition is long, transitional paragraphs may give a pithy reminder of the points already made and a forecast of what is to follow.

> Let us now pass to the second division of the argument, and dismissing the supposition that any of the received opinions may be false, let us assume them to be true, and examine into the worth of the manner in which they are likely to be held, when their truth is not freely and openly canvassed. However unwillingly a person who has a strong opinion may admit the possibility that his opinion may be false, he ought to be moved by the consideration that, however true it may be, if it is not fully, frequently, and fearlessly discussed, it will be held as a dead dogma, not a living truth.—JOHN STUART MILL, *On Liberty.*

> I have now spoken of the education of the scholar by nature, by books, and by action. It remains to say somewhat of his duties.
> —RALPH WALDO EMERSON, *The American Scholar.*

(2) Transitional expressions are needed when the writer leaves the main line of his discussion to make some quick contrast, or to overthrow some mistaken conception, or merely to make a remark "by the way." Such a divergence should always be noted. There is no need to apologize for it, but it must be recognized as a purposeful divergence. The reader must not be permitted to think that the composition has run out of control.

Let us suppose that, in an essay on flood control, the writer wishes to compare the dikes of Holland with the levees along the Mississippi. Such a digression will be marked by a transitional passage:

> *Although it is not particularly important for this discussion,* I may note here the obvious fact that the dikes of Holland furnish no true parallel to the levees at New Orleans, Vicksburg, and Cairo. The dikes of Holland hold back the ocean, which is larger than the Mississippi. That is so. But the ocean receives floods; it never rises in floods, except on the rare occasion of a tidal wave. Its ordinary tides are measurable; their rise and fall can be exactly predicted. The Mississippi, on the other hand, is a fresh-water stream, racing to the ocean. It is turbulent and unpredictable. Nobody ever knows how much it will rise at any given season, because nobody knows how much rain is going to fall within a given time.

If the divergence is considerable, a transitional paragraph may be necessary. If it is slight, a sentence or even a part of a sentence (as above) may be enough to make the connection clear.

(3) It may be necessary to prepare the reader for some change of thought or for a transition from one sub-topic to another. The *transitional sentence* is commonly used to mark a transition between paragraphs or parts of long paragraphs. It is particularly useful in rather formal discussions, in which the logical structure of the composition needs to be emphasized. The following paragraph, taken from a formal essay, begins with such a sentence:

> *This brings us to another kind of thought which can fairly easily be distinguished from the three kinds described above.* It has not the usual qualities of the reverie, for it does not hover about our usual complacencies and humiliations. It is not made up of our homely decisions forced upon us by everyday needs, when we review our little stock of existing information, consult our conventional preferences and obligations, and make a choice of action. It is not the defense of our own cherished beliefs and excuses for remaining of the same mind. On the contrary, it is that peculiar species of thought which leads us to *change* our mind.—JAMES HARVEY ROBINSON, *The Mind in the Making.*

Words, phrases, and clauses are the most common transitional devices. Some of these devices are *pronominal:* they are pronouns (or pronominal adjectives); or they are phrases containing pronouns, with the antecedent in a preceding clause. Others are *directive expressions.* That is, they direct us how to interpret or approach a given passage. Generally these "directives" are parenthetical expressions, without much grammatical function in the sentence where they are placed. As transitional devices they point out the path of thought. They do not make the path. They mark a coherence which already exists; they help to make clear the sequence of ideas.

The following passages contain examples of pronominal devices:

> Indeed, the actual dimensions of the fireplace were even larger. A whole ox, a stag, or an elk could be roasted *there,* or a bear upon occasion.—HERVEY ALLEN, *Bedford Village.*

> 'Tis next alleged we must not expose ourselves to temptations without necessity, and next to *that,* not employ our time in vain things. To *both these* objections one answer will serve, out of the grounds already laid, that to all men *such* books are not temptations or vanities, but useful drugs and materials wherewith to temper and compose effective and strong medicines.—JOHN MILTON, *Areopagitica.*

> It is well to begin with the superficial; and *this* is the superficial effectiveness of Shaw; the brilliancy of bathos. But of course the vitality and value of his plays does not lie merely in *this;* any more than the value of Swinburne lies in alliteration or the value of Hood in puns.—G. K. CHESTERTON, *George Bernard Shaw.*

The following paragraphs contain examples of directive expressions:

> Water is a dominant factor in sculpturing the landscape and in determining the depth, fertility, and productivity of the soil. *Consequently,* it plays an important role in the development of civilization—BERNARD FRANK and ANTHONY NETBOY, *Water, Land, and People.*

> The two great points of difference between a democracy and a republic are: *first,* the delegation of the government, *in the latter,* to a small number of citizens elected by the rest; *secondly,* the greater number of citizens, and greater sphere of country, over which the latter may be extended.
> —JAMES MADISON, *The Federalist,* No. X.

Study the best writers and observe the kinds of transitional

devices they use and the occasions where they find it necessary to mark transition. The following list will suggest some
of the brief transitional devices that you should look for,
but remember also to look for transitional sentences and
paragraphs.

Brief Transitional Devices

Words: previously, afterwards, however, moreover, nevertheless, also, first, last, next.

Phrases: on the contrary, on the whole, in addition to, by
the way, to repeat, in conclusion, generally speaking, for instance.

Clauses: we now see; I suppose; it must be admitted; as I
implied earlier; as I have said.

Such brief transitional devices are less often used to link
paragraphs or sections of a composition than to link sentences
and groups of sentences within the paragraph. The subject
of transition within the paragraph will be studied fully later.
(See Chapter 4.)

EXERCISES

1. Read an article in the *Atlantic Monthly, Harper's Magazine,*
or in one of the literary quarterlies, such as the *Yale Review, Virginia
Quarterly Review, Georgia Review, Sewanee Review.* Make a list
of all brief transitional devices used in the article; classify these
expressions according to form and function. Make a record, also,
of transitional sentences used in the article.

2. Make a classified list of the transitional expressions used in
"The Boys' Ambition" (page 8).

3. Find and bring to class at least one good example of a transitional paragraph.

5. PROPORTION AND EMPHASIS

There remains one final question: *How much* shall I write
on the different parts of the subject? The parts of the composition must not only be set in order; they must be put
together in a right *proportion,* so that *emphasis* falls where
it is intended, and yet no one part of the composition is out
of balance with the rest.

The answer to questions of proportion may be given first
in general terms: Make the composition a well-balanced
piece of writing within the limits chosen or allowed. The

space given to any part depends upon two things: (1) the importance of that part in relation to other parts; (2) the scale of the composition as a whole—that is, its prescribed limits and the necessity of giving each part its proportionate space within those limits. A map that covers a wall can show the windings of the Mississippi River in greater detail than a map made to fit within the pages of a book; but in both maps the Mississippi retains the same *relative* size: it is the largest river compared with other rivers, as Alaska is the largest state compared with other states.

The writer's judgment is the guide in determining what is most important; and to that most important part he will naturally give the largest space. But he must give only so much *proportionate* space; that is, he must conform to the scale of relative proportions set up by the limits within which he is obliged to work. In a criticism of intercollegiate athletics, it would be possible to write at length on football as an entertaining show; but that part is a relatively minor part, which could be discussed briefly. Still more space could well be given to a much more important point—that football is the modern youth's substitute for feats of arms and chivalric adventure. If the theme is 2500 words in length, the writer may decide to give about 500 words to his first point and about 1000 words to his last one. If he is allowed only 600 words in all, he will give about one-fifth of his space (or about 120 words) to his first point and two-fifths (about 240 words) to his last point.

In theme writing the problem of proportion is not a precise mathematical problem. It is enough to understand that each division of the subject should receive as much or as little discussion as it deserves, within the scale decided upon. If any doubt arises as to the relative importance of any single part, the outline can be consulted. The outline will show the relation between one part and another, and of each part to the whole. For the outline is like a map, a blueprint, or an architect's drawing. It shows the scale on which the completed composition is to be carried out.

The inexperienced writer needs to guard against the temptation to write at length when he is treating parts of the subject in which he has a special interest, and then to rush hastily through parts of the discussion which interest him less. If you are writing about dams, do not allow your ad-

miration for Norris Dam or Hoover Dam to tempt you to
neglect such less spectacular matters as reforestation and
cover crops.

The good writer avoids such temptations by keeping always before him the demands of the subject as a whole. He
deals justly with his subject; he is fair to his reader. For he
knows that if he puts an emphasis where it does not belong,
he falsifies the subject and cheats his reader. If his composition is ill-balanced, it is awkward; if it is awkward, it
will be so much the less likely to be convincing.

CHAPTER 3

EXPOSITORY WRITING

EXPOSITION is that kind of writing or speech which sets forth knowledge, ideas, facts, problems, or situations in such a way as to convey information and meaning. The purpose of expository writing is to explain rather than to describe, relate, or convince. Exposition is therefore ordinarily distinguished from description, narration, and argument. In the older rhetorics these four kinds of writing are rather strictly divided and are called the four kinds of discourse. In practice, however, these four types of discourse rarely appear in a pure form. One shades into the other. An explanation of a power dam may be descriptive in part, for the writer will want to give his reader a picture of the concrete structure in all its massiveness. The explanation of a process may be as much narration as exposition. Hilaire Belloc's "Mowing a Field" (pages 44–46) is an instance. Narratives, in turn, may contain exposition. History, for example, is a blending of narration and exposition, for the events are related and explained. Argument contains definition and analysis, which are expository in nature. It is best, therefore, to use the terms *expository writing, descriptive writing, narrative writing*. Expository writing is writing that tends toward exposition, even though it may not be pure exposition. Descriptive writing is mainly descriptive; narrative writing is mainly narrative. Argument will necessarily appear when it is proper to support an opinion. Instead of dealing with formal argumentation, we shall study, in a later chapter of this book, the problems of argumentative writing.

By far the greater number of occasions for writing bring us to exposition and therefore call for expository writing. The most familiar questions of human experience are proba-

39

bly these: *How is it done? How is it made? What do you mean? Why does so-and-so behave like that? What is the truth about this situation?*

From childhood to old age, we are asking and answering such questions. The answers are expository. Expository writing finds its use in the most familiar tasks of everyday life and in highly involved questions of science, philosophy, and art. The boy who explains to his friend how to play marbles is grappling with the same essential problem of expression as the learned astronomer who explains his calculations in terms of light-years. The big-league pitcher who explains (perhaps through a ghost writer) how he learned to throw a curve ball is using expository writing; and so is the flower expert who tells us how he developed a prize-winning dahlia. The chapter in the history textbook on the causes of the American Revolution is expository writing. So, too, are the report of a congressional committee, the literary critic's review of the latest novel, the newspaper editorial which interprets some foreign event.

PROJECT 1. A PROCESS

Explanations of processes answer the question: *How it is done?* or *How is it made?* In themes of this sort the two major problems of composition are easily solved. The guiding purpose is generally nothing more than the writer's intention to explain the steps of the process, in clear sequence; and the organization is a simple matter of putting these steps in their right order. The principle of the process theme is the same as the principle of the process itself. As in the process it is necessary to do the right thing at the right time, so in the theme it is necessary to give the right information at the right place.

If the process is simple and is within the range of ordinary experience, it presents no special difficulties. The beginning of the process is the beginning of the composition. After the steps of the process have been explained in detail, the theme comes to an end. A theme entitled "How to Build a Campfire" may have the following topical outline:

   I. Preparatory steps.
      A. Choice of a convenient spot.
      B. Gathering kindling and fuel.
  II. Building the fire.
      A. How to arrange the kindling.

      1. The bungling amateur's way.
      2. The Indian way.
   B. How to feed the fire.
   C. How to provide for cooking.
   D. What to do in rainy weather.
III. Safety precautions.
   A. During dry weather.
   B. During the night.
   C. When leaving camp-site.

If the process is technical or complex—such as the manufacture of cotton fiber into rayon, the process of renovating a colonial house, or the building of a set for an amateur play —then the problem of organization is not so simple. A complex process will subdivide into several related processes. Each of these has an order of its own. When all are put together in their right order, the theme is organized. To form a plan for a complex process, therefore, you should divide the complex process into simple processes and develop each one in turn. Sometimes it may be difficult to make such a division. Try to state the central problem involved in the process itself and build your organization around that problem. For example, the central problem in the process of reconstructing a colonial house might be how to introduce modern conveniences without destroying the original design and character of the house.

The following outline illustrates the organization of a theme which deals with a complex process. Observe that each main division of the outline (with the exception of the first main division) deals with one of the lesser processes, which is subdivided into its steps.

HOW BLACK TOBACCO IS PRODUCED

Theme Sentence: Black tobacco culture is an all-the-year task which involves varied types of skill and knowledge.

  I. What is black tobacco?
   A. It is black, or "dark," in comparison with Burley or "light."
   B. It is a "strong" tobacco.
   C. It is grown mainly in "The Black Tobacco Patch," a restricted upland region in Kentucky and Tennessee.
 II. Planting is done in the very early spring.
   A. The beds must be put in order.
     1. They are "burned off" or steamed to kill weeds and pests.

2. The soil must be carefully prepared.

B. The tiny seed must be mixed with ashes or fine soil to be sown.

C. The beds must be protected from cold and from plant diseases.

III. The transplanting or "setting out" is done in late spring or early summer.

A. The field must be carefully prepared.

B. The tobacco farmer must have weather wisdom if he is to judge the best time for "setting out."

C. The young plants are set out in rows wide enough apart to allow room for cultivation and later growth.

D. The labor of transplanting is back-breaking and tedious.

IV. The tobacco plants require constant attention during the growing season.

A. A certain amount of cultivation is necessary during the early summer.

B. At all times each individual plant must be tended like a growing infant.

1. Tobacco worms are picked off by hand.

2. Plants are "topped" to promote leaf growth.

3. "Suckers" must be pulled off, in order that all the strength of the plant may go into the large leaves.

V. The tobacco is "cut" or harvested in September and October before frost begins.

A. The tobacco farmer must judge when to "cut."

1. He must know when the plants are mature.

2. He must be a judge of weather conditions.

B. The tobacco is "cut" in the following manner:

1. Using a peculiarly shaped knife, workers split each stalk from the top to a point a few inches above the ground.

2. The stalk is cut at this point and placed upside down on the ground.

3. The stalks are placed over "sticks" inserted in the split.

4. The sticks are hung on racks until transported to the tobacco barn.

VI. The next step is "firing" or curing the tobacco.

A. Burley tobacco is generally air-cured.

B. Black tobacco is cured by smoke.

1. A slow fire of hickory or some other good wood is kept smouldering in the barn.

2. It must be watched day and night.

3. "Firing" tobacco is nevertheless a kind of festival.

a. Men may swap yarns, eat, drink.

b. One well-known character used to read Walter Scott only when he "fired" tobacco.

VII. The crop is marketed during the winter or early spring.
   A. A wet "season" is necessary for transporting the tobacco to the neighboring market town.
      1. Dry tobacco cannot be handled without damage.
      2. In wet weather the leaves take up moisture from the air.
      3. It is then "in order" and can be "stripped" for marketing.
   B. It is hauled to town and deposited on a "floor" in the warehouse.
   C. It is then sold at auction.
   D. Some farmers, however, sell their crops from the barn.
   E. The new crop is often planted before the old one is sold.

The above outline illustrates how each main division of a complex process breaks up into parts, some of which may be subdivided. It is not always advisable to make outlines in such detail.

The beginner is advised not to attempt at once the most complex and technical subjects. It is best to choose a simple process for the first theme of this type.

Whether the process is simple or complex, familiar or strange, do not forget the reader. Define special terms that are peculiar to the process—such as *black tobacco, suckers, sticks, firing, in order,* in the outline given above. Do not assume that the reader knows the meaning of such terms. Some of the simplest and most interesting processes have their technical vocabularies. If you are explaining how to play golf, give the meaning of the terms *mashie, niblick, tee, putter, green.* If you are explaining how to harness a horse, you must make sure that the reader knows the meaning of such words as *halter, bit, crupper, traces, single-tree, check-rein.* Do not omit essential steps in the process, on the assumption that the reader's knowledge may be taken for granted. If you are explaining how to roast beef, you cannot take for granted a reader's knowledge that the time for cooking depends upon the size of the roast. Remember that clearness of explanation is a first essential. The process of roasting beef can be explained in such a way as to be intelligible only to hotel chefs. Your task is to explain the process so that it will be intelligible to the nonexpert reader.

Last, do all you can to make your explanation interesting. If you keep your eye on the subject and take pains to present details concretely and exactly, your explanation will be interesting and will need no devices to "make" it interesting. Do not depend upon stylistic flourishes, clever remarks, pretentious language to "add" interest. Such attempts at ornament attract attention away from the subject. Your duty is to the subject, which ought to be chosen so that it is interesting in itself.

There are, however, certain aids to interest which are quite legitimate. Often they will be aids to clearness as well. If the process is one in which mistakes can easily be made, note the nature of those mistakes and warn the reader against them. It is always interesting to show the difference between the right way and the wrong way of doing things, and such a contrast may help the reader to understand your explanation. Hilaire Belloc, in "Mowing a Field," gives a ludicrous picture of an awkward mower; it makes an effective contrast with his explanation of the right way to mow. Second, remember that any introduction of a human element is an aid to interest. Much of the charm of Belloc's explanation comes from the fact that his explanation is also an account of his personal experience. You may tell how you caught tarpon off the coast of Florida, or how you learned to ski. Or you may create characters who play the role of novice and expert in the process that you are explaining: a Percy Dub who slices his golf shots and digs up hunks of turf, and a Bobby Eagle who is an old hand at the game. You may introduce actual characters that you have known: an old Vermonter who has carried his thousands of sap-buckets and knows how to make maple syrup; a Southern planter who knows the ways of cotton; a head bell-boy who knows what happens at the hotel desk; a guide of the North woods; a hairdresser; a steelworker; a Cape Cod fisherman.

MOWING A FIELD[1]   *By Hilaire Belloc*

WHEN I got out into the long grass the sun was not yet risen, but there were already many colors in the eastern sky, and I made haste to sharpen my scythe, so that I might get to the cutting before the dew should dry. Some say that it is best to wait till all the dew has risen, so as to get the grass quite dry from the very first. But, though it is an advantage to get the grass quite dry, yet it is not worth while to wait till the dew has risen. For, in the first place, you lose many hours of work (and those the coolest), and next—which is more important—you lose that great ease and thickness in cutting which comes of the dew. So I at once began to sharpen my scythe.

[1] Reprinted from *Hills and the Sea* by Hilaire Belloc, with permission of Methuen & Co., Ltd.

There is an art also in the sharpening of the scythe, and it is worth describing carefully. Your blade must be dry, and that is why you will see men rubbing the scythe-blade with grass before they whet it. Then also your rubber must be quite dry, and on this account it is a good thing to lay it on your coat and keep it there during all your day's mowing. The scythe you stand upright, with the blade pointing away from you, and put your left hand firmly on the back of the blade, grasping it; then you pass the rubber first down one side of the blade-edge and then down the other beginning near the handle and going on to the point and working quickly and hard. When you first do this you will, perhaps, cut your hand; but it is only at first that such an accident will happen to you.

To tell when the scythe is sharp enough this is the rule. First the stone clangs and grinds against the iron harshly; then it rings musically to one note; then at last, it purrs as though the iron and stone were exactly suited. When you hear this, your scythe is sharp enough; and I, when I heard it that June dawn, with everything quite silent except the birds, let down the scythe and bent myself to mow.

When one does anything anew, after so many years, one fears very much for one's trick or habit. But all things once learnt are easily recoverable, and I very soon recovered the swing and power of the mower. Mowing well and mowing badly—or rather not mowing at all—are separated by very little; as is also true of writing verse, of playing the fiddle, and of dozens of other things, but of nothing more than of believing. For the bad or young or untaught mower without tradition, the mower Promethean, the mower original and contemptuous of the past, does all these things: He leaves great crescents of grass uncut. He digs the point of the scythe hard into the ground with a jerk. He loosens the handles and even the fastening of the blade. He twists the blade with his blunders, he blunts the blade, he chips it, dulls it, or breaks it clean off at the tip. If any one is standing by he cuts him in the ankle. He sweeps up into the air wildly, with nothing to resist his stroke. He drags up earth with the grass, which is like making the meadow bleed. But the good mower who does things just as they should be done and have been for a hundred thousand years, falls into none of these fooleries. He goes forward very steadily, his scythe-blade just barely missing the ground, every grass falling; the swish and rhythm of his mowing are always the same.

So great an art can be learned only by continual practice; but this is worth writing down, that, as in all good work, to know the thing with which you work is the core of the affair. Good verse is best written on good paper with an easy pen, not with a lump of coal on a whitewashed wall. The pen thinks for you; and so does the scythe mow for you if you treat it honorably and in a manner that makes it recognize its service. The manner is this. You must regard the scythe as a pendulum that swings, not as a knife that cuts. A good mower puts no more strength into his stroke than into his lifting. Again, stand up to your work. The bad mower, eager and full of pain, leans forward and tries to force the scythe through the grass. The good mower, serene and able, stands as nearly straight as the shape of his scythe will let him, and follows up every stroke closely, moving his left foot forward. Then also let every stroke get well away. Mowing is a thing of ample gestures, like drawing a cartoon. Then, again, get yourself into a mechanical and repetitive mood: be thinking of anything at all but your mowing and be anxious only when there seems some interruption to the monotony of the sound. In this, mowing should be like one's prayers—all of a sort and always the same, and so made that you can establish a monotony and work them, as it were, with half your mind: that happier half, the half that does not bother.

In this way, when I had recovered the art after so many years, I went forward over the field, cutting lane after lane through the grass, and bringing out its most secret essences with the sweep of the scythe until the air was full of odors. At the end of every lane I sharpened my scythe and looked back at the work done, and then carried my scythe down again upon my shoulder to begin another. So, long before the bell rang in the chapel above me—that is, long before six o'clock, which is the time for the Angelus—I had many swathes already lying in order parallel like soldiery; and the grass yet standing, making a great contrast with the shaven part, looked dense and high. As it says in the Ballad of Val-es-Dunes, where—

>The tall son of the Seven Winds
>Came riding out of Hither-hythe,

and his horse-hoofs (you will remember) trampled into the press and made a gap in it, and his sword (as you know)

>was like a scythe
>In Arcus when the grass is high
>And all the swathes in order lie,
>And there's the bailiff standing by
>A-gathering of the tithe.

So I mowed all that morning, till the houses awoke in the valley, and from some of them rose a little fragrant smoke, and men began to be seen.

OUTLINES

The making of outlines is generally a part of the instruction in a composition course. It is best to think of an outline as a tool, like a carpenter's square and level, which are used in construction but which in themselves have no great value. An outline *tests* the structure of a composition, much as square and level test the angles of planks and the horizontal condition of a building. It is also a blueprint or working plan which gives a skeletonized picture of organization. Outlines in themselves are nothing; they have merit only in connection with a work in progress. For this reason, it is well to look at an outline of a composition, since only thus can we see the relation of outline to completed work.

The two types of outline in common use are: (1) the complete sentence outline, (2) the topical outline. Below are given outlines of Hilaire Belloc's "Mowing a Field," constructed in each of the two ways. All outlines are analytical: they show the divisions of the subject. The complete sentence outline shows the important main divisions and the subdivisions of these divisions, sometimes in detail. Every division of the complete sentence outline must be a complete sentence, whether it pertains to an important or an unimportant division of the subject.[1] The various divisions of the outline are indented and grouped to show the relative importance of each division and its connection with the other divisions. A topical outline differs from a complete sentence outline only in using topics (phrases or words) rather than complete sentences. In making outlines, remember that you must be consistent: that is, do not make an outline which uses complete sentences for some divisions and topics for other divisions. The complete sentence outline is useful for planning an extended composition or for noting the organization of a complex composition. The topical outline is useful as a preliminary to writing; it furnishes an economical way of planning and testing a short composition.

Both complete sentence outlines and topical outlines must meet these logical requirements: (1) the major divisions, taken together, must be logically equal to the whole content of the composition; (2) the subdivisions of any part, taken together, must equal that part—that is, cover the topic indicated, no more and no less; (3) divisions must not overlap. In addition, the wording of an outline should be simple,

[1] It is permissible for a subdivision to be less than a complete sentence if, with the preceding item of which it is a subdivision, it forms a complete sentence.

the sentences compact. Punctuation, lettering, numerals should follow the scheme indicated in the models.

Complete Sentence Outline

MOWING A FIELD

Guiding Purpose: Mowing a field is a traditional process.

I. It is best to begin mowing before the dew is dry.
  A. Some argue that grass cuts better after the dew is dry.
  B. But it is not worth while to wait.
    1. You lose good hours of work by waiting.
    2. The grass cuts more easily when it is wet.
II. The scythe must first be sharpened carefully.
  A. Both blade and whetstone must be dry.
  B. A certain procedure must be followed.
    1. Stand the scythe upright, blade away from you.
    2. Grasp the back of the blade with the left hand.
    3. Begin whetting near the handle.
    4. Move toward the point, stroking downward alternately on each side.
  C. The sound of the scythe against the stone will tell you when it is sharp.
III. Skill in mowing comes from experience.
  A. As in art, the difference between bad and good mowing is slight but important.
    1. The bad mower makes the following mistakes:
      a. He leaves grass uncut.
      b. He digs his scythe into the ground.
      c. He injures the scythe by bad handling.
      d. He endangers bystanders.
    2. The good mower makes none of these mistakes.
  B. Good mowing consists in letting the scythe do the work for you.
    1. Regard it as a pendulum.
    2. Stand up to your work.
      a. The bad mower leans forward.
      b. The good mower stands straight and follows his stroke through.
IV. In my own mowing I soon recovered this ancient rhythm of work.
  A. I went forward in the traditional manner.
  B. At the end of every lane I sharpened the scythe and looked back.
  C. Long before six o'clock I had many swathes down.
  D. Thus I mowed all the morning.

A Topical Outline

MOWING A FIELD

   I. When to begin work.
     A. Advantages of starting late.
     B. Advantages of starting early.
  II. Sharpening the scythe.
     A. Condition of blade and whetstone.
     B. Position of scythe and hands.
     C. Nature of the stroke for sharpening.
     D. Testing sharpness.
 III. The secret of good mowing.
     A. Slight difference between the good job and the bad job.
       1. How the bad mower works.
       2. How the good mower works.
     B. Letting the scythe work for you.
       1. The pendulum swing.
       2. Correct position.
       3. Mood.
 IV. How I recovered this rhythm.

PRÉCIS-WRITING

A précis is not an outline, but a summary or digest. It is useful as an exercise in grasping the essential ideas of an already completed composition and in stating these ideas in concentrated form. The précis shears away all elaborations of the thought and gives only what is left, in such a way as to make the summary a complete composition. It does not, therefore, skeletonize the original composition so much as it reduces its scale. Many of the articles in the *Reader's Digest* are only précis, so skillfully done that the average reader does not know that he is reading a summary. Since the précis says a great deal within a brief space, it is of great service in taking notes on library assignments and general reading. It is often better to make a précis of an article or a chapter than to write a detailed outline or to record passages verbatim.

Précis of "Mowing a Field"

Some prefer not to begin mowing until the dew has risen. I prefer to begin early so as not to lose the early morning hours. Furthermore, the grass cuts easily when it is wet. The first step is to sharpen the scythe carefully, with alternate downward strokes from handle to point. You will know

that the scythe is sharp when it makes a purring sound
under the stone.

Mowing well is separated from mowing badly by slight
but important differences. The bad mower, ignoring the
mower's tradition, works too energetically, and so leaves
grass uncut, digs into the ground, injures the scythe, and
even imperils bystanders. The good mower goes forward in
a steady rhythm. He knows that the scythe will work for
him if he treats it honorably. Therefore he lets it swing like
a pendulum, and he follows its stroke. He does not lean
forward, like the bad mower, to force the scythe, but stands
up straight and moves with his stroke. He also yields himself to a mechanical mood and thinks of anything but the
scythe.

Thus recovering the art, I went forward in a steady rhythm
and had mowed many swathes before six o'clock; and so
I mowed all that morning.

EXERCISES AND SUGGESTIONS FOR THEMES

1. In what ways does Belloc's explanation of mowing differ
from the technical instructions that might be secured from a
modern agricultural school on how to mow a certain kind of
hay? Or from the instructions that might be given by a city
"garden center" for mowing a lawn? These questions, you will
note, amount to asking how a difference in subject matter, point
of view, guiding purpose may affect vocabulary, tone, emphasis,
proportion. Will such differences also affect the *order* of such an
explanation? Does Belloc, in "Mowing a Field," use natural order
or logical order?

2. Write a process theme somewhat more technical than Belloc's
"Mowing a Field," to which you strive to give the feeling of
human activity and joy in natural surroundings which is an attractive element in Belloc's piece. Titles for such a theme might
be: Men without Scythes, The New Kind of Plowing, Apple Picking in a Commercial Orchard, Fighting Frost in the Orange Groves.

3. Other subjects for process themes:

Cake-baking in a Modern
    Kitchen
Sheep-shearing: Old and New
    Styles
How to Sharpen a Knife
Teaching a Young Horse to
    Jump

Fly-fishing in a Mountain
    Stream
What Happens When It Snows
The Hibernation of a Wood-
    chuck (or other wild animal)
Natural Reforestation in an
    Upland Meadow
How a Patchwork Quilt Is Made

PROJECT 2. MECHANISMS AND ORGANIZATIONS

To write of mechanisms and organizations it is not necessary that the writer be an expert mechanical or social engineer. All that is required is attention to the scheme, plan, or working design of some mechanism or organization with which the writer is familiar—or which he may want to study and explain. Mechanisms are not confined to the inorganic world. The human hand is a kind of mechanism. It makes mistakes, but no robot will ever have a hand as flexible as your own human hand. The building in which you attend classes is an organization of a kind; it was built according to a plan, to serve a certain purpose. Charles D. Stewart has an essay entitled "The Bee's Knees." It is a fascinating explanation of the strangely complex mechanism (essentially a set of tools fitted to an insect body) used by the bee to gather honey. Your college is an organization; and the sociologist will argue that your family is also an organization. If you have a special knowledge of some kind of machinery or organization, you can use that knowledge to advantage. In a society as complex as ours there is hardly anybody without some knowledge of mechanisms and organizations. You will not need to go far afield for a subject or to acquire expert knowledge. Take what is nearest at hand, if you wish. The advantage of the assignment is that you do not need to make up the subject matter. You have only to study it and decide how it must be presented.

In the explanation of a process, this question generally decides itself. Chronological order is inevitable. You must give the steps of the process in their right sequence. Chronological order can also be used in an explanation of a mechanism or an organization. One might, for example, explain a saw-mill by following the progress of a log until the lumber emerges to be stacked for curing; or of a cotton gin by describing the several steps involved in the separation of fiber and seed. Such a treatment would really be a process exposition in which the emphasis has been shifted from the process to the mechanism or organization. In the same way it would be natural to explain the mechanism of the human heart by tracing the passage of the blood from auricle to ventricle; or to explain the organization of a football team by showing what happens in a series of plays and what functions are performed by various members of the team. The difficulty in using this method is that the parts of the machine or the organization must be properly identified and named while the explanation of the process is going on. To give this information at the right time and in the right way is not always easy.

Logical order rather than natural order is therefore generally preferred in expository writing that deals with mechanism and organizations. But logical order cannot be established until the writer has simplified his problem by searching out and determining the *central or basic principle* of the mechanism or organization. An automobile may be only a mysterious collection of metal, rubber, glass, and upholstery until one begins to think of it as a device for using the expansive power of exploding gases. As soon as this central principle is determined, an explanation of an automobile begins to make sense. Considered in relation to this principle, an automobile resolves itself into three essential parts: (1) a motor or *mover*, which is a mechanism for exploding vaporized gasoline in such a way that the resulting power may be used; (2) a transmission system, for applying the power to the wheels; and (3) a vehicular body, where a driver can sit and control the rolling wheels even while he is rolled along.

Working at the subject in this way, we establish three major divisions of the theme. Logic calls for an explanation of the motor first of all. The three major divisions, in turn, break into logical subdivisions. An explanation of the motor requires an explanation of how the internal combustion principle works in relation to the cylinders, the pistons, and the ignition and fuel-supply systems. Then the explanation proceeds logically to drive-shaft, gears, rear axle, and brakes; and last to the structural arrangements of the chassis and body.

If the subject is an organization, the central principle is likely to be identified with the purpose for which the organization exists. Thus a newspaper can be explained as an organization designed to distribute current information as rapidly and cheaply as possible. All the functions of news-gathering, news-writing, editing, printing, distributing, and financing can easily be related to this central principle.

Sometimes it may be preferable to explain an organization or mechanism in the light of conditions that called it forth. Thus feudalism can be explained as a system of land tenure devised to meet a social emergency—the emergency being the social and economic breakdown of Roman civilization. Eli Whitney's cotton gin was produced, not merely by the genius of the individual inventor, but by the growing demand for cotton textiles that could not be manufactured rapidly and in great quantity by the old handicraft system. The historical approach to a subject gives the writer a natural beginning: he takes hold of his subject at the point where it became significant in human affairs. Furthermore, he can set up a contrast between old and new conditions, and from this contrast he goes on to the important features of the new machine or organization which he wishes to explain.

Whatever approach is used, it is generally best to state the central principle early, perhaps even in the first paragraph. This statement, the *theme sentence,* constitutes the nucleus of the discussion. Thus, the first paragraph of an explanation of the Southern plantation might read:

> In the romantic literature of the past, the old Southern plantation is generally represented in either of two ways. It was a white-pillared mansion, inhabited by a genial and courtly master and mistress and surrounded by cotton fields in which contented slaves caroled happily at their work. Or it was, to a more hostile eye, a sinister mask behind whose suave front lurked the hideous evil of slavery. A later view, often called the realistic view, tends to consider the plantation as nothing more than a kind of factory for producing the raw material, cotton. But none of these explanations really hits the truth. *The plantation, in reality, was many things in one: an economic institution, if you wish, but at the same time a farm, a school, a parish, a social center, and above all a home.* If we would understand the plantation, we must consider these many sides of plantation life and see how they are united in one institution.

The theme sentence may forecast important divisions of the discussion, as does the sentence italicized in the paragraph given above. But such forecasting is not absolutely necessary. It is undesirable if it makes the beginning of the theme too formal.

Remember that the main object of themes of this sort is to convey information. Seek to help the reader to visualize the mechanism or organization which you are explaining. Illustration is the most practical method of aiding visualization. You may illustrate by making comparisons, as by saying that the human heart is the world's most efficient pump or that the student council is a miniature Congress. You may illustrate by giving examples: a manufacturer's association, a farmers' league, a labor organization may offer an example of a "pressure group." Or, in technical expositions, you may make a drawing or chart to illustrate your remark. Such charts and drawings are not a substitute for clear explanation, but merely a help.

As in process themes, avoid using technical terms which you do not explain. See that the transition from section to section is clearly marked. Be sure that you have not omitted any important aspect of your subject.

ROCKET POWER: THE PRINCIPLE OF THE REACTION MOTOR[1]
By G. Edward Pendray

1

JET propulsion is rocket power. Thermal-jet engines, duct engines, jet motors, jet-propelled planes, robot bombs, jet-propelled gliders, war rockets, thrusters and skyrockets—all of these are merely different aspects of rocket power. All of them, as we shall see, operate on exactly the same basic principle: the principle of a motor that *thrusts* or pushes, instead of producing rotary motion in a shaft or wheel.

This is the one simple difference that makes rocket power unique —and incidentally makes it so difficult at first for our wheel-conditioned minds to grasp. A few thousand years ago some person, now unknown and long forgotten, invented the wheel. It was such a successful device, so easily adapted to doing its share of the world's work, that when fuel-burning engines were first developed they naturally were made to be harnessed to it. The reciprocating motion of their pistons was transformed by means of a crank into a rotary movement for only one purpose: to turn wheels. Even when we set the engine to the task of moving us through the air, we did so through the medium of a kind of wheel, the propeller.

To understand the principle of jet propulsion, we must think therefore in terms of an engine that does not turn a wheel; a new kind of engine, working on a totally new principle; differing from all the other engines of the world; an engine that *thrusts*.

Such an engine is known as a reaction motor, and reaction motors of all kinds, whether rocket motors, jet engines or duct engines, produce their thrust by a unique method. They simply jet out a stream of gas or other material at high velocity. The

[1] From *The Coming Age of Rocket Power* by G. Edward Pendray. Copyright 1945, 1947, by Harper & Row, Publishers, Inc., and reprinted with their permission.

resulting reaction is what provides the push. That is why, of course, the principle of the reaction motor is known as *jet propulsion.*

The first apparatus ever proposed to make use of jet propulsion was described by Heron, or Hero, a philosopher of old Alexandria, about the beginning of the Christian Era. Heron was an ingenious man who also invented a slot machine and a fire engine. In one of his books, the *Pneumatica,* he outlined plans for building a little device called the "aeolipile." It consisted of a hollow sphere mounted on pivots, equipped with two opposed bent metal spouts. Steam under pressure was introduced into the sphere through a pipe in one of the supports. The vapor, spurting from the curved spouts, caused the sphere to spin rapidly.

A similar demonstration of rudimentary rocket power is to be seen in the ordinary kind of rotating lawn sprinkler. The streams of water, jetting from the sprinkler nozzles, produce reaction against the nozzle arms to make the sprinkler spin.

Some sea creatures, especially the squid, have been using jet propulsion for hundreds of millions of years. The squid fills his mantle cavity with water, then squirts it out with a powerful convulsive motion of his muscles. The water-jet drives him forward; the movement being proportional to the speed and volume of the water thrust out behind.

2

The skyrocket, which aside from Heron's toylike contrivance was the first artificial device to make use of jet propulsion, was invented more than seven hundred years ago. But neither Heron nor the hundreds of generations of fireworks makers, nor presumably the squid, had any real understanding of the principle of jet propulsion. They only knew it worked.

It remained for Sir Isaac Newton, some 265 years ago, to give us the basis for understanding what rocket power really is, and the unique things it can do. Newton, formulating in simple language the three Laws of Motion his mathematics and observation had helped him to discover, wrote out in Latin this observation: "To every action there is always an equal and contrary reaction; the mutual actions of any two bodies are always equal and oppositely directed."

Thus, the hand that pushes a cradle is itself pushed by the cradle, to exactly the same degree and in the opposite direction. The foot that thrusts downward on the earth is thrust upward by the earth in precisely the same amount. The bullet that is ejected by a gun causes the gun to recoil—and the two actions are not only opposite in direction, but are equal in amount.

This is the statement of Newton's Third Law of Motion. Although it describes a phenomenon we daily experience throughout our lives, few people consider or even recognize the reaction that necessarily is a part of every movement of every object. It is important that we recognize it now, for the Third Law is a complete statement of the principle upon which the reaction motor operates.

In most human activities the action is what is wanted; the reaction is thrown away or ignored. In jet propulsion the "action" is thrown away. The reaction is the particular harvest we are seeking.

3

The simplest form of reaction motor—and the best known—is the one that drives an ordinary skyrocket.

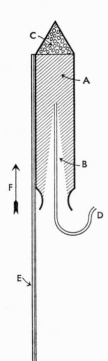

Here is a cross-section drawing of a skyrocket. At the tip is a cone-shaped cap which provides rudimentary streamlining to aid the rapid upward flight of the projectile. Immediately under the cap usually are nested the combustible pellets, the "stars" that cascade brilliantly into the sky at the top of the flight. These are the payload of the skyrocket; they are not a basic part of the rocket itself.

Into the main body of the rocket, usually contained in a heavy paper tube, a quantity of black powder is packed. This is the fuel or *propellant* charge, (A). The material is usually a form of ordinary gunpowder, often mixed with extra charcoal or some other material to slow down the rate of combustion. It is squeezed into the rocket under high pressure, thus packed tightly into a solid cake. Because it is solid, the flame cannot permeate the cake, so combustion takes place only at the exposed surface of the cone-shaped *blast chamber*, (B).

The simple thrust mechanism—or *motor*— of the rocket is completed by constricting the walls of the case below the blast chamber to form a nozzle. Sometimes the throat of the nozzle is reinforced with clay or other hard material to prevent its burning out. A fuse (D) and a long stick—a crude balancing device—complete the rocket.

On firing, what happens is this:

Heat from the fuse ignites the surface of the powder on the walls of the cone-shaped blast chamber. The powder does not explode, but a continuous combustion takes place very rapidly, releasing large quantities of gas at high temperature. Considerable pressure builds up instantly in the chamber, since the hot gas is formed at a much faster rate than it can easily escape through the restriction at the nozzle. The net effect is to eject a stream of gas at great velocity, directed backward. This thrusts the rocket forcibly in the opposite direction.

As the fuel burns, the blast chamber rapidly enlarges, but the restriction at the nozzle continues to keep the pressure high and guides the escaping jet. The rocket takes off with a tremendous swish, emitting a stream of sparks and fire, and flies until the fuel is completely consumed. Then an arrangement at the top of the tube fires the "stars" and the bursting charge in which they are packed.

In a jet motor such as that of the skyrocket there are no moving parts—except the stream of escaping gas. It is by no means easy to grasp just how this jet with nothing to push against, exerts the surprising power that thrusts the whole body of the rocket so violently toward the sky.

The common notion is that the jet does its work by pushing against the air. Superficially this seems reasonable. The air is certainly a resisting medium. But a stream of gas, no matter how rapidly it is moving, or how dense it may be, is no solid connecting rod, capable of pushing against something and transmitting the push back against whatever is adjacent to its starting end. Gas consists of billions upon billions of tiny hard pellets—the molecules of which it is composed. These are not connected together in any way. On the contrary, they are seeking to escape from each other as fast as possible, expanding like a cloud of steam.

The surrounding air similarly consists of random, flying molecules. When a molecule of ejected gas strikes a molecule of air, the collision sends both off in other directions and with altered speeds. But how could such a collision, even when multiplied by the thousands of billions, drive a rocket which is not in any way connected to them? Drive it, moreover, in a specific direction?

The answer, of course, is that they couldn't. The air in no way helps to drive the rocket. It only impedes the action—by getting in the way of the projectile in front, and hindering the rapid, straight-line ejection of the gas behind.

It is something else that drives the rocket—and this brings us back to Newton and his Law of Motion: "To every action there is always an equal and contrary reaction; the mutual actions of any two bodies are always equal and oppositely directed."

Consider the ejected gas as one "body"; the rocket as the other.

The rocket, forcing the gas to escape, pushes it violently toward the earth. The gas, escaping, pushes the rocket as violently toward the sky.

This is jet propulsion, or rocket power, the simple principle of the reaction motor.

EXERCISES

1. The preceding selection exemplifies the method that may be used for an explanation of a mechanism which is a simple and relatively ancient prototype of various complex modern mechanisms like those named in Pendray's first paragraph. The basic principle of the reaction motor is stated in this first paragraph but not fully explained. At what point or points of the discussion is it more fully explained? At what point is the explanation completed?

2. Throughout the discussion the author relies heavily upon comparison and contrast. Why? Point out all such instances of comparison and contrast. What is the value of the reference to Heron and his *Pneumatica*? Of the reference to the squid? What is the importance of the reference to Newton?

3. Is the discussion organized in terms of natural or logical order or of a combination of the two? To what extent is the explanation of the rocket mechanism also an explanation of a process? What is the advantage of the cross-section drawing? If it were not used, what changes would be necessary in section 3?

4. Look up the word *jet* in the dictionary. Is it a new or an ancient term? How are its earlier meanings adapted to modern use? To what extent does Pendray rely upon new technical terms? Do you find any so unfamiliar that you need the help of a dictionary to understand them?

THE HIGHLAND CLAN IN 1746[1]   *By John Prebble*

To AN Englishman of the eighteenth century, and to most Lowland Scots, the Highlands of Scotland were a remote and unpleasant region peopled by barbarians who spoke an obscure tongue, who dressed in skins or bolts of parti-coloured cloth, and who equated honour with cattle-stealing and murder. The savagery with which the Lowland Scots and the English were to suppress the Rebellion [of 1745] is partly explained by this belief, it being a common assumption among civilised men that brutality is pardonable when exercised upon those they consider to be uncivilised.

The Highlanders were a constant threat to the people of the Lowlands, or were believed to be. In England very little was known of them. Their mountains were a week or two weeks from London by fast horse. The Government was as prejudiced and as ill-informed as the people, although in a man like Duncan Forbes, Lord President of the Court of Session, it had a sober and sensible adviser on Highland affairs, did it choose to use him. From the

[1] From *Culloden* by John Prebble. Copyright © 1961 by John Prebble. Reprinted by permission of Atheneum Publishers and Martin Secker & Warburg Limited.

windows of his noble house at Culloden, below Drummossie Moore, he watched the mountain people with a critical eye, and only occasionally looking down his long nose. He was sincerely concerned with the need to bring to them the soft and civilising influence of the south, and when he was severe in his judgments it was with parental disapproval. One day in the summer of 1746, when the Rebellion was over and the Government was taking steps to see that there should not be another, Duncan Forbes sat down and penned a thoughtful essay on what was and what might be now that the blood had been let. It contained a sharp picture of his wild neighbours.

"What is properly called the Highlands of Scotland is that large tract of mountainous Ground to the Northwest of the Forth and the Tay, where the natives speak the Irish language. The inhabitants stick close to their antient and idle way of life; retain their barbarous customs and maxims; depend generally on their Chiefs as their Sovereign Lords and masters; and being accustomed to the use of Arms, and inured to hard living, are dangerous to the public peace; and must continue to be so until, being deprived of Arms for some years, they forget the use of them."

The feudal framework which the power of the chiefs gave to the Highland way of life enclosed a tribal system much older in time. The ties of blood and name were strong among the people, and pride of race meant as much to a humbly[1] in his sod and roundstone house as it did to a chieftain in his island keep.[2] All claimed lines of gentility, and the meanest of them believed himself the superior of any soft-breeked creature living south of his hills. By 1746, however, the clan society was dying, and, for once, history was to show an appreciation of dramatic effect by ending it abruptly and brutally. For more than a hundred years the politics and the economy of the south had been entering the glens. Military roads, driven through the Highlands from garrison to garrison, and sea to sea, broke cracks across the hard geography of the land, but still the past lingered behind its defence-work of the Irish tongue, the memories kept alive by pipes and the songs. The clan remained a man's only identity, and the broadsword his only understandable law outside it.

"A Highland Clan," wrote old Duncan Forbes, "is a set of men all bearing the same sirname, and believing themselves to be related the one to the other, and to be descended from the same common stock. In each clan there are several subaltern tribes, who own their dependence on their own immediate chiefs but

[1] The lower class of Highlanders were denominated humblies from wearing no covering on their heads but their hair. Literally, a humbly is a polled cow; also a person whose head has been shaved or his hair cut.

[2] A stronghold fort.

all agree in owing allegiance to the Supreme Chief of the Clan or Kindred and look upon it to be their duty to support him at all adventures."

No law of the country, none put down on sheepskin anyway, determined the right of a chief to his title, nor need he have title to an acre of ground. "Some Chiefs there are that have neither property nor jurisdiction, and the cutting off of the present Chief does no more than make way for another." For a Highland chief's right to the name sprang from a dawn of society before the writing of laws. So the difficulty of imposing the Law on a race of tribesmen, who had not the understanding or will to accept it, was a matter of extreme concern to men like Duncan Forbes. For him the Rebellion, and the constant feuding forays in the hills, were sad obstacles to the progress of civilisation. But to soldiers like Cumberland, and his rough general of division Henry Hawley, there was a common sense in the argument that if men are all the better for a little blooding so must nations be also. If the Law and loyalty could not be brought into the hills by persuasion and argument it must be brought by the musket, the bayonet and the gibbet.

Still Forbes persevered. "It has been for a great many years impracticable (and hardly thought safe to try it) to give the Law its course among the mountains. It required no small degree of Courage, and a greater degree of power than men are generally possessed of, to arrest an offender or debtor in the midst of his Clan. And for this reason it was that the Crown in former times was obliged to put Sheriffships and other Jurisdictions in the hands of powerful families in the Highlands, who, by their respective Clans and following could give execution to the Laws within their several territories, and frequently did so at the expense of considerable bloodshed."

Great chieftains, men ennobled by the Crown like the Campbells of Argyll and Breadalbane, were thus responsible for the Law in the hills, and by the execution of it would have been less than men if they had not thereby increased their own power and property. They could put the greatest number of broadswords in the greatest number of hands, and dress the settlement of ancient feuds in the livery of the King. The Government had not solved the problem by acknowledging and confirming the Hereditary Jurisdictions of the chiefs, it had merely given quasi-legal authority to the primitive savagery of Highland life. Although, in 1746, Europe and America were within half a century of revolution and the Rights of Man, North Britain still slumbered in tribal twilight four hundred miles from London.

The social system of a Highland clan was fixed, and the barriers were crossed emotionally only. A chief's son, wet-nursed by the wife of a humbly, would never call his foster-brother his equal, but the milk shared by them imposed a life-long obligation that could and often did compel the one to give his life for the other. And if the compulsion were not strong enough, if the clansman were reluctant to come out with sword and target when needed, the chief would feel himself justified in burning the roof of his milk-brother's hut.

The geography of their land determined the economy of the clans. It was, and is, a hard land. Before Man, the moving floors of ice cut the glens, and so flayed the earth skin that at its best the rock is covered by shallow soil. In such harsh and unrewarding surroundings men could be herdsmen only, raising black and shaggy cattle, hardy sheep and goats. And being tribal herdsmen they became warriors to protect their flocks, until in the end history stood on its head and they were men of war rather than minders of cattle. Forays against the herds of their neighbours became affairs of honour, and only the people south of the mountains saw it as robbery. A quarrel between men of different tribes might be settled by a dirk-thrust at night, by single combat, or by whole clans pulled out on to the heather by the fiery cross. One cattle-raid would be answered by another, year after year, and the bards of the clans composed heroic poems about each bloody incident, the pipes played rants in honour of men dead for centuries.

The land, once held by the tribe in common, had by the eighteenth century become the chief's, his title to it being no more tangible than the approval of his tribe, a situation that proved most awkward for some of them when the great chiefs of Argyll, or Seaforth, or Lovat, discovered that a sheet of sheepskin could be a more effective weapon than a broadsword or a Lochaber axe. Yet, though the land was the chief's, the clan's interest in the soil was deep and strong. Part of it was "mensal land,"[1] used by and for the chief himself. Parts, too, might be given in perpetuity to families of officials of the clan, men like the Bard, the Harper and the Piper. The rest was held by tenants under "tacks"[2] or leases granted by the chief. Thus the tacksman, though not of the chief's family, was a man of importance in the tribal society, and his rank entitled him to be a junior officer or senior noncommissioned officer when the clan formed itself into a regiment for war. In their turn the tacksmen sub-leased part of their land, and so each social stratum was formed, each man owing economic allegiance to those above him, and all bound in fealty to the chieftain whose direct and known progenitor had been the strong-loined hero who had started the whole tribe.

The chief was a man of contradictions, a civilised savage whose interests and experience were often far wider than most English-

---

[1] Land set apart for the supply of food for the table (Lat., *mensa*) of the king, prince, or chief.

[2] Leases.

men's. He could speak Gaelic and English, and very often French, Greek and Latin as well. He sent his sons to be educated at universities in Glasgow and Edinburgh, in Paris or Rome. He drank French claret and wore lace at his throat. He danced lightly, his own Highland reels and southern measures. He swore oaths in which God and Celtic mythology were mixed. He would boast, as did the MacGregors, that Royal was his race, or that he bore a King's name if he were an Appin Stewart, but his allegiance to Kings was quixotic. In his glens he was king, and there was no appeal higher than he among his clan. A woman was once brought before Macdonald of Clanranald and accused of stealing money from him. He ordered her to be tied by the hair to sea-weed on the rocks, and there she stayed until the Atlantic tide rolled in and drowned her. Although Clanranald's people may have trembled at the violent justice of their chief, none could have questioned the punishment, for who stole from the chief stole from the clan.

The chief protected the clan and the chief punished the clan. At the best, offenders were driven from the glens; at the worst they might be sold to the merchant captains who called at Inverness, looking for servants for the Americas. Seven years before Culloden Sir Alexander Macdonald of Sleat and his brother-in-law Macleod of Dunvegan, chiefs of the Isles, drove one hundred of their people aboard ships for deportation to Pennsylvania, and swaggered their way out of the uproar this caused in the Lowlands when the ship was discovered and the deportees released at an Irish port. No protest was heard or recorded from a Macdonald or a Macleod clansman.

Although now and then a chief might whet his talents on the politics or society of the Lowlands or England, most of them, once their youth was past, stayed in their hills, where they were not known by their surnames but by their land, by the glen or loch, the strath or clachan[1] that was their home. And the wife of a chief, whether or not her husband would have been plain Mister in Glasgow or London, was always Lady. A chief's amusement came from the land and the culture of his people, from bardic poems and wild pipe music. More actively, when he was not away on a cattle-raid, he hunted. The high mountains, at one time, were running with the stag, the wolf and the cat, and the hunting of them was a fine and barbaric spectacle even after the fire-arm came to the Highlands. Sir Ewen Cameron of Lochiel, chief of a clan that was "all gentlemen" by its own estimate, once organised a splendid deer-hunt for the pleasure of his guests. He called out hundreds of his men and stretched them over the hills at the head of Loch Arkaig. They moved forward, shouting and crying, sounding the pipes and beating sword on shield, so that the deer bounded from cover and ran toward the mouth of a narrow glen.

[1] A small village in which there is a parish church.

There stood Lochiel and his guests with broadswords in their hands. By the swinging and the cutting of the long blades they slew many animals, and the Cameron Bard and the Cameron Harper made an epic of it. Tacksmen and humblies, because they were blood of blood with Lochiel, felt that some of his valour and some of his pride was theirs, too. So where he went they would go, and if he passed by their door they would have a plaid for his head and brawn[1] for his dogs.

Duncan Forbes, in his painstaking efforts to enlighten a usually obtuse Government in London, once numbered the fighting-men of the Highlands, naming them clan by clan, from Macdonald of Glencoe's 130 broadswords to the 4,000 well-armed kerns[2] whom Campbell of Argyll and Campbell of Breadalbane could put into battle if they wished. Altogether, Forbes estimated that the warrior strength of the mountains was 31,930, and he regarded this as a conservative figure. Had all these found common cause they could have tumbled the House of Hanover from the throne merely by assembling and marching down to the Lowlands. Less than 6,000 advancing south to Derby under Prince Charles four months before Culloden, had forced George II to think seriously of immediate retirement to Hanover. But, in fact, there had never been unity in the Highlands, nor could ever be. Religion, feuds, the political ambitions of chiefs, the natural jealousies of men who live remote and primitive lives, made common cause impossible. Each clan was enough to itself, and the world ended beyond the glen, or with the sea that locked in the islands.

The patriarchal system of clanship, the fact that there was never at one time more than half the people of the Highlands profitably employed, the ancient stories of valour and combat, all fostered the warlike spirit of the clans. Thus a chief was judged by his attitude toward military matters, by his courage, and by his sensitivity in affairs of honour. As soon as a chief's son came to manhood he was watched carefully by his father's people. If he were quick to revenge an insult by tugging out his dirk, if he were always ready to lead high-spirited young men on a cattle foray, then he was greatly esteemed and accepted as worthy to succeed his father. If, however, his brief encounter with softer living in the Lowlands, or on the Continent, had turned his mind to more sedentary interests, he would be despised, and the allegiance of the clan might turn to a younger brother. The milksop might remain the chief in name, none could take that from him, but hard sinews and a fine cunning in war were expected of the man who led the clan in battle.

Every man and boy old enough or fit enough to carry arms was automatically a soldier in the regiment of the clan, his rank fixed

[1] Scraps of meat, usually swine.

[2] Foot soldiers, armed with a dart or dirk.

by his social position. The chief, or that man of the chief's family named by him, was the colonel. The chief's brothers or sons commanded the flanks and the rear. The head of each family was an officer or a sergeant, bringing in his brothers, sons and tenants to form companies or platoons. Each family, too, stood in line of battle according to its importance in the clan, so that the common humbly, the raw-thighed, half-naked sub-tenant of a sub-tenant would find himself in the rear rank of all, and think it no more than his right. Brother fought beside brother, father by son, so that each might witness the other's courage and valour and find example in them.

The clan gathered when the fiery cross was sent across its country, two burnt or burning sticks to which was tied a strip of linen stained with blood. The cross was passed from hand to hand, by runners in relay. One of the last occasions on which it was sent was when a Campbell, the Earl of Breadalbane, rallied his people against the Jacobite clans in 1745. It travelled thirty-two miles about Loch Tay in three hours. A clan that had been gathered by the cross was moved by deep and distant superstitions. An armed man it met with by the way was a portent of good fortune and victory. A stag, fox, hare or any beast of game that was seen and not killed promised evil. If a barefooted woman crossed the road before the marching men she was seized, and blood was drawn from her forehead by the point of a knife. All this and more. Every tribe had its slogan, a wild and savage exhortation to slaughter or a reminder of the heroic past. It was cried for the onslaught, in the confusion of a night alarm, and it was as much a part of the clan's identity as the badge of heather, gale, ling,[1] oak or myrtle that a man wore in his bonnet. The slogan was yelled, the rant played and the badge worn, be it for a battle such as that now facing the Jacobite clans, or for a dark-of-night *creach*[2] when young men fell upon a neighbour's cattle and sheep.

Because there were no laws to protect a clan against a chief's rights, the past had established a compensating balance. If he had the right of life and death over his people, he was equally responsible for their welfare, and most chiefs honoured this obligation. As landlord, father-figure, judge and general-at-arms his power was great, but it was not always absolute, and on occasions he would debate major issues with the leading members of his family and clan—the settlement of serious disputes between one man and another, the support of children orphaned, the declaration of war and the acceptance of terms for peace. This was something from the tribe's past, when men held things in common,

---

[1] A species of rush, or thin long grass.
[2] A foray for forcibly driving off cattle from the grounds of the lawful owner.

and there were chiefs who felt themselves strong enough in their feudal power to disregard it. They would not ask their council's advice, or would ignore it if they did, and, if they felt their following among the clan to be weak, they would burn a few cottages to encourage the laggards. From boyhood, from the moment his foster-mother weaned him, a Highland chief began to understand, or at least to enjoy, his peculiar position in life. He was of the same blood and name and descent as his people, but he stood halfway between them and God.

His prosperity or poverty depended upon the industry of his clan, and it would have been unnatural if all chiefs recognized this in terms of their responsibility toward their people. A chief's tenants, tacksmen and humblies, followed his standard, avenged his wrongs, supplied his table with the produce of their crofts, reaped his corn, cut his fuel. They paid their rents to him loyally, even when he was an outlaw or in exile. For nine years after Culloden, Macpherson of Cluny lived in a cave on his mountains, nourished by his clan and protected from the soldiers. A chief was not distinguished by the degree of his fortune or by the splendour of his dress, though some walked like peacocks in tartan and silver. His power and importance rested in the cattle on his braes, and in the number of pretty fellows he could have in his tail when he went abroad. Thus did a Macdonald of Keppoch boast that his rent-roll was five hundred fighting-men. In such a climate of pride and sensitive honour the hospitality of the Highlands was more often manifest vanity. When this same Keppoch was told by a guest of the great candelabra to be seen in the houses of England he ringed his table with tall clansmen, each holding aloft a flaming pine-knot. Keppoch grinned at his guest and asked where, in England, France or Italy, was there a house with such candlesticks.

Edward Burt was a heavy-footed Englishman with no sense of humour but a rewarding taste for sociology. He went to the Highlands early in the eighteenth century to help Marshal Wade build his civilising roads, and he found the pride of the Highland chiefs quaintly archaic and faintly alarming. "I happened to be at the house of a certain chief, when the chieftain of another tribe came to make a visit. I told him I thought some of his people had not behaved toward me with that civility I expected of the clan. He started, clapped his hand to his broadsword and said, if I required it, he would send me two or three of their heads. I laughed, thinking it a joke, but the chief insisted he was a man of his word." Honour was honour, it clothed a man better than a fine jacket before the eyes of his neighbours, and the heads of three of his tribe were well-expended if they kept a chief decent. Burt must have talked the Highlander out of the bloody offer, for he does not say that he received the heads, and he was too meticulous a chronicler to have ignored the fact. He had a bumbling respect for this primitive code of honour, and for the simple and barbaric way in which the Highlanders gave their word on any sacred matter. "This oath they take upon a drawn dirk, which they kiss in a solemn manner, consenting if ever they prove perjured to be stabbed with the same weapon." And while, like a good civilised Englishman, he deplored the mountain habit of cattle-lifting, "I cannot approve of the Lowland saying 'Show me a Highlander and I will show you a thief.' I do not remember that ever I lost anything among them but a pair of doe-skin gloves."

Another Englishman who was inclined to accept the Highlanders' claims to gentility was Daniel Defoe. "We see every day the gentlemen born here: such as the Mackenzies, McLeans, Dundonalds, Gordons, Mackays, and others who are named among the clans as if they were *Barbarians,* appear at Court and in our Camps and Armies, as polite and as finished gentlemen as any from other countries, or even among our own, and if I should say, outdoing our own in many things, especially in arms and gallantry as well abroad as at home."

Any Mackenzie or Mackay would have agreed that Defoe was giving them no more than their due.

Edward Burt studied the clans more closely than Defoe, and saw more of the common people among them, and in all that he wrote of them there is curiosity and distaste, a wonder that such a society should exist on one island with men as civilised and as humane as Edward Burt. He never fully understood the peculiar relationship that existed between chief and tribesman. "The ordinary Highlanders esteem it the most sublime degree of virtue to love their chief and pay him a blind obedience although it be in opposition to the government, the laws of the kingdom, or even the law of God. He is their idol; and as they profess to know no king but him (I was going further) so will they say they ought to do whatever he commands."

On the other hand, the love and veneration of his clan was sometimes a trial to the chief, since he was expected to behave at all times with superior courage and superlative hardihood. Burt tells a story of a chief who was once taking his men over the hills in a winter foray against another clan. The raiders sheltered for the night in a high corrie, and when the chief rolled snow into a ball, placing it beneath his head for a pillow, his followers looked sourly at him and murmured among themselves, "Now we despair of victory, since our leader has become so effeminate he cannot sleep without a pillow."

EXERCISES

1. John Prebble states first the views, most of them mistaken, that Englishmen and Lowland Scots had of the Scottish Highlanders: for example, that "the Highlands of Scotland were . . .

peopled by barbarians who spoke an obscure tongue, who dressed in skins or bolts of particoloured cloth, and who equated honour with cattle-stealing and murder." When you set out to explain an organization, what advantages are there in quoting, first, some popular but erroneous views and then proceeding to refute such misconceptions? In what passages does Prebble "attack" the stereotype of the Highlander?

2. In order to understand the events of 1745 we must understand, Prebble tells us, some "historical factors": the ancient phenomenon called "the clan"; feudal concepts of land tenure; matters of geography, climate, language, and custom which differentiated the Scottish Highlands—including the great deference of the Highlanders for poets, pipers, and singers and the persistence of pagan superstitions in a Christian community. Obviously Prebble cannot discourse at length on all these factors. How often does he ask the reader to draw on his own knowledge? Does he demand too much of the reader or is there a reasonable compromise?

3. Study the author's manner of introducing and presenting commentaries from Burt, Forbes, and Defoe. Are these handled with proper attention to transition and clarity? What advantages have direct quotations over paraphrases?

4. List the instances in which the author uses comparison and contrast, either directly or by inference, to explain the clan system.

5. In describing or characterizing a typical Scottish chief the author often uses paradox—"a seeming contradiction that is nevertheless true in fact." List the "seeming contradictions" that go to make up Prebble's image of the "typical" chief.

6. Characterize the tone of Prebble's article. Is it realistic, sympathetic, romantic, impersonal, formal, informal?

7. How does anecdote, embedded in the expository description, help to explain the clan system? Point out examples.

SUGGESTIONS FOR THEMES

1. Write an explanation of a mechanism. Some suggestions are given below. Be sure that you understand the central principle, essential parts, and method of operation of the mechanism that you choose to explain.

An automatic rifle	A chain saw
An automobile starter	A telescope
A transistor radio	A solar heating system
An electric hair-dryer	A compass
A printing press	An electric skillet

2. Look up some American pre-industrial tool or mechanism and explain it: for example, a spinning wheel; a loom; a Navajo

weaving frame; a potter's wheel; a well-sweep; a sleigh; a double-bitted axe.

3. Differentiate some instrument or mechanism from one somewhat resembling it: for example, musket and rifle; "prop"-plane and jet-plane; piano and harpsichord; trumpet and bugle.

4. Look up some notable invention and write an explanation of it: for example, the phonograph; the X-ray; the submarine; the Roman catapult; the arquebus; the English long-bow.

5. Explain some governmental organization: a unit of a modern fire department; the school mothers' patrol; a highway patrol station; a New England town; county government in the South; an irrigation system; a national forest.

6. State the central principle of some organization and use it as the unifying element in an expository theme: a "privateer" ship (as used in the British-American war of 1812); an eleemosynary fraternal organization (such as the Elks, Shriners, B'nai B'rith, etc.); a farmers' cooperative; a Roman legion; a unit of the American Automobile Association; a cattle ranch; an airport.

7. Explain some organism or natural organization. Use the same principles of composition that you have applied to mechanisms and civilized organizations. Marine creatures; "societies" of birds, animals, or insects; flowers; the ecological arrangements of a pond, swamp, beach, or river under natural conditions—these will offer subjects.

PROJECT 3. PEOPLE

Thomas Carlyle contended, in his *Heroes and Hero Worship,* that all history is but the biography of great men. In more recent times our historians have seemed to argue the contrary. They have written of how history makes men rather than of how men make history. Yet history, like conversation, seems to begin and end with talk of men and women rather than of mere things. Even in the daily newspaper names make news. The human subject is the most absorbing of all subjects, and a course in composition would be a queer kind of tomfoolery if it stayed away very long from the big people and little people who provoke our curiosity by behaving like human beings.

In writing about people we may use either of two approaches: (1) we may treat the person as an *individual* with such marked peculiarity or distinction as to stand out from other individuals; or (2) we may consider the person a *type,* representative of a place, a time, a tradition, a fashion, a race, a profession. Queen Elizabeth I stands out as an individual among monarchs, Audubon among naturalists, the eccentric Rube Waddell among baseball pitchers, John Paul Jones among naval heroes, and so on. Such individuals are distinguished by certain odd or highly developed traits of character. On the other hand Sinclair Lewis' famous creation George F. Babbitt is a type. He is thought to embody the ways of the typical businessman. Sinclair Lewis' portrait may or may not do justice to the businessman; it is a good enough likeness to have made the name "Babbitt" a catch-word. It is easy to think of familiar American types: the frontiersman, the Yankee farmer, the Puritan, the cowboy, the Southern planter, the mountaineer, the Irishman, the Swede, the flapper of the nineteen-twenties, the Hollywood movie star, the radio announcer. Exaggerated and made humorous, these types often appear as stereotypes or caricatures: there is a typical stage Irishman, a stage Westerner and Southerner, a stage villain, soubrette, and juvenile leading man in melodramas, and there are the characters of the comic strips. They fit a known pattern; they embody traits common to individuals of the type concerned.

Often enough, of course, the person may be a type and yet be also a striking individual. Both Andrew Jackson and Abraham Lincoln were frontiersmen, in many ways typical frontiersmen; but they were different in their individual traits. Daniel Webster and Ralph Waldo Emerson were both New Englanders; yet as individuals they seem nearly opposite. Every person is a combination of typical and individual traits. A written interpretation of a character will emphasize either one side or the other of the combination, depending on the point of view.

If the subject of the composition is an individual, the problem of the writer is to decide upon the distinguishing traits of character and then to bring these out by giving close attention to supporting details. Robert Louis Stevenson, in writing of Samuel Pepys, finds that one of Pepys's chief traits was his capacity for being interested in a great number of things. Stevenson not only mentions Pepys's "insatiable curiosity," but gives immediately the specific details which support the general statement at the beginning of the paragraph:

> The whole world, town or country, was to Pepys a garden of Armida. Wherever he went, his steps were winged with

the most eager expectations; whatever he did, it was done with the most lively pleasure. An insatiable curiosity in all the shows of the world and all the secrets of knowledge, filled him brimful of the longing to travel, and supported him in the toils of study. Rome was the dream of his life; he was never happier than when he read or talked of the Eternal City. When in Holland he was "with child" to see any strange thing. Meeting some friends and singing with them in a palace near the Hague, his pen fails to express his passion of delight "the more so because in a heaven of pleasure and in a strange country." He must go to see all famous executions. He must needs visit the body of a murdered man, defaced "with a broad wound," he says, "that makes my hand now shake to write of it." He learned to dance, and was "like to make a dancer." He learned to sing, and walked about Gray's Inn Fields "humming to myself (which is now my constant practice) the trillo." . . . He was a member of Harrington's Club till its dissolution, and of the Royal Society before it had received the name. Boyle's *Hydrostatics* was "of infinite delight" to him, walking in Barnes Elms. We find him comparing Bible concordances, a captious judge of sermons, deep in Descartes and Aristotle. We find him, in a single year, studying timber and the measurement of timber; tar and oil, hemp, and the process of preparing cordage; mathematics and accounting; the hull and rigging of ships from a model; and "looking and improving himself of the (naval) stores with"—hark to the fellow!—"great delight."—ROBERT LOUIS STEVENSON, *Familiar Studies of Men and Books.*

It is necessary that each distinguishing trait be exemplified by supporting details. These details must be concrete. High-sounding generalizations, rhetorical flourishes, polite catch-words, loud eulogies, or vehement denunciations—these will not do. The concrete details are the facts, the really significant part of the character study.

Detail is so important that it is often good strategy to begin a character study with a description of personal appearance. Froude's study of Julius Cæsar begins as follows:

> In person Cæsar was tall and slight. His features were more refined than was usual in Roman faces; the forehead was wide and high, the nose large and thin, lips full, the eyes dark gray like an eagle's, the neck extremely thin and sinewy. His complexion was pale. His beard and moustache were kept carefully shaved. His hair was short and naturally

scanty, falling off toward the end of his life and leaving him
partially bald. His voice, especially when he spoke in public,
was high and shrill. His health was uniformly strong until
his last year, when he became subject to epileptic fits.
                    —JAMES ANTHONY FROUDE, *Cæsar: A Sketch.*

Froude follows this description with a discussion of
Cæsar's personal habits and then goes on to discuss his
qualities as statesman and soldier. At every point Froude
supports his general statements with examples of Cæsar's
personal valor, or his devotion to his subordinates, or his
genuine patriotism.

The descriptive beginning gives the reader a "thumb-nail
portrait" which he can carry in his mind while reading the
character analysis which follows. This analysis will generally
fall into obvious subdivisions. Froude discusses, for example,
Cæsar's ability as a politician, his genius as a soldier, his
aims as statesman, and his accomplishments as an orator
and a man of letters. The initial personal description must
be kept within proportionate limits. And it must be vivid—
it must set forth the real individual.

If the subject is a type, the problem of organization is
easier. Center on the qualities of the type and minimize the
individual qualities. Again, it is necessary to give supporting
details to make the portrait clear and interesting.

There are several possible ways of writing a study of a
type:

(1) Sum up the type in a single statement which you can
expand. In discussing the average attendant at a filling station, you might begin thus:

> In off-hours he may be a human individual, as irregular
> and unpredictable (and perhaps as impudent) as any other
> contrary American. But at his glittering pump, lettered uni-
> form on his back, wiping-rag in hand, he is a polite robot,
> a walking tool of quick service that talks by formula and
> moves as if animated by a pushbutton.

The sketch of the filling-station attendant would then
show just how the human robot performs, what formulas he
uses, what typical actions are forced upon him by the
routine of his work.

(2) Begin the discussion with a statement of wrong con-

ceptions which you intend to refute. Thus, in discussing the Puritans, Macaulay warns his readers not to be misled by the "potent ridicule" long directed at the Puritan party in England. After this warning, he states his theme in the following sentence:

> Those who roused the people to resistance, who directed their measures through a long series of eventful years, who formed, out of the most unpromising materials, the finest army that Europe had ever seen, who trampled down King, Church, and Aristocracy, who, in the short intervals of domestic sedition and rebellion, made the name of England terrible to every nation on the face of the earth, *were no vulgar fanatics.*—THOMAS BABINGTON MACAULAY, *Essay on Milton.*

The rest of the essay answers the question: If the Puritans were not vulgar fanatics, then what were they?

(3) The type may be shown in association with the background, habitat, cause that makes him typical. The backwoodsman naturally is not to be dissociated from his cabin in the clearing, or the businessman from his desk, his luncheon club, his golf. This method is particularly valuable for the treatment of regional American types: the Vermont farmer of the East, the lumberjack of the Northwest, the Indian of the Great Plains or of the Pueblo, the rancher or wheat farmer of the Great West, the plantation owner of the Deep South. But the same method can also be used for historical figures. Napoleon Bonaparte, so far as he may be considered a type, may be studied against the background of the French Revolution; William Jennings Bryan, against the background of the Middle West of the eighteen-nineties, when Populism set the prairies afire. General Robert E. Lee may be studied as a product of Virginia.

(4) The type may be revealed dramatically by putting an individual into action. Such a character sketch may begin with an illustrative incident or anecdote. If you are dealing with Calvin Coolidge as a typical New Englander, you may begin with one of the "Coolidge jokes" circulated during his Presidential administration. For example, there is the story of a man who had bet that President Coolidge could be persuaded to say more than two words at a time. The man sat next to Coolidge at a dinner and told the President about his bet. "You lose," said Coolidge.

DAVID WARK GRIFFITH[1]   *By James Agee*

HOLLYWOOD was his invention. Charlie Chaplin said, "The whole industry owes its existence to him." Yet of late years he could not find a job in the town he had invented. He clung to the shadows, a bald, eagle-beaked man, sardonic and alone. At parties, he sat drinking quietly, his sharp eyes panning the room for a glimpse of familiar faces, most of them long gone. David Wark Griffith had been the Master, and there was nobody quite like him afterwards.

It was a long stretch from the genteel poverty of the Kentucky farm where D. W. Griffith was born in 1875 to the international renown he achieved. He had wanted to be a writer, but all that he wrote floundered and failed. In the beginning he was ashamed to be an entertainer: he toured with road shows as Lawrence Griffith. He was stranded in tank towns, fired, overworked and underfed. Between roles, he did slob labor.

Griffith tried writing for pictures, but the Edison Co. rejected his scenarios. When (in 1907) they hired him as an actor, to wrestle with a stuffed eagle in an old-fashioned cliff-hanger, he attached himself to the movies and never, voluntarily, left them again. But until his third contract as a director with Biograph, his pride would not permit him to sign himself David Griffith.

As a director, Griffith hit the picture business like a tornado. Before he walked on the set, motion pictures had been, in actuality, static. At a respectful distance the camera snapped a series of whole scenes clustered in the groupings of the stage play. Griffith broke up the pose. He rammed his camera into the middle of the action. He took closeups, crosscuts, angle shots and dissolves. His camera was alive, picking off shots; then he built the shots into sequences, the sequences into tense, swift narrative. For the first time the movies had a man who realized that while a theater audience listened, a movie audience watched. "Above all . . . I am trying to make you see," Griffith said.

Griffith brought a strange, yet significant, heritage to his work. His father was Colonel Jacob Wark ("Roaring Jake") Griffith, a Confederate cavalry officer given to florid reading of Shakespeare. Like him, young D. W. had a stentorian voice, a tough physical frame, and a character that mixed moral austerity with poetic sentiment. He absorbed the attitude of the post-bellum Southerner to the Northern carpetbagger and the problems of the new freed men. When his talents and his viewpoint merged in *The Birth of a Nation,* a story of the Civil War, the Reconstruction and the first Ku Klux Klan, the cinema had its first "colossal." But on the heels of the picture came race riots and cries of racial bigotry.

---

[1] From *Agee on Film.* Copyright 1958 by the James Agee Trust. Reprinted by permission of Ivan Obolensky, New York City.

Griffith was hurt and astonished at the cries. By way of answer, he sank all the money he had in another super, *Intolerance*. The film ran 20 hours, before cutting, and undertook to prove, in four parallel stories from history, that intolerance and injustice never pay. *Intolerance* itself was a failure at the box office. Like his later successes (*Broken Blossoms, Orphans of the Storm,* and *Way Down East*) it perhaps only proved that Griffith would never again match *The Birth of a Nation*.

Griffith tried the talkies twice. One had Walter Huston as Abraham Lincoln and was a box-office dud. The other, called *The Struggle,* was considered too faulty for general distribution. Yet in his lifetime, Griffith made 432 movies. They grossed about $60 million, some $25 million of it clear profit for Griffith and his associates.

When he died last week at 73 of a cerebral hemorrhage, in the Hollywood hotel where he lived alone, his lawyer said that the estate would not exceed $50,000. Of this, $20,000 had been found in a safe some years ago during the audit of an ancient hotel. It was wrapped in brown paper and marked "D. W. Griffith—Personal." D. W., his mind on the remote intangibles of a lifetime, had forgotten all about it.

In Hollywood last week, many people were offering epitaphs for Griffith. But perhaps the most succinct was the one presented years ago by another man who could claim to know about such things, the Frenchman René Clair. "Nothing essential," he said, "has been added to the art of the motion picture since Griffith."

EXERCISES

Agee's sketch is a good example of a small-scale, terse portrait by an exceptionally serious and skilful critic who is here writing for a popular news magazine and must adapt his style to its requirements. Undoubtedly the factual details that Agee chooses to combine are selected from a mass of information derived from books, newspapers, and magazines as well as from interviews with persons who knew Griffith. In a scholarly biography, salient details would be "documented"—authenticated by references to sources used. In a popular news magazine, such authentication is rarely possible except in the form of direct quotations—as in Agee's quotations from Chaplin and René Clair. The following are some of the aspects of Agee's sketch that naturally invite study.

1. *His method of composition.* Evidently Agee decided to build his portrait upon the sharp contrasts and paradoxes that he discovered in Griffith's career. Trace out this pattern of contrasts and paradoxes from its first appearance to the last paragraph. What are the advantages of this pattern as compared with (a) a plain chronological narrative of Griffith's career or (b) a more exclusive

focus on Griffith's essential contribution to the art of moving pictures, as indicated by Agee in paragraph 4?

2. *Special terms.* What words or phrases belong to the lingo of photographers, the theatre, or Hollywood? Are these special terms so generally understood that Agee is entitled to use them without explanation? Are *The Birth of a Nation* and other titles so well known that Agee can assume public knowledge of them?

3. *Conformity to magazine style.* Is this a typical *Time* article in diction and tone? If you have access to the collection of articles entitled *Agee on Film,* compare it with articles written by Agee for other periodicals.

CAPTAIN OF INDUSTRY, 1925[1]   *By Sinclair Lewis*

HE always wore large grave suits, brown or gray or plain blue, expensively tailored and not very interesting, with decorous and uninteresting ties of dull silk and no jewelry save a watch-chain. But though you were not likely to see what he wore, you noted him as a man of importance, as an executive, tall, deep-chested, his kind eyes never truculent, but his mouth serious, with crescents of wrinkles beside it. His gray-threaded brown mustache, trimmed every week by the best barber at the best hotel, was fully as eccentric and showy as a doormat.

He made his toilet like a man who never wasted motion—and who, incidentally, had a perfectly organized household to depend upon. His hand went surely to the tall pile of shirts (Fran ordered them from Jermyn Street) in the huge Flemish armoire, and to the glacial nest of collars, always inspected by the parlor maid and discarded for the slightest fraying. He tied his tie, not swiftly but with the unwasteful and extremely unadventurous precision of a man who has introduced as much "scientific efficiency" into daily domesticity as into his factory.

He kissed Fran and, while she nibbled at sweetbreads and drank her coffee in birdlike sips and furiously rattled the newspaper in bed, he marched downstairs to the oak-beamed dining-room. Over a second copy of the *Advocate,* and a Chicago paper, he ponderously and thoroughly attended to orange juice, porridge and thick cream, bacon, corn cakes and syrup, and coffee in a cup twice as large as the cup which Fran was jiggling in her thin hand as she galloped through the paper upstairs.

To the maid he said little, and that amiably, as one certain that he would be well served. He was not extraordinarily irritable even when he was informed that Emily, his engaging daughter, had been up late at a dance and would not be down for breakfast. He liked Emily's morning gossip, but he never dreamed of demanding her presence—of demanding anything from her. He smiled over the letter of his son, Brent, now a junior in Yale.

Samuel Dodsworth was, perfectly, the American Captain of Industry, believing in the Republican Party, high tariff and, so long as they did not annoy him personally, in prohibition and the Episcopal Church. He was the president of the Revelation Motor Company; he was a millionaire, though decidedly not a multimillionaire; his large house was on Ridge Crest, the most fashionable street in Zenith; he had some taste in etchings; he did not split many infinitives; and he sometimes enjoyed Beethoven. He would certainly (so the observer assumed) produce excellent motor cars; he would make impressive speeches to the salesmen; but he would never love passionately, lose tragically, nor sit in contented idleness upon tropic shores.

EXERCISES

This sketch purports to be a portrait of an individual, but we soon realize that the Samuel Dodsworth of Sinclair Lewis' novel also represents a well-known type, the American industrialist and businessman of the nineteen-twenties. Does the fact that the portrait is "fictional" make it any the less "true"? If Lewis had been writing a completely matter-of-fact sketch of an actual "captain of industry" (for example, Walter Chrysler, Henry Ford, John D. Rockefeller), how different would it have been in method? In selection of details? What is the function of the parenthetical statement—"so the observer assumed"—in the final paragraph? Is it really necessary? Who is the "observer"? If restated in expository rather than in narrative-descriptive form, would the details selected here by Sinclair Lewis constitute a convincing and accurate portrait of the typical captain of industry?

SUGGESTIONS FOR THEMES

1. Write a sketch of an individual in which—using James Agee's method—you isolate certain important features of the individual's career or temperament.

2. Write a theme in which you emphasize a dominant trait in the life of some notable personage: for example, Dr. Samuel Johnson's dislike of sham and pretense; Benjamin Franklin's practicality; Winston Churchill's "British pluck"; Florence Nightingale's self-sacrificing devotion; Caruso's vitality.

3. Select as your subject an individual who, in your opinion, has been misrepresented or misunderstood. Refute erroneous conceptions and reveal the true person.

4. Compose a portrait of some familiar contemporary type: for example, the connoisseur of antique automobiles; the Ivy League

expert in "country music"; the man who drives a Mercedes-Benz; the man whose trumpet always sounds retreat; the coffee shop singer.

5. The dictionary defines a caricature as "the deliberately distorted picturing or imitating of a person . . . by exaggerating features or mannerisms for satirical effect" (*Webster's New World Dictionary*). Is it necessarily true that a caricature must carry a "satirical"—that is a derogatory—effect? Experiment by writing a favorable caricature of some class of persons often satirized.

PROJECT 4. IDEAS

In explaining a process, mechanism, or organization or in portraying, through expository discussion, a typical or individual character, we enjoy the great advantage of having a tangible, concrete *object* before our eyes—or at least before the "mind's eye." Whatever we may think "about" the object, it is always actually there as the focus of our thinking, and any vagueness of thought or feeling may be corrected by reference to the object itself.

If we take another step and begin to theorize or generalize about the object, we move into the more difficult realm of abstract ideas; yet, as long as we continue to refer closely to the object itself, or compare the particular object with others of the same kind, we should not find it difficult to write about it clearly, definitely, and systematically.

Thus Aldo Leopold, in "Thinking Like a Mountain," begins with a graphic description of a wolf's howl and the interpretation made of it by wild animals or the rancher, then gradually develops a generalization about the relationship of wild life to civilization. He strongly suggests that even predatory animals like the wolf have a "value," but leaves the reader to develop the generalization implied in his suggestion.

This, the method of proceeding from the particular to the general, from the concrete to the abstract, is far easier than its opposite. If we begin with an abstract idea—which may at first be somewhat nebulous and uncertain—and seek to express it, we are in an area of major difficulty. Expression will fail, or will remain incomplete and untrustworthy, unless we can find ways of giving the idea concrete form.

The problem of explaining an idea therefore becomes, first, a problem of discovering *what the idea really is*. Until it is clearly and accurately stated, it cannot be satisfactorily explored. Therefore *definition* is often the first step in a discussion of ideas, for the idea to be discussed must be disentangled from other ideas with which it might be confused, and the area of discussion must be limited accordingly. For further clarification *analysis* is important: the idea is divided into its essential parts, or its significant features are isolated for the purpose of definite discussion. But definition and analysis must be assisted by *illustration*.[1] An idea is never really explained until it is illustrated: that is, until a concrete instance or instances are offered to which the abstract conception can be logically and illuminatingly applied. In this way the "subjective" discussion of an idea (reversing the process earlier described) arrives at its "object."

Example and illustration therefore are supremely important in the discussion of ideas. The examples used may be *actual examples:* a discussion of the value of the pioneer tradition, with reference to Lincoln, Jackson, and other presidents who were "born in a log cabin." Or they may be *hypothetical examples:* that is, imagined instances, possible instances, which correspond closely enough to our common experience to be accepted as plausible and instructive.

In explaining "belief," the American philosopher and psychologist William James resorts to the following hypothetical example:

> Suppose, for example, that I am climbing the Alps and have had the ill-luck to work myself into a position from which the only escape is by a terrible leap. Being without a similar experience, I have no evidence of my ability to perform it successfully; but hope and confidence in myself make me sure I shall not miss my aim, and nerve my feet to execute what without those subjective emotions would perhaps have been impossible. But suppose that, on the contrary, the emotions of fear and mistrust preponderate; or suppose that, having just read the *Ethics of Belief,* I feel it would be sinful to act upon an assumption unverified by previous experience—why, then I shall hesitate so long that at last, exhausted and trembling, and launching myself in a moment of despair, I miss my foothold and roll into the abyss. In this case (and it is one of an immense class) the part of wisdom clearly is to believe what one desires; for the belief is one of the indispensable preliminary conditions of the realization of its object. *There are then cases where*

[1] See Chapter 7 for further discussion of definition and analysis.

faith creates its own verification. Believe, and you shall be
right, for you shall save yourself; doubt, and you shall again
be right, for you shall perish. The only difference is that to
believe is greatly to your advantage.—WILLIAM JAMES, *The
Will to Believe.*

The realm of ideas is of course the high province of religious and philosophical thinkers, the greatest of whom, by
their clear and successful exploration of ideas, have notably
influenced human history. Ideas are also, in another sense,
the province of psychologists, but so far the psychologists
have been less notably successful than the religious and
philosophical thinkers of the past. For the modern psychologist, committed to scientific method, is handicapped by the
obvious fact that ideas do not submit readily to scientific
examination. A biologist can look at a fish. He can cut it
up with dissecting instruments and put parts of it under a
microscope for a very special kind of look. But no psychologist can, in similar fashion, "look" at an idea. His elaborate
arrangements for seeming to do so are rude makeshifts in
comparison with the arrangements of the physical scientist.

To write about ideas, clearly and truthfully, is another
way of "looking" at ideas which, if not quite "scientific" in
the laboratory sense, can still be logical, honest, reliable,
and, if well managed, effective. Ideas are inescapable. They
must be dealt with. Let us not be daunted either by the sublime triumphs of the philosophers or by the special claims
of the psychologists. What the student needs to do is to find
ways of rendering purposeful and exact, in his writing, what
he is inevitably doing all the time, less purposefully, less
exactly, in his conversations and imaginings.

In the selection that follows, Leopold begins his explanation—which at first appears to be a narrative—with a dramatized description of the wolf-howl, which he at first
interprets only through the cryptic statement: "Only the
mountain has lived long enough to listen objectively to the
howl of a wolf." His raw particulars—the concrete items of
experience that support his idea—are thus interpreted *symbolically* before he emphasizes, by direct account, his own
personal experiences. His personal experiences are followed
by brief paragraphs that interpret both symbol and fact and
that bring the total idea into clear and definite focus. Leopold uses an *indirect* method of explanation which, though

it is presented in terms of realistic personal experience, is closely akin to the method of the parables of Scripture and the fables of Æsop.

THINKING LIKE A MOUNTAIN[1]   *By Aldo Leopold*

A DEEP chesty bawl echoes from rimrock to rimrock, rolls down the mountain, and fades into the far blackness of the night. It is an outburst of wild defiant sorrow, and of contempt for all the adversities of the world.

Every living thing (and perhaps many a dead thing as well) pays heed to that call. To the deer it is a reminder of the way of all flesh, to the pine a forecast of midnight scuffles and blood on the snow, to the coyote a promise of gleanings to come, to the cowman a threat of red ink at the bank, to the hunter a challenge of fang against bullet. Yet behind these obvious and immediate hopes and fears there lies a deeper meaning, known only to the mountain itself. Only the mountain has lived long enough to listen objectively to the howl of a wolf.

Those unable to decipher the hidden meaning know nevertheless that it is there, for it is felt in all wolf country, and distinguishes that country from all other land. It tingles in the spine of all who hear wolves by night, or who scan their tracks by day. Even without the sight or sound of wolf, it is implicit in a hundred small events: the midnight whinny of a pack horse, the rattle of rolling rocks, the bounds of a fleeing deer, the way shadows lie under the spruces. Only the ineducable tyro can fail to sense the presence or absence of wolves, or the fact that mountains have a secret opinion about them.

My own conviction on this score dates from the day I saw a wolf die. We were eating lunch on a high rimrock, at the foot of which a turbulent river elbowed its way. We saw what we thought was a doe fording the torrent, her breast awash in white water. When she climbed the bank toward us and shook out her tail, we realized our error: it was a wolf. A half-dozen others, evidently grown pups, sprang from the willows and all joined in a welcoming mêlée of wagging tails and playful maulings. What was literally a pile of wolves writhed and tumbled in the center of an open flat at the foot of our rimrock.

In those days we had never heard of passing up a chance to kill a wolf. In a second we were pumping lead into the pack, but with more excitement than accuracy: to aim a steep downhill shot is always confusing. When our rifles were empty, the old wolf was down, and a pup was dragging a leg into impassable slide-rocks.

We reached the old wolf in time to watch a fierce green fire dying

[1] From *A Sand County Almanac* by Aldo Leopold. Copyright 1949 by Oxford University Press, Inc. Reprinted by permission.

in her eyes. I realized then, and have known ever since, that there was something new to me in those eyes—something known only to her and to the mountain. I was young then, and full of trigger-itch; I thought that because fewer wolves meant more deer, no wolves would mean hunters' paradise. But after seeing the green fire die, I sensed that neither the wolf nor the mountain agreed with such a view.

Since then I have lived to see state after state extirpate its wolves. I have watched the face of many a wolfless mountain, and seen the south-facing slopes wrinkle with a maze of new deer trails. I have seen every edible bush and seedling browsed, first to anemic desuetude, and then to death. I have seen every edible tree defoliated to the height of a saddlehorn. Such a mountain looks as if someone had given God a new pruning shears, and forbidden Him all other exercise. In the end the starved bones of the hoped-for deer herd, dead of its own too-much, bleach with the bones of the dead sage, or moulder under the high-lined junipers.

I now suspect that just as a deer herd lives in mortal fear of its wolves, so does a mountain live in mortal fear of its deer. And perhaps with better cause, for while a buck pulled down by wolves can be replaced in two or three years, a range pulled down by too many deer may fail of replacement in as many decades.

So also with cows. The cowman who cleans his range of wolves does not realize that he is taking over the wolf's job of trimming the herd to fit the range. He has not learned to think like a mountain. Hence we have dustbowls, and rivers washing the future into the sea.

We all strive for safety, prosperity, comfort, long life, and dullness. The deer strives with his supple legs, the cowman with trap and poison, the statesman with pen, the most of us with machines, votes, and dollars, but it all comes to the same thing: peace in our time. A measure of success in this is all well enough, and perhaps is a requisite to objective thinking, but too much safety seems to yield only danger in the long run. Perhaps this is behind Thoreau's dictum: In wildness is the salvation of the world. Perhaps this is the hidden meaning in the howl of the wolf, long known among mountains, but seldom perceived among men.

EXERCISES

Aldo Leopold was a distinguished American naturalist who, after a long experience, reached some important conclusions regarding forestry, conservation, and wild life—conclusions which in many respects are at variance with approved contemporary practices. Some of his experiences and the essence of his thinking are embodied in *A Sand County Almanac*, from which the preceding selection is taken. The selection at first sight may seem "descriptive" and therefore not properly placed under the general heading, "Ideas." Before you reach a conclusion on this point, consider the following questions.

1. What is the meaning of the title? Can a mountain "think"?
2. What generalization can be made in the light of the descriptive and narrative details presented?
3. Is this generalization explicitly stated anywhere in the selection?
4. Use one of Leopold's sentences as the basis of an expanded written discussion: for example, in the last paragraph: "too much safety seems to yield only danger in the long run."

PROJECT 5. CRITICISM

> Read not to contradict and confute, nor to believe and take for granted, nor to find talk and discourse, but to weigh and consider.—SIR FRANCIS BACON, *Of Studies.*

The advice of Bacon is as good today as it was three and a half centuries ago, when the onrush of the New Learning shocked some Englishmen, fired others with enthusiasm, and led many to strut like wordy peacocks. The serious student must be a critic in the meaning of Bacon's words: he must "weigh and consider" while he is getting new knowledge. He must keep his critical powers ever alert, whether his studies lead him to the humanities (language and literature, philosophy), the natural sciences (physics, chemistry, biology), or the social sciences (history, economics, sociology, political science). Merely to learn by rote is a poor sort of education. To "weigh and consider" implies the exercise of free intelligence upon the facts. The student is expected to distinguish between more important and less important, to trace out relationships, to make comparisons— in short, to be equal to the occasion whenever cool-headed judgment is required, whether in a class report, a discussion question on a final examination, or an ambitious term paper.

The word *critic* comes from the Greek *krinein: to judge.* The true critic is neither prosecuting attorney nor counsel for the defense. He is a judge.

The types of expository writing in which judgment is the chief governing factor are the *review* and the *critical article* or *essay.*

a. The Review

The word *review* means "to look back" or "to look again," and has various applications. As here used, it refers to the critical review—that is, "a critical discussion or article, as in a newspaper or magazine, dealing with a book, play, concert, etc., especially with a recent one" (*Webster's New World Dictionary*). It rules out first impressions, or loose impressions of any sort. It abhors "snap judgment." It implies a second look, or indeed a tenth look if that is necessary to secure fairness and completeness of presentation, clearness of interpretation, and balance in judging the book or other work under review. A good review will generally develop as follows:

(1) **Approach to the Subject.** This may be a brief introductory paragraph indicating the general or special nature of the subject reviewed (a book, a play, possibly even a magazine article). This paragraph may refer to the timeliness of the book or article; to other works of a similar or different nature; or to some trend in literature, drama, or art. A striking quotation makes a good beginning if it foreshadows the content of the review or sets the tone of the discussion. But the writer may dispense with preliminaries and launch at once into a presentation of subject matter.

(2) **Presentation of Subject Matter.** In a concise summary, present the theme, characters, plot of the novel or play, the leading ideas of the book or articles, the significant features of the work—be it poem, drama, essay, biography, opera, symphony. Give whatever interpretative discussion is needed. Presentation of the *essential substance* of the work reviewed must accompany any criticism that you may offer.

(3) **Critical Estimate.** Discuss the excellences and defects of the work under consideration, but be judicious and temperate in expressing your views. Base your judgment upon specific facts and refer to those facts. Brief quotation of key passages is a way of referring to "facts." Avoid vague approval or contemptuous dismissal. A sound critical estimate will rest, in the end, upon fair and correct answers to three questions: *What is the author trying to do? Does he succeed in doing it? Is it worth doing?*

(4) **Organization.** There is no prescribed order in a critical review. It is a composition, and, like any other composition, it must be unified and coherent. It should be interesting in itself. But always it must contain two basic elements: information about the work reviewed and judgment of that work.

Observe carefully the principle of proportion. A review

that is all summary is not a true critical review—though it may serve as a "report." A review that is all criticism is not fair to the reader, for the reader deserves information about the subject criticized; and it is not fair to the subject, for the subject must be presented if the basis for criticism is to be understood. Avoid a long and unwieldy summary. Avoid excessive quotation. Above all beware of using the review as a vehicle for your merely personal opinions.

(5) Mechanics of the Review.   Every review must contain exact information as to the author, title, and publication (or production in the case of a play, moving picture, or the like). For book reviews such data may appear in the form of a *headnote* (between the title of the review and the beginning) or as a *footnote* (at the bottom of the first written or typed page). The following example illustrates a standard form for a book review:

> *The Ballad of Tradition.* By Gordon Hall Gerould.
> Oxford: The Clarendon Press. 1932.

Title, author, place of publication, publisher, and date of publication should be given. Book reviews in periodicals also give information as to the price of the book, the number of pages, and, when pertinent, the format or other special features.

If you are reviewing a magazine article, give the title of the article, the name of the author, and the title and date of the magazine. This information may appear in a footnote, or it may be included in the text of the review at some appropriate point near the beginning. Such an identifying reference might read as follows:

> Dr. Jean Mayer's article, "Food Fads for Athletes," in the *Atlantic Monthly* for December, 1961, turns the cold light of scientific analysis upon the superstitions of the old-fashioned training table.

In summarizing or restating the content of the work discussed, distinguish your own comment from the matter summarized. The reader must know whose ideas are being put before him. Use quotation marks when you reproduce a passage *verbatim*. When you paraphrase, insert a directive expression ("according to Dr. Mayer" or "the author says") to make the identification plain. (See pages 260–265 for other examples of citation.)

THE GREAT PAST OF THE CUMBERLAND COUNTRY[1]

Seedtime on the Cumberland. By Harriette Simpson Arnow.
New York: The Macmillan Company. $7.50.

IT IS a rare historian who will assert that his book is not a history. That rare one is Harriette Arnow, who says in the preface to her *Seedtime on the Cumberland:* "This work is not a history, nor is it concerned with the lives of famous men and women. . . . I have tried to recreate a few of the most important aspects of pioneer life as it was lived on the Cumberland by ordinary men and women."

Since Mrs. Arnow's book is not fiction or legend or sociology but well-authenticated facts of the American past, it must be history, despite her disavowal. One can guess what her over-modest statement means. In these days we have no Parkmans. Modern histories tend to be generalized outlines patterned to fit a thesis, or at the other extreme they are the research specialist's pokings into a tiny hole in a small corner of his narrow "field." They carry the aseptic odor of the laboratory. In their selectiveness and dry adherence to method they manage to lose the sense of the past even though that past may often be dramatic and lively in the "sources" that the historians carefully consult.

Seedtime on the Cumberland is not that kind of history. It presents pioneer life in that great crescent of irregular land in Kentucky and Tennessee reaching from the mountainous headwaters of the Cumberland River deep into Middle Tennessee and thence northwest to the Ohio River and the Illinois country. This is what Mrs. Arnow calls—from its shape on the map—the "Old Boot." The several maps specially prepared for her book permit a reader to visualize the "Old Boot" clearly in its internal arrangements and outside relationships.

In her moving prologue that reader will realize that this historian, native to the Cumberland region, can draw upon family tradition and historical imagination as well as "documentary sources." Of her childhood Mrs. Arnow writes:

> Times and places were mingled in my head; the past was part of the present, close as the red cedar bucket in the kitchen, or the big cherry press put together with pegs, or the parched corn a grandmother now and then made for us. This was the same as the parched corn from the old days, or the cornmeal mush we sometimes ate, no different at all from the mush in the stories. An old shirt in a trunk upstairs, square-armholed, stitched by hand, of cotton woven and spun on the Big South Fork of the Cumberland, could have

[1] From the New York *Herald Tribune Book Review,* September 4, 1960. Reprinted by permission.

been the same as that worn by some old gran'pa with many
greats before his name. My people loved the past . . . but it
cannot be said we lived in the past. Two things tied all time
together. . . . These were the land and the Cumberland.

And Mrs. Arnow has her "documentary sources" too. Her visualization of the past is as stoutly pegged to reality as the corners
of the big cherry press of her childhood. From state archives, publications of historical societies, from the great Lyman Draper
manuscript collection, diaries, letters, reminiscences, local histories, Mrs. Arnow has dredged up the rich particulars of the Cumberland pioneer's life in the old, bold, Indian-harried, buffalo-
thundering days from the end of the French and Indian War to
about 1803. Of course professional historians, biographers, and
popular romancers have dipped into these same sources for their
special ends. But Mrs. Arnow is the first historical writer to pull
together into one thoroughgoing, large-scale book so convincing a
mass of what belonged especially, often uniquely, to the Cumberland pioneer's experience. Since it is not a strictly chronological
narrative, it necessarily takes on a good deal of the character of
a grand historical scrapbook, somewhat loosely organized into
fourteen compendious chapters. But that was also the procedure
of Herodotus, the father of history, in his ostensible account of
the Persian wars. Mrs. Arnow does not traffic in myth and fable
as Herodotus did, but she has his earnest solicitude for topography,
even for geology, as well as his love for the illuminating incident
which may not pertain closely to the topic at hand. For example,
she suddenly turns aside from her account of James Robertson's
trip from the French Lick to Kaskaskia in 1779 and tells us that
the forked limb of a white oak made the best pack saddle. She
follows with the story of the preacher who "once stopped short
in his exhortation to a large congregation in the woods, and while
his eyes were still turned devoutly to heaven, suddenly pointed
his finger to a branch and exclaimed, 'Brethren, behold up yonder
a first-rate crotch for a pack-saddle.' "

Stereotypes fall away as Mrs. Arnow develops her account of
the "Shirttail Men" who opened the way into the wilderness, "The
Travelers" who made the actual settlements, "The Woodsmen"
who learned how to turn the forest from enemy into friend, how
to build log-houses, clear the land and farm it while simultaneously
for some decades fighting off Indians at almost any moment. Daniel
Boone, the surprised reader may learn, was not a typical frontiersman. He talked himself into fame, was not a good leader, had a
foolish way of getting captured, was not a reliable founder of
settlements. In the wilderness of the Cumberland country you
had better have that wise and experienced man, James Robertson,
to lead you—or Kaspar Mansker—or Edmund Jennings—not
Boone. Andrew Jackson was not an Indian fighter. That pale-

faced lawyer, storekeeper, and land speculator could shoot a pistol, but never fought an Indian until in 1813 he commanded a military expedition against the distant Creeks. Nor was Colonel John Donelson of Virginia an Indian fighter, either, or very much of a frontiersman, despite his famous exploit in the winter of 1779–80, when his party floated down the Tennessee and poled up the Cumberland to share in the founding of Nashville with the Robertson group and the Eaton group who came overland. "Inept and unseasoned," Mrs. Arnow calls Donelson. Evidently she thinks teen-aged Nancy Gower a better man than Donelson. Nancy, with an Indian bullet in her thigh, guided a boat to safety when the men ran off. "Donelson's boat had a four-pounder," is Mrs. Arnow's sharp comment, "and there was no shortage of ammunition." The Donelson flotilla, she says, though adventurous and colorful, "carried only a few of the men who actually did the hard and ugly work of making Middle Tennessee. It was the few coming overland who built stations, fought Indians, and made the world if not safe at least possible for the Donelsons, the Polks, and others including Andrew Jackson."

These less well-known few are for Mrs. Arnow the true "seed" of the Cumberland country. With firm, accurate, and loving hand she traces, in the fine closing chapters of her book, their complete way of life. In so doing she dispels—one hopes forever—the false legend of the "crudity" of the frontier. She sees the Cumberland life as a genuine culture, basically British colonial transplanted, with some mixture of Scotch-Irish, German, Welsh, and French, and adapted but not sacrificed to wilderness necessity. Settlers had to live in log-houses—until they could build better—but they built those log-houses so well that many have lasted, like the traditions they symbolize, well into the twentieth century. In the hard decades these pioneers could not well be bookish and intellectual, but they were not illiterate. Of the 220 signers of the Cumberland Compact, only one had to "make his mark." One might complain a little against Mrs. Arnow for some small vices of style and a great deal of over-annotation, but these would be niggling complaints. Her book from now on will be an indispensable guide to whoever, for reasons pious or pragmatic, undertakes a mental journey into this stirring portion, now nearly two hundred years away, of the great American past.

b. The Critical Essay

Many of the book reviews in our periodicals—as also reviews of plays, movies, concerts, and art exhibitions—are news items first of all. They emphasize subject matter. Book reviewer and dramatic critic are glorified reporters who "cover" new books and plays and tell us what is going on in the world of entertainment, art, history, science—though always with side-glances of estimation.

The critical essay reverses this emphasis. It is above all a reasoned judgment based upon facts—the facts being the significant features of whatever is under consideration, whether the subject matter of a book, its style, its technique, its underlying philosophy, or its social implications.

Since criticism is a general term, by no means limited to criticism of the arts, the critical essay may have a political or historical subject. It may scrutinize the foreign policy of the United States, Jefferson's idea of democracy in the light of its present results, the character of Charles I of England, the pro's and con's of student government, the architecture of a housing unit. No matter what the subject, the principle is the same: to give a deliberate judgment, rendered after systematic study, and to support it with evidence to justify the position taken. Criticism of this sort naturally develops into the *article of opinion* (see Chapter 9) or, if lightly or humorously presented, into the *informal essay.*

Here, discussion may properly center upon literary criticism, since it offers convenient limits within which methods of criticism may be studied and practiced.

A thoroughgoing review of a single book may well become a critical essay if it places the book in its proper perspective. Generally such a review will subject the book to a searching critical analysis and will discuss issues that arise from the author's treatment of his material. This treatment naturally gives the critic an opportunity to bring his own views into the foreground, if he has good reason to do so.

More often the critical essay is a discussion of a literary or artistic topic rather than a mere review. The subject may be a single author or some aspect of his work, a study of some tendency, a critical examination of technique or style. Typical subjects are: "Poe's Idea of the Short Story," "Sinclair Lewis as Satirist," "Coleridge's Use of the Ballad Form," "Gershwin's Use of the Jazz Idiom."

If the topic requires careful research, and if the criticism is based upon that research, a true critical essay may be the result. But the critical essay, though it must be well informed, is not a research paper. It does not depend upon a mere "looking up" of a subject; it is not a mosaic of quotations and summaries accompanied by documentation. The critical essay may use facts assembled by research, but goes beyond research to make its own original and independent judgment.[1]

On the other hand, a critical essay is not a merely personal avowal of "what I like." To say "this book (or picture, or recording) does something to me" is to retreat into banality. Personal criticism can be written by experienced writers who have undergone long discipline, cultivated both their taste and their wits, and become "persons of importance." From Voltaire to Mencken and Shaw, there have been many such writers—brilliant performers whom we read with excitement, but whose vanity may make them untrustworthy as critics. This does not mean that we should undervalue the personal element. Much can be gained from studying and recording one's own reactions to a book or picture. But the place for indulging freely one's personal opinions, wild notions, private obsessions, splendid intuitions is the *informal essay*. In this form the writer has "king's excuse" to be openly partisan, even mildly "rambunctious," if at the same time he can be good-humored, or at least not unpleasant.

The best criticism is impersonal. The good critic proposes to do justice to his subject, not to parade his strictly personal views. Criticism is neither mere fault-finding nor fulsome praise, but a judicious attempt to discover true worth.

Certain special methods may enter into the process of critical discussion or, on occasion, may govern it.

The *historical method* of criticism is especially useful in the study of old masters if it becomes necessary to review the causes and sources of literary styles and attitudes. If the subject is "Hawthorne's *The Scarlet Letter* as an Interpretation of Puritanism," it is important to know what Puritanism was and what may have led Hawthorne to take a certain attitude toward it. The advantage of the historical method is that it is factual and impersonal. The critic reconstructs the mind of a past age, and this reconstruction becomes a major part of his critical interpretation.

In using the *method of standards* the critic chooses or establishes some aesthetic standard to which he thinks a book, play, or picture ought to conform, and then measures his subject by that standard. If the stories of Ernest Hemingway are to be criticized, by what standard are they to be

[1] See Chapter 8 for a discussion of the function and method of the research paper.

judged? By the classic standards of Aristotle? The popular standard of the "pulp" and "confession" magazines? The standard of the "slicks"—*Atlantic Monthly, Esquire, Harper's* —or of the literary quarterlies, like *Kenyon Review* or *Sewanee Review?* The difficulty is in knowing what standard to use. Mathew Arnold's solution was to urge always the standard of the *best* literature, the *best* art—a lofty view that naturally leaves some room for debate.

In recent decades some notable critics have developed what may be called the *analytical method.* Without entirely excluding the methods mentioned above, these analysts— often called the "New Critics"—emphasize "explication of the text," or the close scrutiny of poem, story, or novel in terms of its own independent being as an art work. The subject matter is interpreted with careful reference to its scheme of presentation—the form, the technique, the rhetoric being viewed as more or less indivisible from the content, idea, or impression. Examples of this criticism can readily be found in such books as *The Well Wrought Urn,* by Cleanth Brooks; *In Defense of Reason,* by Yvor Winters; or *The Great Tradition,* by F. R. Leavis.

LANDSCAPE IN GORIZIA[1]   *By Carlos Baker*

THE opening chapter of Hemingway's second novel, *A Farewell to Arms,* is a generically rendered landscape with thousands of moving figures. It does much more than start the book. It helps to establish the dominant mood (which is one of doom), plants a series of important images for future symbolic cultivation, and subtly compels the reader into the position of detached observer.

> In the late summer of that year we lived in a house in a village that looked across the river and the plain to the mountains. In the bed of the river there were pebbles and boulders, dry and white in the sun, and the water was clear and swiftly moving and blue in the channels. Troops went by the house and down the road and the dust they raised powdered the leaves of the trees. The trunks of the trees too were dusty and the leaves fell early that year and we saw the troops marching along the road and the dust rising and leaves, stirred by the breeze, falling and the soldiers marching and afterward the road bare and white except for the leaves.

[1] Reprinted from *Hemingway: The Writer As Artist* by Carlos Baker, by permission of Princeton University Press and the author. Copyright, 1952, by Carlos Baker.

The first sentence here fixes the reader in a house in the village where he can take a long view across the river and the plain to the distant mountains. Although he does not realize it yet, the plain and the mountains (not to mention the river and the trees, the dust and the leaves) have a fundamental value as symbols. The autumnal tone of the language is important in establishing the autumnal mood of the chapter. The landscape itself has the further importance of serving as a general setting for the whole first part of the novel. Under these values, and of basic structural importance, are the elemental images which compose this remarkable introductory chapter.

The second sentence, which draws attention from the mountainous background to the bed of the river in the middle distance, produces a sense of clearness, dryness, whiteness, and sunniness which is to grow very subtly under the artist's hands until it merges with one of the novel's two dominant symbols, the mountain-image. The other major symbol is the plain. Throughout the substructure of the book it is opposed to the mountain-image. Down this plain the river flows. Across it, on the dusty road among the trees, pass the men-at-war, faceless and voiceless and unidentified against the background of the spreading plain.

In the third and fourth sentences of this beautifully managed paragraph the march-past of troops and vehicles begins. From the reader's elevated vantage-point, looking down on the plain, the river and the road, the continuously parading men are reduced in size and scale—made to seem smaller, more pitiful, more pathetic, more like wraiths blown down the wind, than would be true if the reader were brought close enough to overhear their conversation or see them as individualized personalities.

Between the first and fourth sentences, moreover, Hemingway accomplishes the transition from late summer to autumn—an inexorability of seasonal change which prepares the way for the study in doom on which he is embarked. Here again the natural elements take on a symbolic function. In the late summer we have the dust; in the early autumn the dust and the leaves falling; and through them both the marching troops impersonally seen. The reminder, through the dust, of the words of the funeral service in the prayer-book is fortified by the second natural symbol, the falling leaves. They dry out, fall, decay, and become part of the dust. Into the dust is where the troops are going—some of them soon, all of them eventually.

The short first chapter closes with winter, and the establishment of rain as a symbol of disaster. "At the start of the winter came the permanent rain and with the rain came the cholera. But it was checked and in the end only seven thousand died of it in the army." Already now in the winter, seven thousand of the wraiths have vanished underground. The permanent rain lays the dust and rots the leaves as if they had never existed. There is no excellent beauty, even in the country around Gorizia, that has not some sadness to it. And there is hardly a natural beauty in the whole first chapter of *A Farewell to Arms* which has not some symbolic function in Hemingway's first study in doom.

SUGGESTIONS FOR THEMES

1. A review of a magazine article has certain advantages. A student who is learning how to write reviews can read, digest, and review a magazine article in much less time than he can even read a book. He can practice writing the short critical review within narrow limits and, furthermore, can give himself an introduction to the world of contemporary thought so far as that thought is expressed in periodicals. The review of a magazine article is a natural preparation for writing editorials, articles, essays on current topics. The assignment would then be as follows: (a) examine a selected group of periodicals—preferring the serious monthlies, quarterlies, or special magazines and avoiding the news weeklies and picture magazines; (b) read at least three articles or essays (*not* fiction) from three different magazines; (c) write a review of one of the articles you have read.

2. Review some book that you have read or read a book with this assignment in mind and write a review of it. For further acquaintance with book reviews, make a discriminating examination of book reviews found in the New York *Times Book Review;* the *Saturday Review;* the London *Times Literary Supplement;* and the book review departments of the weekly, monthly, and quarterly periodicals. Observe closely the mechanics of the book review as practiced by the best critics: how the reviewer refers to a book and its author; how much he quotes and in what connection; how he begins and ends his review; how much space he gives to summary and interpretation and how much to criticism.

CHAPTER 4

THE PARAGRAPH

PARAGRAPHS are modern conveniences. Ancient writers got along without paragraphing, as they also got along without much punctuation. For this reason it is difficult for us to read old manuscripts and books, but the lack of paragraph divisions and punctuation may not have bothered ancient writers and readers as it bothers us. In former times people thought of literature as recorded speech. They read aloud more than we do now. Pauses, changes of voice, and gestures served to mark stops and divisions.

Today we are silent readers. We need typographical devices to mark the divisions of thought for the rapidly glancing eye. For this reason we make an indention in the left-hand margin and call the unit of thought thus set off a paragraph. The use of punctuation marks, capital letters, and paragraph divisions has been systematized only since printed books became common. All such devices are aids to the eye. Even the paragraph itself may be considered a form of punctuation. Yet, although paragraphing is sometimes as mechanical as punctuation, the paragraph has undergone a modern development and requires study on its own terms.[1]

NATURE AND FUNCTION OF THE PARAGRAPH

In modern usage, paragraphs are devices for showing the minor divisions of thought within the whole composition.

[1] The word *paragraph* comes from two Greek words, *para* ("by the side of") and *graphein* ("to write"). Writers formerly put a mark by the side of a passage to call attention to a division of thought or to indicate some point of reference. This mark was finally conventionalized in the symbol now used as a printer's correction: ¶. The standard practice now is to indicate a paragraph by the use of an indention on the left-hand margin of the manuscript or printed work.

Paragraphs are units, but, except for certain special purposes, they have no separate role as units. They are functional units, sentence-groups which form links in a chain of thought. The paragraph indention gives notice that one phase of thought-development is ending and another phase is beginning.

A paragraph may be defined as the rounded development of a single idea. The single idea is called the topic of the paragraph. It is a definite part, or sub-topic, of the general subject, and it undergoes a building-up somewhat like the building-up of the general idea within the whole composition. In that sense the treatment of the paragraph topic is a *rounded* development. The paragraph must give the reader a sense of completeness and adequacy. That is to say, the paragraph must have order, or organization, as the whole composition has order. At the same time, it must remain a *functional* unit. It contributes its part to the discussion of the subject. The paragraph must therefore satisfy two requirements: (1) it must deal effectively with its own topic; (2) it must present the topic in clear relation to the whole composition.

The paragraph printed below appears as the fourth paragraph of Chapter XXII in Mr. Van Wyck Brooks's *The Times of Melville and Whitman*. The title of this chapter is "Mark Twain in the East." It tells how Mark Twain, during his residence at Hartford, Connecticut, enjoyed international fame as "a symbol of the new America." The first phrase of the opening sentence, "In dozens of other respects as well," links the paragraph with the discussion that Mr. Brooks is developing. And the opening sentence in its entirety states the aspects of the general discussion that is to be developed in this particular paragraph: "In dozens of other respects as well, Mark Twain's personality was an all but unparalleled emblem of the country and the time, to such a degree that his name evoked in the minds of his contemporaries a picture of America itself in this post-war age." This sentence, then, is the topic sentence of the paragraph. The succeeding sentences associate Mark Twain's writings and personal characteristics with the "picture of America" that his name evoked.

> *In dozens of other respects as well, Mark Twain's personality was an all but unparalleled emblem of the country and the time, to such a degree that his name evoked in the minds*

of his contemporaries a picture of America itself in this post-war age. He was the natural democrat who wrote the story of the prince and pauper to show that they were identical when one removed their clothes; and who was more interested than he in money-making, inventions, machines at a moment when the capitalist system was approaching its zenith? With the instinct of the born promoter or the gambler who had acquired his taste in the "flush times" of Nevada and the Sierra mines, he was driven to invest in a dozen schemes for making money quickly, a patent steam-generator, a new process of engraving, and what not. With all the buoyant hopefulness that was also a typically American note, he was drawn to these money-making schemes as a fly to a jam-pot, although he lost fortune after fortune, and he negotiated with another inventor, an Austrian with a new machine, when he had been struggling for a year to pay his debts. He hoped to control the carpet-weaving industries of the world. He was the first author ever to use a typewriter, and he had the first telephone ever used in a private house. This house was like Beecher's Boscobel, the spreading edifice with the broad verandahs, the cupolas and columns and acres of rare shrubs and trees—it was almost a rival of Barnum's Iranistan. For the rest, Mark Twain had become a national pet.—VAN WYCK BROOKS, *The Times of Melville and Whitman.*[1]

LENGTH OF THE PARAGRAPH

The length of the paragraph will ordinarily depend upon the degree of elaboration needed to bring out the topic clearly. The answer to the question, "How long must a paragraph be?" must be as unsatisfactory as the countryman's description of his lost cow: "She has a tail about as long as a piece of rope and a white spot on the side next the fence." The length of the paragraph is relative. A paragraph must be long enough to do its work properly, but not so long as to weary the reader.

Instruction on this point cannot, therefore, be specific. Some authorities suggest a minimum length of 100 to 150 words and a maximum length of 350 to 400 words. Others say that the reader, especially the American reader, expects at least one break on every page and will not endure long passages of unparagraphed material. It may help to keep

[1] From *The Times of Melville and Whitman* by Van Wyck Brooks. Copyright 1947, by Van Wyck Brooks. Reprinted by permission of E. P. Dutton & Co., Inc., and New American Everyman's Library.

such instructions in mind as a working standard, provided we remember that no absolute rule can be made. Much depends upon the nature of the subject and the skill of the writer. Thoreau, in his *Walden* and elsewhere, has paragraphs fully a page in length. Yet Thoreau is universally admired for his excellent prose. Scientific treatises often contain long, cumbersome paragraphs. On the other hand, our current journalism, over-conscious of typographical patterns, cultivates brevity of paragraphs. The following selection illustrates the "short and snappy" paragraphs of newsweeklies and newspapers; but they are not good models for non-journalistic writing:

> When Congress in 1961 added Cape Cod National Seashore to the U. S. system of national parks, it started something.
> Today, plans are being made which would create as many as a score of new national parks. In addition, other recreation areas would be opened up. All told, around 20 million acres would be added to the 26 million of the present parks.
> Not since the time of President Theodore Roosevelt have plans been so ambitious.—From *U. S. News and World Report,* January 22, 1962.

The extremes to avoid are evidently under-development of the paragraph, which leads to choppy composition, and over-development, which makes the composition tedious. Choppy paragraphs sometimes result from failure to see the full implications of the topic; in this instance the remedy is further development. But perhaps in a sequence of seemingly undeveloped paragraphs (as above) some of the separate topics are actually one topic; such separate paragraphs should then be combined. Over-development may result from needless repetition. Then the remedy is to prune away non-essential matter. But over-development may also result from failure to perceive the real divisions of the subject. The writer of an over-developed paragraph may be trying to treat two or three ideas as one idea. Then the remedy is to divide the paragraph. In general, bad paragraphing results from careless thinking. Good organization in the whole composition tends to bring about good paragraphing, for in the end we determine paragraph length by seeing the paragraph as a functioning part of the entire scheme, doing its proportionate share, no more and no less.

THE TOPIC SENTENCE

The topic sentence states the central idea to be developed in the paragraph. It unifies the paragraph, as the guiding purpose unifies the whole composition. In most expository paragraphs, the topic sentence will appear at or near the beginning of the paragraph, but it may be placed at the end of the paragraph, to summarize what has been said. Or it may appear in the middle of the paragraph. Sometimes a paragraph may have a topic sentence at the beginning and a sentence at the end which repeats or restates the idea of the topic sentence, and thus serves to clinch the thought and to make the paragraph ending firm.

It is quite possible to write a good paragraph without a topic sentence. Such paragraphs are fairly common in the work of practiced writers. The topic may be implied rather than expressed, if the paragraph is actually a unit. The paragraph may lack a topic sentence, but it must not lack a topic or have two topics. The test of a good paragraph is: Can its central idea be stated in a single compact sentence?

PARAGRAPHS AS RELATED PARTS OF THE
WHOLE COMPOSITION

The topics of the paragraphs, taken in order, mark the sequence of thought of the composition. In good expository writing it often happens that the topic sentences, with little change, will make a fairly good outline of the composition. The following are the topic sentences of four successive paragraphs in an essay by Gilbert Highet.

1. "I must say that I am fascinated, in a horrible way, by motion pictures about ancient Greece and Rome."
2. "It is the active parts which are so funny."
3. "The Greek and Roman armies are usually wrong, too."
4. "The reason for these mistakes is quite obvious."

The logical organization of the thought, if represented in a topical outline, would be as follows:

I. The "horrible fascination" of motion pictures about Greece and Rome.
   A. Good photography, but
   B. Ludicrous historical mistakes.
II. "Active" parts funnier than the "static."

A. The Hollywood idea of Roman chariots.
B. Actual Roman usage of chariots.
III. Hollywood's wrong notions about Greek and Roman armies.
IV. The reason for such mistakes.

The four closely related paragraphs of which this topical outline is a representation are as follows:

I MUST say that I am fascinated, in a horrible way, by motion pictures about ancient Greece and Rome. However silly they may be, they are usually photographed quite beautifully; the costumes are very becoming, particularly to the women; there is a certain thrill in seeing all the famous buildings, like the Acropolis at Athens, looking brand-new and so clean; and then the mistakes and the distortions are uproariously funny. They are just as funny as George Washington waving a machine gun, or Meade's troops headed by a detachment of Sioux Indians. And sometimes they are far funnier. The unconscious humor of the movies is one of their strongest assets.

In movies about ancient Greece and Rome, the static parts often look quite real and convincing—no doubt because they have been modeled on pictures and statues. It is the active parts which are usually so funny. Almost every motion picture about ancient Rome I have ever seen showed somebody driving through the streets of the city in a chariot, while the citizens cringed away from his mad career. This is as absurd as showing a cowboy on horseback galloping along the sidewalk of Fifth Avenue, New York. Chariots and such things were absolutely prohibited in the streets of Rome; they were kept for war, or else for hot-pole driving on the highways outside the cities. Everybody walked. The average Roman never rode in a chariot from the day of his birth to the day of his death.

The Greek and Roman armies are usually wrong, too. Most Hollywood producers know very little about military tactics, and still less about the more difficult science of strategy. Even in modern movies, they constantly make both the Good Ones and the Bad Ones commit elementary blunders in the art of war.

In *The Robe* we see a group of Roman legionaries rushing into a town and shooting at everyone visible with bows and arrows. In other pictures about Rome we see the legionaries throwing spears with great care and accuracy, as though those were their essential weapons. The reason for these mistakes is quite obvious. The people in Hollywood think that everyone fights by shooting; if not *bang bang,* then *fft fft;* if not smoking guns, then whizzing arrows and hissing spears. But this is nonsense. The Romans conquered the world with swords—short, strong, efficient swords which were used both for cutting and for thrusting. Spears were thrown at the opening of a battle, much as grenades are thrown now, without very careful aim, merely as a device to disrupt the enemy's line; what mattered was the body-to-body conflict. As for bows and arrows, these were left to Arabs and the like, who stayed out in the wings together with slingers. It is as ridiculous to show the Roman soldiers using bows and arrows as it would be to show the U.S. Marines using blowpipes and poisoned darts. The Romans, like the Marines, were realists; they knew that if you want to kill an enemy and defend yourself, the surest way is to face him, eye to eye, and put a sword into him.—GILBERT HIGHET, "History on the Silver Screen." [1]

METHODS OF DEVELOPING THOUGHT
WITHIN THE PARAGRAPH

Since the paragraph is the *rounded development* of an idea, it cannot be simply a loose collection of sentences. The content of the paragraph is determined by its function as a part of the whole composition. Its *form* is determined by the kind of treatment which is used to give the paragraph topic a rounded development.

The organization of a paragraph will depend upon the nature of its topic and upon what the writer proposes to do with that topic at the particular stage of thought which it is intended to mark in the total scheme of the composition. In descriptive and narrative writing, and particularly in narrative writing, paragraph divisions may seem rather arbitrary. They may indicate the stages of the action, or may emphasize some phase of an incident or quality or aspect of an object, upon which a writer wishes to dwell, or which he prefers to indicate briefly. The descriptive or narrative paragraph cannot generally be held to strict rules; it raises special problems which need not be considered here. But the rounded development mentioned above is normal in the paragraphs of expository and argumentative writing. Such paragraphs, indeed, will commonly have logical organization,

[1] From "History on the Silver Screen" in *Talents and Geniuses* by Gilbert Highet. Copyright 1957 by Oxford University Press, Inc. Reprinted by permission.

and the topic may be developed by any one of the various methods of logical organization, or by such combination of methods as need may suggest.

The method chosen, for any given paragraph, must be the one that will express the thought most clearly and adequately. A writer does not set out in cold blood to develop a paragraph by this or that method. It will do him no good to have at hand a check-list of methods of development and use them mechanically, without regard to his subject and his purpose. Rather, he must determine what method his subject-matter demands, at any particular point. If he schools himself in thinking logically, if he has a proper respect for his subject and for his readers, he will soon learn to use apt and right methods.

There are several common methods of logical organization. They are not peculiar to the paragraph as a form. They are nothing less and nothing more than the methods by which expository writing, as well as most argumentative writing, generally proceeds. They are explained here separately, one by one, that the student may become aware of them and may consciously strive to master them. It would be perfectly proper to say that they represent studies in the possibilities of expository—or argumentative—techniques; but they may be practiced, with profit, within the small scale of the paragraph. Such methods are discussed more broadly in Chapter 7.

There are at least seven methods of logical development.

1. Particulars and Details

Expand the topic statement by giving the particulars that substantiate it or the details which are the components of the topic. This is one of the most convincing ways to amplify a general statement. Only through clear and lively detail can the writer convey to the reader the total impression of the topic that exists in his own mind. A general statement, when unsupported by specific detail, is vague and unconvincing.

In the paragraph that follows, Constance Rourke first makes a general statement about the bold, legendary Crockett. Next come the specific details.

> Then Crockett reappeared in popular stories as though he had never died, assuming an even bolder legendary stature

than before. The story of his life in one of the almanacs began by picturing him as a baby giant planted in a rock bed
as soon as he was born and watered with wild buffalo's milk.
Another declared that as a boy he tied together the tails of two
buffaloes and carried home tiger cubs in his cap. In another
he wrung the tail off a comet, and announced that he could
"travel so all lightnin' fast that I've been known to strike fire
against the wind." Lightning glanced through all the stories.
By leaping astride the lightning Crockett escaped from a tornado on the Mississippi when houses came apart and trees
walked out by their roots. He could make lightning by striking
his own eye. He could make fire by rubbing a flint with his
knuckles. On one of his adventures he was barred by an
"Injun rock so 'tarnal high, so all flinty hard that it will turn
off a common streak of lightnin' and make it point downward
and look as flat as a cow's tail." Once he escaped up Niagara
Falls on an alligator. "The alligator walked up the great hill
of water as slick as a wild cat up a white oak."—CONSTANCE
ROURKE, *American Humor*. [1]

To set forth in this way the details that constitute the
parts of a whole is actually *analysis*. Crockett's legendary
career (his *bolder legendary stature*) is analyzed, in the
paragraph quoted, as follows: (1) tales of Crockett's mythi-
cal babyhood; (2) tales of his cosmic feats; (3) tales of his
strength and daring. For a complete discussion of analysis,
see Chapter 7.

2. Illustration and Example

The purpose of illustration is to clarify a statement or
discussion by referring to some definite case, instance, or
example. To illustrate is, literally, to "illuminate," to "throw
light on."

In the following paragraph by Frederick J. Turner, the
reference to "our American anthem" illustrates the general
statement "that it is almost impossible to see the situation
except through sectional spectacles":

> Although political sectionalism is still a term of reproach,
> implying unfairness and a disregard of national interests, the
> section reproved is seldom conscious that its action is ad-
> verse to the common good. We are so large and diversified a
> nation that it is almost impossible to see the situation except
> through sectional spectacles. The section either conceives

[1] From *American Humor* by Constance Rourke. Reprinted by
permission of the publishers, Harcourt, Brace & World, Inc.

of itself as an aggrieved and oppressed minority, suffering
from the injustice of the other sections of the nation, or it
thinks of its own culture, its economic policies, and well-
being as best for the nation. It thinks, in other words, of the
nation in terms of itself. "I love thy rocks and rills, thy woods
and templed hills," runs our American anthem. It was written by a New Englander and its scene is that of New England,
not of the snowcapped mountains, the far stretches of Great
Plains, or Arid America. We think sectionally and do not
fully understand one another.—FREDERICK JACKSON TURNER,
"Sections and Nations," *The Significance of Sections in
American History.*

Somewhat different is illustration which proceeds by
analogy: that is, by stating a possible or imagined likeness
between two things. Analogy is a resemblance that may be
reasoned from, so that from the likeness in certain respects
we may infer that other and deeper relations exist. A family
may be thought of as a "state" in its unity, in its organization with a head and subordinate parts, and in its autonomy.
From certain observed resemblances others are inferred; and
so in every analogy. Although we may doubt the exactness of
the parallel, by analogy we somehow accept many inferences
from the known phenomena.

Furthermore, the use of analogy enables the reader to
visualize, and through visualization to understand. Analogy
explains the unknown in terms of the known, the unfamiliar
in terms of the familiar, as in the examples that follow:

The American Constitution is brief, elegant, ambiguous,
and in many ways mysterious. It is very unlike the Constitution that its framers planned; it is highly unlikely that the
dominant interpretation of that Constitution, fifty years
hence, will be that held by any American political school
today. American unity is not a simple, coherent, easily defined, and limited idea; the Constitution is not a simple
means of living happily ever after. Institutions of that simple
kind are left to the more old-fashioned and romantic novelists. For them marriage is as definable a means to happiness
as a political doctrine is to a Frenchman. For the Frenchman
who would not, for a moment, think of taking seriously so
simple a view of life in a novel will often accept it in a
political programme. And the American who may be ready to
read a nice, simple story, a "western" if he is a man, a "love
story" if the American is a woman, rarely expects these elegant and happy solutions in political life. That things are not
what they seem, that persons and problems change, while

preserving the same names, that we create the world of illusions in which we live and love, these are truths about the human situation that the political American does not need to be told. He feels them. The Constitution has undergone as many changes, if you like, as many degradations, as a character in Proust. It is to themes like these that the American—lawyer, politician, great businessman—devotes his mind and his passions; and one possible price is an obvious simplicity in literature and philosophy. (It is not wise, however, to be too sure even of this. The federal attorney who convicted Alger Hiss is an enthusiastic Proustian, and Calvin Coolidge translated Dante on his honeymoon.)—D. W. BROGAN, "So You're Going to America? A Letter to a French Friend." [1]

In the above paragraph D. W. Brogan, an Englishman, is telling a French friend how things really are in the United States. The use of analogy begins in the fourth sentence with the statement: "The Constitution is not a simple means of living happily ever after." The analogy is slightly complex, inasmuch as Mr. Brogan assumes that the Frenchman will think the American Constitution is as simple as a "Western" or a "love story," when actually it is more like a novel by Proust. The analogy between the Constitution and a "marriage" implies also the American view that the Constitution is a "compact" that in effect marries the States and the Federal government. In the following paragraph by Oliver Wendell Holmes the analogy between a tree and an animal is developed in a much more direct, less subtle way.

A tree is an underground creature with its tail in the air. All its intelligence is in its roots. All the senses it has are in its roots. Think what sagacity it shows in its search after food and drink! Somehow or other, the rootlets, which are its tentacles, find out that there is a brook at a moderate distance from the trunk of the tree, and they make for it with all their might. They find every crack in the rocks where there are a few grains of the nourishing substance they care for, and insinuate themselves into its deepest recesses. When spring and summer come, they let their tails grow, and delight in whisking them about in the wind, or letting them be whisked about by it; for these tails are poor passive things, with very little will of their own, and bend in whatever direction the wind chooses to make them. The leaves make a deal of noise

[1] From *The Virginia Quarterly Review,* Vol. 33 (Autumn, 1957). Reprinted by permission of the author.

whispering. I have sometimes thought I could understand them, as they talk with each other, and that they seemed to think they made the wind as they wagged forward and back. Remember what I say. The next time you see a tree waving in the wind, recollect that it is the tail of a great underground, many-armed polypus-like creature, which is as proud of its caudal appendage, especially in the summertime, as a peacock of his gorgeous expanse of plumage.

—OLIVER WENDELL HOLMES, *Over the Teacups.*

3. Comparison and Contrast

Comparison and contrast are among the commonest methods of logical development. They are distinguished from analogy by the fact that the thinking is done always in terms of the real and actual. One of the terms is not imaginary, as is often the case in analogy, but both of the things compared or contrasted actually exist. Thus Macaulay, when he is explaining Francis Bacon's contribution to modern thought, compares the philosophy of Bacon, the modern, to the philosophy of Plato, the ancient Greek. When the automobile made its appearance, people called it a horseless carriage; they were saying, in effect, that the automobile was like a carriage without a horse. The effort in such explanations is to bring the idea or thing discussed within the reader's own experience—to get him to see the new thing in terms of something that he already knows.

Comparison and contrast may be used in a single brief passage, in order to make a swift illustration, or they may occupy a pair or a group of paragraphs. The following paragraph is developed by comparison and contrast. It also moves from the general to the particular and in further illustration uses the reactions of the child approached by a person wearing a mask.

> Tears may be considered as the natural and involuntary resource of the mind overcome by some sudden and violent emotion, before it has had time to reconcile its feelings to the change of circumstances: while laughter may be defined to be the same sort of convulsive and involuntary movement, occasioned by mere surprise or contrast (in the absence of any more serious emotion), before it has time to reconcile its belief to contradictory appearances. If we hold a mask before our face, and approach a child with this disguise on, it will at first, from the oddity and incongruity of the appearance, be inclined to laugh; if we go nearer to it, steadily, and without saying a word, it will begin to be alarmed, and be half in-

clined to cry: if we suddenly take off the mask, it will recover
from its fears, and burst out a-laughing; but if, instead of
presenting the old well-known countenance, we have concealed a satyr's head or some frightful caricature behind
the first mask, the suddenness of the change will not in this
case be a source of merriment to it, but will convert its surprise into an agony of consternation, and will make it scream
out for help, even though it may be convinced that the whole
is a trick at bottom.—WILLIAM HAZLITT, "On Wit and
Humour."

4. Repetition

The value of repetition is that it strengthens the topic
statement by repeating it in different forms. The thought is
not so much developed as it is reinforced and clarified by
being displayed in different lights. In argumentative writing,
particularly, the repetition of an opinion or claim "drives
home" the point. The repeated statements are so many hammer blows.

> One terrible idea occurs in reference to this matter. Even
> supposing the war should end tomorrow, and the army melt
> into the mass of the population within the year, what an in-
> calculable preponderance will there be of military titles and
> pretensions for at least half a century to come! Every country
> neighborhood will have its general or two, its three or four
> colonels, half a dozen majors, and captains without end—
> besides non-commissioned officers and privates, more than
> recruiting offices ever knew of—all with their campaign
> stories, which will become the staple of fireside talk forever-
> more. Military merit, or rather, since that is not so readily
> estimated, military notoriety, will be the measure of all
> claims to civil distinction. One bullet-headed general will
> succeed another in the Presidential chair; and veterans will
> hold the offices at legislatures, and fill all the avenues of
> public life. And yet I do not speak of this deprecatingly, since,
> very likely, it may substitute something more real and genu-
> ine, instead of the many shams on which men have hereto-
> fore founded their claims to public regard; but it behooves
> civilians to consider their wretched prospects in the future,
> and assume the military button before it is too late.
> —NATHANIEL HAWTHORNE, "Chiefly about War Matters."

5. Definition

A paragraph may be developed by definition, that is, by
explaining the meaning of the topic or of some term connected with the topic. Definition sets bounds to a discussion.

It establishes the limits within which a topic or a term is valid. In logical definition the term is first set forth as a member of a class (*genus*) of ideas or objects. Then are given the qualities which distinguish it from other members of the class. These constitute the *differentia,* or "that property or mark distinguishing a species from other species of the same genus" (*Webster's New Collegiate Dictionary*). In the two paragraphs following, *incline* and *slides* are defined (and explained) as terms used in logging operations.

> An incline is a mechanical means of raising or lowering logs, generally in cars on a track, on grades which are so steep as to make operation of locomotives impossible. In its simplest form an incline consists of a hoisting engine at the top of the incline which hauls up the loaded cars or drops down the loaded ones by means of a drum and steel cable. Some inclines are designed on a principle of counterbalancing, which brings up an empty car as the loaded one goes down.
>
> Slides are just what the name indicates: an arrangement by means of which it is possible to slide the logs downhill. They generally follow the topography of the land on a downward grade, and are mostly used where the construction of logging railroads is not desirable or economically feasible. A slide may be merely a smoothed-off track down a slope in the shape of a trough or furrow; or it may consist of a sort of chute constituted of parallel logs or poles a few inches apart, supported on cross skids like railroad ties. Logs may be hauled along these slides by teams or other power; or, if the grade is sufficient, may descend by gravity.—STANLEY F. HORN, *This Fascinating Lumber Business.*

6. Logical Relationships: Causes and Effect; Proof

A paragraph may be developed by showing logical relationships: by following out a chain of reasoning from one idea to another or from one thing to another. A chain of reasoning may go from cause to effect or from effect back to cause. Thus one might explain how the need for zoning cities arises out of the need of protecting residence values, real-estate investments, or merely out of civic pride. A paragraph on cosmetics might trace the use of rouge and lipstick to feminine vanity or to mere convention; or it might show the results of the use of cosmetics—a notion of beauty as something to be artifically cultivated and a corresponding dislike of the natural and non-artificial.

Explanations made in terms of historical background and origins are likely to use cause and effect as a method of development. The feudal system, the English Reform Bill of 1832, or the disestablishment of the Anglican Church in Virginia might be discussed in terms of the social and political conditions that produced the changes.

Closely allied to this procedure is the method of giving reasons for belief in a certain view or the method of presenting evidence in proof of a certain statement. A geologist may report that a certain spot will not yield oil because the rock formations in that locality are not of the right type. A scholar may argue that one of Shakespeare's plays derives from Plutarch's *Lives* and sustain his point by tracing similarities between the stories told in the play and in Plutarch.

In the following paragraphs Charles and Mary Beard trace out the effect of mass production upon American life.

> The whole scheme of American life, as well as the structure of classes and the economy of the family, felt the impress of the changing machine process as mass production and the vivid selling operations which attended it scattered the same commodities and identical ideas over the entire country. Even distant lands were being transformed by an Americanization on the pattern which Matthew Arnold had so dreaded fifty years before, their more ancient arts and moralities corroding under the invasion of technology and standardized wares. Queens on thrones were soon endorsing American facial creams, for a price, and ex-premiers approving American cigarettes. With all his energies every great manufacturer in the United States strove to capture at least the national market. Makers of phrases also wrought for a continent. The slogans and catchwords of advertising sped from sea to sea on the morning of their publication—photographs and designs eventually flying as quickly as words on the wings of electricity.
>
> Within a week of their announcement the modes of New York, Boston, and Chicago became the modes of Winesburg, Gopher Prairie, and Centerville and swept on without delay into remote mountain fastnesses. Thus the technology of interchangeable parts was reflected in the clothing, sports, amusements, literature, architecture, manners, and speech of the multitude. The curious stamp of uniformity which had arrested the attention of James Bryce at the dawn of the machine age sank deeper and deeper into every phase of national life—material and spiritual. Even those who bent their energies to varieties of social reform, to the improve-

ment of education, the management of drives for benevolence, the distribution of knowledge, and the advancement
of public health brought the nation within their purview and
utilized the advertising courage of the marketplace. And all
these tendencies, springing naturally out of the whirl of business, were encouraged by the conscious struggle for efficiency
in every domain, by the discovery and application of the
most economical apparatus for the accomplishment of given
ends.—CHARLES and MARY BEARD, *The Rise of American
Civilization,* Vol. II. [1]

7. Combined Methods

A study of the paragraphs given above will show that
even in those specimens which illustrate particular methods
of paragraph development, there is some combining of
methods. The paragraphs from *The Rise of American Civilization* use cause and effect along with details and specific
instances. It is common to find definition followed by illustration; and repetition may make use of detail, comparison,
analogy. Combining methods is not exceptional; rather it is
a normal method. Probably the majority of paragraphs in
any piece of good writing will use more than one method
of thought development.

In practice, writers do not stop to ask themselves whether
they are giving a neat example of this or that method of
paragraph development. If they did so, writing would become as stiff and formal as the laws of the old-fashioned
rhetoric. Everything would seem to be cut to fit a pattern.

There is only one rule: use the paragraph development
that seems to fit the situation. Try different methods as the
orderly development of the thought may suggest. Remember
that the paragraph is a flexible unit, but its substance must
always be firm, and the development of the thought must
be a rounded development.

LINKING THE PARTS: TRANSITION WITHIN THE PARAGRAPH

In the paragraph as in the whole composition an orderly
sequence of thought best guarantees that the thought will
move smoothly from beginning to end. In many paragraphs,

[1] Reprinted with permission of the publisher from *The Rise of
American Civilization* by Charles and Mary Beard. Copyright
1927, 1930, 1933 by The Macmillan Company. Copyright 1955,
1958 by Mary Beard. Copyright 1963 by William Beard and
Miriam B. Vagts.

however, the sequence needs occasional markings to suggest and to emphasize the relation between the parts of the paragraph. Many paragraphs can be divided into subordinate parts which, taken together, constitute the topic. In other words, a paragraph can often be outlined, much as a whole composition can be outlined.

For example, in the second paragraph by the Beards, on page 107, the topic statement, in paraphrase, is this: "The technology of interchangeable parts standardized American habits." The Beards then show that technology brought uniformity to country districts as well as to metropolitan areas; that this uniformity affected every phase of national life; that it affected even those who sought to change American life—the reformers; and that the whole process was a by-product of the struggle for efficiency. The outline of this paragraph would be as follows:

Topic statement: The technology of interchangeable parts standardized American habits.
1. Metropolitan modes swept into country districts.
2. There was uniformity in every phase of American life.
3. Even social reformers used the methods of business.
4. All of these tendencies were encouraged by the struggle for efficiency.

The directive expression *thus* joins the first two sentences. The phrase, *curious stamp of uniformity,* repeats the idea of standardization. The phrase, *every phase of national life,* is a further repetition, and because it is a repetition of an idea it is a linking phrase. The word *even* connects the third point with the two preceding points. The phrase, *and all these tendencies,* links the final point with all that has gone before; *all these* is not only a connecting but a summarizing phrase.

An examination of the paragraphs in good expository prose will disclose a variety of connectives, or transitional expressions, like those pointed out above. Ordinarily such expressions are used at the junction of the parts of the paragraph. They are not to be used where the junction is already evident. To overweight a paragraph with such words as *and, but, nevertheless, moreover,* is worse than to have no connectives at all. A spare style is better than a fat style. Transitional devices should be used where they actually help, and not otherwise.

The way to acquire a feeling for smooth transitions is to examine critically one's own writing and to study the practice of the best writers. The following list of transitional devices will be helpful.

1. *Simple connectives:* and, but, for.

    Use these sparingly. It has never been wrong to use them at the beginnings of sentences. Good writers, of all periods of our literature, have felt free to begin sentences, at times, with *and* or *but*. But it is wrong to use them often in this way.

2. *Pronouns and pronominal adjectives:*

    The personal pronouns: he, she, it, they.

    Pronominal adjectives: this, that, these, those.

    A pronoun connects because it refers to an antecedent. When the antecedent of a pronoun or pronominal adjective is in the sentence preceding, then the two sentences are joined economically and often quite effectively.

3. *Repetitions of significant words or phrases, or variant repetitions through synonyms.*

    In the paragraph from Hawthorne, given above (p. 105), note the repetition in *military . . . general . . . veterans.*

4. *Directive expressions:*

    (a) *Indicating addition to or continuance of the thought:* furthermore, moreover, finally, for example, similarly, likewise, best of all, last and worst, etc.

    (b) *Indicating subtraction from or reversal of the thought:* however, on the contrary, strange as it seems, none the less.

    (c) *Result:* in consequence, accordingly, therefore, hence, as a result, thus.

SPECIAL USES OF THE PARAGRAPH

The typical paragraph has the rounded development described in the preceding pages, but in practice the paragraph is an adaptable and highly flexible instrument, changeable and various as the thought that produces it. In the hands of the best writers it assumes many shapes and has many degrees of complexity. No theoretical instruction in the principles of paragraph writing can set forth all the possible degrees of complexity, or all the varieties of form. A student's observation of what the best writers do, coupled with his own exercises in paragraph writing, will achieve more than all the theoretical instruction that could be given him. Instruction is given him, in fact, by way of guidance rather than of prescription. Instruction opens his eyes to the available technical devices. It teaches him what to look for when he is analyzing paragraph structure. It encourages him to cultivate a sense of form in his own paragraphing.

Although the typical paragraph of expository and argumentative writing has a rounded development, there are certain other kinds of paragraphs which do not always have this typical rounded development. Such paragraphs serve special functions in the whole composition. The most important of these special kinds of paragraphs are: (1) introductory paragraphs; (2) concluding paragraphs; (3) transitional paragraphs; (4) short paragraphs used for emphasis; (5) paragraphs in dialogue.

1. Introductory Paragraphs

Introductory paragraphs may announce the guiding purpose or thesis of the whole composition, or, in outline, may forecast a plan of treatment, or may strike the keynote of the composition. An introductory paragraph should tend toward brevity rather than length. A labored and pompous introductory paragraph wearies the reader's attention and defeats rather than helps the writer's purpose. The introductory paragraph should be interesting. If it does not catch the reader's attention and tempt him to go on, it is worse than useless.

The following are examples of introductory paragraphs.

> The year 1880 is a key-date in the history of ciphers. The experience of the Franco-Prussian and the Russo-Turkish Wars had now confirmed what the American Civil War had foreshadowed—that an age of mass armies had come, in which it would no longer be possible for the general to keep his battle under observation and to control its course by aides carrying word-of-mouth orders. He must work from the map, and map strategy demands communications fast as lightning, fast as the electric telegraph, and secret as the grave. Ciphers had been raised from the status of something a soldier could have with advantage to something he must have.—FLETCHER PRATT, *Secret and Urgent: The Story of Codes and Ciphers.*

> Jet propulsion is rocket power. Thermal-jet engines, duct engines, jet motors, jet-propelled planes, robot bombs, jet-propelled gliders, war rockets, thrusters and skyrockets—all

of these are merely different aspects of rocket power. All of
them, as we shall see, operate on exactly the same basic
principle: the principle of a motor that *thrusts* or pushes,
instead of producing rotary motion in a shaft or wheel.—G.
EDWARD PENDRAY, "Reaction Motors: How They Work and
Some Experiments with Them."

2. Concluding Paragraphs

A concluding paragraph rounds off discussion of the subject. It aims to give the reader a sense of completeness and
finality. It should not be a formal résumé, but it may sum up
the discussion pithily, perhaps by some brief restatement
which is likely to be an emphatic generalization or some
forceful comment on the significance of what has been said.
In composing his final paragraph the writer strives to make
the best possible impression on his reader, for last impressions are often decisive and enduring. At the same time, one
must remember that every paragraph, the last no less than
the first, is to be judged in the light of what it does within
the composition as a whole. *It is not necessary to make up a
special concluding paragraph if the composition brings itself
naturally to an end at a certain paragraph.* The concluding
paragraph must not seem to be added as an afterthought or
as an ornamental peroration.

The following paragraph taken from James Truslow
Adams's "The American Dream," is a good example:

It seems to me that it can be only in one such way, carried
out in all departments of our national life, that the American
dream can be wrought into an abiding reality. I have little
trust in the wise paternalism of politicians or the infinite wisdom of business leaders. We can look neither to the government nor to the heads of the great corporations to guide us
into the paths of a satisfying and humane existence as a great
nation unless we, as multitudinous individuals, develop some
greatness in our own individual souls. Until countless men
and women have decided in their own hearts, through experience and perhaps disillusion, what is a genuinely satisfying
life, a "good life" in the old Greek sense, we need look to
neither political nor business leaders. Under our political
system it is useless, save by the rarest of happy accidents,
to expect a politician to rise higher than the source of his
power. So long also as we are ourselves content with a mere
extension of the material basis of existence, with the multi-
plying of our material possessions, it is absurd to think that
the men who can utilize that power for themselves will aban-

don both to become spiritual leaders of a democracy that despises spiritual things. Just so long as wealth and power are our sole badges of success, so long will ambitious men strive to attain them.—JAMES TRUSLOW ADAMS, *The Epic of America*.[1]

3. Transitional Paragraphs

A transitional paragraph marks a division between groups of paragraphs (sections) of a composition or at times between paragraphs that in themselves develop aspects of the discussion which need a clearly accented transition from one aspect to the next. In either instance, a transitional paragraph is a device for making the junction of parts evident and smooth. It may be a *summarizing* paragraph, in which the preceding discussion is briefly restated and the direction of the ensuing thought-development is foreshadowed. Occasionally it may be a *one-sentence* paragraph of a purely conjunctive type. In any case it is functional in nature; it both divides and links; and its content is generally slight. (See pages 32–33.)

The following are examples of transitional paragraphs:

> It is impossible to answer the question categorically because the items are intangible. But we find ourselves reasoning about it as well as we can—which is as follows.—JOHN CROWE RANSOM, "Poets Without Laurels."

> If now we are not resigned to the teaching of sophistry or of etiquette, there remains only the severe and lofty discipline of *vere loqui*. This means teaching people to speak the truth, which can be done only by teaching them the right names of things. We approach here a critical point in the argument, which will determine the possibility of defining what is correct in expression; we come in fact to the relation of sign and thing signified.—RICHARD M. WEAVER, "To Write the Truth."

4. Short Paragraphs for Emphasis

In many magazines and newspapers, the practice is to "break" the solidity of the printed column or page by making paragraph divisions arbitrarily, with no particular regard for actual paragraph structure. This practice carries to an ex-

[1] From *The Epic of America* by James Truslow Adams, by permission of Little, Brown & Co.

treme the principle of eye-convenience suggested at the beginning of this chapter. Such paragraphing is a cheap means of securing emphasis. It is not to be commended as a standard practice.

In rare instances, nevertheless, a good writer may paragraph a single sentence, merely for emphasis, as this sentence is paragraphed.

5. Paragraphs in Dialogue

The quoted speeches of persons engaging in dialogue are always paragraphed separately. Quoted matter of any sort may be set off in an independent paragraph, especially when the quotation is lengthy.

The following brief selection illustrates the paragraphing of dialogue.

> "Why, foolish!" said he, "all things converge as they lie further away from your eye. That's perspective."
> "But then parallel lines do meet far, far away."
> "No. But they seem to."
> "But how can they seem to, if they really don't?"
> "Well, er—" the bright boy hesitated painfully. "It's all in your eye."
> "My eyes don't converge——"
> "I don't mean that. When you look at things far off, you see them as smaller than when they are close. Lines that are four feet apart close up seem only an inch or two apart a mile off."
> The bright boy gave up. But I worried him.
> —WALTER B. PITKIN, *On My Own.*

SPECIMEN PARAGRAPHS FOR ANALYSIS

Analyze the paragraphs given below. Point out the topic sentence of each paragraph; note where it is placed; note instances of paragraphs without topic sentences; study the use of transitional devices and methods of developing the topic. As guides for your analysis, note particularly the discussions of specimen paragraphs in the preceding pages, especially pages 99–109.

1. When I gaze upon the stately and beautiful Parthenon, I do not wonder at the greediness of the moderns to appropriate it. I do wonder at the obtuseness which allowed them to persevere in trying to make it work in the towns. It seems like the enthusiasm of him who should squander much money to transfer an Arabian stallion from his desert home, that, as a blindfolded gelding, he might turn the mill. The lines in which Byron paints the fate of

the butterfly that has fallen in the clutches of its childish admirer would apply not inaptly to the Greek temple at the mercy of a sensible building committee, wisely determined to have their money's worth.—HORATIO GREENOUGH, "American Architecture," *Form and Function.*

2. The distressing fact is that most of our urban universities are singularly lacking in any of the amenities of cultural life. How unlovely, how discouraging, are most of our great urban universities! The "bookstores" filled with textbooks and athletic equipment and toilet articles. The hideous cafeterias with their clutter and noise and dirt, the food antiseptic but tiresome; service nonexistent; popular music piped in relentlessly to drown out all conversation. If there must be music, why not Beethoven and Bach? The residence halls with their Coca-Cola machines (the impoverished English provide every student with facilities for making tea), and their television, and the students packed three to a room. The student unions designed to look and feel like hotel lobbies, with the local paper (never the *Times*) and *Playboy* for sale at the newsstand and a bowling alley in the basement. The student newspaper invariably featuring the most recent athletic contest or the forthcoming prom. You would as soon look at a Hearst paper for news of the world scholarship as to a university paper! Even the playing fields are closed to all but members of the varsity teams; the best facilities of the gymnasium set aside for teams; the hours of access to swimming pool or squash court rigidly fixed for the convenience of the coaches or of the teams.—HENRY STEELE COMMAGER, "Is Ivy Necessary?" [1]

3. The true greatness of Mr. Jefferson was his fitness for revolution. He was the genius of innovation, the architect of ruin, the inaugurator of anarchy. His mission was to pull down, not to build up. He thought everything false as well in the physical as in the moral world. He fed his horses on potatoes, and defended harbors with gunboats, because it was contrary to human experience and human opinion. He proposed to govern boys without the authority of masters or the control of religion, supplying their places with Laissez-faire philosophy, and morality from the pages of Lawrence Sterne. His character, like his philosophy, is exceptional—invaluable in urging on revolution, but useless, if not dangerous, in quiet times.—GEORGE FITZHUGH, *Cannibals All! or Slaves without Masters.*

4. Critics are rarely faithful to their labels and their special strategies. Usually the critic will confess that no one strategy— the psychological, the moralistic, the formalistic, the historical—or

[1] From the *Saturday Review,* September 17, 1960. Reprinted by permission of the *Saturday Review.*

combination of strategies will quite work the defeat of the poem. For the poem is like the monstrous Orillo in Boiardo's *Orlando Innamorato*. When the sword lops off any member of the monster, that member is immediately rejoined to the body, and the monster is as formidable as ever. But the poem is even more formidable than the monster, for Orillo's adversary finally gained a victory by an astonishing feat of dexterity: he slashed off both the monster's arms and quick as a wink seized them and flung them into the river. The critic who vaingloriously trusts his method to account for the poem, to exhaust the poem, is trying to emulate this dexterity: he thinks that he, too, can win by throwing the lopped-off arms into the river. But he is doomed to failure. Neither fire nor water will suffice to prevent the rejoining of the mutilated members to the monstrous torso. There is only one way to conquer the monster: you must eat it, bones, blood, skin, pelt, and gristle. And even then the monster is not dead, for it lives in you, is assimilated into you, and you are different, and somewhat monstrous yourself, for having eaten it.—ROBERT PENN WARREN, "Pure and Impure Poetry." [1]

5. There are two schools of thought regarding the pretzel's origin, but both start at the church. The crossed dough ends of the bread are said to represent the crossed arms of the priest or the acolyte at prayer. From this point forward pretzel authorities differ. (Don't smile; there are pretzel experts, and they take themselves quite seriously.) One story is that glazed hard pretzels encrusted with coarse salt were given out at monastery doors to passing pilgrims. The hole in the center had a functional purpose— pretzels could be strung on a pilgrim's staff.—CLEMENTINE PADDLEFORD, *How America Eats.*

6. The fourteenth century was an age of profound social and spiritual change: an age of ruin and rebirth, of apocalyptic fears and mystical hopes. It was the age of the Great Schism and the Black Death and the Hundred Years War, but it was also the age of Dante and Petrarch, of St. Catherine and St. Bridget, of Tauler and Suso and Ruysbroeck, an age of poets and mystics and saints. It saw the breakdown of the universal theocratic order of medieval Christendom and the rise of political nationalism and religious division, and at the same time it witnessed the passing of the old agrarian feudal society and the rise of capitalism and urban industrialism. Western Europe was stirred from end to end by a wave of social unrest which showed itself in revolutionary movements and bitter class warfare. At no other time in European history has the common people asserted itself more vigorously or found more

---

[1] Copyright 1943 by Robert Penn Warren. Reprinted from *Selected Essays* by Robert Penn Warren, by permission of Random House, Inc.

remarkable leaders. It was the age of the Jacquerie and the Peasants' Revolt, of the wars of the Swiss peasants and the German towns against the princes, and the still more heroic struggle of the Flemish proletariet against their own ruling classes and the power of the French monarchy.—CHRISTOPHER DAWSON, "The Vision of Piers Plowman." [1]

7. Just why President Davis selected John T. Pickett to represent the Confederacy as diplomatic commissioner to the Mexican government is not at all clear. True, he was forceful, bold, and shrewd and was widely acquainted in Mexico, for he had been consul at Vera Cruz for a number of years and had had a rather intimate association with Juarez and the small group of Liberals who made up his advisers and principal officers. But, to offset these advantages, he was quick-tempered, sharp of tongue, and, when angry, somewhat of a trouble hunter. In other words, Pickett was no diplomat.—FRANK LAWRENCE OWSLEY, *King Cotton Diplomacy.*

8. We have an English proverb that says: "He that would thrive, must ask his wife." It was lucky for me that I had one as much disposed to industry and frugality as myself. She assisted me cheerfully in my business, folding, and stitching pamphlets, tending shop, purchasing old linen rags for the paper-makers, etc., etc. We kept no idle servants, our table was plain and simple, our furniture of the cheapest. For instance, my breakfast was a long time bread and milk (no tea), and I ate it out of a twopenny earthen porringer, with a pewter spoon. But mark how luxury will enter families, and make a progress, in spite of principle: being called one morning to breakfast, I found it in a China bowl, with a spoon of silver! They had been bought for me without my knowledge by my wife, and had cost her the enormous sum of three-and-twenty shillings, for which she had no other excuse or apology to make, but that she thought *her* husband deserved a silver spoon and a China bowl as well as any of his neighbors. This was the first appearance of plate and China in our house, which afterward, in a course of years, as our wealth increased, augmented gradually to several hundred pounds in value.—BENJAMIN FRANKLIN, *The Autobiography of Benjamin Franklin.*

9. It is doubtful whether we are a nation materially rich. The movies and the radio and television tell us we are, and so does the press. But after the movies we go home to the tiny "ranchtype" cottages of stucco that stretch (already decaying) mile on mile about Los Angeles, or to the dog-kennel shanties which house

[1] From *Medieval Essays,* by Christopher Dawson. Copyright, 1954, by Sheed & Ward, Inc., New York. Reprinted by permission of The Society of Authors and the author.

the poor of Memphis, or the interminable dreariness which rings around the core of Detroit; and we read our newspapers in houses that line the filthy old lanes of North Boston, or the mean streets off Cleveland's Euclid Avenue, or the howling South Side of Chicago. Some of us live in better places, of course; but commonly we pay a price for decency which means great sacrifice in certain other values of civilized life. A contemplative man may be inclined to think that most Americans still are as fond of magniloquent exaggeration of their resources as they were in the days of Mr. Jefferson Brick. If America is wealthy, very often her wealth is of a sort peculiar to the twentieth century and alien to the traditional standards of prosperity. We all know the new Pontiac beside the rotting cabin in the swamp, the comic-books and movie-magazines strewn in the backyards of the tenements, the soda-fountain and cocktail lounge prodigality of our time; and the television set now dominates every slum flat.—RUSSELL KIRK, "The Problem of Wants." [1]

EXERCISES

1. Develop the following paragraph beginnings into fully rounded paragraphs.

    a. In pioneer times a few brave souls could hack out a clearing in the wilderness, throw up some log cabins, fight off the Indians, and establish a settlement—a real center around which a town, even a city, might grow up. Today a center is quite a different thing. It starts overnight, almost anywhere, with bulldozers . . . .

    b. To a summer motorist, worn down by road-heat, motor-heat, and eye-fatigue, any decent roadside restaurant is a help. But most inviting is that rare haven where the car can be parked in the shade.

    c. The relationship between automobiles and ladies' fashions is seldom discussed, but is nevertheless one of the realistic facts of modern life. If every Jill, as well as every Jack, must drive a car many times a day, then . . . .

    d. It is a real question whether national student organizations are operated for the benefit of students in the member institutions or for the far-off bureaucracy at the national headquarters. The student-body is perpetually changing; the inevitable bureaucracy . . . .

    e. If the President of the United States goes to the airport to meet a distinguished foreign visitor, that is "protocol." If

[1] From *Program for Conservatives* by Russell Kirk. Copyright 1954, Henry Regnery Company, Chicago. Reprinted by permission of the publishers.

you should make a "bread-and-butter call" on some one who has entertained you, that is "etiquette."

2. Write paragraphs, as your instructor may direct, in which you imitate the patterns of thought development used by various writers in the specimen paragraphs that you have analyzed.

CHAPTER 5

THE SENTENCE

THE sentence is the basic unit of expression by which the rounded development of the whole composition is achieved. We must write in sentences if the writing is not to be like a tale told by an idiot. And if the writing is to be good writing, the sentences must be good sentences.

What is a good sentence? The question cannot be answered briefly. Hamlet's "The rest is silence," in Shakespeare's play; "Mistah Kurtz—he dead!" in Conrad's *Heart of Darkness* (though not elegant); and Arnold's famous "The future of poetry is immense, because in poetry, where it is worthy of its high destinies, our race, as time goes on, will find an ever surer and surer stay"—all these, in their places, are good sentences. We may have the plain sentences of scientific prose, the lively sentences of journalism, the elaborate sentences of Ruskin, James, or Faulkner, in patterns of endless variety.

This chapter considers the sentence as employing a basic threefold pattern of grammar, logic, and rhetoric. For the good sentence, whatever its word-content, length, and structure, must satisfy three requirements:

(1) It must have correct form (*grammatical pattern*).

(2) It must "make sense" (*logical pattern*).

(3) It must be effective (*rhetorical pattern*).

The good sentence is a successful interweaving of these three patterns. For purposes of study we shall momentarily separate them.

1. GRAMMATICAL PATTERN

A good sentence is first a grammatical sentence: that is, a sentence which meets the requirements of grammar and syn-

120

tax. These requirements should be familiar to the student of composition, but may here need some review.[1]

The common grammatical definition of a sentence is: *A sentence is a group of words expressing a single complete thought.* This brief definition—as will later appear—requires a great deal of qualification. But it should be clear that "single complete thought" implies strict application of the principle of *unity.* The single thought, expressed through the *subject-verb-object* (or *-complement*) combination, must be self-sufficient. It must be an independent grammatical construction, not a functional part (*clause*) in some construction of which it is a member. At the same time, "single complete thought" does not exclude sentences that are unified structures of multiple related thoughts. The sentence—like the composition and the paragraph—has *unity* in its wholeness and completeness; *coherence* in the proper relation of its parts to one another; and *emphasis* if rightly written both grammatically and rhetorically.

Considered grammatically, sentences have the following characteristics:

(1) Every sentence must have a *subject:* that is, a noun, pronoun, or substantive expression (a word, phrase, or clause used as a noun). The subject is that about which something is said—or "predicated"—in the sentence. In each of the following sentences the *simple subject* (the subject without its modifiers) is italicized.

> a. The cold *sleet* struck my face.
> b. Smiling, *he* took off his hat.
> c. *To think* clearly is the first requirement.
> d. *What you think* will make little difference to the officer.
> e. *Riding* was his chief hobby.

(2) Every sentence must have a *predicate.* The predicate is that which is said about the subject. Its essential part is a *finite verb.* Without a finite verb, no predication can be made, and there is no sentence. A subject may be "understood" or unexpressed, as in the elliptical sentences "Go!" (*You* go!) or "Help!" (*You* help!). But the finite verb cannot be omitted. A finite verb is a verb form capable of person and number—a *limited* form of the verb, not an infinitive,

[1] For a thorough review or occasional reference the student should have at hand some textbook like Marckwardt and Cassidy's *Scribner Handbook of English* or other standard manual.

participle, or gerund. The finite verb, without its modifiers or complements, is the *simple predicate* of the sentence.

    a. The cold sleet *struck* my face.
    b. Smiling, he *took* off his hat.
    c. To think clearly *is* the first requirement.
    d. What you think *will make* little difference to the officer.
    e. The lecture being over, George *closed* his notebook.
    f. Riding *was* his chief hobby.

In the sentences given above, *smiling* (a participle), *to think* (an infinitive), *being* (a participle), and *riding* (a gerund) are non-finite verb-forms, or verbals. None of these verbals constitutes a predication. The predications are built upon the finite verbs *struck, took, is, will make, closed, was.*

The completeness of a sentence depends upon its having both a subject and a predicate. Subject and predicate may have modifiers, and in grammatical terms the structure of the sentence may be simple, compound, or complex. But always the sentence must contain at least one subject-verb combination of the "independent" type—not introduced by a subordinating conjunction, relative pronoun, or relative adverb.

Certain seeming exceptions to this rule are discussed below under the heading "Deliberate Fragmentations." Ignorant violations of the rule—essentially violations of the principle of unity—result in the error of the fragmentary sentence or, at another extreme, the fused sentence.

Deliberate Fragmentations:

(1) The Broken Sentence. Occasionally a writer may deliberately isolate fragments of a sentence (or of sentences) in order to obtain a special effect. Such use of sentence fragments is quite different from a careless failure to complete a sentence. The type of deliberate fragmentation here called the "broken sentence" may appear in a descriptive passage where a writer is building up a series of impressions:

> The mountains are clothed smokily with pine, *ocote,* and, like a woman in a gauze *rebozo,* they rear in a rich blue fume that is almost cornflower blue in the clefts. It is their characteristic that they are darkest-blue at the top. Like some splendid lizard with a wavering, royal-blue crest down the ridge of his back, and pale belly and soft, pinky-fawn claws, on the plain. Between the pallor of the claws, a dark spot of

trees, and white clots of a church with twin towers. Further away, along the foothills, a few scattered trees, white dot and stroke of a hacienda, and a green, green square of sugar cane.—D. H. LAWRENCE, *Mornings in Mexico.*

Deliberate fragmentations of the broken sentence type have only a special and limited use, and are not recommended for normal prose composition. Generally, in passages like that quoted above, the fragmentations constitute a single sentence, parts of which are separated by terminal punctuation in order to emphasize vivid details, presented in series.

(2) The Elliptical Sentence. An elliptical sentence may be defined as a legitimate abbreviation of a complete sentence. Only a part of the complete sentence is written or spoken. The remainder, although omitted, is clearly implied. Some examples of elliptical sentences follow:

(a) Jottings made in a diary or in similarly abbreviated records:

A snowstorm in the morning, and continuing most of the day. But I took a walk of over two hours, amid the falling flakes. No wind, yet the musical low murmur through the pines, quite pronounced, curious, like waterfalls, now still, now pouring again. All the senses, sight, sound, smell, delicately gratified.

—WALT WHITMAN, *Specimen Days and Collect.*

(b) Various kinds of customary exclamations, public notices, signs, labels:

Help!   Man overboard!   No Parking.   Price, 25 cents.

(c) The answer to a question or even the question itself:

"Did you see the prowler?" "No." (*Meaning:* "I did not see him.")
"I have one true friend." "Who?" (*Meaning:* "Who is your friend?")

(d) Proverbial expressions:

The sooner, the better. Least said, soonest mended.

The Error of the Fragmentary Sentence

The following groups of words do not satisfy the requirements for a grammatically complete sentence and are not to be considered allowable as deliberate fragmentations. They illustrate the error of the fragmentary sentence.

1. Sirens wailing, bells clanging, whistles screeching, people
   shouting and screaming as if sudden calamity had descended.
2. The rudder of an airplane, wrongly thought to function
   like a ship's rudder, to which it has a superficial resemblance.
3. To order a dinner at this particular restaurant, on the
   assumption that it is like other restaurants you have heard
   praised.

None of these word-groups is grammatically complete.
Group 1 contains a series of nouns (*sirens . . . bells . . .
whistles . . . people*) that might be used as a compound subject. But this possible subject lacks a predicate. The finite
verb, *had descended,* which stands in the subordinate clause
introduced by *as if,* has its own subject, and thus does not
furnish a predication for the noun series. In group 2 the
noun *rudder* lacks a predication; the verb-form *thought,*
which is associated with it, is a participle modifying *rudder,*
not a finite verb. *To order,* in group 3, is an infinitive, not a
finite verb.

The word groups are therefore "fragmentary" sentences.
They are meaningless as they stand, or at best are but fragments of a meaning not yet stated. But if finite verbs are
used, the word groups become complete sentences.

1. Sirens wailed, bells clanged, whistles screeched, people
   shouted and screamed as if sudden calamity had descended.
2. The rudder of an airplane is wrongly thought to function
   like a ship's rudder, to which it has a superficial resemblance.
3. To order a dinner at this particular restaurant, on the assumption that it is like other restaurants you have heard
   praised and may have visited, may result in an embarrass-
   ing social situation.

Sometimes the sentence fragments may be parts of a complete sentence which has been split by terminal punctuation
on the mistaken assumption that to begin a word-group with
a capital letter and close it with a period is enough to establish that word-group as a sentence. The error, when it occurs
in this form, is often treated as an error of punctuation and
is called "the period fault." But it arises, of course, from
failure to comprehend grammatical and syntactical rela-

tionships—from lack of understanding of what a sentence really is.

> WRONG: He is a most inconsiderate and tactless kind of person. Who is eternally dropping in just as the cook is setting the table for dinner.
> RIGHT: He is a most inconsiderate and tactless kind of person, who is eternally dropping in just as the cook is setting the table for dinner.
> WRONG: At the end of this long, shady street, we found a good hotel. Overlooking the lake, yet conveniently near a shopping center.
> RIGHT: At the end of this long, shady street we found a good hotel, overlooking the lake, yet conveniently near a shopping center.

The caution against the error of the fragmentary sentence should not be taken as a mere prohibition. The negative statement, *Do not mistake fragments for sentences,* is but a way of illustrating the positive principle of completeness. The subject and the predicate are the essential elements of completeness. They are the grammatical foundations of the sentence, and within the small scale of the sentence they parallel the topic and the discussion of a large-scale composition. Observe that the length of a sentence has nothing to do with its completeness. The shortest sentence in the Bible, "Jesus wept," is a complete sentence; but the conglomeration, "Weeping, groaning, tearing their hair, beating their breasts, and rending their garments," is only a series of phrases and not a complete sentence. Nor does complexity of structure have anything to do with completeness. We shall presently consider the nature of the structural complications that may be introduced in a sentence. But first it is advisable to issue another caution against another typical error—the error of the fused sentence.

Fusion of Sentences: The Comma Fault (or Comma Splice)

Improper fusion of sentences occurs when a writer fails to perceive that each single and complete thought is also a *separate* thought and must be kept apart from a single and complete thought that follows it. Terminal punctuation is the remedy for such errors, if the sentences thus fused (or "run together") are obviously separate sentences. But if the sentences can be treated as independent clauses of a compound sentence, then the semicolon may be used.

WRONG: Hotels and tourist courts will be crowded, you must make a reservation if you expect to stay overnight.

RIGHT: Hotels and tourist courts will be crowded. You must make a reservation if you expect to stay overnight.

WRONG: Councilman Brookhart has been faithful to his pledge, therefore he should be re-elected.

RIGHT: Councilman Brookhart has been faithful to his pledge; therefore he should be re-elected.

The error of improper fusion is sometimes classified as an error of punctuation and is called the "comma fault" or the "comma splice." If no punctuation at all appears in the fused sentence, it is sometimes called the "run-on" sentence.

But the error of the fragmentary sentence and the error of the fused sentence are errors of unity. They violate the principle explained above: that the sentence must be a single, complete unit of thought.

TYPES OF SENTENCE ORGANIZATION

But the principle of unity (singleness and completeness of thought) applies in sentence situations far more varied than might be inferred from the explanations given thus far. A sentence may consist of few parts or many parts. We may now extend the discussion of sentence unity by pointing out that unity of thought implies unity of organization. Sentences may be classified according to the way in which their parts are organized. The parts of a sentence are not only the subject and predicate, but also the modifiers of subject and predicate; and these modifiers may be single words or phrases or clauses. The grammarian rigidly classifies sentences as *simple, compound, complex, compound-complex;* but the writer must understand that each of the types is capable of much variation within the limits of its strict grammatical pattern.

1. The Simple Sentence

a. Simple sentence without modifiers:

SUBJECT	VERB	OBJECT
Water	*quenches*	*thirst*

b. Simple sentence with adjective and adverb modifiers:

This cool water completely quenches my thirst.

The cool water of this spring completely quenches a traveler's thirst.

This spring water, cool and pleasant, completely quenched my thirst, long aggravated by a hot and dusty walk.

c. Simple sentence with compound subject:
Good water and fresh air are among the first requirements.

d. Simple sentence with compound predicate:
The water quenched my thirst and revived my drooping spirits.

A simple sentence is a sentence consisting of one independent clause. Or, negatively, it is a sentence that does *not* have two or more independent clauses and that does *not* contain a dependent clause.

Observe that modifiers do not change the *organization* of the simple sentence, so long as they are single words (adjectives and adverbs) or phrases (a phrase is a group of words not having a subject and predicate and used as a part of speech). Observe also that a compound subject or a compound predicate (or both) does not prevent the sentence from being still a simple sentence.

2. The Compound Sentence

a. Compound sentence without modifiers:
Dogs barked, and chickens squawked.

b. Compound sentence with modifiers:
Aroused by the sudden noise, the dogs barked furiously, and the chickens, hearing the commotion, began to squawk.

c. Compound sentence of three members, with modifiers:
Jim was impressed by the man's courage, and I was moved by his evident sincerity, but neither of us could quite approve his methods.

A compound sentence is a sentence consisting of two or more independent clauses. Sentence *a* is not at all complicated, but since it has two independent clauses, it is compound. In sentences *b* and *c* the complication has greatly increased, but it is built up around coördinate clauses. The characteristic of the compound sentence is that it observes the principle of coördination. It combines clauses of equal rank (always independent clauses) and generally clauses that express closely parallel or complementary thoughts.

3. The Complex Sentence

a. Principal clause, with adverbial clause following:
> *We will go whenever you are ready.*

b. Principal clause, with relative clause beginning with *who:*
> *Probably the canteen was left in this gully by some soldier, who paused here for a moment, seventy-five years ago, to take refuge from the enemy's fire and to wet his blackened lips.*

c. Adverbial clause, followed by principal clause:
> *If you are ready, we will go now.*

d. Adverbial clause, principal clause, and noun clause:
> *Although you may think poorly of his conclusions, you must admit that the speaker has shown great originality.*

A complex sentence consists of an independent clause (principal clause) and at least one dependent clause. The dependent clause may be used as an adjective or adverbial modifier. In sentence *a,* above, the clause *whenever you are ready* is an adverbial clause modifying the verb *go.* In sentence *b,* the relative clause *who . . . lips* is used as an adjective and modifies the noun *soldier.* Dependent clauses may also function as nouns. In sentence *c,* the clause *that . . . originality* is a noun clause, and is the direct object of the verb *admit.* A noun clause may also be used as the subject of a verb: "*Whoever wins the match* will be champion."

Observe that complexity has nothing to do with length. The essential feature of the organization of a complex sentence is that it contains the principal clause + dependent clause relationship. The dependent clause, of course, contains its own subject and predicate, but the statement that it makes is not independent. The dependent clause functions as a part of speech, as can be seen if one substitutes an adverb like *soon, now, presently,* for the adverbial clause, *whenever you are ready,* in sentence *a,* above. If the wrong clause is subordinated, then the sentence does not possess unity. The unity of the complex sentence comes from the fact that the dependent thought is put in right relation to the main thought.

4. The Compound-Complex Sentence

a. Two principal clauses, with introductory dependent clause:

> *If you are ready, we will go; but do not expect me to carry all your packages.*

b. Two principal clauses, with four dependent clauses:

> *When all the packages had been assembled, and when all the baggage had been carried out to the car, it seemed at last that we were ready to go; but from past experience we knew how little to count on a quick start, and so were not surprised when Susanna began to think of more things to do.*

A compound-complex sentence consists of two or more principal clauses and at least one dependent clause in one of its members. It represents the highest degree of complication obtainable in a sentence. Sometimes a compound-complex sentence may seem to be a group of sentences rather than one clearly unified sentence. If it is really a group of sentences, then it ought to be broken up into separate sentences. The true compound-complex sentence is a real unit, a single sentence. Sentence *a*, above, consists of two independent clauses so closely related as to be two aspects of a single idea: *We will go . . . but do not expect me . . .* Each of these clauses has its own modifiers. In sentence *b*, we have two independent clauses, *It seemed at last . . .* and *but we knew . . . and so were . . . ,* which unify around the central idea of seeming-but-knowing. Each of these clauses has a group of its own modifiers.

SENTENCE ANALYSIS

A good working knowledge of grammar and syntax is essential to a mastery of the sentence. The student of composition should realize that what he formerly learned by rote—and perhaps thought dull and foolish—can now be put to really practical use. It is impossible to study sentence structure without knowing the terms and principles of grammar and syntax. In no other way is it possible to understand what happens in a sentence. And unless one understands what happens in a sentence, he will write blindly. He will work like a craftsman who does not know the names of his tools, or the qualities of his materials, or the physical laws of the structure that he is attempting to create.

Sentence analysis is a means of studying what happens in a sentence. For those who have learned to read by taking in "eyefuls" and "getting the general drift," practice in sentence analysis may well be a prerequisite for exercises in sentence writing. For such readers may not have learned to pay close attention to the parts of a sentence and to the relationship of part to part. Sentence analysis is simply a device for cultivating such close attention. It is, indeed, a highly specialized kind of reading which may become very useful to blind readers (people who do not see what they are reading) or rapid readers. But any reader and any writer will profit by close attention to the elements of the sentence and their function in the sentence.

EXERCISES

Unity of Sentence Structure. Correct errors in the following sentences. Distinguish any sentences that may rightfully be classified as deliberate fragmentations or permissible fusions.

1. Mr. Bonami is the center of a vast system of newsmen stationed through the globe and across the U. S. A. Organized to give you up-to-the-minute stories solidly backed by picture coverage. Using the very latest techniques.

2. This fellow had money, too, and hair-oil. Also an ignorant silver watch and a showy brass watch-chain.

3. "The Bill of Rights is a series of legal rights of individuals against the state and federal governments," the report says, "it does not apply unless the right is one that may be enforced or protected in the courts."

4. The advertiser does not own the view of which we are deprived, so why should a handful of large outdoor advertisers desecrate our great scenic roads?

5. As the hart panteth after the water brooks. So panteth my soul after Thee, O God.

6. As I say, she'd of divorced Jim, only she seen that she couldn't support herself and the kids and she was always hopin' that Jim would cut out his habits and give her more than two or three dollars a week.—RING LARDNER, "Haircut."

7. To get consideration, you must have letters from your pastor and other reputable persons. This being necessary to prove that you are a man of good character.

8. She worried about leaving the screen door unlatched, that was how a prowler broke in, one time.

9. Look. On that icy cliff. Number Four is slipping, he is falling, all are lost.

10. Then that haunted room—in which old Mrs. Battle died—whereinto I have crept, but always in the day-time, with a passion of fear; and a sneaking curiosity, terror-tainted, to hold communication with the past. How shall they build it up again?—CHARLES LAMB.

Classification and analysis. Classify the following sentences (as simple, compound, complex, compound-complex). Make a grammatical analysis of at least four.

1. Greatly agitated by the telephone call, Jenny returned to her pleasant bedroom, but could not sleep.

2. Police and fire departments are prompt to answer a call, no matter what time of day or night.

3. Do not fail to study both the risks and the rewards of the program you choose.

4. When shrimps learn to whistle, to borrow a proverb from Nikita Khrushchev, Soviet agriculture will provide enough food for Russia.

5. Dinner will be served at 7 P. M., and please be on time.

6. If you want to be on time for dinner, you must be ready by 7 P. M., and that does not mean 7:30 or 8:00 P. M.

7. The body of the community, whenever it can come to act, can meet with no effectual resistance; but till power and right are the same, the whole body of them has no right inconsistent with virtue, and the first of all the virtues, prudence.—EDMUND BURKE.

8. One would see her then as possessed of all things, all but the single most precious assurance; freedom and money and a mobile mind and personal charm, the power to interest and attach; attributes, each one, enhancing the value of a future.—HENRY JAMES.

9. Love of flattery, in most men, proceeds from the mean opinion they have of themselves; in women, from the contrary.—JONATHAN SWIFT.

10. The mystic chords of memory, stretching from every battlefield and patriot grave to every living heart and hearthstone all over this broad land, will yet swell the chorus of the Union when again touched, as surely they will be, by the better angels of our nature.—ABRAHAM LINCOLN.

2. LOGICAL PATTERN

The conventions of grammar represent the ways in which we have come to use the meanings, forms, and arrangements of words. Words have a meaning in their mere content, as spoken or written symbols of things, persons, ideas, qualities, relationships. Thus the word *man,* for all that speak English, calls up the idea of *homo sapiens.* Grammar is a kind of code by which we understand, also, that words have meaning according to their changes of form, or inflections. We change the vowel *a* in *man,* singular, to form the plural *men,* and instantly know that more than one man is meant. Furthermore, words have meaning according to their syntax—that is, their relationship to one another in the sentence where they appear. In English this relationship is closely dependent upon the order of words in the sentence. Thus the sentence "The batter hit the ball" has an entirely different meaning from "The ball hit the batter." We can, then, readily conclude that grammar is the servant and ally of logic. Ignorance or disregard of the conventions of grammar inevitably does injury to meaning, or to what we designate, in this part of our study, as the logical pattern of the sentence. Errors resulting from such abuse of grammar fall into two broad groups: errors of form and errors of structure.

Some Typical Errors of Form

Errors of form—to which the term *solecism* is often applied—occur when inflectional changes are not used correctly. In some instances, as in the *errors of case,* the meaning may not be destroyed. But the user of such solecisms will not command respect in good company.

> WRONG: Mrs. Goodwin invited Sarah and *I.*
> (The speaker, straining to be polite, falls into crudity and uses the nominative form *I* where the objective is required.)
> RIGHT: Mrs. Goodwin invited Sarah and *me.* (Objective form.)
> CORRECT BUT EVASIVE: Mrs. Goodwin invited Sarah and *myself.*
> (The speaker timidly avoids a choice between *I* and *me,* and drafts the reflexive pronoun to camouflage his ignorance.)
> WRONG: It is a matter of *whom* should be appointed.
> RIGHT: It is a matter of *who* should be appointed.
> WRONG: I shall lend the book to *whomever* speaks first.
> RIGHT: I shall lend the book to *whoever* speaks first.
> WRONG: Father deplored *Jimmy* marrying so young.
> RIGHT: Father deplored *Jimmy's* marrying so young.

In the last pair of examples the sentence marked "wrong" contains a small but clearly perceptible distortion of meaning. Father does not really deplore *Jimmy;* he deplores *Jimmy's marrying* so young. The verbal *marrying* is not a participle modifying *Jimmy* but a gerund, or verbal noun. *Jimmy* must be put into the possessive case, as it would be if the speaker said: "Father deplored Jimmy's rashness."

Slight distortion of meaning may also occur when *adjective and adverb forms are confused:*

> WRONG: The critic rates Faulkner *highly* as a novelist.
> RIGHT: The critic rates Faulkner *high* as a novelist.

Similar distortion of meaning appears in the too common but nevertheless regrettable *errors of agreement:*

> WRONG: The instructor asked everybody to sign *their* name.
> RIGHT: The instructor asked everybody to sign *his* name.
> WRONG: The shriek of sirens, racing through the dark streets, *make* me nervous
> RIGHT: The shriek of sirens, racing through the dark streets, *makes* me nervous.

But such crudities, bad as they may be, weigh less than the gross errors of structure.

Word Order and Syntax

During the long historical process of the blending of Norman-French and later Latinistic elements with the original Anglo-Saxon, the English language lost the greater part of the inflections that once characterized it. In the English sentence, therefore, the *position* of words and groups of words, more often than their form, indicates their syntactical relation to one another.

We may illustrate the difference between a highly inflected and a relatively uninflected language by comparing the English sentence used above—"The batter hit the ball"—with its Latin equivalent. We may put the Latin words in any order—

> Piliator pilam pepulit.
> Pilam piliator pepulit.
> Pepulit pilam piliator.

And still the logical meaning would be, "The batter hit the ball." The syntax, and therefore the meaning, is shown by the inflectional endings (pilia*tor* pil*am* . . .), not by the word order. The *emphasis*—or the rhetorical effect—shifts as the word order changes, but the basic meaning does not. If we wish to say in modern Latin, "The ball hit the batter," we should have to change the inflectional endings and write, "Pil*a* piliator*em* pepulit."

If we examine a line from Vergil which describes the threshing of grain—

Surgentem ad zephyrum paleae jactantur inanes.
(III *Georgic*, 134)

we know at once from the inflectional ending of the participle *surgentem* that it modifies the noun *zephyrum*. But in English we cannot without confusion approximate the Latin word order. "Rising on the west wind the empty chaff is tossed" is a mistranslation because in the English sentence the position of the participle *rising* affiliates it with the subject, *chaff,* and not with *west wind (zephyrum).* A correct translation would be "Upon the rising west wind the empty chaff is tossed" or, if we wish to keep something of Vergil's effect, "Upon the rising west wind the chaff is tossed, empty."

Normal Word Order

In English, through centuries of usage, we have become accustomed to the familiar sequence: *subject—verb—object* (or *—predicate complement*). We call this sequence *normal word order.* From childhood we are so habituated to this normal order that in common discourse we need no instruction to place a noun or other substantive in the position of the subject; a finite verb adjacent to it, agreeing with its subject in number and person; another noun or substantive expression after the verb where the direct object belongs—or a predicate adjective or predicate noun when the verb is "intransitive." Our way of putting "proper things in proper places" is illustrated by the following examples of normal order:

The mechanic repaired our automobile. (*subject—verb—direct object*)

An indirect object always *precedes* the direct object:

The manager handed *me* the bill. (*subject—verb—indirect object—direct object*)

Predicate adjectives and predicate nouns follow the verb:

The automobile was *new*. (*predicate adjective*)
It was our first *automobile*. (*predicate noun*)

The addition of modifiers will cause no confusion if they are *properly placed:*

A clever mechanic at the filling station easily repaired our automobile.

Through some manipulation we may discover that we can change the position of the phrase *at the filling station* and of the word *easily* without changing the meaning:

(1) At the filling station a clever mechanic easily repaired our automobile.
(2) A clever mechanic easily repaired our automobile at the filling station.

Then, more doubtfully:

(3) Easily at the filling station a clever mechanic repaired our automobile.

But a more drastic shift gets us into the *Looking Glass* world of Lewis Carroll:

(4) A clever automobile filling at the station repaired our mechanic easily.

If we are using words that undergo considerable inflectional change—for example, personal pronouns—we can juggle the word order, though not without some risk. In the sentence, "Her I love, and no other," the meaning is clear, but here the inverted order (object preceding subject and verb) seems un-English and a little forced. "Her he loves, and no other" is a grammatically correct but an unlikely construction. "Her loves he" is absurd; it invites us to wonder whether some illiterate person is trying to say "She loves him, and no other."

Change of Function without Change of Form

The importance of position can be further observed by the construction of sentences in which the same word functions in different parts of speech without undergoing a change of form. The function, and with it the meaning, is then determined from position alone.

In the sentence "Brave men deserve fair women," *brave* and *fair* function as adjectives. From their position they are naturally and correctly taken to modify the nouns following them, *men* and *women*. But in a famous line from Dryden's poem, "Alexander's Feast," we find *brave* and *fair* functioning as nouns: "None but the *brave* deserves the *fair*." From their position we know that *brave* and *fair* are nouns, used as subject and object. Also, from the position of the words alone we know that "a fair American" is something quite different from "an American fair." In the sentence, "You must *brave* the danger," we know from its position that *brave* functions as a verb.

Position of Modifiers

In the preceding group of sentences (page 135) we have noted that caution must be observed in the placing of modifiers. It is now important (1) to state the general principle that governs the position of modifiers and (2) to illustrate, by examples, the dangers awaiting writers who do not understand and apply this principle.

General principle: A modifier, whether word, phrase, or clause, must be so placed in the sentence that a reader can instantly associate it with the word to which it logically and grammatically belongs. Except in the case of *predicate adjectives,* a modifier will generally stand next to, or close to, the word it modifies. But some modifiers, especially adverbial modifiers, can stand in more distant positions provided no injury to meaning results from such placement.

Adjectives and Adjectival Modifiers. Adjectives normally precede the substantives that they modify:

> An *honest* man is needed.
> The hitch-hiker gave us a *long, elaborate, evasive* harangue.

But for rhetorical emphasis they may follow the substantive:

> To our relief the door opened on a patio, *bright* and *peaceful*.

Predicate adjectives regularly follow the verb:

> The desk is *rickety*.
> The house is *in poor condition*.

Adjective phrase and relative clauses regularly follow the substantive that they modify:

Adjective phrase	We can see that he is a man *of the people.* (In Greek one could say "an of the people man", but not in English.)
Relative clause	Richard was dancing with a blonde girl *whom he had just met.*

Participles: Participles are verbal adjectives and require particular attention, since an absurd distortion of meaning may occur from improper placement. For example, a present participle, if placed at the beginning of a sentence, is taken to modify the subject of the sentence. In the sentence, "*Coming,* I saw him," the participle modifies the subject *I.* In the sentence, "I saw him *coming,*" it modifies the pronoun *him,* which it immediately follows. But in such a sentence as "Coming home at noon, my faithful dachshund welcomed me as usual," confusion of meaning is evident. Probably the writer meant to say, "Coming home at noon, I was welcomed as usual by my faithful dachshund."

Adverbial Modifiers. To some extent, adverbs may be distinguished by the form. Of these there are two important classes:

(1) Adverbs formed by adding the suffix *-ly* to an adjective (hopeful*ly,* tru*ly,* pardonab*ly*). But since some adjectives also end in *-ly*—usually those formed from the addition of *-ly* to nouns (hour*ly,* year*ly,* mother*ly,* etc.)—the distinction between adverb and adjective will often depend upon word order.

(2) Adverbs formed by the addition of the following suffixes: *-day, -long, -meal, -place, -side, -time, -ward, -wards, -way, -ways, -wise, -where,* and *-s.* For example: nowa*days,* head*long,* piece*meal,* in*side,* some*time,* in*wards,* half*way,* side*ways,* length*wise,* any*where,* evening*s.* Of these adverbs, some may function as adjectives (a *headlong* rout, an *inside* look); but many are used as adverbs only (*everywhere, sometimes, always,* etc.) and can be distinguished by their form, regardless of their place in the sentence.

On the other hand, there are more than fifty adverbs that have no characteristic adverb forms and that can function as other parts of speech: as prepositions (*about, above, in, near*); nouns (to the *right,* I learned *much*); adjectives (*down, fast, hard, north,* etc.); even as verbs (*back* a candidate, *up* the price, etc.). Position in the sentence, then, is the most reliable way for distinguishing the adverbial function of a word and for directing its meaning as the writer and speaker intends.

As we experiment with the placing of adverbs, we note at once that adverbs, in comparison with adjectives, are highly mobile, and can occupy various different positions without necessarily losing a clear relationship with the words they modify:

Tomorrow a chartered bus will be waiting at this corner.
A chartered bus will be waiting at this corner *tomorrow*.
A chartered bus will be waiting *tomorrow* at this corner.

Similarly, if the single adverb is replaced by a phrase:

At eight o'clock a chartered bus will be waiting here.
A chartered bus will be waiting here *at eight o'clock*.

Or if an adverbial clause is used:

When you telephone, a taxi will come to the side entrance.
A taxi will come to the side entrance *when you telephone*.

But if the following word order is used, the meaning becomes ambiguous:

A taxi will come *when you telephone* to the side entrance.

Now we do not know whether the clause *when you telephone* refers to the verb *will come* or to the phrase *to the side entrance;* and if we do not know the relationship of this particular adverbial modifier to its referent, we do not know what the sentence means.

Logic and grammar, indeed, are so closely bound that any failure to observe their close relationship will produce slovenly writing or outright nonsense.

Inversions and other changes of order made for rhetorical purposes are of course not only allowable but necessary for variety and emphasis, as will be explained in the study of rhetorical patterns (pages 144–176). But such deviations cannot be allowed when they upset grammatical arrangements so as to destroy the logic of the sentence.

Let us examine again two sentences used above.

1. A clever mechanic at the filling station easily repaired our automobile.
2. A clever automobile filling at the station repaired our mechanic easily.

In sentence 2, no less than in sentence 1, the grammar

could be taken as "correct." Sentence 2 contains no solecisms, no illiteracies. But it is nonsense. There is no "sense" for the correct grammatical pattern to set forth. The lesson of the nonsensical sentence might well be: *Do not write nonsense, even in a grammatical form.* But for our purpose at this point we might also say: *If grammatical pattern and logical meaning do not correspond, the result is nonsense.* Or if, in view of the preceding discussion as a whole, we wish to make a full statement of the principle involved, the lesson is this: *The good sentence is not only a sentence that is grammatically unified and correct. It is a sentence in which the forms and conventions of grammar bring out the intended meaning clearly and accurately.*

Typical Errors of Sentence Structure

It would be interesting to speculate why human thought, as expressed in language patterns, behaves as it does. But such a discussion would require a title like that of a certain famous book, *The Meaning of Meaning*, and would lead us aside into complex studies of semantics and linguistics. Here we need only lay down those cautions that illustrate negatively the principle that grammar must conform to logic.

1. Dangling Modifiers

> Descending the slope to Antietam Creek, the famous Burnside Bridge, scene of McClellan's last great onslaught, comes into view.

The present participle *descending* is a "dangling participle." There is no substantive that it can modify both grammatically and logically. The reader follows his well-established grammatical inclination to attribute the participle to the subject of the sentence, *Bridge*. Thus an absurdity is created. The writer surely meant to indicate that the *traveler*, not the *Bridge*, is descending the slope. He should have written: "As the traveler descends the slope, the famous Burnside Bridge . . . comes into view." Or: "Descending the slope, the traveler will see the famous Burnside Bridge. . . ." The first correction changes the participle to an adverbial clause; the second inserts a subject, *traveler*, that *descending* can modify both logically and grammatically.

Participles, gerund phrases, and elliptical clauses are peculiarly subject to the difficulty illustrated above. Examples:

WRONG: Reassured by his manner, it seemed a good time to ask my question.

RIGHT: Reassured by his manner, I thought it a good time to ask my question.

WRONG: On receiving your check, the order will be filled.

RIGHT: On receiving your check, we will fill the order.

WRONG: Though defeated by a small score, the game was a triumph for our team.

RIGHT: Though we were defeated by a small score, the game was a triumph for our team.

Absolute expressions have a special grammatical status and should not be confused with dangling modifiers:

RIGHT: Our mission having been accomplished, the lieutenant gave the signal to withdraw. (*nominative absolute*)

RIGHT: To tell the truth, we never did attend the meeting. (*absolute infinitive phrase*)

2. Misplaced Modifiers. The logic of the sentence, no less than the grammar, requires that all modifiers *clearly* modify the word or words to which they belong. The rule that modifiers should be placed as near as possible to the word they modify, though good for most adjectival modifiers, will not always work for adverbial modifiers and has other limitations that become evident in practice. The following sentences illustrate some of the situations that may arise:

WRONG: He always ate a light breakfast before taking a bath, *consisting of coffee and toast.*

Here we have an adjective modifier, the participial phrase *consisting of coffee and toast.* The absurdity created by misplacement is easily remedied by placing the phrase immediately after its substantive, *breakfast.*

RIGHT: He always ate a light breakfast, *consisting of coffee and toast,* before taking a bath.

But if a sentence contains a complex arrangement of prepositional phrases, some of which are adverbial modifiers, it will be impossible to place all such modifiers close to the word that they modify. In the following sentence all the modifiers of the verb *met* cannot be placed adjacent to it:

POORLY COMPOSED: The congressional leaders, *in response to this summons,* met *with the President* to discuss the question of armed intervention *at nine o'clock at the White House.*

The sentence is overloaded with adverbial modifiers. Some rewriting, as well as change of word order, is needed:

BETTER: Responding to this summons, the congressional leaders met with the President at nine o'clock at the White House to discuss armed intervention.

Squinting Modifiers. In the following sentence the adverbial modifier looks two ways and therefore permits ambiguity of meaning. This type of modifier is called the "squinting modifier."

WRONG: What you decide *during this interval* may shape your destiny.

The meaning of the sentence changes as we shift the position of the adverbial phrase *during this interval.* The following sentences are correct and clear:

During this interval, what you decide may shape your destiny.
(The prepositional phrase modifies *decide.*)
What you decide may shape your destiny *during this interval.*
(The phrase now becomes an *adjectival* modifier of *destiny.*)
What you decide may, *during this interval,* shape your destiny.
(Allowable for emphasis. The phrase modifies *may shape.*)

In the following sentences note that the underlined modifiers, though placed at some distance from the words they modify, cause no absurdity or ambiguity, but are readily associated with the words to which they belong; from their position, indeed, they give the sentences a certain emphasis.

Lord Lovell stood at the castle gate, *combing his milk-white steed.*

The piping chorus came back on the still air, *high-pitched, assertive, impudent.*—JAMES BOYD, *Drums.*

To me it seemed as though the mist itself had screamed, so *suddenly,* and apparently from all sides at once, did this tumultuous and mournful uproar arise.—JOSEPH CONRAD, *Heart of Darkness.*

Forward, through the muttering crowd that parted before him, that calm face pressed.

3. Errors of Coördination and Subordination. The principle of coördination requires that only elements of equal grammatical rank be joined by the simple conjunctions *and, but, or.* The *logic* of the sentence requires, in addition, that the elements thus joined have a natural affinity for each other—that is, logically belong together.

> WRONG: I have heard a story with a moral that interests me and which I wish to tell you.

This is an example of *false coördination.* The form of the sentence misleads the reader into thinking, momentarily, that the two relative clauses *that interests me* and *which I wish to tell you* are to be grouped in thought as modifiers of *moral.* But the *that*-clause refers to *moral,* the *which*-clause to *story.*

> TECHNICALLY   I have heard a story which I wish to tell you
> CORRECT: and which has a moral that interests me.
> BETTER: I have heard a story which I wish to tell you. It has a moral that interests me.

Such failures of proper coördination also violate the principle of *parallelism,* which will be explained in our later study of the rhetoric of the sentence. In the following sentence there is an obvious violation of parallelism as well as of coördination:

> WRONG: She is a young woman of peculiarly haunting beauty and who also has a powerful intellect.

The first modifier of *young woman* is the adjective phrase *of a peculiarly haunting beauty.* The reader expects the next modifier to have the same grammatical pattern—as the conjunction *and* signals him to expect. But he finds a relative clause instead. To eliminate the false coördination, change the relative clause to a phrase:

> RIGHT: She is a young woman of peculiarly haunting beauty and of great intellectual power.

No less damaging to the logic of the sentence is the failure to use subordinate constructions for sentence elements that actually are subordinate as thoughts. The writer of the following sentence has failed to distinguish between principal and subordinate elements. Through his indolent linkage of clauses by *and* and *but* he has coördinated elements that are not logically coördinate.

WRONG: The ballad tells about Lord Randal, and he has been dining with his true love, but she has poisoned him, and he is sick at heart.

IMPROVED: The ballad tells about Lord Randal, who has been dining with his true love. She has poisoned him, and he is sick at heart.

The illustrations given above suggest only a few of the typical errors that occur because of failure to make the grammatical pattern of the sentence conform to its logical meaning. It would be impossible here to give examples of all such errors. It is far more important to observe and apply the positive principles to which these errors do violence. In brief summary these principles are:

(1) Logic must govern grammar. Use grammatical constructions that clearly and precisely express the intended meaning.

(2) Remember that word order and position are of first importance in the English sentence. Modifiers must be placed so as to adhere clearly and unmistakably to the words that they modify. Modifiers must always have words to modify.

(3) In writing sentences of two or more clauses be sure (a) that only ideas of logically equal value are put into coördinate constructions; (b) that the clauses are so handled as to express the right degree of subordination where subordination is logically demanded and coördination where coördination is logically demanded.

EXERCISES

Revise or rewrite the following sentences.

1. Motoring through the tree-lined streets, the peacefulness of the old Virginia town brought back memories of its historic past.

2. Judging from the number of new faces among spectators and dancers, the annual square dance festival was a success.

3. After the show, we stopped at a curb service restaurant and had sandwiches and coffee, but I could feel a headache coming on, which is not unusual when I look at a movie for a couple of hours, and I was all for going home instead of another show which the other boys insisted on, but they said, "Just take a couple of aspirins and come on."

4. While repairing the chimney, a brick fell on the farmer's head.

5. Lord Byron wrote a poem about the Bridge of Sighs at Venice and which my grandfather would recite on the slightest excuse.

6. Stopped like other motorists by high water in the underpass, it seemed impossible for us to keep the appointment.

7. The crowd fell back grudgingly before the police, and evidently not really intimidated but still looking for trouble.

8. The girl in the red dress that I spoke to is his fiancée.

9. After Ewell's corps had entered Gettysburg, and previous to the arrival of Meade's army in force on Cemetery Hill, was the time when Lee could have won the battle.

10. The principles of the present liberal arts program are: required courses at the freshman level or later to insure basic uniformity; the principle of distribution to provide broad culture; and we think concentration in a major field will guarantee thoroughness.

11. We only had one gallon of gasoline in the tank.

12. The headmaster would lecture us on how to develop our characters in the old chapel nearly every morning in the good old-fashioned way.

3. RHETORICAL PATTERN

A sentence may be grammatically correct and perfectly logical, yet still not adequate for its intended purpose. The good sentence must be grammatical, logical, and *effective*. It must do *well* the work that it is intended to do. To write well, you must acquire skill in using grammar and syntax as tools of expression. Knowledge of grammar and syntax will help you to understand the nature of the word-stuff that goes into the sentence. But only through another kind of study can you learn to control this word-stuff so as to obtain the kind of expression that will best suit your purpose.

Perhaps grammar is to language what chemistry, physics, and mechanical engineering are to building materials. Then rhetoric, as the giver of laws of design, corresponds to architecture. Through mastery of rhetoric the writer or speaker exerts a higher kind of control than can ever be obtained from the study of grammar alone. Grammar is the law of the language, considered as language; rhetoric is the art of language, considered as thought. Grammar marks the limits within which you are to stay. Rhetoric teaches how to profit by limitations or at times to transcend them. Grammar leads to good form. Rhetoric, well practiced, leads to style.

Grammatical Form and Rhetorical Form

Although we distinguish here between grammar and rhetoric, the relationship between them is very close. It is impossible to discuss the form of the sentence without speaking of its grammatical constructions; but these grammatical constructions also have certain *qualities,* aside from their correctness or incorrectness, that mere grammatical analysis will not reveal. In order to see what happens in a sentence, we must add rhetorical analysis to grammatical analysis.

The following sentence, often quoted, is taken from Emerson's *Self-Reliance:*

> A foolish consistency is the hobgoblin of little minds, adored by little statesmen and philosophers and divines.

Let us first make a grammatical analysis. The sentence is a simple sentence. The simple subject, *consistency,* is modified by the article *a* and the adjective *foolish. A foolish consistency* is the complete subject. The simple predicate, *is the hobgoblin,* consists of a copulative verb, *is,* and its complement, *the hobgoblin. Hobgoblin* is modified by the prepositional phrase, *of little minds,* and the participial phrase, *adored by little statesmen and philosophers and divines.* The part of the sentence from *is* to *divines* constitutes the complete predicate.

Such a grammatical analysis does not tell us *why* Emerson wrote the sentence as given above. He could have satisfied the requirements of grammar in four words: "Consistency is a hobgoblin." Evidently, to make his statement logically exact and complete, he said "a *foolish* consistency" and added the further qualification that consistency is the hobgoblin only of *little minds,* which we find attributed to certain adorers of consistency. The modifying elements round out the declarative statement into its full logical meaning.

Rhetorical analysis must go further. It shows us at once what grammar ignores, that the explosive word *hobgoblin* is a strong figurative expression, greatly reinforced by its participial modifier *adored.* Emerson is putting the slavish followers of consistency into the class of heathen worshippers of a bogy or other false god. Further examination discloses that the sentence is organized around two powerful word-groups: (1) *a foolish consistency;* (2) *the hobgoblin of little minds.* Each of these word-groups is a rhetorical unit. Each contains a strong word: *foolish,* in word-group 1; *hobgoblin,* in word-group 2. These two strong words carry much more force than the plain grammatical subject *consistency* and the colorless verb *is*. The deliberate repetition of *little* drives home the point. There is a possible fault in Emerson's use of *divines,* which gives the teasing effect of a near-rhyme with *minds;* and rhymes are objectionable in prose. But the blemish is negligible. It is a clean and economical sentence, shrewdly constructed.

How different the effect would have been if Emerson had written the sentence as follows:

> Little statesmen, philosophers, and divines make consistency into a hobgoblin, which they adore. That kind of consistency is foolish.

The one strong sentence has been turned into two sentences, without any resulting improvement, but rather the contrary. The subject has been shifted, and the whole emphasis has been changed for the worse. The two sentences are grammatical and logical, but *not* effective.

Whether or not you may wish to follow Emerson as a model, you will do well to study good sentences of all kinds as closely as the sentence from Emerson has just been studied; and you must follow the implications of such a study if you are to gain control over the sentence as an instrument of expression. How may the student of composition attain such mastery?

First, he must know the grammar of the sentence so well that his use of grammar becomes almost instinctive. He must know the forms of words and their *qualities;* the kinds of sentences, clauses, phrases, and their *qualities;* the idiom of the language. He must be able to feel and to use what the poet William Butler Yeats called "the natural momentum of the syntax."

Second, he must know the *effect* within the sentence of the constructions that he uses—and must be able to revise his rough drafts in order to secure the effect he wants. He must be prepared to discard one construction and choose another, to expand or contract, to compound ideas or to separate them, to manipulate word order, and so through conscious design to make both meaning and effect count for the reader.

Two disciplines will help him to gain this skill: (1) rhetorical analysis of sentences; (2) conscious attempts to follow definite patterns in his own sentences.

Rhetorical Analysis of Sentence Patterns

Rhetorical analysis of sentences is less precise than grammatical analysis but far more interesting because it deals with the effects of combinations of words rather than with their merely formal relationships. Grammatical analysis reveals the anatomy of the sentence much as a scientist, by dissection, might study the anatomy of a horse. Rhetorical analysis deals with the "points" of a sentence very much as a lover of fine horses studies the "points" of a living horse.

For such analysis no scheme can be devised as methodical as the once commonly practiced grammatical "diagrams" of sentence structure. We can, however, look carefully at a sentence, see how it is put together, identify its notable features, and, with a few simple graphic devices, indicate its rhetorical pattern.

Often the notable features will be found to consist of striking words or word-groups that give the sentence its peculiar quality. These are sometimes called "pivot" words or expressions, since the rhetorical force of the sentence may be said to "turn" or "rest" upon them. Whatever term may be applied to them, rhetorical analysis may disclose that "pivot" words do not necessarily coincide with "subject" and "verb" as grammatical study might have led us to expect. Subject and verb are of supreme *functional* importance, but they may be words with little content and no rhetorical force. We have already noted, for example, that in Emerson's sentence the subject, *consistency,* and the verb, *is,* impart no emphasis. A large part of rhetorical analysis consists in studying how the rhetorical pattern interweaves with, but does not necessarily coincide with, the grammatical pattern.

To carry out this study it is highly important to determine what various words and word-groups contribute to the effectiveness of the sentence. Since any variation in normal order attracts attention and therefore gives emphasis, it is important to note the *position* of modifiers—and of all "pivot" words or word-groups—in the *order* of the sentence.

Special effects of any kind should be noted and examined: for example, repetition of single words and phrases; or the kind of repetition called *parallelism*—which is a repeating of patterns or constructions. Variation is no less important than repetition. A good prose style is often the result of a skilful combination of repetition and variation.

The *diction* of a sentence—and especially the use of *figurative* or metaphorical language—is an essential element in rhetorical effectiveness and must be considered in all rhetorical analysis. (See Chapter 6, "Words," for a detailed treatment of this subject.)

Last, sentences may be grouped in rhetorical classifications according to whether their structure is *loose, periodic,* or *balanced;* whether they tend to "segregate" or "aggregate" details; whether they employ a plain or an elaborate style.

Examples of Rhetorical Analysis

The rhetorical analyses that follow deal with simple, complex, compound, and compound-complex sentences. In order to show the basic grammatical structure, the simple subject and main verb are underlined. Important rhetorical groups are marked with horizontal braces, above the type. These are numbered for convenience in reference. Vertical lines mark divisions between minor phrasal units. In some instances "pivot" words or word-groups are underlined with a wavy line.

After studying the analysis carefully, the student should read the sentence aloud and indicate the rhetorical pattern by slight pauses and shadings of his voice.[1]

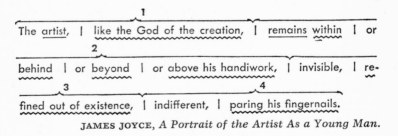

JAMES JOYCE, *A Portrait of the Artist As a Young Man.*

Simple Sentences. Grammatically, the preceding example is a simple sentence, of which *artist* is the simple subject. *Remains,* the verb, is followed by a series of word-groups

[1] See Robert M. Gay's *Reading and Writing* (Houghton Mifflin Company) for many interesting and practical suggestions as to rhetorical analysis, the study of phrasal units, and the imitation of sentence patterns. In certain particulars, this chapter follows—though with modifications—the approach suggested by Professor Gay.

which must be considered as predicate complements, adjectival in function, rather than as adverbial modifiers of *remains*. These are: (a) *within . . . handiwork,* a long prepositional phrase; (b) *invisible,* a single adjective; (c) *refined out of existence,* a participial phrase; (d) *indifferent,* a single adjective; (e) *paring his fingernails,* another participial phrase. The five predicate complements give the sentence a complicated rhetorical twist. Nevertheless, grammatically considered, it is not a complex sentence but a simple sentence.

Rhetorically considered, it is a sentence of subtle elaborateness and complexity. The subject, *artist,* and the verb, *remains,* are matter-of-fact, colorless, noncommittal. The force of the sentence comes, first, from the bold modifying phrase, *like the God of the creation.* This phrase overshadows the noun, *artist,* which it modifies. And, second, this force is intensified by the powerful accumulation of predicate complements that follow the verb. A remarkable amount of emphasis falls upon the four prepositions, *within, behind, beyond, above*—words that ordinarily have a purely functional character. In group 3, the phrase *refined out of existence* seems to give an explanation of *invisible,* although it does not modify *invisible* and is in fact grammatically coördinate with it. In the same way the strongly ironic closing phrase, *paring his fingernails,* seems to qualify *indifferent,* although it does not modify *indifferent.* Groups 3 and 4 thus have symmetrical structure with respect to each other, but are asymmetrical (unbalanced) in internal structure.

Thus, by the cross-pattern of rhetorical emphasis, the "strong" element of the sentence lies in its adjectival, or grammatically "weak" elements. In total effect, the sentence exhibits a peculiar kind of rhetorical syncopation; it emphasizes elements that, like the prominent elements of a musically syncopated pattern, receive an accent on the "offbeat." If we removed the syncopation and made a somewhat more "regular" statement, the sentence might read: "The God of the creation remains within his handiwork, invisible and indifferent; the artist thus resembles God." This interesting rhetorical effect might be graphically illustrated if we should write the minor ("offbeat") elements in capitals, as follows: "The artist, like THE GOD OF CREATION, REMAINS WITHIN (or behind, or beyond, or above) HIS HANDIWORK, INVISIBLE, refined out of existence, indifferent, PARING HIS FINGERNAILS."

She | was very good-natured, and not above forty foot high, being

little for her age.

JONATHAN SWIFT, "A Voyage to Brobdingnag," *Gulliver's Travels.*

This sentence refers to "Glumdalclitch," the "little nurse" —in fact a young giantess—who in Swift's account of the Brobdingnagians was assigned to the care of Lemuel Gulliver. Much of the effect of the sentence, as of the entire "voyage," derives from Swift's relentlessly ironic application of "perspective" to his story. Gulliver, the English sailor, is made to describe the monstrous world of the giants in the level commonplace terms that he would use in everyday life. Since the scale of measurement has been almost unimaginably enlarged, we get, through a telescopic magnification of human nature, an extraordinary point of view.

But the sentence illustrates, as well as any sentence could, how a rhetorical pattern may serve to produce explosive effects, even though the language itself is simple to the point of plainness. Again, as in the sentence from Joyce, the force of the sentence lies in the adjectival constructions, not in the subject and verb. Grammatically considered, the adjectival constructions, *very good-natured* and *not above forty foot high,* form a pair which constitute the predicate complement, while the participial phrase, *being little for her age* modifies the subject, *she.* Rhetorically considered, the sentence divides into three word-groups, which are rhetorically but not grammatically coördinate—in effect a rhetorical series. Instead of proceeding in climactic order, the series develops a jolting and ludicrous anti-climax as it moves from the commonplace *very good-natured* to the vast surprise of *not above forty foot high* and then drops to *being little for her age*—which comes like a casual afterthought. Although parallel construction might be expected, Swift very carefully twists his sentence away from a too precise parallelism. He does not say, as he might have said: "She was very good-natured, approximately forty foot high, and little for her age" or "She was approximately forty foot high, little for her age, and very good-natured." Instead, he weaves the grammatical and rhetorical arrangements into a skillful cross-pattern that gives the sentence exactly the kind of poker-faced irony he wishes to attain.

Complex Sentences. In the simple sentence the modifiers are always words and phrases. The sentence design is shaped up by minor accretions placed at strategic points—that is, if modifiers are used. In the complex sentence there are major structural complications. The distinguishing feature of the complex sentence is that it uses clauses as modifiers. This feature makes a great difference in the rhetorical pattern of the sentence. In the simple sentence the structural details are likely to assume a coördinate relationship. We often have a series of adjectives, phrases, adverbs, or, when subject or predicate is compounded, a series of nouns or verbs. The simple sentence thus moves, as it were, always on the same level, as in the following sentence by Blake: "The roaring of lions, the howling of wolves, the raging of the stormy sea, and the destructive sword, are portions of eternity, too great for the eye of man." In the complex sentence the organization (to continue the figure of speech) is both horizontal, as in the simple sentence, and vertical. That is, the complex sentence has both coördinate and subordinate units, and its subordinate units are clauses. It is very important to understand that the dependent clauses of the complex sentence are structural *units* and are to be viewed as groups, and that each dependent clause has its own internal organization, elaborate or simple in nature.

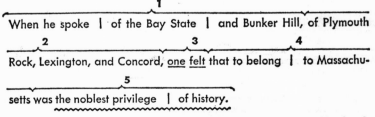

VAN WYCK BROOKS, *The Flowering of New England.*

Group 3 is the subject-verb group. It is of minor rhetorical importance. The greatest rhetorical emphasis is on groups 4 and 5, which together make up a noun clause, the object of *felt*. We should be justified in saying that the "rhetorical subject" of the sentence (if there could be such a thing) is in this subordinate clause and is the phrase, *to belong to Massachusetts;* and the "rhetorical predicate" would then be the rest of this clause—group 5. The sentence really leads up to the phrase, *noblest privilege of history,* which is therefore marked as a pivot expression.

The preparation for this strong final effect (which probably is intended to imitate the rolling majesty of Webster's speeches) is in the clause with which the sentence begins. The effectiveness of this clause is in the concrete power of the series of proper names. Note the rhetorical grouping of these proper names. The first pair are grouped with *when he spoke* (group 1); the next three, although they also are the grammatical and logical objects of *spoke,* form a rhetorical group of their own, echoing the pattern of the first group, while they amplify and extend the meaning.

Compound Sentences.   In grammar, a compound sentence consists of two or more independent clauses. In rhetoric, we must qualify this definition by saying, *not any two or more* independent clauses, but only those independent clauses which will make an effective as well as a logical and grammatical combination. In the good compound sentence, the "two or more" independent clauses must be facets of one idea—statements that really supplement each other and can stand side by side as coördinates. Consider the following three ways of handling a matter-of-fact statement:

(1) There were seven rooms in the house. Only two of them were of public note. (Two sentences.)
(2) There were seven rooms in the house, but only two of them were of public note. (Compound sentence.)
(3) Only two of the seven rooms of the house were of public note. (Simple sentence.)

Probably there is little to choose among these three ways of stating a simple fact. The *effect* of the compound sentence, however, is to establish a contrast between the seven rooms and the two rooms; but the two clauses are of equal importance and combine readily in one sentence because they really express but one basic idea—the idea contained in sentence 3.

The pattern of the compound sentence is naturally relaxed and easy. Its structure is that of the simple sentence repeated and prolonged. It is without the tension of the complex sentence. It develops as if by addition, subtraction, alternation. The coördinating conjunctions *and, but, or* may be compared to mathematical symbols. *And* is equivalent to the sign $+$; *but* to the sign $-$; *or*, perhaps, to the sign $\pm$. Compound sentences are useful for setting forth ideas that involve comparison, contrast, or balance.

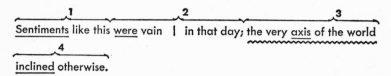

Sentiments like this were vain | in that day; the very axis of the world inclined otherwise.

JOHN DONALD WADE,
"Profits and Losses in the Life of Joel Chandler Harris."

This is a common type of compound sentence. It uses few modifiers. The weight of the sentence is carried by the nouns and verbs, and the "rhetorical subjects" and "rhetorical predicates" of the two clauses coincide rather closely with the grammatical subjects and predicates.

There is some contrast between the two clauses. The first clause is plain and abstract in its form of statement. The second clause is powerfully metaphorical and concrete. If the first clause understates the idea (perhaps ironically), the second clause overstates. (See *hyperbole* and *litotes*, Chapter 6.)

The rhetorical groups divide each of the coördinate clauses into two phrasal units of about equal importance, but these divisions are not very sharp.

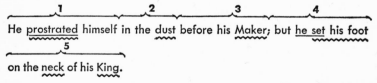

He prostrated himself in the dust before his Maker; but he set his foot on the neck of his King.

THOMAS BABINGTON MACAULAY, *Essay on Milton.*

In this sentence of Macaulay's, the contrast is much sharper than in the sentence of John Wade's. The two clauses, furthermore, are not only put in contrast, but are carefully balanced, almost word for word, one with the other. Note that the pivot words of the second clause follow the order of the pivot words of the first clause. The sentence illustrates parallelism, balance, and antithesis. It is much more artificial and much less natural than Wade's sentence, which has much the same structure. Macaulay's art is so apparent as to make his sentence seem like a piece of verbal gymnastics. The art of Wade's sentence is subtly hidden but works none the less powerfully.

Compound-Complex Sentences. The compound-complex sentence is a mixed type. It combines a compound structure with a complex structure. Remember that the mixed construction of the compound-complex sentence is a matter of structure, not of length. The following sentence from Thoreau contains only fifteen words, and yet is compound-complex: "This was manly as the world goes; and yet it was idle, if not desperate." The difficulties of analyzing the compound-complex sentence are greater when the sentence is rather long as well as involved in structure.

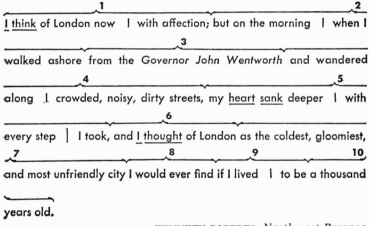

KENNETH ROBERTS, *Northwest Passage.*

The theme of this very elaborate sentence is a very simple one: the contrast between a man's thoughts about London at the time when he first saw it and at some later time. The complexity and elaborateness of the sentence arise from the writer's wish to show this man's feelings in detail.

The contrast is managed in the following way: the first independent clause of the sentence contains a very general statement—the rhetorical unit, group 1. All that follows is the detailed contrast between what the man thinks *now* and what he thought *on the morning when I walked ashore.* Group 1 is very simple in structure; but the rhetorical groups that follow (groups 2–10) are necessarily crowded with detail. The compound-complex structure is the only good means for organizing so much detail.

The contrast is emphasized by the repetition in the statements, *I think of London now* (group 1) and *I thought of London* (group 6).

Groups 4 and 7 contain a series of adjectives—*crowded, noisy, dirty* and *coldest, gloomiest, and most unfriendly.* It is doubtful whether this accumulation of adjective modifiers really helps the effect very much. Fewer adjectives might do the work just as well.

Imitation of Sentence Patterns

Imitation of sentence patterns is a useful means of getting experience in writing sentences that have an effective design. It has exactly the same purpose that the copying of a master's work may have for an art student. From doing, or trying to do, what the master does, the student learns what good work is. Imitation is a means of acquiring skill; it is the way in which we naturally learn a great many things, from infancy on into later life. There are limits to the value of imitation, of course; a mere copyist never attains real excellence. But imitation is useful in acquiring skill in so many fields of attainment that there is no reason to neglect it in writing. It is the kind of exercise that ought to establish good habits of writing.

The exercise is not to be done blindly. It must be preceded by a careful study of the model which is to be imitated. With a good sentence before you, examine its structure closely, as has been done in the rhetorical analyses of the preceding section. When you have determined what the pattern of the sentence is, then reproduce the pattern of the model in a sentence of your own which has an entirely different content. You may find it necessary to retain some of the words of the model, especially the purely functional words; but change the words wherever you can. The result should be a new sentence constructed upon the pattern of the old one.

The following sentence from Thomas Hardy may be imitated in the ways suggested:

MODEL

The sky was clear—remarkably clear—and the twinkling of all the stars seemed to be but throbs of one body timed by a common pulse.

IMITATION 1

The field was green—extraordinarily green—and the luster of all its furrows appeared to be but flashings of one surface, blended in the slanting light.

IMITATION 2

Her smiles are secretive—queerly secretive—and the quietness of all her ways seems to disclose only rumors of her mystery, guarded by her quivering mouth.

EXERCISES

1. Write imitations of the sentences analyzed in the preceding section (pages 148–154).

2. Make rhetorical analyses of sentences given below, as your instructor may direct. Then write imitations of the sentences that you have analyzed.

   a. The inner man is at times a tyrant, parasitical, wasteful, and voluptuous.—GEORGE SANTAYANA, *Character and Opinion in the United States.*

   b. At seventeen years old I was already an old-fashioned cannon full of shot, and nothing had kept me from going off but a doubt as to my capacity to shoot straight.—WILLIAM BUTLER YEATS, *Autobiographies: The Trembling of the Veil.*

   c. The proper study of mankind is woman, and, by common agreement since the time of Adam, it is the most complex and arduous.—HENRY ADAMS, *Mont-St.-Michel and Chartres,* Chapter XI.

   d. As Hitler remarks in one of his shrewd chapters on propaganda, you don't sell your brand of soap by pointing out that a rival brand is just as good.—JAMES BURNHAM, *The Managerial Revolution.*

   e. No man can read a fine author, and relish him to the very bones while he reads, without subsequently fancying to himself some ideal image of the man and his mind.—HERMAN MELVILLE, "Hawthorne and His Mosses."

f. I did not wish to take a cabin passage, but rather to go before the mast and on the deck of the world, for there I could best see the moonlight amid the mountains.—HENRY D. THOREAU, *Walden.*

g. Our Revolution, so wise in its conception and so glorious in its execution, was the mere assertion by adults of the rights of adults, and had nothing more to do with philosophy than the weaning of a calf.—GEORGE FITZHUGH, *Cannibals All! or Slaves without Masters.*

h. I have sometimes heard of an Iliad in a nutshell; but it hath been my fortune to have much oftener seen a nutshell in an Iliad.—JONATHAN SWIFT, *A Tale of a Tub.*

i. We shall fight on the beaches, we shall fight on the landing grounds, we shall fight in the fields and in the streets, we shall fight in the hills; we shall never surrender, and even if, which I do not for a moment believe, this island or a large part of it were subjugated and starving, then our Empire beyond the seas, armed and guarded by the British Fleet, would carry on the struggle until, in God's good time, the New World, with all its power and might, steps forth to the rescue and liberation of the old.—WINSTON CHURCHILL, *Speech on Dunkirk,* June 4, 1940.

j. There is a new feeling in the old American books, far more than there is in the modern American books, which are pretty empty of any feeling, and proud of it.—D. H. LAWRENCE, *Studies in Classic American Literature.*

Phrasal Units

A feeling for the right phrase is as important as a feeling for the right word. In order to cultivate such a feeling it is important to understand that a phrase in rhetoric is not always the same thing as a phrase in grammar. The rhetorical groups marked in the preceding analyses may be considered rhetorical phrases or, more properly, *phrasal units.* It was frequently observed in those analyses that such phrasal units represent combinations not classified as phrases in grammar. In grammar a phrase is a group of words not containing a subject and predicate and used as a part of speech. In rhetoric a phrase is any group of words that makes an effective rhetorical combination rather than a merely grammatical combination. There is some analogy here between rhetorical phrasing and musical phrasing. Groups of notes in a musical composition have a certain time value, established by a regular beat; but they are also grouped in "phrases" to form melodic patterns.

A sentence from Bacon's essay "Of Truth" may be used to illustrate the two kinds of phrases:

> The first creature of God, in the works of the days, was the light of the sense; the last was the light of reason; and his sabbath work, ever since, is the illumination of his Spirit.

Grammar says that *of God* is a prepositional phrase modifying *creature*. Rhetoric views *the first creature of God* as a phrasal unit which includes the prepositional phrase *of God,* the noun that it modifies, and the adjective and definite article that modify the noun. *The light of the sense, the light of reason, his sabbath work, the illumination of his Spirit* are similar phrasal units.

In grammar we commonly have the following kinds of phrases: verb phrase (*have bought, will go, having been scattered*); prepositional phrase (*in my house, by his order*). In rhetoric we are likely to have phrases consisting of some important word and its modifiers or of words paired or grouped in series: a noun and its modifiers (*a large, unwieldy, shapeless mass; a doubtful bundle of rags*); a verb and its associated words (*cut corners, titter emptily, flashed like a bullet*); two or three nouns, verbs, or adjectival modifiers (*a gentleman and a scholar; beg and beseech; groaning, hissing, and booing*). A subject and predicate may constitute a phrasal unit (*Remember now thy Creator; we cannot dedicate*).

Very likely many people do not write well because they have never learned to read well. When studying the following exercises, read the sentences aloud and indicate by slight pauses and changes in your voice the phrasal units of which a reader should take notice. Draw vertical lines (see sentence 1) to indicate divisions between phrasal units, and study the composition of these units and their rhetorical importance.

EXERCISES

1. The heavens declare | the glory of God; | and the firmament showeth | His handiwork. | Day unto day | uttereth speech, | and night unto night | showeth knowledge.—Psalm 19.

2. In accumulating property for ourselves or our posterity, in founding a family or a state, or acquiring fame even, we are mortal; but in dealing with truth we are immortal and need fear no change, nor accident.—HENRY D. THOREAU, *Walden.*

3. To invent good stories, and to tell them well, are possibly very rare talents, and yet I have observed few persons who have scrupled to aim at both: and if we examine the romances and novels with which the world abounds, I think we may fairly conclude that most of the authors would not have attempted to show their teeth (if the expression may be allowed me) in any other way of writing; nor could indeed have strung together a dozen sentences on any other subject whatever.—HENRY FIELDING, *The History of Tom Jones,* Book IX, Chapter I.

4. Being an invalid, Joseph Sedley contented himself with a bottle of claret, besides his madeira at dinner, and he managed a couple of plates full of strawberries and cream, and twenty-four little rout cakes that were lying neglected in a plate near him, and certainly (for novelists have the privilege of knowing everything), he thought a great deal about the girl upstairs.—W. M. THACKERAY, *Vanity Fair.*

5. The mystic chords of memory, stretching from every battlefield, and patriot grave, to every living heart and hearthstone, all over this broad land, will yet swell the chorus of the union, when again touched, as surely they will be, by the better angels of our nature.—ABRAHAM LINCOLN, *First Inaugural.*

6. The world stage is like those theatrical productions that fill the proscenium with a dozen different sets from among which spotlights pick out first a bedroom, then a street corner, office, bar.— JAMES BURNHAM, "France Is the Fulcrum," *National Review.*

7. He that hath wife and children hath given hostages to fortune; for they are impediments to great enterprises, either of virtue or mischief.—FRANCIS BACON, "Of Marriage and Single Life."

8. Now the ring, shining with the serene purity of fine gold on her rather grubby thumb, turned her feelings against her overalls and sockless feet, toes sticking through the thick brown leather straps.—KATHERINE ANNE PORTER, "The Grave."

9. A strong common sense, which it is not easy to unseat or disturb, marks the English mind for a thousand years: a rude strength newly applied to thought, as of sailors and soldiers who had lately learned to read.—RALPH WALDO EMERSON, *English Traits.*

10. The paths made by deer and bear became roads and then highways, with towns in turn springing up along them and along the rivers Tallahatchie and Sunflower which joined and became the Yazoo, the River of the Dead of the Choctaws—the thick, slow,

black, unsunned streams almost without current, which once each
year ceased to flow at all and then reversed, spreading, drowning
the rich land and subsiding again, leaving it still richer.—WILLIAM
FAULKNER, "Delta Autumn."

Conventional Phrases

Certain kinds of phrases may be called conventional. These
are the word-combinations that through long use have become standard and relatively unchanging features of the
language. Whenever they are used, they must be used in
their conventional form because any attempt to change them
would probably result in misunderstanding.

Transitional phrases are for the most part of a very conventional type. Their function has already been explained in
preceding chapters (see pages 32–36). They link sentences,
parts of paragraphs, or paragraphs. They also have a connec-
tive function within the sentence, especially within the compound or the compound-complex sentence. In long and complicated sentences, like the one which follows, transitional
phrases serve as guides to remind the reader of what has
gone before and what is to come after.

> The method of "approaching," being practised on foot, has
> many advantages over that of "running"; *in the former,* one
> neither breaks down his horse nor endangers his own life;
> he must be cool, collected, and watchful; must understand
> the buffalo, observe the features of the country and the course
> of the wind, and be well skilled in using the rifle.—FRANCIS
> PARKMAN.

The paragraph given below contains a number of transitional phrases of the conventional type. Observe that some of
the expressions italicized are clauses. In view of their function, however, and of our natural tendency to think of them
as units, they, too, may be classified, from the rhetorical
standpoint, as phrases or phrasal units.

> A book *of this kind* does not differ very much, *it will be
> observed,* from a collection made in Maine or North Carolina
> or Texas. *Indeed,* songs *of this sort* are much more widespread
> than earlier collectors believed. Francis J. Child noted the
> universal diffusion of the ballad in Europe; but apparently
> he could not get it into his head that the diffusion might be
> equally universal in his own country. The great Harvard
> scholar, George Lyman Kittredge, continued the error, at least
> in his own edition of Child's collection; he could not, *I sup-*

pose, bring himself to believe that anything existed if it had not been brought to his attention in a manuscript, and *therefore* wrote, in 1904: "Ballad-making, so far as the English-speaking nations are concerned, is a lost art; and the same may be said of ballad-singing." This book not only *proves the contrary;* it proves that ballads are still made and sung, *surprisingly enough,* in the city itself.

The common transitional phrases are well known and do not need to be listed here (a list is given on page 36). They are such expressions as *in the first place, to sum up, to go back, of course, I suppose, you know, if I may differ.* Some of the single words used for transitional purposes are really two-word or three-word combinations that have been fused: *indeed* (for *in* + *deed*); *nevertheless* (*never* + *the* + *less*); *however* (*how* + *ever*).

Idiomatic Phrases. By far the greater number of conventional phrases are idioms. That is, they are word-combinations peculiar to the language, not always susceptible to easy grammatical explanation, and not always capable of ready translation into another language.

Although some idiomatic phrases have become not only conventional but trite, many of them are inescapable because we have become accustomed to saying certain things in an American-English way and in no other way. Idiomatic phrases make up a very considerable part of our conversation. Most of us would be rather helpless if by some miracle they were suddenly eliminated. In writing we need to be more careful; we should not use, as in conversation, the first expression that comes to mind, which is often not only a conventional but a trite phrase. Yet it is also praise of writing to say that it is idiomatic. An idiomatic style is one that makes use of the peculiar native excellences of the language. Idiomatic expressions have a wiriness, homeliness, raciness for which there is often no adequate substitute. Familiarity with idioms is a first necessity to any one who wishes to write genuine American-English. And unfamiliarity with idioms may often lead to grotesque mistakes, as we all know when we hear a foreigner struggling with the language.

Remember that idioms, like the rules of etiquette, are often arbitrary and inexplainable. There could be no greater evidence of the strength of tradition than in the compulsions set up by the idiomatic phrases of our language. Why is it

that we say *brother and sister* and rarely *sister and brother?*
Why can we say *none the less* and *not the least,* but never
nothing the less or *none the least?*

The following are examples of idiomatic phrases. Note
that they come in large part from the Anglo-Saxon and perhaps reflect, more vividly than the Norman-Latin portion of
the English vocabulary, our ancient experience as a people.[1]

VERB PHRASES:	make up to, hem and haw, nail down, break up, watch and wait, to have and to hold, care about.
ADJECTIVE PHRASES:	short and sweet, rough and ready, high and dry, dark and deep, slow but sure.
ADVERB PHRASES:	now or never, here and there, here and now.
FIGURATIVE PHRASES:	fat as a pig, cool as a cucumber, hard as nails, tough as whitleather, an axe to grind, split the difference, laugh up one's sleeve, the end of his rope, play out, peter out, hog the road.
TECHNICAL AND CANT PHRASES:	rank and file, put one's oar in, rock the boat, quick on the trigger, hew to the mark, toe the line.
PHRASES DEALING WITH ANIMALS:	lead a dog's life, from the horse's mouth, crooked as a snake, a pig in a poke.
SOMATIC PHRASES:	make the mouth water, hip and thigh, have it on the tip of the tongue, lick one's chops.

EXERCISES

1. The following idiomatic phrases were collected from current
issues of magazines. Classify these idioms according to the scheme
indicated above. Add new classifications if necessary.

not out of the woods yet	on the run
take a stand	on my mind
the skin of his teeth	count on
break away from	count out
field a slate (of candidates)	count-down
shrug off	run for (the Senate)
command respect	stage a walkout
look into the matter	at the grass-roots level
from head to tail	high time that

[1] For lists of idioms, see Logan Pearsall Smith's *Words and
Idioms* and Fowler's *Dictionary of Modern English Usage.*

pull over (to the curb)	a sweeping assertion
throw a fit	keep cropping up
take over (the government)	serve a hitch

2. Make a similar list of your own from popular magazines. Then examine literary magazines (*Sewanee Review, Kenyon Review, The American Scholar,* or the like) to see whether you find the same type of idiomatic phrases.

3. Custom—rather than textbook rules—ordains certain verb-preposition combinations. For example, we "call *up*" a friend by telephone, "call *down*" a rude person, "call *out*" a person who is to be summoned or challenged, "call *over*" a list, etc. Make a list of the preposition combinations that belong with the following: *make, dig, rub, break, hit, climb, muster, cut.*

Parallelism in the Sentence

The principle of parallelism might be stated in the form of an axiom: *Like ideas require like expression.* Grammar looks at this principle rather negatively; it rejects, as ungrammatical, an attempt to join in coördinate relationship any expressions that are not actually of equal rank. In the sentence "The society chooses its members by secret ballot, and which must be unanimous," the error is an error of false coördination. An independent clause and a dependent clause are wrongly joined by the conjunction *and.* The grammatical error can be remedied in either of two ways: (1) We may strike out the conjunction and make the sentence read "The society chooses its members by a secret ballot, which must be unanimous"; but the sentence is not yet quite correct, since the word *ballot* is really being used in two senses. (2) We may make the two clauses parallel in structure:

The society chooses its members by secret ballot, and the election must be unanimous. (Two independent clauses.)

The members of the society are chosen by secret ballot and by unanimous vote. (Two phrases.)

The illustrations indicate that parallelism, as a rhetorical device, rests upon grammatical coördination, but that it involves something more: the notion of consistency of form as well as of equality of rank. By repeating the structural pattern, we emphasize the similarity between two ideas or in a series of ideas. Or, once committed to a certain train of ideas, we maintain a consistent point of view and emphasize that point of view by using a close similarity of expression. Parallelism is therefore, first, a grammatical necessity for parts of a sentence that are actually in a certain kind of coördinate relationship; it means that elements of the same grammatical rank must have the same structure. But, second, parallelism is a rhetorical device used for organizing parts of sentences or even groups of sentences so as to emphasize the similarity of the thoughts.

EXERCISES

In the sentences given below, study carefully the elements which have parallel structure. Give the grammatical construction of those elements. Note particularly any instances where the parallelism is not perfectly carried out, and be able to say why such variations are used.

1. Whoever wishes to attain an English style, familiar but not coarse, and elegant but not ostentatious, must give his days and nights to the volumes of Addison.—SAMUEL JOHNSON, *Lives of the English Poets.*

2. His tenants grow rich, his servants look satisfied, all the young women profess to love him, and the young men are glad of his company.—RICHARD STEELE, *The Spectator*, No. 2.

3. I must observe also that, as Virgil, in the poem which was designed to celebrate the original of the Roman empire, has described the birth of its great rival, the Carthaginian commonwealth, Milton, with like art, in his poem on the fall of man, has related the fall of those angels who are his professed enemies.—JOSEPH ADDISON, *The Spectator*, No. 267.

4. And always America is the place of the deathless and enraptured moments, the eye that looked, the mouth that smiled and vanished, and the word; the stone, the leaf, the door we never found and never have forgotten.—THOMAS WOLFE, *Of Time and the River.*

5. Common sense sometimes errs by excess of conservation; but it is better to err with Pope, who thought "Whatever is, is right," than with Jefferson, whose every act and word proves that he held that "Whatever is, is wrong."—GEORGE FITZHUGH, *Cannibals All!*

6. Every single poem written regular is a symbol small or great of the way the will has to pitch into commitments deeper and deeper to a rounded conclusion and then be judged on whether it has been strongly spent or weakly lost; be it in art, politics, school, church, business, love, or marriage—in a piece of work or in a career. Strongly spent is synonymous with kept.—ROBERT FROST, "The Constant Symbol."

7. The hard, pertinacious little paragon, softened now, romantically picturesque with his luxuriant white hair and his formal

black gown, had turned out to be one of the most authentic of Christian saints, serene, unbreakable, heroic—an epitome, in a sense, of the English genius, part and parcel of the English scene.— JOHN DONALD WADE, *John Wesley.*

8. Where once the American artist had to wage the Emersonian fight for self-reliance and for freedom from a sense of provincialism, his main fight now is for acceptance in a culture that values the pecuniary.—MAX LERNER, *America As a Civilization.*

9. An environment is an abstraction, not a place; Natchez is a place but not an environment.—ALLEN TATE, "The Profession of Letters in the South."

10. What the Greeks only suspected, we know well; what their Aeschylus imagined, our nursery children feel.—THOMAS HARDY, *The Return of the Native.*

Practice in Parallelism. A too constant use of parallelism will make a style too ornate and dull for the modern taste. In the sentences of the preceding exercise you should note a great difference between the studied, highly wrought, interlocking parallelisms of Addison, Steele, and Emerson and the less rigid, more subtle parallelisms of John Wade, Robert Frost, and other modern authors.

Yet, although there is a danger in carrying parallelism too far, a certain amount of deliberate practice in parallelism is valuable. It directs one's attention to structural units, and it enforces careful organization of the sentence.

The following exercises are intended to give a practice of this kind.

EXERCISES

1. Write sentences to illustrate the use in parallel structure of the indicated elements.
   - a. A sentence beginning with a series of infinitives which are the subject of the main verb or are in apposition with the subject.
   - b. A sentence containing a series of noun clauses used as the object of a verb.
   - c. A sentence containing a series of participles modifying the subject of the sentence or of a clause.
   - d. A sentence containing a series of gerund phrases.
   - e. A sentence containing a series of independent clauses.
   - f. A compound sentence in which the second independent clause repeats, with some agreeable variation, the pattern of the first clause, yet without violating the principle of parallelism.

2. Copy and bring to class ten examples of parallelism selected from such sources as the following.

    a. The Bible (see especially Psalms, Ecclesiastes, Job, Revelation).

    b. The essays of Sir Francis Bacon.

    c. A collection of famous orations, classic or modern.

    d. The prose works of Sir Thomas Browne, John Donne, Herman Melville.

    e. The stories and novels of William Faulkner, Thomas Wolfe, Joseph Conrad.

3. Point out and correct all violations of parallelism in the following sentences.

    a. If you decide to go fishing on these lakes in a small boat, safety precautions will have to be observed by a novice.

    b. After some years of experience with this firm, John was promoted from road grading to office manager.

    c. Circling at a discreet distance, but bristling and showing their teeth, and with a considerable barrage of ugly barks and growls, the wild dogs moved with us, no matter which way we turned.

    d. Timothy knew the deer were in the woods, but with no way of luring them out, and they could not be reached through the blowdown.

    e. Thackeray's *Vanity Fair* is not only esteemed for its accurate description of British society, but he also achieved permanent fame in creating the character of Becky Sharp.

    f. She is a girl who somehow gets invited to all the parties; the boys are always tagging after her; though all the time caring about nothing but art and never seeming to value such attention.

    g. Because the birth rate increased sharply during the 1940's and also on account of the public's enthusiasm for college education, the colleges and universities of the nation face the problem of a greatly expanded enrollment in the 1960's.

    h. Newspapers today are influenced by various factors unknown to Benjamin Franklin, such as new economic complications, steadily increasing competition from radio and television, and the public demands diverse kinds of news and information, to say nothing of labor troubles.

Types of Sentence Structure

In writing we rarely take the trouble to make each sentence conform to some rigid structural scheme. We follow the progress of the thought, shaping it as best we can to fit the need of the moment, and correcting and revising the sentences from time to time to secure an effective expression.

Nevertheless, even a cursory examination of any passage of good prose will reveal that sentences fall into three structural types; and, if we would govern the structure of our sentences, it is helpful to keep these typical structures in mind.

The three types of sentences are *loose, periodic,* and *balanced.* (We may, of course, have a combination of types—a *mixed* structure—especially in long, elaborate sentences.)

Loose Sentence.   A loose sentence is a sentence which has a predicate early in the sequence of its sentence elements. Its assertion is complete, in a sense, long before the final punctuation mark is reached. A loose sentence ends with a modifier—a phrase, a subordinate clause, a coördinate clause, or some other element not absolutely necessary to the meaning of the sentence.

EXAMPLE

> Charles had a habit of taking early morning walks, perhaps because his aunt had commended the birds, if not the worms, to his attention, or perhaps because he just could not sleep late, anyway.

The term "loose," as applied to sentence types, means nothing derogatory. In rhetoric, a loose sentence is not a sentence that is written in a slipshod, careless way. It is a sentence in which the focal point is reached, and the essential meaning is disclosed, before the full content is rounded out. It does not keep the reader in suspense, but it *adds* its qualifications, explanations, reservations *after* its assertion has been made. The loose sentence is, in fact, the normal type of sentence organization. The majority of sentences in any passage of prose will be loose sentences.

Periodic Sentence.   A periodic sentence is a sentence which withholds its predicate until the end, or near the end, of the sentence; or which, in rhetorical terms, is "massed according to the principle of suspension." Its meaning is generally not complete until the final word or word-group of the sentence is reached. A periodic sentence ends, therefore, with a verb or a predicate complement or, if the sentence order is inverted, with the subject. The arrangement of the periodic sentence is generally climactic.

EXAMPLES

Either because his aunt had once commended the birds, if not the worms, to his attention, or perhaps because he could never sleep late, Charles, as had been his habit, continued his early morning walks.

How much of this morbid feeling sprang from an original disease of the mind, how much from real misfortune, how much from the nervousness of dissipation, how much was fanciful, how much was merely affected, it is impossible for us, and would probably have been impossible for the most intimate friends of Lord Byron, to decide.—THOMAS BABINGTON MACAULAY.

The periodic sentence employs the principle of suspension, as the loose sentence does not. A loose sentence seems natural and spontaneous; a periodic sentence, since it is deliberately organized so that its focal point is at the end, achieves its intended effect by methods that, to a modern reader, may often seem artificial. It does, in fact, set a premium upon artifice. It is best adapted to stately and dignified prose of a ceremonious and oratorical nature, but it may be used effectively in ordinary prose, when some sharp or highly concentrated effect is desired. Overuse of the periodic sentence will inevitably make writing seem stilted, falsely rhetorical.

Balanced Sentence. A balanced sentence is a sentence in which there is a close correspondence of parts in a symmetrical arrangement. It may be a correspondence of phrase with phrase: *"An acre in Middlesex is better than a principality in Utopia."* Or it may be a part-by-part correspondence of two independent clauses, as in Macaulay's sentence: "He prostrated himself in the dust before his Maker; but he set his foot upon the neck of his King." The following schematic arrangement shows how careful is the balance in this sentence:

He	←————————→	he
prostrated	←————————→	set
himself	←————————→	his foot
in the dust	←————————→	upon the neck
before his Maker	←————————→	of his King

Parallelism is of course an important structural feature of the balanced sentence. The most obvious and effective uses of parallelism are found in balanced sentences. The balanced sentence, with its perfect symmetry, has an air of contrivance that limits its use in modern composition. It is good for sudden strokes, for witty sallies, for pithy descriptions and thumbnail sketches. But modern critics consider a style like Macaulay's abominably artificial—"rhetorical" in the bad sense. Modern taste abhors rigid patterns and prefers merely a suggestion of similarity of pattern, with an immediate suggestion of irregularity—in other words, as much variation as repetition, and perhaps more variation than repetition.

The following sentences illustrate a less precise and formal type of balance:

> Not only do we at the feast of Christmas celebrate at once
> Our Lord's Birth and His Death; but on the next day we cele-
> brate the martyrdom of His first martyr, the blessed Stephen.
> —T. S. ELIOT, *Murder in the Cathedral.*

> It is a useful accomplishment to be able to say *no,* but
> surely it is the essence of amiability to prefer to say *yes*
> where it is possible.—ROBERT LOUIS STEVENSON, *Familiar
> Studies.*

Mixed Structure. In long sentences, especially in long compound or compound-complex sentences, the principle of suspension may be followed through only a part of the sentence. This part of the sentence may justly be classified as periodic, and the sentence as a whole may be regarded as of a mixed type, partly periodic, partly loose.

EXAMPLES

> I think that in England, partly from the want of an Acad-
> emy, partly from a national habit of intellect to which that
> want of an Academy is due, there exists too little of what I
> may call a public force of correct literary opinion, possessing
> within certain limits a clear sense of what is right and wrong,
> sound and unsound, and sharply recalling men of ability and
> learning from any flagrant misdirection of their advantages.
> —MATTHEW ARNOLD (From *that in England* to *opinion,* the
> sentence is periodic. The rest of the sentence is loose.)

> If all men are mortal (an assumption), and if Socrates
> was a man (in the sense assumed), no doubt Socrates must
> have been mortal; but we suspect that we knew all this before
> it was submitted to the test of a syllogism.—CARL BECKER,
> *The Heavenly City of the Eighteenth Century Philosopher.*
> (From *If all* to the semicolon, the sentence is periodic; the
> rest is loose.)

EXERCISES

1. Determine which of the following sentences are loose, which are periodic, and which are balanced.

   a. Judges and lawyers during tedious trials, legislators during debates, men relaxing during hot noons and rainy days, snow-bound farmers—all shaved away on sticks of wood they loved to feel, experiment with, and shape into useful models.—RICHARD B. LILLARD, *The Great Forest.*

   b. The young man looked at him still; he looked at the young man; and the issue, by a rapid process, was that the knowledge of a perched privacy appeared to him the very last of luxuries.—HENRY JAMES, *The Ambassadors.*

   c. The sleep of a laboring man is sweet, whether he eat little or much; but the abundance of the rich will not suffer him to sleep.—Ecclesiastes V, 12.

   d. Violence shall no more be heard in thy land, wasting nor destruction within thy borders; but thou shalt call thy walls Salvation, and thy gates Praise.—Isaiah LX, 18.

   e. Like all great churches that are not mere storehouses of theology, Chartres expressed, besides whatever else it meant, an emotion, the deepest man ever felt—the struggle of his own littleness to grasp the infinite.—HENRY ADAMS, *Mont-St. Michel and Chartres.*

   f. Among all these immigrant groups who shared the slums and tenements, who looked at the police with fear and trembling, who offered their untaught skills for whatever wages industry chose to offer, there stood out only one that could speak the tongue of the land—the Irish.— THEODORE H. WHITE, *The Making of the President, 1960.*

   g. Children sweeten labors, but they make misfortunes more bitter: they increase the cares of life, but they mitigate the remembrance of death.—SIR FRANCIS BACON.

   h. It was at Rome, on the 15th of October 1764, as I sat musing amidst the ruins of the Capitol, while the barefooted friars were singing vespers in the temple of Jupiter, that the idea of writing the decline and fall of the city first started to my mind.—EDWARD GIBBON, *Autobiography.*

2. Write five sentences of your own in loose structure.

3. Rewrite the same sentences in periodic structure.

4. Compose five balanced sentences.

THE SENTENCE AS A UNIT OF COMPOSITION

So far we have studied the sentence without considering its relation to the paragraph or passage of which it is a part. But the sentence as a unit of composition cannot be studied in such isolation. The sentences of good prose support and continue each other. Grammatically, each is a separate unit, but the effectiveness of the passage will often depend upon the way in which the sentences are related to each other. Sometimes they may be so closely related that an individual sentence will not "make sense" logically if it is taken out of its context.

The grouping of sentences to develop the topic of a paragraph has been dealt with in a previous chapter. The problem, thus considered, is a matter of *composition*—the structural organization of thought. The effect of this grouping upon the form of individual sentences is a matter of *rhetoric,* concerning which it is impossible to lay down strict rules. The interdependence of sentences, one upon another, can best be understood by close examination of sentence-to-sentence relationships in specimen passages of good prose.

1. I have a great deal of company in my house; especially in the morning, when nobody calls. Let me suggest a few comparisons, that some one may convey an idea of my situation. I am no more lonely than the loon in the pond that laughs so loud, or than Walden Pond itself. What company has that lonely lake, I pray? And yet it has not the blue devils, but the blue angels in it, in the azure tint of its waters. The sun is alone, except in thick weather, when there sometimes appear to be two, but one is a mock sun. God is alone,—but the devil, he is far from being alone; he sees a great deal of company; he is legion. I am no more lonely than a single mullein or dandelion in a pasture, or a bean leaf, or sorrel, or a horse-fly, or a humble-bee. I am no more lonely than the Mill Brook, or a weathercock, or the north star, or the south wind, or an April shower, or a January thaw, or the first spider in a new house.—HENRY D. THOREAU, *Walden.*

2. Leaving the highway I turned off into the woods toward the pond, which was apparent through the foliage. The floor of the forest was strewn with dried old oak leaves and *Transcripts.* From beneath the flattened popcorn wrapper (*granum explosum*) peeped the frail violet. I followed a footpath and descended to the water's edge. The pond lay clear and blue in the morning light, as you have seen it so many times. In

the shallows a man's waterlogged shirt undulated gently. A few flies came out to greet me and convoy me to your cove, past the No Bathing signs on which the fellows and the girls had scrawled their names. I felt strangely excited suddenly to be snooping around your premises, tiptoeing along watchfully, as though not to tread by mistake upon the intervening century. Before I got to the cove I heard something which seemed to me quite wonderful: I heard your frog, a full, clear *troonk,* guiding me, still hoarse and solemn, bridging the years as the robins had bridged them in the sweetness of the village evening. But he soon quit, and I came on a couple of young boys throwing stones at him.—E. B. WHITE, "A Letter to Thoreau."[1]

Paragraph 1, by Thoreau, presents his cherished belief that individual man, dwelling close to unviolated nature, can be self-sufficient and needs little or no support from society (*company*). Thoreau chooses to state his topic in the form of a paradox: he has *company,* though *alone*—in fact, most of all when most *alone.* In its logical organization, the paragraph consists of a general statement (*I have a great deal of company . . . when nobody calls*) which is supported by a series of particulars; but the particulars are cast, as he himself indicates, into the form of *comparisons.*

Such a logical organization, however, would not necessarily require a group of sentences expressed in the rhetorical form that Thoreau has used. Since he is engaged in exploring a paradox (a seeming contradiction which indirectly affirms a truth), Thoreau chooses to express his thought in sentences that make use of parallelism and antithesis. These devices necessarily lead to a certain amount of deliberate repetition of sentence patterns. But Thoreau is careful not to let this procedure become mechanical. By unobtrusive variation he contrives to avoid the monotony that his parallelisms and repetitions might otherwise produce. And the antithesis between *company* and *alone,* as it runs through the several sentences, appears with a changing emphasis achieved by manipulation of the rhetorical pattern.

The strong paradox of the topic sentence, *I have a great deal of company . . . when nobody calls,* is followed by an entirely colorless, matter-of-fact statement, *Let me suggest . . . ,* which makes a transitional bridge to the graphic

[1] From *One Man's Meat* by E. B. White. By permission of Harper & Row, Publishers, Inc.

sentences that develop the paradox. Three sentences begin with *I am no more lonely than*—each, with its negative form, being the first part of a comparison; the particulars of the second part follow in series. But the three sentences beginning *I am no more lonely than* do not come in monotonous succession. Between the first and the second appears an intervening passage, the first sentence of which is a rhetorical question, *What company has . . . ?* This question is answered in the next three sentences. Two of these begin with statements that echo, in impersonal form, Thoreau's personal negative (*I am no more lonely than*). *The sun is alone* and *God is alone,* with their trains of particulars, are thus not mere mechanical repetition. The comparisons involved in these two sentences are not developed directly, by the use of "than," but by antithesis: *sun* is set off against *mock sun; God* against *devil. Company,* which appears to have an ordinary social meaning in the topic sentence, acquires a disreputable meaning when it appears as an attribute of the devil; while *lonely* and *alone,* repeated several times, gradually acquire dignity as attributes of *sun* and *God.* The cosmic antitheses are developed in clauses. The two series *than a single mullein* and *than the Mill Brook* are developed so as to give *humble-bee* and *spider* climactic positions.

Paragraph 2, by E. B. White, done in a much less formal, more modern prose, achieves its effects by echoing, in a deliberately ironic pattern, the procedure and style of Thoreau. Mr. White achieves his "comparisons" (which are intended as an implied commentary on Thoreau's belief in nature) less by direct comparison and antithesis than by couplings which put oddly assorted objects into juxtaposition. Beginning with two sentences that seem to copy exactly the manner of Thoreau, Mr. White explodes his first hidden mine at the end of sentence 2 (*dried old oak leaves and Transcripts*). Changing to inverted order in the next sentence, he deliberately brings *popcorn wrapper* and *frail violet* into jarring contrast. Next comes a Thoreau-like sentence in normal order, followed by a sentence which begins with seeming emphasis upon the natural scene, in the phrase (transposed out of normal order) *In the shallows.* Whatever expectation the reader may have of another Thoreau-like sentence is destroyed by *a man's waterlogged shirt.* The two sentences are therefore set in bold antithesis to each other. A similar procedure is followed, with subtle variations, throughout the remainder of the paragraph. It is important to note that, although Thoreau's sentences in paragraph 1 are closely related, one to another, they are more "quotable," as separate sentences, than any of White's. If lifted out of their context, Thoreau's sentences retain a certain self-sufficiency and are in themselves notable. But White's sentences, if thus severed from the context, lose all force and hardly carry a meaning. White's prose is therefore much more closely woven than Thoreau's. It has less gravity of content. It is the prose of a skilful essayist. Thoreau's is the prose of a thinker and philosopher.

Variation of Sentence Pattern

In the section dealing with rhetorical analysis we have called attention to the ways in which good writers shift phrases and clauses and words and in other ways manipulate the rhetorical groups to obtain some effect. We also noted that sentences might be classified, according to their rhetorical pattern, as loose, periodic, balanced, and mixed.

All these studies of the structure of single sentences may be utilized in the study of variety. Vary the rhetorical pattern of your sentences if you wish the whole composition to be pleasing. In good writing there will probably be a majority of sentences of the loose type; some will be of mixed pattern; a much slighter proportion should be periodic or balanced.

Keep steadily in mind the importance of *position* in the English sentence. Any alteration of normal order is allowable, provided it does not disturb grammatical relationships or confuse meaning. The shifting of the order of sentence elements is therefore one of the easiest and most practical means of getting variety in sentence patterns.

The examples given below illustrate some of the common ways in which the order of a sentence may be changed from the normal order or otherwise altered to secure variety.

1. Sweet are the uses of adversity.
   (Predicate complement first; subject and verb reversed.)
2. Why he did it, nobody will ever know.
   (The object, a noun-clause, stands first; the rest of the sentence is in normal order.)
3. Bristling with anger, he rushed out of the office.
   (Participial phrase at beginning; then normal order.)
4. In the sober light of morning, the whole affair assumed a quiet different aspect.
   (Adverbial phrase first.)

5. There, plain as a pikestaff, stood the fugitive himself, bold and evidently unruffled by the sudden encounter.
   (Complete inversion of the normal order. The order is: predicate complement—verb—subject.)
6. If you want to form a plan, then you must consider, coldly and objectively, and of course without fear, the nature of the problem before you.
   (Adverbial clause first; then the subject and verb; then several adverb modifiers; then the object.)
7. And then Oedipus, in a fit of mental blindness ironically parallel to Tiresias' physical blindness, is most fatally impelled, with complete dramatic logic, to pronounce unwittingly his own doom.
   (Simple sentence in normal order, but with modifiers intervening between subject and verb; between the elements of the compound verb; and between this verb and its complement.)

EXERCISES

1. Compose sentences in which you follow the variations from normal order in the examples given above.

2. Study the order of the sentence elements in the following sentences. Compose sentences in which you use similar patterns.

a. First in the ragged procession, jaunty as ever, came Moffitt Hydes-Lee; the swing of his Alpenstock and the tilt of his hat told me he meant to be first.

b. In this upland meadow, just beyond the beaver dams on the rocky side of the stream, stands a single dead sugar-maple, boughs white and spectre-like against the green.

c. Modern dress fits modern ways; but stylish shorts rarely beautify the human leg.

d. All lecturers, all professors, all schoolmasters, have ruts and grooves in their minds into which their conversation is perpetually sliding.—OLIVER WENDELL HOLMES, *The Autocrat of the Breakfast Table.*

e. Every nail driven should be as another rivet in the machine of the universe, you carrying on the work.—HENRY D. THOREAU, *Walden.*

f. The Colorado today roars down through its lonely mile-deep canyons exactly as it did in the days of the Spaniards—sullen, treacherous, inimicable to man.—WELDON F. HEALD, "The Colorado River."

g. That night the Mexicans played the accordion and other

instruments in the ward and it was cheerful and the noise of the inhalations and exhalations of the accordion, and of the bells, the traps, and the drum came down the corridor.—ERNEST HEMINGWAY, "The Gambler, the Nun, and the Radio."

h. A people alone are a great river; and that is why I am persuaded that where a people has died, a nation is about to die.—WILLIAM BUTLER YEATS, *Ideas of Good and Evil.*

3. Rewrite the following sentences. You are expected not only to correct all errors, but also to make the sentences rhetorically effective.

a. When the captain called time I realized that all it was for was to give Robb a chance to catch his breath before shooting the foul shot and make the point that might win the game which would surely make us champions.

b. Death can strike so close to one, and no one knows where it will strike next, or whom it shall strike next, this dealt an important blow to my life.

c. Seeing Jerry brought to Wendell's remembrance that Jerry had asked him only the day before if he could go watch football practice with him.

d. When Christmas vacation from school came and I began working downtown all day long, I was so tired that I did not think that I could drag to work another day but I did.

e. As the holder of Farmers National Savings Account, this is an ideal time to reflect on the relative values of the various investments available to you during such an uncertain period.

f. In most of these ballads the friend is given power, not to exactly corrupt, but he takes possession of one who he finds to be already corrupt.

g. Rather than setting up a government monopoly, it was agreed that a corporation would be established in which private companies could own 50 per cent of the stock and individuals 50 per cent, and the corporation would be government-regulated.

CHAPTER 6

WORDS

GRAMMAR is the foundation of word-study, but it cannot tell us which word, out of many correct words, is the *best* word for a given situation. The choice of the best word is a matter of taste, judgment, and skill, which the principles of rhetoric must govern. We are now concerned with *diction,* the rhetorical term commonly employed to refer to the manner in which words can effectively express thought. We do not discard grammar, but take it for granted. The study of the grammar of words is a study of limitations. The study of diction is a study of possibilities.

The familiar phrase "a good command of words" implies first of all a good stock of words, a sizable vocabulary. If a writer has relatively few words at his command, his range of choice is limited. A man with a "Basic English" vocabulary of a few hundred words can doubtless survive in modern traffic. If he has learned to write legibly, he can—with some help—fill out an application for a job or for unemployment relief. But he will be incapable of writing the kind of prose composition expected of an educated person—incapable of even a good letter.

All of us have three vocabularies—or it might be better to say, three kinds of vocabularies. First, and smallest, is the stock of words we command for ordinary conversation—a simple, elementary stock consisting of a few nouns and verbs, and a few adjectives and adverbs, rather shopworn, with a spice of slang added for liveliness. (The "Basic English" vocabulary contains only this small stock, or little more.) Second, and considerably larger, is the stock of words that we can summon to mind when we think and consider. Third, and largest, is the stock of words that we can recognize and understand when we hear them spoken or see them written.

177

Obviously the good writer must work systematically to narrow the gap between the second and the third vocabulary. He must bring his writing vocabulary nearer to the content of his recognition vocabulary.

To achieve this end, he must first of all become familiar with the resources of the language. It is true that some individuals can read and listen and somehow acquire a large vocabulary by sheer contagion. For most of us, however, positive effort is necessary. It is of course quixotic to try to memorize the dictionary, as did one of the unsuccessful suitors in Hans Christian Andersen's story, "Jack the Dullard." In that story it is supposedly worthless Jack who has a ready wit and so wins the princess. His older brother, who had memorized the dictionary, could think of nothing to say at the crucial moment. Andersen's story is a reproach to pedants, not to people who seriously wish to speak and write well. No good writer scorns the dictionary. But it is also important to make memorable words one's own by early and judicious use.

Next, a good command of words implies that one's control over words be intelligent and discriminating. A large vocabulary will not of itself make a good writer. With justice we laugh at Mrs. Malaprop's notion that an educated young lady should have "a supercilious knowledge of accounts," and with less justice, we may accept Goldsmith's charge that Dr. Samuel Johnson "made little fishes talk like whales." But flat mediocrity of diction is no less to be avoided than violent error or pompous verbosity.

Increase of vocabulary will bring *quantity* of words. Only a study of what happens in the written composition itself will give us knowledge of the *quality* of words. The purpose of the good writer should be to unite *quantity* and *quality* in his writing vocabulary. This chapter deals first with quantity: the vocabulary of English, as the student finds it set before him; and second with quality: or vocabulary in action.

1. USE OF THE DICTIONARY

The dictionary is a storehouse of words and a guide, as authoritative as we possess, in matters of usage. An unabridged dictionary contains—theoretically, but not actually —all the words in the language, both those in current use and those encountered in the works of English and American authors of the past. No dictionary of a living language can ever be quite complete or absolutely authoritative. New words are always coming into a living language, and old words are dropping out of use or are changing their forms and meanings. The dictionary makers can never catch up. But the dictionaries of our time are complete and authoritative enough. They put before us, in a compact and wonderfully convenient form, the resources of our language.

For complete information on words and the history of words the student should consult such unabridged dictionaries as the *New English Dictionary* (often called the *Oxford English Dictionary*) and other comprehensive dictionaries available in libraries.[1] For desk use, a good abridged dictionary of college grade is an absolute necessity. It is assumed here that the student will have such a dictionary for his personal use.

Intelligent use of the dictionary calls for an understanding of the nature and variety of the information that it gives and of the meaning of the abbreviations and symbols used in presenting that information. The dictionary itself will give, in its preface and at other convenient places, the key to all abbreviations and symbols. The most important kinds of information given in a dictionary are as follows.

1. Correct spelling; both preferred spelling and allowed spelling if more than one spelling is in use.

2. Pronunciation, indicated by phonetic symbols and diacritical marks.

3. Grammatical functions and inflections; the use or uses of words as parts of speech; the principal parts of verbs, idiomatic combinations.

4. Etymology; the derivation of words when the derivation from Anglo-Saxon, Latin, French, Greek, or other language is known.

5. The meaning of words; the different meanings, when words have several meanings.

6. The standing of words in respect to usage; that is, whether they are obsolete, archaic, provincial, dialectal, colloquial, slang, poetic, historical, technical.

7. Synonyms.

Dictionary Entries

The following entries, reprinted from three widely used dictionaries, illustrate the methods used by dictionary makers to present information.

---

[1] See pages 250–253 for a list of these and other reference books.

thwart (thwôrt), *v.t.* **1.** to oppose successfully; prevent from accomplishing a purpose; frustrate (a purpose, etc.); baffle. **2.** *Archaic.* to cross. **3.** *Archaic.* to extend across. —*n.* **4.** a seat across a boat, esp. one used by an oarsman. **5.** a transverse member spreading the gunwales of a canoe or the like. See diag. under **gunwale.** —*adj.* **6.** passing or lying crosswise or across; cross; transverse. **7.** *Archaic.* perverse; obstinate. **8.** adverse; unfavorable. —*prep.*, *adv.* **9.** across; athwart. [ME *thwert*, adv., t. Scand.; cf. Icel. *thvert* across, neut. of *thverr* transverse, c. OE *thweorh* crooked, cross] —**thwart′er,** *n.*
—**Syn. 1.** THWART, FRUSTRATE, BAFFLE imply preventing one, more or less completely, from accomplishing a purpose. THWART and FRUSTRATE apply to purposes, actions, plans, etc.; BAFFLE, to the psychological state of the person himself. THWART suggests stopping one by opposing him, blocking him, or in some way running counter to his efforts. FRUSTRATE implies rendering all attempts or efforts useless or ineffectual, so that nothing ever comes of them. BAFFLE suggests causing defeat by confusing, puzzling, or perplexing, so that a situation seems too hard a problem to understand or solve.

In the above entry from the *American College Dictionary* we find in parentheses, immediately after the word *thwart,* its pronunciation, indicated by a phonetic respelling. The key to the phonetic symbols appears in complete form on the inside cover of this dictionary and in shortened form at the foot of odd-numbered pages. The abbreviation *v. t.* signifies that *thwart* is used as a transitive verb in the senses recorded under 1, 2, and 3. Note that two of these meanings are labelled *Archaic.* The abbreviation *n.* signifies that the meanings of *thwart* as noun are to follow. Looking further, you may be surprised to discover that *thwart* may also be used as adjective, preposition, or adverb. In this particular dictionary the etymology is placed last—after the definitions. An Old English (*OE*) word meaning "crooked" or "cross" is cited as among various North European words from which the derivation may be traced. After listing the noun *thwarter* the entry records and briefly discusses certain synonyms of *thwart.*

cor·ral (kə-ral′), *n.* [Sp. < *corro,* a circle, ring < L. *currere,* to run], **1.** an enclosure for holding or capturing horses, cattle, and other animals; pen; stockade. **2.** an enclosure surrounded by wagons, for defense against attack. *v.t.* [CORRALLED (-rald′), CORRALLING], **1.** to drive into or confine in a corral. **2.** to surround or capture; round up. **3.** to arrange (wagons) in the form of a corral. **4.** [Slang], to take possession of; lay hold of.

In the above entry from *Webster's New World Dictionary: College Edition* the etymology of the noun *corral* comes immediately after the phonetic respelling, followed by the definitions, with the older meanings first. The forms and meanings of *corral* as a transitive verb are given next, in order of age, from oldest to newest. Within this brief space we may note the origin and usage of a word that comes to us directly from the Spanish and carries rich associations from the historic past. It is "American English"—in this instance represented by a word that passed from the vocabulary of the western frontier into literary usage and then, with a general rather than a particular meaning, into the popular vocabulary as slang.[1]

¹re·cord \ri-'kȯ(ə)rd\ *vb* [ME *recorden*, lit., to recall, fr. OF *recorder*, fr. L *recordari*, fr. *re-* + *cord-, cor* heart — more at HEART] *vt* **1 a** (1) **:** to set down in writing   (2) **:** to deposit an authentic official copy of   **b** (1) **:** to register permanently   (2) **:** INDICATE, READ   **2 :** to cause (as sound) to be registered (as on a phonograph disc) in reproducible form ~ *vi* **:** to engage in recording
²rec·ord \'rek-ərd *also* -ˌȯ(ə)rd\ *n* **1 :** the state or fact of being recorded   **2 :** something that records; as   **a :** something that recalls or relates past events   **b :** an official writing that records the acts of a public body or officer   **c :** an authentic official copy of a document deposited with a legally designated officer   **d :** the official copy of the papers used in a law case   **3 a :** the known or recorded facts regarding something or someone   **b :** an attested top performance   **4 :** something on which sound or visual images have been recorded; *specif* **:** a disc with a spiral groove carrying recorded sound for phonograph reproduction
³record *like* ²\ *adj* **:** surpassing others of its kind

In the above entries from *Webster's Seventh New Collegiate Dictionary*,[2] you should note that the word *record* appears first as a verb, second as a noun, third as an adjective, with the same spelling for each entry but with the accent for the verb differing from that for the noun and adjective. The superior numerals (¹, ², ³) signal differences of function and meaning sufficient to require three separate entries for the word. Pronunciation is indicated by the phonetic spellings that follow ¹*record* and ²*record*. The extensive "Guide to Pronunciation" contained in the front matter of this dic-

---

[1] See Krapp, *The English Language in America;* Marckwardt, *American English;* Mencken, *The American Language;* Pyles, *Words and Ways of American English;* Craigie, *Dictionary of American English;* Bergen and Evans, *A Dictionary of Contemporary American Usage.*

[2] This edition of *Webster's Collegiate Dictionary* is abridged from the much debated *Webster's New International Dictionary.*

tionary explains these phonetic symbols, which for immediate convenience are briefly illustrated through examples at
the foot of the odd-numbered pages. The etymology of the
word is of special interest since it tells us that *record* comes
to us through the Middle English and Old French from the
Latin *cor,* meaning *heart.* The phrase "more at HEART" indicates a cross-reference to the entry for *heart,* under which
you will find certain meanings that associate *heart* with
memory. You may then recall that the common expression
"learn by heart" means "to memorize"—or record in the
memory. For *record* as a transitive verb (*vt*) you will note
two groups of definitions; for *record* as an intransitive verb
(*vi*) only one. For *record* as a noun (*n*) four definitions
appear. For the adjective (*adj*) *record* the pronunciation is
indicated as like that of the noun *record* (*like²*).

Word Origins

Only by close and careful examination of the complete
entry can we make the best use of the resources of the dictionary. Hasty scanning is not enough and may lead to deception and error.

There may be, for example, a temptation to pass over the
etymology of words. The etymology looks forbiddingly technical and learned, as indeed it is. Yet there are times when
knowledge of the derivation of a word may help to fix its
meaning and associations. "Even the plainest-looking words,"
writes Max Eastman, "will sometimes reveal to one who likes
them well enough to look for it, a lucid perception out of
which they sprang. *Sarcasm* is a 'tearing of the flesh.' . . .
Retort is 'a twisting back.' *Enthusiast* is 'full of God.' . . .
Such is the poetry which you find in the dictionary, the un-
premeditated art of men for centuries dead, whose utterance
in a vivid moment rose to heights of genius and could not be
forgotten." The person who knows that *plebeian* comes from
the Latin word *plebs,* meaning "common people," and that
aristocracy derives from two Greek words, *aristos,* meaning
"best," and *kratein,* "to rule," will use the terms with a nicer
sense of their meaning than if he had never known their
derivation at all. He who remembers (or learns by consulting
a dictionary) that *unique* comes from the Latin *unus,* meaning "one," will never write that an experience was "unique"
unless it really was the one and only experience of the sort;
and he will not speak of *fundamental* values unless they are

really "foundations." A knowledge of derivations is sure to be of general use in giving a writer a feeling for the "undertones" of words and should guide him in his search for exact shades of meaning as well as warn him away from outright improprieties.

The most practical modern use of etymology, however, appears in the place where those who value education only for its "practical" worth may be startled and embarrassed to find it—that is, in the vocabulary of the physical and social sciences. Many an ambitious technical student has found out too late, and much to his sorrow, how large a debt engineering, psychology, medicine, chemistry, political science, and the like owe to Greek and Latin. Such terms as *hydraulics, psychosomatic, pathology, corporation* derive from classical sources. Such formidable polysyllables as *osmosis, autarchy, pyromagnetic, stearoptene, cardiograph, metalliferous, deciduous* are scientific word coinages, all of fairly recent origin, direct from Latin and Greek sources, and most of all from Greek sources. The student who does not know his Greek (and few students in the middle twentieth century get the opportunity to learn that language) has every right to reproach the educational system which has encouraged him to study modern science but handicapped him in acquiring the vocabulary of modern science. He may repair his deficiency to some extent by learning the etymology indicated in the dictionary. It is also practical good sense to study and master the common prefixes and suffixes that are taken from the classic language—prefixes such as *ad, bi, inter, pro, retro,* from the Latin, and *amphi, anti, dia, hypo, syn* from the Greek; and suffixes such as *osity, ation, ic, ous.*[1]

OTHER USES OF THE DICTIONARY

The dictionary can be consulted on a number of grammatical questions. Since its word-list is comprehensive, it may often be a more convenient reference book than the ordinary textbook of grammar, which is necessarily selective

[1] The following books may be consulted for further study of the relationship between the classic languages and English: Bradley, *The Making of English;* Earle, *Philology of the English Tongue;* Greenough and Kittredge, *Words and Their Ways in English Speech;* Hoffman, *Everyday Greek: Greek Words in English, Including Scientific Terms;* Johnson, *Latin Words of Common English;* McKnight, *English Words and Their Background.*

in its illustrations. Should a preposition be used as an adjective, as in expressions like "a *through* train" or "the *under* dog"? As to *through* and *under,* the dictionary says yes. May *plenty* be used as an adverb, as in the phrase "plenty good"? *The American College Dictionary* and *Webster's New World Dictionary* list the adverb *plenty* as "colloquial." *Webster's Seventh New Collegiate Dictionary,* which has dropped "colloquial" as a term indicating level of usage, simply lists *plenty* as an adverb. What is the past tense of the verb *plead?* Is it *pleaded, plead,* or *pled?* Should *gotten* be used as the past participle of *get?* Is *dived* or *dove* the correct past tense of *dive?* All three of the dictionaries mentioned above agree that *pleaded* is the preferred form of the past tense of *plead.* They are in slight disagreement as to whether the other three forms are "standard," or "dialectal or colloquial." Both *got* and *gotten* are respectable as the past participle form of *get.* *The American College Dictionary* lists *dove* as "U. S. Coll. and British Dial."* The dictionaries also list the correct forms of troublesome words. *Indexes* is the preferred plural of *index,* but *indices* is allowed; *criteria* is the preferred plural of *criterion,* but *criterions* is allowed. The plural of *medium* is *media* or *mediums.*

Above all, the dictionary shows us in exact detail how changes of meaning accompany changes of syntax. The word *form,* for example, is listed in one dictionary as having more than two dozen meanings or shades of meaning when used as a noun; many less when used as a transitive verb; only three when used as an intransitive verb.

The dictionary is likewise useful in recording the idioms of the language. If we are in doubt, it can tell us that the best American practice is to say *different from;* but that in colloquial use, especially in England, *different to* and *different than* are to be found. It will note that one *agrees to* a proposal; that the climate or the dinner *agrees with* us; and that we *agree in* our attitudes.

Last, the dictionary gives a classification of words according to their usage. A word not found in a recent edition of a good dictionary has not yet been given a respectable place in the language, or else is so new in currency that it has not been recorded. Words recorded without special annotation are to be regarded as "good English" or "standard English." Words marked *obsolete* have passed out of use; those marked *archaic* are tending to pass out of use. A *colloquial* word or expression is proper in conversation but not, without special reason, in formal composition. The designation, *slang,* indicates a word in the lower and more doubtful levels of the colloquial class. Besides these common distinctions of usage, the dictionary makes other distinctions by marking words that belong to the special vocabularies of sciences and professions, and notes such special varieties of usage as *historical, poetic, heraldic.* Wherever there is a point of difference between English and American usage, it notes that difference. It also makes due record of the more important dialects.

The student who makes intelligent use of his dictionary will have his reward in increased knowledge and mastery of words. Yet with all these admonitions, it is still wise to remember that a mere dictionary knowledge is no knowledge and is therefore rightfully despised. The dictionary is a tool, not a master. And even as a tool, the dictionary has its limitations. To compile and publish an authoritative dictionary requires the patient labor of a large staff of editors and readers over a long period of years. The result is that the best of dictionaries, no matter how scrupulous and catholic its editors may be, will inevitably lag behind current usage to some extent; or it may—because the human mind is not perfect or omniscient—fail to record what people here or there may expect to find in it. "A good dictionary," says the great scholar, George Philip Krapp, "is an important aid. But even the best dictionary cannot render absolute and universal decisions. It provides material only for adaptation, not for blind acceptance. The actual vital moment in which it is necessary to use a word in speaking or in writing is of infinitely greater importance than all the authority of the dictionary." [1]

SUGGESTIONS FOR STUDY

1. Look up the following words in the dictionary. Make a study of the several meanings given in the entry for each word. Write sentences in which you use at least two meanings for each word.

contend	glaze	conjure	reckon	evolution
progress	hold	pastoral	shoot	corporation

2. Determine, by use of the dictionary, the profession, trade, sport, or special occupation to which the following belong:

[1] From *The Knowledge of English* by George Philip Krapp.

reeve	rivet	dibble	camber	whipper-in
joinery	bedder	buntline	timpani	wicket
sauté	ginner	grounder	nol-pros	spinner

3. Determine whether the following words are colloquial archaic, obsolete, slang—or in good usage:

fritter	beck	wont	squeegee	irregardless
leastwise	friz	gab	shimmy	thingumajig
gumption	thole	tote	unkempt	coffin nail

4. Establish from the dictionary the correct pronunciation of the following:

grievous	schism	status	ration	beaux arts
naïveté	height	sumac	a priori	meridional
athlete	rigmarole	often	harass	irreparable
sherbet	ribald	defect	arctic	perspiration

5. Use the dictionary to determine, if possible, the etymological relationship between the words listed in each of the following pairs or groups. Determine, if you can, the historical background involved in that relationship.

tangent, contact	animal, unanimous
paper, papyrus	economy, metronome
clerk, cleric, clergy	hospital, hospitality, hotel
lyre, lyric	engine, cotton gin

6. Determine which of the following words are specifically "American" and which are "British":

roundup	goober	bootlegger
heath	kerb	scuttlebutt
barrens	beatnik	gin mill
treacle	spinney	layby
be-bop	pram	haggis

7. From each group of words given in parentheses choose the word nearest in meaning to the word italicized. Give your reasons for your choice.

  a. Although at times humorous, his report of the conference was generally *flippant.* (glib, gossipy, voluble, frivolous)
  b. He was *lenient* with his sons—through the first offense. (mild, gentle, tolerant, indulgent, forbearing)
  c. I would prefer not to locate my office in a *congested* area. (packed, impeded, swollen, crowded, overloaded)
  d. Gambling nearly always has *pernicious* results. (unsocial, destructive, deadly, wicked, diseased)
  e. Talkative with one or two intimates, he was *taciturn* and

reserved in a large group. (depressed, gloomy, silent, quiet)

   f. That style of decoration seems *gaudy* in a Georgian house. (vulgar, ostentatious, cheap, flashy, brilliant, excessive)

8. Using your dictionary as a source of reference, study the following words as examples of prefixes and root words in combination. For each word in the list give the meaning of the prefix and the meaning of the root word with which it is combined.

contradiction	symmetrical	postlude
amphitheatre	effect	protocol
polyphonic	heterogeneous	quasi-judicial
suspicion	commotion	proceed
annotate	incredible	consonant
pseudonym	epithet	resume
precede	superficial	biennial

9. Establish the derivation of all the words italicized in the following sentence:

> I copied over his [David Hume's] *lectures* twice in my own hand, from notes taken in the class, and when I have had *occasion* to consult them, I can never sufficiently admire the *penetration* and clearness of *conception* which were necessary to the arrangement of the *fabric* of law, formed originally under the strictest influence of *feudal* principles, and *innovated, altered,* and *broken* in upon by the change of times, of habits, and of manners, until it *resembles* some ancient castle, partly entire, partly ruinous, partly *dilapidated, patched* and altered during the succession of ages by a thousand additions and combinations, yet still *exhibiting,* with the marks of its *antiquity,* symptoms of the *skill* and *wisdom* of its founders, and capable of being *analyzed* and made the subject of a methodical plan by an *architect* who can understand the various styles of the different ages in which it was *subjected* to alteration.—SIR WALTER SCOTT, *Memoir of His Early Years.*

10. Rewrite the following sentences, correcting all carelessness and inexactness in the use of words. Avoid wordiness.

   a. Maria tried to form a mental picture in her mind of what the word meant.
   b. Whenever legislation was being carried out, all the people turned out to speak up on opinionated matters.
   c. From his ideas one can see the advantage that a fraternity plays in the college life.
   d. From that simple political equality women have reached out to greater achievements.

e. Emotional development is very important and is sometimes still in a growth stage when a person reaches college age.

f. College not only can change an individual's viewpoint of life but will definitely strengthen their character, if not will power, if given a chance.

g. The principal influences the teachers never to be close with the pupils and to push rules and regulations down their throats.

h. Then the laughter would smoulder into various giggles.

i. Another reason which stops crime in small towns is that the people in small towns are usually regular church-goers.

j. There is only one thing I can think of where high school has preparatory school beat.

k. According to some accounts, the Great Plague of London was imported into the city by bales of merchandise from Holland, but by some authorities it was introduced by Dutch prisoners of war.

l. The doctor's position has risen to that of, perhaps, the most valuable member of modern society—certainly an essential element.

2. VOCABULARY AND USAGE

Despite all its neat convenience as a bureau of general information, the dictionary only provides materials; it does not teach methods. It can tell a writer whether a word is standard or colloquial, but not whether a colloquialism *ought* to be used in a given passage. It will mark certain words as obsolete or archaic—words like *quoth, whilom, wend, certes* —and so steer the writer away from a high-flown, affected style. It may also help the writer to eliminate dialectal expressions (*nowheres near*), vulgarisms (like *gent* for *gentleman*), and outright improprieties (like *muchly* for *much*); yet many problems will be left unsettled.

Formal and Informal Diction

One of the most important of these problems concerns the tone of the diction in the composition as a whole rather than the mere selection or rejection of isolated words. This is the problem of how to draw the line between formal and informal usage. Differently stated, it is the question of how rigorous a writer should be in excluding words and phrases that lie in the borderland between severely correct English and "bad" English. The answer to the question is in the principle that Chaucer got from Plato: "The word must be the cousin to the deed." The diction must fit the idea, purpose, character, context of the discourse, and will be prevailingly formal or informal accordingly.

The difference between formal and informal diction is illustrated in the passages given below. Passages 1 and 2 are formal; passages 3 and 4, informal, in varying degrees.

> 1. From this view of the subject it may be concluded that a pure democracy, by which I mean a society consisting of a small number of citizens, who assemble and administer the government in person, can admit of no cure for the mischiefs of faction. A common passion or interest will, in almost every case, be felt by a majority of the whole; a communication and concert result from the form of government itself; and there is nothing to check the inducements to sacrifice the weaker party or an obnoxious individual. Hence it is that such democracies have ever been spectacles of turbulence and contention; have ever been found incompatible with personal security or the rights of property; and have in general been as short in their lives as they have been violent in their deaths.—JAMES MADISON, *The Federalist,* No. 10.

> 2. When I meet a government which says to me, "Your money or your life," why should I be in haste to give it my money? It may be in a great strait, and not know what to do: I cannot help that. It must help itself; do as I do. It is not worth the while to snivel about it. I am not responsible for the successful working of the machinery of society. I am not the son of the engineer. I perceive that, when an acorn and a chestnut fall side by side, the one does not remain inert to make way for the other, but both obey their own laws, and spring and grow and flourish as best they can, till one, perchance, overshadows and destroys the other. If a plant cannot live according to its nature, it dies; and so a man.—HENRY D. THOREAU, "Civil Disobedience."

> 3. Crime, as they [the new criminologists] depict it, becomes a sort of disease, either inherited or acquired by contagion, and as devoid of moral content or significance as smallpox. The criminal is no longer a black-hearted villain, to be put down by force, but a poor brother who has succumbed to the laws of Mendel and the swinish stupidity of society. The aim of punishment is not to make him sweat, but to dissuade and rehabilitate him. In every pickpocket there is a potential Good Man. . . . Men do not sit in prisons

as long as they used to; the parole boards shove them out almost as fast as the cops shove them in.—H. L. MENCKEN, "Criminology," *Prejudices, Sixth Series.*

4. "Football will never see another as great as Jim Thorpe," stated Amos Alonzo Stagg, who had seen them all in his 100 years.

"Here was the theoretical super player in flesh and blood," said Percy Haughton of Harvard.

The big Indian was a wraith in an open field with his speed. He had a swivel hip that could—and did—knock tacklers cold with a twist. His stiff-arm was as lethal as the jab of Joe Louis. Not only could he run the tackles and ends like Red Grange; he also could split the middle of the line like Bronko Nagurski. As a punter—well, in one game against Lafayette every kick was more than 70 yards. He was a deadly field goal kicker from inside midfield.—ARTHUR DALEY, "The Noble Red Man," The New York *Times.*

In passages 1 and 2, both Madison and Thoreau use formal diction. There are no colloquialisms, no slang expressions. They take no liberties with the language. But the two passages differ much in the kind of formal diction chosen to convey the ideas. Madison, writing with cool, systematic logic on the differences between a pure democracy and a republic, uses a large proportion of words of Latin origin— words abstract and general, as might be expected in view of his subject. The diction of Thoreau, as he argues his personal view of the citizen's relation to the State, is simple, direct, energetic. It is prevailingly monosyllabic, rather Anglo-Saxon and homely. It gives much of the effect of informality without ever crossing the border-line between "good English" and doubtful English. It is plain English of the highest quality.

The other selections, written for different purposes and in an entirely different tone from the selections by Madison and Thoreau, naturally use a more informal diction. H. L. Mencken deliberately and sarcastically mixes scientific terms and high-flown language, as if to parody the manner of social scientists and preachers. Literary terms mingle with near colloquialisms (*a poor brother who has succumbed to the laws of Mendel*) or even with the racy Americanisms of the police court reporter (*the parole boards shove them out almost as fast as the cops shove them in*). The passage by Arthur Daley, on the other hand, is a straightforward bit of journalism from the sports page, written with the skill of a seasoned reporter, with no descent into clichés or flashy vulgarisms.

The difference between Madison and Thoreau, on the one hand, and Mencken and Daley, on the other, is not, then, a difference between "good" and "bad." It is a difference between two kinds of diction which we distinguish—roughly and none too exactly—as formal and informal.

The principal governing the use of formal and informal diction can be stated as follows:

(1) In *formal* writing—a serious essay, a learned paper, a scientific treatise, a dignified exposition or argument—use the "good English" of the educated world. Avoid slang and, except for special purposes, avoid colloquialisms.

(2) In *informal* writing—a personal essay, a light magazine article, a newspaper report or sketch, a personal letter— you should still use this same "good English." But you are allowed (not required) to use colloquialisms and even an occasional slang expression if by so doing you improve— and do not cheapen—the effectiveness of your writing.

The danger in the use of informal diction is that it tempts the writer to be lazy, vulgar, or even offensively incorrect. Good taste alone, in the end, will tell us how far we may go in borrowing colloquial vigor without falling into raw error. In all great civilizations of the past a firm distinction has been maintained between the written and the spoken language, and all have maintained a stricter standard for the written. The common usage of everyday speech, though it may supply words that sooner or later creep into the formal vocabulary, cannot determine the rhetoric of written composition. In conversation we may say that Napoleon "couldn't make the grade at Waterloo," but we reject the phrase as too flippant for a careful essay on Napoleon's strategy.

Slang

The standard prohibition against slang is definite. Slang, according to Noah Webster, for example, is "language consisting either of new words or phrases often of the vagrant or illiterate classes, or of ordinary words or phrases in arbitrary senses, and having a conventional but vulgar and inelegant use." The great defect of slang, however, is as much in its lazy inexactness and triteness as in its "vulgar and inelegant" associations. Slang expressions like *swell guy,*

grand time, raw deal are omnibus terms with no clear outline of meaning and suggest an impoverished vocabulary.
Most such expressions represent momentary fads and soon
lose their meaning. The college sophomore who says "Beat it"
to the intruding freshman in the nineteen-sixties said "Skid-
doo!" in other days. A slang term can be dead or bromidic in
ten years, a year, or a season. Only if it meets some real need
of expression will it survive indefinitely. Among former slang
words that have survived into our time and become proper
words are *mob, cad, bus, radio.* It is possible that *ad, phone,
flunk* and other words now deemed "vulgar and inelegant"
in written composition will have similar survival value. But,
in the absence of good precedent, it is best for the inexperienced writer to avoid doubtful words.

Except in some special context, it is also necessary to
avoid words marked by the dictionary as *jargon, cant,* or
argot. "Toonerville's cats will jazz along with the team for
the tilt with Boonetown tossers" is a mixture of jargon and
cant—and in excessively bad taste. The word *grand* when
used by a gangster to mean a thousand dollars is argot.
Bulls and *bears* are cant expressions of the stock exchange.
Quilling or *apple polishing* (for *flattering* a professor) is collegiate cant.

The opposite fault occurs when a writer "over-writes" or
indulges in "fine writing" out of some fear of being incorrect
or some desire to be really literary. The writer of the following has made a strained effort to be literary:

> Perhaps the ancient pedagogue, as he scowled upon his
> lowly aspirants, would have been astounded had he been of a
> prophetic nature. But how was he to prognosticate that the
> succeeding centuries would infest the seats of his academic
> temple with scheming creatures who adjudicated the inquisi-
> tion into his own character and idiosyncrasies the most bene-
> ficial and valuable of educational curricula? Especially
> would this fact have amazed him if he had foreseen the
> identity of the individuals who would most avariciously be
> subjected to intensive research.—*Student Paper.*

The accompanying diagram, reproduced from the *Oxford
English Dictionary,* will illustrate the relationship of the various levels of usage to one another and their place in the
vocabulary. The student writer will do best to keep a middle
position close to the upper level of usage, designated as
Scientific-Literary-Foreign, and yet not so far away from the
lower level as to make his writing priggish and artificial.

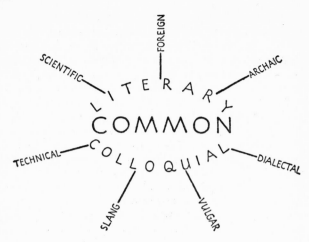

The center is occupied by the "common" words, in which literary and colloquial usage meet. "Scientific" and "foreign" words enter the common language mainly through literature; "slang" words ascend through colloquial use; the "technical" terms of crafts and processes, and the "dialect" words, blend with the common language both in speech and literature. Slang also touches on one side the technical terminology of trades and occupations, as in "nautical slang," "Public School slang," "the slang of the Stock Exchange," and on another passes into true dialect. Dialects similarly pass into foreign languages. Scientific terminology passes on one side into purely foreign words; on another it blends with the technical vocabulary of art and manufactures. It is not possible to fix the point at which the "English Language" stops, along any of these diverging lines.—*Oxford English Dictionary.*

The temptation to write or speak more grandly than the occasion requires is with us always. Our natural wish to be impressive is well set forth in the following passage:

A man gives ten cents to a beggar, but he makes a dona-tion when the amount of the gift is larger. The beggar asks alms for himself, but the collector for charity solicits sub-scriptions. A house or barn or railway station is built, but a church is an edifice and is erected. The workman pays his bills, but the master settles his accounts. The public speaker makes a speech or addresses an audience, according to his sense of the importance of the occasion.—GEORGE PHILIP KRAPP, *The Knowledge of English.*

The desire to be polite, like the desire to seem impressive, may also lead to the use of "elegant variation." In common intercourse we have many formulas by which we soften harsh experience or avoid words deemed to suggest ugliness and dirtiness. People do not die, but "pass away." For some queer reason, "illness" is thought to be more elegant than "sickness." Delicate ladies were formerly bothered not by the "bad smell" of a gutter, but by its "offensive odor." Such attempts to substitute a polite or over-literary term for a plain term are called *euphemisms*. In ordinary life they are among the inexorable conventions of social intercourse, the rituals by which we live with as much dignity as we can command. But what is politeness in social intercourse may seem only affectation in written composition.

Resist the desire to be ostentatious. Do not fear the large word, but above all do not fear the small word, the plain word, the homely word. Prefer the simple word to the polysyllable if no logical content or no valuable shade of association is lost by the preference. There is no virtue in saying *prestidigitation* rather than *sleight-of-hand, similitude* rather rather than *likeness, protuberance* rather than *bump, perspiration* rather than *sweat*. The great vigor of American literature in certain of its best periods comes in no small measure from the supple, easy plainness of the language. The language of Thoreau, for example, is rarely literary in any affected sense. The letters of Jefferson, the writings of Franklin, the diaries of William Byrd of Westover, the papers written for *The Federalist*—all these, and many more, are notable for their directness and simplicity.

EXERCISES

1. Read the following selections from this text and note the degrees of formality and informality in each of them:

> Agee's "D. W. Griffith" (page 73)
> Leopold's "Thinking Like a Mountain" (page 80)
> Specimen paragraphs from this chapter

2. Make a comparative study of the degrees of formality and informality observed in such publications as are indicated below. Choose one group for intensive study.

> a. Signed articles about sports events published in metropolitan newspapers.
> b. News reports or feature articles by the press services as compared with columns by your favorite political commentator or local columnist.

    c. Compare the diction and phrasing of any two of the following essayists: James Thurber, Rebecca West, Robert Louis Stevenson, Agnes Repplier, Charles Lamb, Aldous Huxley, Christopher Morley, E. B. White.

    d. Compare Vernon L. Parrington's discussion of Davy Crockett (*Main Currents in American Thought*) with Crockett's "Autobiography" (*A Narrative of the Life of David Crockett*) published in 1834.

    e. Characterize the diction and "tone" of a speech delivered by Webster, Lincoln, Calhoun, Bryan, Churchill, or Kennedy.

3. Consider the diagram on page 193 and compile seven short lists of words which may be entered under the seven sub-categories designated in the chart.

4. Compile a list of stock expressions that commonly appear in the conversation of your friends and acquaintances. Classify them under the following heads.

    a. Campus slang—peculiar to your own institution

    b. "Collegiate" slang—terms and expressions with a wider application than merely in your own college

    c. Current American slang

    d. Expressions once considered slang but now on the borderline of good usage—for example, *fan, fanletter, stag, stagline*

    e. Expressions once classified as slang (see older dictionaries) but now accepted in good usage

3. THE QUALITIES OF WORDS

To study the qualities of words it is necessary to analyze their action and effect in the written composition itself. In the word-lists of the dictionary they are inert and all but dead; on the written page or in the spoken utterance their latent qualities awaken and may be identified and judged. These qualities are so various that they do not submit to one principle of classification; several different classifications, upon several different principles, are necessary if the critical analysis is to be practical and complete.

Functional Words and Content Words

Most sentences are made up of two kinds of words: functional words and content words. Functional words express relationships. They have but one meaning, and that meaning never changes. Conjunctions, prepositions, articles, pronouns, and auxiliary verbs are functional words (*and, but, or; because, when, how; in, by, with; a, an, the; I, he, it;*

shall, will, have—as auxiliaries). Our main concern with functional words is to use them correctly. They are colorless. Whatever quality they have is grammatical and syntactical; and therefore, essential though they are, our study here is not of them. Content words are nouns, verbs, adjectives, adverbs (*justice, cabin, road, police; go, worry, insinuate, block; virtuous, helpful, slimy, bizarre; awkwardly, late, sonorously, acutely*). Content words of course also have function, but their quality derives from their meaning. The content words of a sentence convey the meanings out of which, with the assistance of the purely functional words, the total meaning of the sentence is built up. It is impossible to construct a sentence without at least one content word. Sometimes, of course, content words may be implied without being actually given in the sentence.

> Good fences make good neighbors. (All the words are content words.)
> If we *keep* up our *fences,* we shall *stay* on *good terms* with our *neighbors.* (Six content words; nine functional words.)
> If we . . . up . . ., we shall . . . on . . . with. (All functional words; no content words; no meaning; no sentence.)

To study the qualities of words we must evidently direct our attention mainly to the content words, which are the solid building material of the sentence.

Denotation and Connotation

Content words possess two kinds of meaning—denotative meaning and connotative meaning. The denotative meaning is the bare logical meaning, and only that. In chemistry, *proton* and *ion,* and in mathematics, *surd* and *hypotenuse,* "denote" certain concepts or objects which are precisely set forth in those sciences. We may speak of the denotative meaning of a word as the "core of meaning" that it has when applied to the object or class of objects, quality, idea to which it consistently and usually refers. Dictionary definitions generally state the denotative meaning of a word. Thus *clan,* according to the dictionary, denotes "a social group comprising a number of households the heads of which claim descent from a common ancestor, especially in the Scottish highlands." Similarly, the words *knight, vassal, serf* denote certain degrees of status which are defined at great length in the histories of feudalism.

The connotative meaning of a word is generally regarded

as being the meaning, or various meanings, added to a word by the associations that it acquires from its common uses, or that may be attributed to it from a figurative use. The chemical and mathematical terms mentioned above have a very exact denotation but very little connotation, since they are not likely to be used outside the province of the strict sciences, to which they belong. The word *clan,* on the other hand, brings up suggestions of tartans, bagpipes, and claymores, the novels of Sir Walter Scott, and tales of border warfare. So, too, the words *knight, vassal, serf* are rich in associations of the Middle Ages. An abstract word like *substance* has very little connotation, but concrete words like *marmalade, eggnog, mud, glue, opium* have a great deal of connotative meaning. The verbs *ask, beg, request, beseech, implore* have about the same denotative meaning but different connotative meanings. The adjectives *vigorous, strong, powerful, Herculean* all denote strength, but they have slightly different connotations.

All matter-of-fact writing, since it aims to be logical and informative and no more, will prefer words that have an exact denotation and little or no connotation. The scientist, for example, must strive for logical exactness and therefore attempts to make his vocabulary as strictly denotative as is possible. Science communicates facts as facts. It does not want unruly human emotions to intrude upon its explanations. The language of mathematics probably comes nearest to the ideal of a scientific language. The symbols of mathematics—$x, y, z; (x - 6)^2; x \cos a$—have a pure logical content. The axioms and theorems of mathematics approach the clear exactness of its symbols. The mathematical statement, "A straight line is the shortest distance between two points," is a plainly denotative use of words. But the saying, "The longest way round is the sweetest way home," is freighted with connotations, or overtones of meaning, that science does not want and cannot use. Yet it is difficult to isolate old words from the associations that have gathered about them in the course of time; and therefore science must spend a great deal of effort in inventing new words free of the multiple meanings that the old ones possess.

In other kinds of writing, we turn to advantage the multiple meanings that so much embarrass the scientist. In descriptive writing, in narrative, in essays, in criticism, in argument, indeed in any kind of writing that tries to interest or convince the reader as well as to convey a matter-of-fact content, words may be chosen *because* they have rich associations and multiple meanings. In this sentence from Sir Thomas Browne, words are chosen partly for their rolling dignity of sound and partly for the contrasting associations between phrases like "thin walls of clay" and "specious buildings":

> Now since these dead bones have already outlasted the living ones of Methuselah, and in a yard underground, and thin walls of clay, outworn the strong and specious buildings above it, and quietly rested under the drums and tramplings of three conquests, what Prince can promise diuturnity to his relics . . . ?

In these simpler but equally rhetorical sentences from Stephen Crane's *The Red Badge of Courage,* words are chosen which suggest as well as state the condition of panic that seizes an inexperienced soldier's mind:

> The fight was lost. The dragons were coming with invincible strides. The army, helpless in matted thickets and blinded by the overhanging night, was going to be swallowed. War, the red animal, war, the blood-swollen god, would have bloated fill.

Stephen Crane's phrase, describing war as a "blood-swollen god," *contains* the idea that war is destructive, but *suggests,* with that idea, images of drunken abandon, cannibalism, blood-sacrifice to Moloch or Baal, and pagan slaughter in general.

With such possibilities open to him, the writer must realize that exactness in the choice of words depends on two considerations: his words must have both the right logical meaning, or denotation, and the right associational meaning, or connotation. As Herbert Read says, "A word must *mean* the thing it stands for, not only in the sense of accurately corresponding to the intention of the writer but also in the visual sense of conjuring up a reflection of the thing in its complete reality." Thus, while the possibilities of choice may be often so wide as to be confusing, and will seem only to increase the writer's difficulties, his opportunities for gaining subtle degrees of exactness and new and powerful effects are enormously increased by the multiple meanings that words take on, and by the great variety of synonyms available to him, each with its own aura of connotation. Consider, for example, the varieties of connotation in the following groups of words. The words in any given group have the same denotative core of meaning.

> hateful, odious, obnoxious, offensive, repugnant, abhorrent, loathsome
> leader, commander, conductor, director, boss, chief, captain, head
> stubborn, obstinate, headstrong, resolute, inflexible, pertinacious, intractable, dogged, hard-headed
> teacher, pedagogue, school-teacher, school-ma'am, professor
> choose, elect, select, pick, single out, cull, prefer

Many of the associations that gather around words come from traditional usage. We speak of the *chief* of an Indian tribe, a Scottish clan, a fire department; the *boss* of a ward, a section-gang, a factory; the *commander* of an army; the *leader* of a political party; the *captain* of a ship or a team; the *head* of a family. The people gathered at a football game are a *crowd;* at a church, a *congregation;* at a theater, an *audience.* A teacher is a *teacher* when we speak merely of his function, but a *pedagogue* when he takes himself too seriously or when we make light of his teaching. We *close* a door, or emphatically order it to be *shut,* or in anger *bang* or *slam* it. We may *move, scrape, shuffle,* or *scuffle* our feet. We *eat, bolt, gobble,* or perhaps only *consume* our food. We may be *moved,* or *stirred, aroused, excited, inflamed.* We *shrink* from a blow, *quail* at danger, *wince* with pain. We *cut* cake, cards, and acquaintances, but *sever* diplomatic relations. Grandfather is *hoary* with age; good wine is *old;* furniture is *antique;* tin bathtubs are *antiquated;* the thousand-year-old redwoods of California are *ancient* or *venerable.* Many associations of this sort are so well established as to have become idioms of the language and are therefore useful, indeed necessary.

Triteness and Originality

On the other hand we have many expressions that have become worn-out and trite: the "counters" of speech; the *clichés* or stereotyped expressions of the commonplace mind, the uninventive writer. These are to be avoided. We have long since had enough of the old romantic stereotypes—the *forlorn nightingales, ivy-mantled towers, villages nestling in valleys.* Modern rubber-stamp words and phrases are just as reprehensible, and perhaps duller—*social awareness, stream-lined efficiency, heritage of culture, march of science.*

But originality will not automatically result from mere avoidance of the trite. The original writer builds new associations by making new combinations of words. One of the readiest ways to make new combinations, and therefore new associative values, is through transferring words from some familiar category into a new and striking application. This procedure is of course opposite to the procedure of science. *Valence,* in chemistry, has a narrow, specific meaning of which science is jealous. The chemists made up this technical term. They did not borrow *value,* which has a flavor of the market, or *virtue,* which suggests morality, or *strength,* which suggests the gymnasium.

In literary practice we can appropriate whatever seems good in any special vocabulary and make it do service in the general vocabulary. Long ago, *electric,* a scientific term, was taken over in the familiar phrase *electric thrill.* An experience as well as a taste can be *bitter.* We can *mask* a doorway as well as a face. Such expressions of course are metaphorical. They suggest a likeness without asserting that it is literally there and must later be discussed more fully under the heading, "Figures of Speech." Here they are noted only as examples of word transfers, used for their connotative quality.

In the following illustrative passage, the words underlined twice have been transferred from a purely denotative category to a connotative-denotative category; those underlined once are not word transfers, yet are used for their connotative force.

> Yes, news by noon is stale. But surely that is comment enough upon it. In very truth, it would have been just as stale in the morning. The events you read of so eagerly happened yesterday, or the day before, or if it was a Krakatoa that has blown its head off at the antipodes, last week. No matter; the editor claps the latest date line on the event and he hands you the hoax for which you pay him tithe every day.—DONALD CULROSS PEATTIE, *A Book of Hours.*

EXERCISES

1. From the specimen paragraphs given in Chapter 4, select one in which the choice of words is prevailingly denotative, and another in which there is a large proportion of connotative words. What has determined, in each case, the author's choice of words?

What differences of style and effect are produced by the choice of words?

2. In the pairs of passages given below, determine, in each instance, which has the greater number of connotative words and account for the difference in the effect produced by the use of connotative words. Are the more "denotative" passages to be criticized unfavorably because of the author's preference for denotative words?

a. (1) The spinnaker is a large, lightweight sail shaped like a cup, or a cone cut in half. It was first developed for racing, but now is found on many small sailboats to improve their speed and performance. It is used only for sailing downwind, when the jib loses its function of funnelling wind to the mainsail and flaps uselessly. At this point, the spinnaker's vast size and ability to face at right angles to the wind makes it a far more effective sail.—BILL WALLACE, "The Spinnaker," *Sailing*.[1]

(2) Just at sunset there was a rush to shorten sail before the menace of a sombre hail cloud. The hard gust of wind came brutal like the blow of a fist. The ship, relieved of her canvas in time, received it pluckily: she yielded reluctantly to the violent onset; then, coming up with a stately and irresistible motion, brought her spars to windward in the teeth of the screeching squall. Out of the abysmal darkness of the black cloud overhead white hail streamed on her, rattled on the rigging, leaped in handfuls off the yards, rebounded on the deck—round and gleaming in the murky turmoil like a shower of pearls. It passed away. For a moment a livid sun shot horizontally the last rays of sinister light between the hills of steep, rolling waves. Then a wild night rushed in—stamped out in a great howl that dismal remnant of a stormy day.—JOSEPH CONRAD, *The Nigger of the Narcissus*.[2]

b. (1) I attempted to rise, but was not able to stir; for, as I happened to be on my back, I found my arms and legs were strongly fastened on each side to the ground; and my hair, which was long and thick, tied down in the same manner. I likewise felt several slender ligatures across my body, from my arm-pits to my thighs. I could only look upwards; the sun began to grow hot, and the light offended

[1] Reprinted by permission of Golden Press, Inc. and The Ridge Press from *Sailing: A Golden Handbook*. Copyright 1961 by Golden Press, Inc.

[2] Reprinted by permission of J. M. Dent & Sons Ltd., London.

my eyes. I heard a confused noise about me; but in the posture I lay, could see nothing except the sky. In a little time I felt something alive moving on my left leg, which advancing gently forward over my breast, came almost up to my chin; when bending my eyes downward as much as I could, I perceived it to be a human creature, not six inches high, with a bow and arrow in his hands, and a quiver at his back.—JONATHAN SWIFT, "A Voyage to Lilliput."

(2) In the gravelled parking space before the station several cars were drawn up. Their shining bodies glittered in the hot sunlight like great beetles of machinery, and in the look of these great beetles, powerful and luxurious as most of them were, there was a stamped-out quality, a kind of metallic and inhuman repetition that filled his spirit, he could not say why, with a vague sense of weariness and desolation. The feeling returned to him—the feeling that had come to him so often in recent years with a troubled and haunting insistence—that "something" had come into life, "something new" which he could not define, but something that was disturbing and sinister, and which was somehow represented by the powerful, weary, and inhuman precision of these great glittering, stamped-out beetles of machinery.—THOMAS WOLFE, "Proteus: The City."[1]

c. (1) The column that had butted stoutly at the obstacles in the roadway was barely out of the youth's sight before he saw dark waves of men come sweeping out of the woods and down through the fields. He knew at once that the steel fibers had been washed from their hearts. They were bursting from their coats and their equipments as if from entanglements. They charged down upon him like terrified buffaloes.—STEPHEN CRANE, *The Red Badge of Courage.*

(2) Unfortunately for Ney and d'Erlon, they were faced by a general who understood the French tactics, and in part, at least, knew how to neutralize them. Instead of lining the ridge along which the Braine-'Alleud-Wavre Road ran, Wellington drew up the bulk of his forces in the rear of it, where they were sheltered from the shot and shell of the enemy's great battery which, as it was composed of guns and not howitzers, could not search the rear slope. The result was that his men suffered little from the

---

[1] From *Of Time and the River,* by Thomas Wolfe. Copyright, 1935, by Charles Scribner's Sons. Reprinted by permission of Charles Scribner's Sons.

preliminary bombardment. All they had to do was to lie down in ranks behind the ridge, and when the enemy's columns approached its summit, rise, advance a few paces and deliver a crashing volley on their heads before they could deploy.—MAJOR-GENERAL J. F. C. FULLER, "The Battle of Waterloo," *A Military History of the Western World.*

Abstract and Concrete; General and Specific

The division of words into the classifications *abstract-concrete, general-specific* offers another useful and important angle of approach to problems of diction. In making this approach, however, the student must bear in mind: (1) that the classifications overlap to some extent; and (2) that the classification of words as *abstract-concrete, general-specific* may vary according to their use in different contexts and for different purposes.

Abstract-Concrete. An *abstract* word expresses a quality or characteristic considered apart from any particular object or action. A *concrete* word makes a particular application of a quality or characteristic or distinguishes some individual object or action. *Abstract* and *concrete* denote not only different but opposite types of meaning.

Thus *sweetness* is abstract; *sugar, honey, molasses* (objects to which the term *sweetness* may be applied) are concrete. The quality of a soldier's behavior may be expressed in the single abstract word *gallantry.* The concrete instance of his gallantry, not to be expressed in a single word, was that *at Okinawa he brought in a wounded comrade under enemy fire.* An automobile driver was *reckless* (abstract); he *ran through a traffic light* (concrete). *Anatomy* is abstract; *eyetooth, hair, kneecap* are concrete.

Abstract words, we soon discover, refer to ideas or qualities as such. They are a necessary and inescapable feature of the diction when the writing deals with ideas and non-material subjects. There are no substitutes for such terms as *love, truth, beauty, honesty, legality, virtue.* When properly used, abstract words do the work that no other words can do. Without them, the human reason could not function at its highest potential level; and religion, art, philosophy, and science would lack a proper language. At the same time, all abstractions, whether represented in single words or phrases or in processes of thought, need to be supported by details and examples; and when not so supported, they tend to be-

come vague and meaningless. Abstract terms, when loosely
defined or deliberately perverted, can cause endless confusion and trouble in human affairs. Perhaps it was a vague
use of the abstract word *patriotism* (and its loose attachment
to wrong particulars) that led Doctor Samuel Johnson to
explode with an angry definition: "Patriotism is the last
refuge of a scoundrel." The abuse of noble abstractions is
one of the continuing vices of humanity. Paraphrasing Doctor Johnson, we might say that abstract terms like *progress,
tradition, fundamental values, social awareness, constructive, outstanding* are often the refuge of writers who do not
know what they want to say, yet wish somehow to be impressive and seem important.

In the following passage, which might be entitled "A
Typical Speech at an Alumni Meeting," the speaker is using
abstract words in order to seem impressive; but since the
abstractions are not associated with definite particulars, nobody can be sure exactly what the speaker means:

> I wish to take advantage of this occasion to emphasize the
> significance of the relationship between the Alumni and the
> College. We have always felt it to be of the greatest impor-
> tance to this institution to maintain contact with our sons
> and daughters who have gone forth to wider fields of accom-
> plishment. Yet we also have the conviction that they profit by
> fostering a spirit of coöperation with their Alma Mater as it
> goes ever forward upon its great constructive tasks.

On the other hand, in the passages following, abstract diction is correctly and effectively used; and although the points
made may be arguable, they could not be adequately expressed without the use of abstract terms, and, in the sources
from which these passages are excerpted, the abstract statements are supported by concrete particulars:

> We hold these truths to be self-evident, that all men are
> created equal, that they are endowed by their Creator with
> certain unalienable Rights, that among these are Life, Lib-
> erty, and the pursuit of Happiness.—THOMAS JEFFERSON,
> *The Declaration of Independence.*

> Society never advances. It recedes as fast on one side as
> it gains on the other. It undergoes continual changes; it is
> barbarous, it is civilized, it is christianized, it is scientific; but
> this change is not amelioration. For everything that is given
> something is taken.—RALPH WALDO EMERSON, *Self-Reliance.*

The value of concrete words is in the directness and sharpness of the image that they bring to a reader's mind. They are physical and, to use a psychological term, *sensational:* they appeal to the senses. They enable a reader to see, hear, touch, at least in imagination. In description and narration, as well as in much of the detail of expository writing, concrete diction is a prime necessity. Without it there may be only windy generality and dullness, and nothing really substantial or interesting. The following selection indicates how a writer of fiction may use concrete diction:

> He walked on. The sibilant grass brushed his thighs; the moist air, heavy with the smell of mould and earth, saturated his lungs and filled out his flagging muscles with borrowed strength. The floor beneath was spongy now except where rock lay scattered, as by a petulant hand. Once he looked up and high above the dark slick trunks he saw sunlight pelting the interlocked branches, a luminous cloudburst, too high for it to reach the quiet basin's floor over which he was beginning to feel himself pass as through some forbidden place. To his front and side the basin appeared as open as a meadow, and yet his vision was everywhere blocked by clumps of laurel and honeysuckle. Neither barred the way, nor opened it up. He passed on, as though he moved always through the same place, his ears deadened by the quiet, his sight by a sensuous glaze. Without beginning or end the basin was there, and he was there. Deep within it he trod the green light. He dared not speak, lest he drown.—ANDREW LYTLE, *The Velvet Horn.*[1]

In all good writing both concrete and abstract diction will appear. Neither, in its proper place, is better than the other. It is impossible to give absolute rules for the use of abstract and concrete words. Their value and use must be learned by the process of trial and error. The division of words into abstract and concrete simply affords another method for studying the qualities of words. It is a good idea to examine what you have written for its proportion of abstract and concrete words and to see how a change from one to the other will affect the diction as a whole.

General-Specific. General words refer to class, kind, or type; specific words refer to the particular members of a class, kind, or type. *Dwelling* is a general word; *house, hut, cabin, tent, barracks, mansion* are specific. But *dwelling* is specific

---

[1] Copyright 1957 by Andrew Lytle. *The Velvet Horn.* Reprinted by permission of Ivan Obolensky, New York City.

with reference to the general term *building*, which includes all classes of structures erected for human use. A general term like *architecture* can be made specific by the addition of qualifying adjectives or phrases: *Georgian architecture, early New England architecture, the architecture of Versailles.*

The overlapping of abstract-concrete with general-specific classifications, as well as the relativity of the terms, can best be indicated by examples. Thus *communicate* is both abstract and general. *Speak* is concrete and specific with reference to *communicate*, but it is general with reference to the still more concrete and specific terms, *rant, shout, whisper. Virtue* is general and abstract. *Honesty, truthfulness, chastity,* considered with reference to *virtue,* are specific but still abstract qualities.

Writing that has a preponderance of general words is likely to seem heavy and pretentious. But general terms are as necessary to the vocabulary as specific terms. When the subject is scientific or philosophical—whenever, indeed, the subject calls for generalizations—the writing will have a large proportion of general terms; but in descriptive and narrative writing the tendency will be toward the specific. The ideal is a judicious balance. The general terms must have enough specific terms to support them; but specific terms should not be used so freely and exclusively that the reader is confused by sheer detail. The writer who urges us "to cherish the fundamental values of civilization" or "to uphold the constructive ideals of Americanism" is thinking vaguely and writing badly. He needs to be specific. But Shelley's saying, "Poetry is the record of the best and happiest moments of the happiest and best minds," is an apt generalization which we would not wish to alter, all the more because it is convincingly supported, in *A Defense of Poetry,* by Shelley's remarks upon the specific nature of the poet's experience. The choice between "careful preparation was fundamental in the planning of our campaign" and "the establishment of bases in North Ireland and England was the first step in the Allied reconquest of the European mainland" is a choice between the general and the specific. Whether a writer will use one or the other will depend partly upon his subject and his purpose. But where no meaning is sacrificed, it is best to use the specific terms, for they give a clarity and liveliness rarely conveyed by general terms. Other things being equal, it is better to say *football game* than *athletic exercise, the professor of chemistry* rather than *science teacher.*

EXERCISES

1. Identify all the abstract and concrete words in the last four paragraphs of Leopold's "Thinking Like a Mountain" (page 80).

2. In the following passage, would it be possible to improve the diction by substitution of concrete for abstract words?

> The task of building and of maintaining a high civilization in which man may develop his latent potentialities is our one all-inclusive social purpose. It is a continuous task. If we relax our efforts, even for a short period, the work of centuries may be lost. If we take our civilization for granted, our own future may be endangered.—HAROLD H. TITUS, *Living Issues in Philosophy.*

3. Would the following passage be improved by the use of a more concrete diction? If you think so, rewrite the passage.

> Daily, at regularly recurrent times, each family assembles for the consumption of food. On such occasions sociology may identify values which must be associated with fundamental aspects of the family life. At such times food consumption is not a purely dietary procedure. Raw material and functional goals are merged in a context of significant social awareness which, although it may seem not to extend beyond the bounds of family interest, nevertheless carries broad human implications.

4. In the following passages, determine, so far as you can, the prevalence of abstract or concrete, general or specific words. Determine also, in each instance, whether the diction is adapted to the subject and the author's purpose.

> a. Everything was perfectly open. The Commodore was cleared with a cargo of arms and ammunition for Cuba. There was none of that extreme modesty about the proceeding which had marked previous departures of the famous tug. She loaded up as placidly as if she were going to carry oranges to New York, instead of Remingtons to Cuba. Down the river, furthermore, the revenue cutter Boutwell, the old isosceles triangle that protects United States interests in the St. John's, lay at anchor, with no sign of excitement aboard her.— STEPHEN CRANE, "Stephen Crane's Own Story."

> b. Times and places were mingled in my head; the past

was part of the present, close as the red cedar water bucket in the kitchen, or the big cherry press put together with pegs, or the parched corn a grandmother now and then made for us. This was the same as the parched corn from the old days, or the cornmeal mush we sometimes ate, no different at all from the mush in the stories. . . . Two things tied all time together; these had run through most of the old stories to shape the lives of men, and so did they shape our lives and the lives of people about us. These were the land and the Cumberland.—HARRIETTE SIMPSON ARNOW, *Seedtime on the Cumberland.*

c. Memory is all chance, and I have learned that you remember things not because they are important; you remember the important things because they help you to fix in mind the trifles of your early life, or the trifles simply drag with them through many years the incidents that have altered your fortunes.—ALLEN TATE, *The Fathers.*

Figures of Speech

The effectiveness of diction, whether in prose or poetry, may very well depend, in the last analysis, upon the writer's skill and resourcefulness in the use of *figurative* (i.e., *metaphorical*) language. The two terms, *figurative* and *metaphorical,* are used almost interchangeably to describe language that refers to one thing in terms of another which it actually or symbolically resembles. (A *flood of sound poured* from the loudspeaker. Thought and care had *furrowed* his brow.)

Although the use of figurative language always carries the danger of extravagance or loose fancifulness, it is nevertheless true that diction can be made subtly exact or richly concrete by suggesting a correspondence between two objects, as in *simile* and *metaphor;* or by impressing an image upon a reader's mind in some unusual and powerful way, as in *hyperbole, litotes, synecdoche, metonymy, personification.* These traditional names for figures of speech come down to us from the Greek and Roman rhetoricians; but the student should not be misled into thinking, for that reason, that these learned polysyllables stand for something pedantic, strange, and quite outside his experience. Actually, figures of speech are natural and even commonplace ways of using language. The rhetorical categories serve only to make systematic what men do every day in familiar discourse and have done since words were invented. (The first sentence in this paragraph contains two metaphors: "richly concrete" and "impress an image.") In ordinary conversation we rarely frame half a dozen sentences without using one or more of the figures of speech that have become stock phrases in the language:

quick as lightning	pluck up courage
cold as ice	starry-eyed
smooth as silk	swallow his words
a voice like a fog-horn	cool as a cucumber
the last one on earth to	tired to death

Slang is almost entirely figurative in cast. The sports page may say that "the Yanks trim the Indians"; "the locals shell" an opposing pitcher; "football embarks on another season"; "the Pirates marked time in the drive for the National League pennant"; and Turnesa and Abbott "landed in the finals of the national amateur golf championship, the latter completing the longest nonstop flight ever made by a freshman in the annual fairway frolic."

The student of prose composition should avoid both the wearisome triteness of the old commonplace comparisons listed above and the flashy, too easy novelty of slang, which often cheapens its figures of speech by overuse and careless abandon. A good figure of speech will have novelty and freshness; it will state or imply a comparison that nobody ever thought of before. Yet it will seem as inevitable as old expressions like "cold as ice" and "warm as toast"; and people who hear or read the new expression will wonder why they did not think of it first themselves. Since human experience is an infinitely changing thing, the opportunities for making new comparisons, and hence new figures of speech, are as great as they ever were. But the *methods* and *forms* of figures of speech do not change. They are the same as they were in the time of Homer. By reviewing those methods and forms and by analyzing the figures of speech invented by good writers, the student should learn to do with conscious purpose what he has been doing all his life without knowing or caring.

Simile and metaphor are the commonest and most important of all figures of speech.[1] In a simile the comparison is stated explicitly: "Mist lay thick in the valley, flooding the

---

[1] In modern literary criticism there is a tendency to make *metaphor* a very broad, inclusive term, applicable to figurative language and constructions in general.

ravines like a great river of greyish vapor pouring up from
an unknown source." Usually a simile is introduced by the
words *like, as, as if,* or *as when.* Explicit comparison is the
essential feature of the simile; length is of no importance.
A simile may be very brief: "He was gone like a shot"; or
it may be elaborated to great length, as in the following
passage:

> Many were the wit-combats betwixt him [Shakespeare]
> and Ben Jonson: which two I behold like a Spanish great
> galleon and an English man-of-war; master Jonson (like the
> former) was built far higher in learning; solid, but slow, in
> his performances. Shakespeare, with the English man-of-war,
> lesser in bulk, but lighter in sailing, could turn with all tides,
> tack about, and take advantage of all winds, by the quickness
> of his wit and invention.—THOMAS FULLER, *Worthies of
> England.*

There are two requirements for a simile. First, the comparison must be between objects of different classes, so that
the likeness, when pointed out, will be surprising and yet,
because of its appropriateness, will be interesting. Thus the
Psalmist says of the godly man: "He shall be like a tree
planted by the rivers of water." The comparison between
man and *tree* is a comparison between objects of different
classes, but we are struck with the felicity of the figure
because the goodness of the godly man is, imaginatively
speaking, like the vitality of a flourishing tree. But the
objects compared must not be of such different classes that
the unlikeness is greater than the likeness. It is incongruous
to compare an elephant to a lily, or virtue to an onion.

The second requirement for a simile is that, if extended,
it must be carried out with consistency. Any shifting of the
basis of comparison will result in a *mixed figure of speech:*
"Your contribution will seem like a drop in the bucket of
this great bundle of red tape."

Examine the following similes to see how well they meet
these requirements. Note in each instance what kinds of
objects are compared, how great the degree of likeness and
unlikeness is, and whether the comparison is fitting and
consistent.

> 1. Some people have no good of their dreams. Like fast
> feeders, they gulp them too grossly, to taste them curiously.
> We love to chew the cud of a foregone vision; to collect the

scattered rays of a brighter phantasm, or act over again, with firmer nerves, the sadder nocturnal tragedies; to drag into daylight a struggling and half-vanishing nightmare; to handle and examine the terrors, or the airy solaces.—CHARLES LAMB, *Popular Fallacies,* III.

2. He had a hairless, square, tallowy chin which trembled slightly as he talked, and his nose, nipped bright red by the sharp air, looked like a false nose of painted cardboard between the sallow cheeks.—JOSEPH CONRAD, *Under Western Eyes.*

3. Up scrambles the car, on all its four legs, like a black beetle straddling past the schoolhouse and the store down below, up the bare rock and over the changeless boulders, with a surge and a sickening lurch to the skybrim, where stands the rather foolish church.—D. H. LAWRENCE, *Mornings in Mexico.*

4. The earth immediately about the door was bare. It had a patina, as though from the soles of bare feet in generations, like old silver or the walls of Mexican houses which have been plastered by hand.—WILLIAM FAULKNER, *The Sound and the Fury.*

Metaphor is immediate, and often intense, in its comparison, where simile is deliberate and illustrative. In metaphor the comparison is implied. The likeness between the two objects is assumed to be so apparent that they are identified. The simile will say, *She looks like an angel;* the metaphor, *She is an angel.* The metaphor, far more often than the simile, will consist of a single word or a phrase:

The Dean *punctured* my excuses with a question.

The policeman gave me a *hot look.*

The conversation *back-fired* suddenly.

Prisoned among his test-tubes, he forgot the world.

The headlines *leaped noisily* before my eyes.

The language is full of metaphorical expressions that have lost their meaning as metaphors as the sense of imagined comparison has faded away. We have forgotten that *keystone* refers to the central supporting stone (hence the "key") of an arch, and the metaphorical content of many other words—such as *backbite, craftsman, henchman, broadside, blueblood, degrade, curfew, firebrand, fire-eater,* or even *postmaster*—has been lost in the same way.

At the same time, the making of new metaphors goes on continually. All good metaphors are rich in connotative quality. They make diction vivid and interesting, as no other single rhetorical device can; and, in addition, they enable the writer to say much in little space—they are compact and economical. For these reasons, metaphorical diction is the staple diction of poetry, of all imaginative writing whether poetry or prose, and of all those portions of the personal essay, the literary criticism, or the argument in which the effects of imaginative writing may seem desirable.

Metaphor is subject to the same requirements as simile: the likeness must be found between objects of different classes, and, if a metaphorical passage is prolonged, it must be consistent; it must not "mix the figures." But metaphor perhaps tolerates a greater degree of incongruity than simile, and hence produces often a more effective surprise, a greater imaginative leap.

The following passages contain metaphors of various kinds. Identify the metaphors and discuss their effectiveness.

1. This sort of discourse does well enough with the lamp-post for its second; to men who *may* reason calmly it is ridiculous.—EDMUND BURKE, *Letter to Captain Mercer.*

2. The new American showed his parentage proudly; he was the child of steam and the brother of the dynamo, and already, within less than thirty years, this mass of mixed humanities, brought together by steam, was squeezed and welded into approach to shape; a product of so much mechanical power, and bearing no distinctive marks but that of its pressure.—HENRY ADAMS, "Vis Nova," *The Education of Henry Adams.*

3. When it came night, the white waves paced to and fro in the moonlight, and the wind brought the sound of the great sea's voice to the men on shore, and they felt that they could then be interpreters.—STEPHEN CRANE, "The Open Boat."

4. I felt as if I were walking with Destiny, and that all my past life had been but a preparation for this hour and for this trial. Eleven years in the political wilderness had freed me from ordinary party antagonisms.—WINSTON CHURCHILL, *The Gathering Storm.*

5. No man is an island, entire of itself; every man is a piece of the continent, a part of the main; if a clod be washed away by the sea, Europe is the less, as well as if a promontory were, as well as if a manor of thy friend's or of thine own were; any man's death diminishes me, because I am involved in mankind; and therefore never send to know for whom the bell tolls; it tolls for thee.—JOHN DONNE, *Meditation XVII.*

6. A school is a hopper into which children are heaved while they are still young and tender; therein they are pressed into certain standard shapes and covered from head to heels with official rubber-stamps.—H. L. MENCKEN, "The Human Mind."

Hyperbole and *litotes* are figures of speech which obtain an effect by intensification rather than by comparison. Hyperbole is deliberate over-statement or fanciful exaggeration, such as appears in many common expressions: "a thousand thanks for your kindness"; "tired to death of such movies"; "sing his praises to the skies." The following passages contain examples of hyperbole.

1. He never got to be President, but he was the biggest man. There were thousands that trusted in him right next to God Almighty, and they told stories about him and all the things that belonged to him that were like the stories of patriarchs and such. They said, when he stood up to speak, stars and stripes came right out in the sky, and once he spoke against a river and made it sink into the ground.—STEPHEN VINCENT BENÉT, "The Devil and Daniel Webster."

2. He had a face of great acreage.—O. HENRY, "A Municipal Report."

3. There are no longer any citizens in the world; there are only subjects. They work day in and day out for their masters; they are bound to die for their masters at call.—H. L. MENCKEN, "From the Memoirs of a Subject of the United States," *Prejudices, 6th Series.*

Hyperbole, when overdone, inevitably makes the diction bombastic, ranting, or, when it is applied to trivial objects, absurd. Both hyperbole and litotes are common in humorous writing.

Litotes is deliberate understatement, which generally takes the form of negation of an opposite in order to make an indirect affirmative: "a citizen of no mean city" (that is, of a famous or great city); "not a bad tennis player" (that is, a good tennis player). The following passages illustrate the use of litotes.

> To fall out of a tree in early childhood is not a particularly reassuring experience. It does one's ego comparatively little good to get personally involved, all of a sudden, with the law of gravitation.

> He had been ransomed by the sweat of no vulgar agony, by the blood of no earthly sacrifice.—THOMAS BABINGTON MACAULAY, *Essay on Milton.*

Synecdoche and *metonymy* are forms of indirect statement in which a part of an object or some important association connected with the object is used to symbolize the object itself. In the strict sense, synecdoche is the use of some striking part to symbolize a whole: "The regiment mustered fifteen hundred rifles." (Men equipped with rifles.) "When the speaker finished, we knew we had been listening to a great mind." (A man of great mind.) Metonymy (from the Greek words *meta* and *onyma,* meaning "change of name") substitutes some quality or aspect of the object for the name of the object itself: "In 1940, after the fall of France, England had no defense left but her ancient valor." (That is, citizens who were capable of ancient valor.) Generrally, metonymy differs from synecdoche in emphasizing symbolically some large and significant aspect of an object. Some authorities, however, hold that metonymy is the more general term, and that synecdoche is really a form of metonymy. In modern writing, which is constantly alert to emphasize the concrete and particular, synecdoche is the more common figure. The following are modern examples of synecdoche.

> At midnight I went on deck, and to my mate's great surprise put the ship round on the other tack. His terrible whiskers flitted round me in silent criticism.—JOSEPH CONRAD, *The Secret Sharer.*

> So I walked past the eyes of which the whites were like peeled hard-boiled eggs and past the big sad mouth which didn't know what to say now and just hung open to show the pink, and walked on back to the library, and entered into the deep, shuttered shadow which depended from the high ceiling and the walls of books laid close like stone and which lay on

the deep-red Turkey carpet like a great dog asleep and scarcely breathing.—ROBERT PENN WARREN, *All the King's Men.*

Personification consists in endowing an inanimate object or abstraction with human qualities. It is not often used today in serious writing, but may appear in humorous or satirical prose. The following passage is an illustration:

> Corporations fill but one cage in a large menagerie. Let us glance at some of the other queer creatures created by personifying abstractions in America. Here in the center is a vast figure called the Nation—majestic and wrapped in the Flag. When it sternly raises its arm, we are ready to die for it. Close behind it rears a sinister shape, the Government. Following it is one even more sinister, Bureaucracy. Both are festooned with the writhing serpents of Red Tape. High in the heavens is the Constitution, a kind of chalice, like the Holy Grail, suffused with ethereal light. It must never be joggled. Below floats the Supreme Court, a black-robed priesthood tending the eternal fire. The Supreme Court must be addressed with respect or it will neglect the fire and the Constitution will go out. This is synonymous with the end of the world.—STUART CHASE, *The Tyranny of Words.*[1]

Special Effects in Prose

Alliteration, assonance, and *onomatopœia* are sometimes classified as figures of speech. More properly they have to do with what may be called the "texture" of prose, or with the division of rhetoric known as euphony: pleasant or agreeable sound. Alliteration, assonance, and onomatopœia all are "sound effects" and have a greater technical importance in poetry than in prose; but, if used with subtle discrimination, and not with glaring obviousness, they may at times be useful in prose. *Alliteration* is the repetition of the same sound at the beginnings of words in pairs or in series; or, more rarely, in a series of stressed syllables within a word.

> 1. *L*ength of days is in her *r*ight hand, and in her *l*eft hand *r*iches and honor. Her *w*ays are *w*ays of *p*leasantness, and all her *p*aths are *p*eace.—Proverbs 3: 16–17.

> 2. A *n*ick-tailed, bow-*n*ecked, long, *p*oor, *p*ale sorrel *h*orse, *h*alf dandy, *h*alf devil.—GEORGE W. HARRIS, *Sut Lovingood's Yarns.*

[1] From *The Tyranny of Words* by Stuart Chase. Reprinted by permission of the publishers, Harcourt, Brace & World, Inc.

3. The *dry* leaves in the *d*itch *s*immered and *b*oiled in the *s*ame *b*reezes, a tongue of air occasionally *f*erreting out a *f*ew, and *s*ending them spinning across the grass.—THOMAS HARDY, *Far from the Madding Crowd.*

Assonance is the repetition of the same vowel sound in syllables that have different consonants: *break, gape, became.* Assonance may be viewed as a form of inexact rhyme. True rhyme uses the principle of consonance; that is, the repetition of the same vowel sound in syllables that have the same terminal consonants but different initial consonants: *break, take, wake; resume, perfume.* Rhyme should be avoided in prose, and a writer should take good care to revise passages into which rhyme may have crept by accident. The following passages illustrate the use of assonance in prose:

The barking of the *house* dogs, from the *loud*est and hoarsest bark to the *faint*est *a*erial palpit*a*tion under the *eaves* of heaven.—HENRY D. THOREAU, *A Week on the Concord and Merrimack Rivers.*

In the *ov*er-mastering *lone*liness of that *mo*ment, his *whole* life seemed to him nothing but vanity.—ROBERT PENN WARREN, *Night Rider.*

Onomatopœia is the conformation of sound to sense, or, as the dictionary has it, the "formation of words in imitation of natural sounds"; the words *boom, hiss, quack, whiz* imitate the sounds of which they are the names. Onomatopœic effects are common in descriptive and narrative prose. They are likely to appear in any passage where a writer seeks to intensify his rendering of an action by suggesting the sounds that accompany the action.

He saw nothing and heard nothing but he could feel his heart pounding and then he heard the clack of stone on stone and the leaping, dropping clicks of a small rock falling.— ERNEST HEMINGWAY, *For Whom the Bell Tolls.*

The swish of water on the roofs became rhythmical. The tongues of flame sputtered and went out. A pile of hay burst into lurid flame, and was quenched. A crackle of rifle fire began from the opposite banks of the rivers. The bullets whizzed and moaned into the post. Here and there wood splintered. The tinkle of a smashed window light sounded ominous.—HERVEY ALLEN, *The Forest and the Fort.*

CHAPTER 7

DEFINITION AND ANALYSIS IN EXPOSITORY WRITING

THERE are two important kinds of thought in which sooner or later we find ourselves involved. In one we are called upon to state and explain the nature of things and ideas. We are expected to set forth their meaning, and no more than their meaning, and to do so without bothering overmuch about their merit or demerit, without, indeed, offering opinion or taking sides. It is of the highest importance that this kind of thinking be *disinterested*. It should not be colored with personal opinions but should be concentrated upon the task of clear, non-partisan, impersonal explanation.

In the other kind of thinking we are called upon to exercise judgment. We are asked not only to state and explain the nature of things and ideas but also to declare their degree of truth or falsity, or to distinguish between truth and falsity, and, if necessary, to take sides and argue a case. Writing which uses this kind of thought is argumentative and critical. It is *interested* to the extent that we constitute ourselves judges and uphold a definite position for or against something. But it should never be *interested* to the point of being unfair. The disinterested temper of the expository writing must carry over into the argumentative writing if the latter is to seem firmly grounded and not merely an effusion of personal opinion.

There are two ways in which we may think disinterestedly about a subject. First, we may seek to disengage it from all other ideas or things from which it is different but with which, despite differences, it may be confused, as, for example, we might distinguish chattel slavery from serfdom, which is like slavery in some respects. Such a distinction leads to, and in fact is, a process of definition; and after

217

definition comes a further, still more intensive, exploration of the idea or thing under discussion.

Second, we may follow an opposite, or perhaps a complementary procedure. We put the emphasis on the class in which the idea or thing belongs and make a study of likenesses and differences within that class. The exploration may then be either intensive or extensive. It builds up divisions and classifications. This is the process of analysis. It may be applied, for example, to the problem of farm tenancy. When we endeavor to establish and describe the degrees and types of farm tenancy and undertake to study the causes and results of farm tenancy, we are engaging in analysis.

Definition and analysis are the foundation of good thinking, and a study of definition and analysis is the best practical preparation for the complex problems of the research paper, the critical essay, and the article of opinion.

1. DEFINITION

In its formal and literal sense, definition is a process of limitation. Given a term to define—the amateur spirit, circle, osmosis, Platonism, high standard of living—we draw a boundary line. Within the line is everything to which the term can logically be applied. Outside the line is everything to which the term cannot be applied. A logical definition begins by placing the term to be defined in the class, or *genus,* to which it belongs, and then states the characteristics, or *differentia,* which distinguish it from other objects of the same class.

An axe may be defined by placing it in the class of tools. Next, it must be distinguished from other tools, such as chisels, saws, hammers, files. If we say, "An axe is a tool used for cutting," we have not distinguished the axe from the pocket-knife. If we say, "An axe is a tool used for cutting down trees," we have not distinguished the axe from the saw. We can come close to logical exactness only by elaborating the *differentia:* for example, "An axe is a tool which has a shape like a hammer and a cutting edge, single or double; and which is fitted with a helve so as to adapt it specially to cutting, chopping, hewing, or splitting wood."

The difficulties of composing a perfectly logical definition within the limits of a sentence are plainly very great. We feel at once the need of explaining some of the terms used in the definition, such as *helve* or *hewing*. We may feel impelled to note that while most axes are made of steel, they can be made, and were once made, of flint. We may also be mindful of a time when men fought with axes and used them for splitting heads.

Probably the only really satisfactory one-sentence definitions are those found in the exact sciences. The following are some examples:

TERM	GENUS	DIFFERENTIA
A rectangle	is a quadrilateral	which has four right angles.
A circle	is a plane figure	contained by one line everywhere equally distant from a point within called the center.
Osmosis	is the diffusion	which takes place between two miscible fluids separated by a permeable partition, as in an animal membrane.

—*Webster's Collegiate Dictionary*

The following one-sentence definitions, although not quite so exact as scientific definitions, are in the form of logical definitions and probably would meet the tests of logic:

> Language is the agent or medium by which men communicate their thoughts to one another.—STUART ROBERTSON, *The Development of Modern English.*

> Metaphor is the synthesis of several units of observation into one commanding image.—HERBERT READ, *English Prose Style.*

The one-sentence logical definition is in itself a useful exercise. It is a salutary check upon one's thinking simply to define the terms that have been floating familiarly, but often far too vaguely, in one's mind. We can also test the thinking of others through logical definition. Writers easily fall into the vice of not defining their terms or of defining them loosely; or sometimes they imply a definition without really making it. In such instances we may use the resources of logical definition and ask whether the idea as set forth will fit the *genus* and *differentia* given or implied.

In composing logical definitions, observe the following rules:

(1) In assigning the term to a class, or *genus,* choose the smallest class to which the term can conveniently be assigned. An axe can be assigned to the class of *things,* but not much is gained when that is done. *Instrument* is a further narrowing of class, but that class is still too large. *Tool* is probably as narrow a class as should be chosen.

(2) The definition, when stated, must include everything that properly belongs to the term defined. If you define a boat as a vessel equipped with sails or steam-engine and intended for traveling upon water, you have failed to allow for rowboats and boats moved by gasoline power or (as canal boats) by horse power.

(3) The definition must exclude everything that does not properly belong to the term defined. If you define a bicycle as a two-wheeled vehicle, you must take care to state your definition so as to exclude carts, racing sulkies, and other two-wheeled vehicles.

(4) The language of the definition should meet certain requirements. Use simple and familiar language as far as possible. Even if the definition is highly technical, try to simplify the language. The language must at any rate be of a less complex order than the term defined. Do not use a synonym or a derivative of the term that you are defining. A synonym or derivative is only a repetition of the original term in another form. You must not think in circles.

Formal and Informal Definition

Both formal and informal definition are extensions of logical definition. Each has, as its core of thought, a logical definition. This will generally stand at the beginning of the discussion, as a topic statement which is to be expanded. Each will make use of the devices common in all explanations: illustration; comparison and contrast; amplification through details; elimination; discussion of origin, cause, effect.

The difference between the two kinds of definition is in the manner of treatment. The formal definition continues, in extended form, the precise method of the strict logical definition. It is economical in language and chary of literary effects. Its sole aim is to set forth its explanation clearly and exactly. It does not attempt to awaken the reader's interest or to stir his feelings. Its concern is with facts, not with how the facts may affect the reader. Formal definition is used in textbooks, encyclopedias, and in all writing where the aim is serious instruction.

> A Spenserian stanza is a group of nine verse lines organized as a structural unit. The lines are rhymed in the following pattern: a-b-a-b-b-c-b-c-c. The first eight lines are written in iambic pentameter: that is, each line consists of five iambic feet. The last line, which is called an Alexandrine, after the French line which it resembles, has six feet. The stanza was invented by the Elizabethan poet, Edmund Spenser, who is thought by scholars to have adapted the stanza from the Italian *canzone*. Spenser used the stanza in his epic poem, *The Faerie Queene*. In his hands, the stanza has an easy melodic flow, largely because of the system of link rhymes used to join the first and second quatrains, and the second quatrain with the last line. Because of the fact that only three rhymes are used within nine lines, the stanza is difficult to write, but since Spenser's time it has been used by Byron, Shelley, Keats, and other English poets.

Informal definition aims to give the reader pleasure as well as instruction. It attempts to attract his interest as well as meet the demands of his intellectual curiosity. Although it must rest upon a logical basis, it is not written with the severity of purely logical definition. Its tone is easier and often is personal.

> A sound is a pressure disturbance; a sonic boom, like other explosive sounds, is the result of an abrupt change in pressure. An airplane in subsonic flight produces weak changes in pressure. Because these disturbances travel at the speed of sound, they move faster than the airplane and stay in front of it. In other words, the airplane sends a message ahead warning the air to get out of the way. The air does just that, parting in smooth, curving streamlines to pass around the airplane's surfaces. But a supersonic jet gets ahead of its own pressure disturbances. The air has no advance notice that the jet is coming; it must therefore get out of the way abruptly. A wave of suddenly compressed air—a shock wave —builds up and is thrown off to the sides like the wave that spreads from the bow of a speedboat. The streamlines develop sharp angles where they cross the shock wave.—HERBERT A. WILSON, JR., "Sonic Boom."[1]

[1] *Scientific American,* January, 1962, p. 36.

The student will be called upon to write informal definition more often than formal definition, but he should remember, even though he is writing in a relaxed manner, that the laws of logic cannot be relaxed. Pleasantry must not take the place of thought. He must strive for disinterestedness, he must look steadily at his subject, he must never offer opinions and prejudices as substitutes for genuine definition.

Methods of Definition

Choice of a method of definition will depend largely upon the nature of the term to be defined. If the term is an abstract concept, perhaps difficult to understand, it is advisable to use some familiar illustration. Thomas Henry Huxley, in defining the inductive method of reasoning, uses the illustrative method.

> Suppose you go into a fruiterer's shop, wanting an apple—you take up one, and, on biting it, you find it sour; you look at it, and see that it is hard and green. You take up another one, and that too is hard, green, and sour. The shopman offers you a third; but, before biting it, you examine it, and find that it is hard and green, and you immediately say that you will not have it, as it must be sour, like those you have already tried.
>
> Nothing can be more simple than that, you think; but if you will take the trouble to analyze and trace out into its logical elements what has been done by the mind, you will be greatly surprised. In the first place, you have performed the operation of Induction. You found that, in two experiences, hardness and greenness in apples went together with sourness. It was so in the first case, and it was confirmed by the second. True, it is a very small basis, but still it is enough to make an induction from; you generalize the facts, and you expect to find sourness in apples where you get hardness and greenness. You found upon that a general law, that all hard and green apples are sour; and that, so far as it goes, is a perfect induction. Well, having got your natural law in this way, when you are offered another apple which you find is hard and green, you say, "All hard and green apples are sour; this apple is hard and green, therefore this apple is sour." That train of reasoning is what logicians call a syllogism, and has all its various parts and terms—its major premise, its minor premise, and its conclusion.—THOMAS HENRY HUXLEY, "The Method of Scientific Investigation," *The Method of Discovery.*

Comparison and contrast will obviously be suggested when

you are dealing with a term which in certain respects is like another term, and yet has differences. If you are defining wit, you may say that wit is like humor, is indeed a kind of humor, in so far as it is a capacity for not taking the world too seriously, for provoking laughter, for making persons and things seem ridiculous. But, you go on to say, wit is narrower than humor; it is more intellectual and less emotional; it may show brilliance of mind but seldom generosity of mind.

In the following paragraphs this method of definition is followed out, but emphasis is placed on the contrast between wit and humor.

> I am quite positive that of the two, humor is the more comfortable and more livable quality. Humorous persons, if their gift is genuine and not a mere shine upon the surface, are always agreeable companions and they sit through the evening best. They have pleasant mouths turned up at the corners. To these corners the great Master of marionettes has fixed the strings, and he holds them in his nimblest fingers to twitch them at the slightest jar. But the mouth of a witty man is hard and sour until the moment of its discharge. Nor is the flash from a witty man always comforting, whereas a humorous man radiates a general pleasure and is like another candle in the room.
>
> I admire wit, but I have no real liking for it. It has been too often employed against me, whereas humor is always an ally. It never points an impertinent finger into my defects. Humorous persons do not sit like explosives on a fuse. They are safe and easy comrades. But a wit's tongue is as sharp as a donkey driver's stick. I may gallop the faster for its prodding, yet the touch behind is too persuasive for any comfort.
>
> Wit is a lean creature with sharp inquiring nose, whereas humor has a kindly eye and comfortable girth. Wit, if it be necessary, uses malice to score a point—like a cat it is quick to jump—but humor keeps the peace in an easy chair. Wit has a better voice in a solo, but humor comes into the chorus best. Wit is sharp as a stroke of lightning, whereas humor is diffuse like sunlight. Wit keeps the season's fashions and is precise in the phrases and judgments of the day, but humor is concerned with homely eternal things. Wit wears silk, but humor in homespun endures the wind. Wit sets a snare, whereas humor goes off whistling without a victim in its mind. Wit is sharper company at table, but humor serves best in mischance and in the rain. When it tumbles, wit is sour, but humor goes uncomplainingly without its dinner. Humor laughs at another's jest and holds its sides, while wit sits

wrapped in study for a lively answer. But it is a workaday world in which we live, where we get mud upon our boots and come weary to the twilight—it is a world that grieves and suffers from many wounds in these years of war: and therefore as I think of my acquaintances, it is those who are humorous in its best and truest meaning rather than those who are witty who give the most comfortable companionship.— CHARLES S. BROOKS, *Chimney-Pot Papers*.[1]

The method of comparison and contrast is especially useful when it becomes necessary to distinguish the real meaning of a term from erroneous meanings. Thus used, it often appears in combination with the method of negation: that is, defining a term by stating what it is not. When thus combining methods, be sure to follow your negative statements with a well-reasoned affirmative. The following definition employs the two methods in combination:

Now, we have warped the word "economy" in our English language into a meaning which it has no business whatever to bear. In our use of it, it constantly signifies merely sparing or saving; economy of money means saving money—economy of time, sparing time, and so on. But that is a wholly barbarous use of the word—barbarous in a double sense, for it is not English, and it is bad Greek; barbarous in a treble sense, for it is not English, it is bad Greek, and it is worse sense. Economy no more means saving money than it means spending money. It means, the administration of a house; its stewardship; spending or saving, that is, whether money or time, or anything else, to the best possible advantage. In the simplest and clearest definition of it, economy, whether public or private, means the wise management of labor; and it means this mainly in three senses: namely, first, *applying* your labor rationally; secondly, *preserving* its produce carefully; lastly, *distributing* its produce seasonably.

I say first, applying your labor rationally; that is so as to obtain the most precious things you can, and the most lasting things, by it: not growing oats in land where you can grow wheat, nor putting fine embroidery on a stuff that will not wear. Secondly, preserving its produce carefully: that is to say, laying up your wheat wisely in storehouses for the time of famine, and keeping your embroidery watchfully from the moth; and lastly, distributing its produce seasonably; that is to say, being able to carry your corn at once to the places

[1] From "On the Difference between Wit and Humor" in *Chimney-Pot Papers* by Charles S. Brooks. Reprinted by permission of Yale University Press.

where the people are hungry, and your embroideries to the places where they are gay; so fulfilling in all ways the Wise Man's description, whether of the queenly housewife or queenly nation: "She riseth while it is yet night, and giveth meat to her household, and a portion to her maidens. She maketh herself coverings of tapestry, her clothing is silk and purple. Strength and honor are in her clothing, and she shall rejoice in time to come."—JOHN RUSKIN, "A Joy Forever."

The nature of a thing can often best be stated if we define it with reference to its origin or cause, and a consideration of cause will frequently lead to a study of effects. Many words can be defined according to their etymology, and the etymological definition (which is a definition by origins) will suggest a definition made in terms of the social or historical context in which the word first arose. The word *tithe* means "a tenth part"; and the custom of "tithing," or the giving of a tenth part of one's income to the church, arose during the Middle Ages. A definition of *tithe* would therefore naturally be built up out of these circumstances. Such words as *dictator, romance, lyric, ballad, republic, philosophy,* may be defined in terms of their etymological origins and remote historical associations. *Guild socialism, feudalism, the plantation system, Puritanism,* may be defined in terms of the social and economical causes that produced them.

Certain cautions are necessary. The etymology and ancient history of such terms as *romance* and *plantation* are interesting and revealing but do not shed a great deal of light upon the meaning of those terms today. Definition in terms of origins and causes is most useful when the thing or idea defined represents an ancient rather than a present usage, or when the history of the term actually clarifies its present meaning. Some new words, like *racketeering* and *hitch-hiking,* can readily be defined in terms of the conditions that caused racketeering and hitch-hiking to spring up.

In the following series of definitions, Mark Sullivan shows how the growing materialism of America in the years from 1909 to 1914 brought about a change in the meaning of the words *sell, publicity,* and *propaganda.*

> The emphasis on material things in the new words that came into the language has unmistakable meaning. Equally significant is a new meaning that was acquired by an old word.
> The verb "sell" in "Webster's Dictionary" for 1929 was still

defined as to transfer goods for a price. But in universal practice, to an extent that the dictionary must soon record, "sell" and the process it connotes, had enlarged its domain. To the material world that had been the word's habitat since Christ said, "Go and sell that thou hast and give it to the poor," and in a direction different from Christ's admonition, "sell" had invaded the spiritual and intellectual world. To convert a man to a new conviction or point of view was to "sell him the idea." To impress yourself favorably upon another's attention was to "sell yourself to him." The missionary who a generation before would have described his function as to convert unbelievers, might now have described it, or certainly it would have been so described in the common idiom, as to "sell religion to the heathen." A political leader who in the time of Abraham Lincoln would "go to the people" on the question of abolition, or in 1896 would "educate the people" on the gold standard, would at a later date "sell the League of Nations to the country" or the World Court, or the high tariff or the low tariff. And he would have expressed success in the transaction by saying, in terms of conclusion of a deal, that he had "put it over."

If a commercial interest wished professional aid in "putting over" a new idea, it could find paid practitioners of the art, who called themselves "public relations counsel." That euphemism was successor to "publicity agent"—the substitution being achieved as a commercial adaptation of Talleyrand's epigram, "The chief business of statesmen is to find new terms for institutions which, under their old names, have become odious to the public."

The word "publicity" had passed through a transition similar to that of "sell," but in the reverse direction. As late as the time of Theodore Roosevelt, "publicity" meant letting in the light. Usually it was used in a sense of disinfection, of destroying something undesirable by making the people see and understand it—Woodrow Wilson thought that "pitiless publicity" would cure many of the ills of government. Almost at once "publicity" was annexed by the material world as part of its jargon for acquiring advantage in the world of the mind. "Publicity" was now mainly an art for causing the world to take notice of, and think well of, goods; or of policies which the makers of goods wished to make popular. The word was coming to be synonymous with advertising.

A word that suffered even greater demeaning was "propaganda." In the 1890's it meant, generically, any institution or faith propagating a doctrine; specifically, it was most familiar as the name for an institution in the Catholic Church, the College of Propaganda, founded at Rome in 1622 for the oversight of foreign missions and the education of missionary priests. During almost three hundred years the word retained that sacred connotation without taint from the secular world. During the Great War it came to be used for indoctrinating enemy troops or civilians behind the enemy line with ideas designed to undermine their morale—in plain English, to disseminate deceit artfully. Then it came to be used, with "reverse English," so to speak, as a word for disseminating a different sort of falsehood among the home peoples, with the design of stiffening their morale, or stirring them to greater exertions, or to more bitter hatred of the enemy. From its military use, the word during the 1920's passed into political use. Propaganda became, to each side of a controversy, a word used to describe ideas expressing the other's point of view. Soon the business world annexed it as in part a new synonym for "publicity."

—MARK SULLIVAN, "New Words," *Our Times,* Vol. IV.[1]

In the following selection Thomas B. Costain is preparing to re-examine historical evidence in the case of Richard III of England, who, he argues, was not actually the deformed and cruel villain that Shakespeare and early historians make him out to be. Instead, Costain holds that King Richard III is "the most notorious whipping boy in all history"; but first he defines the expression *whipping boy* in terms of its origin.

THE WHIPPING BOY[2]   *By Thomas B. Costain*

THE whipping boy was an unfortunate youngster appointed to receive any chastisement earned by the son of a royal family, on the theory that princes were above physical punishment. Sometimes the king might take it on himself to doff his crown, roll up his ermine sleeves, and lay the erring son across his august knee, but that was outside the rule. Under no circumstances should stinging whip or menial hand be laid on the hide of an heir apparent. It was supposed that the sight of someone else suffering for his wrongdoing would create a feeling of shame in the princely breast and be fully effective, therefore, as a good, sound, personal beating.

The custom was not universal. The whipping boy was not a fixture in all royal households as was, for instance, the court jester and the dancing master. But references creep into the pages of history often enough to indicate that it was frequently the practice. It is recorded that one Barnaby Fitzpatrick was on hand to receive the hidings which ordinarily would have been the lot of Edward VI. That delicate little fellow, who resembled his burly father, Henry VIII, in so few respects, could not have been guilty often of offenses against discipline.

There seems to have been in the main a more common-sense approach to the problem in England, a feeling that the lesson would be more effective if the beating were administered to the one who had earned it.

The classic example of vicarious punishment was placed on the scroll of time by a ceremony at Rome when permission was granted Henry of Navarre to abjure the Huguenot faith and become king of France. Pope Clement VIII had a stubborn streak in him which had to be overcome first. It may have been not too difficult for Henry to consider Paris worth a Mass, but he, Clement, was not convinced that Henry was worth receiving into the church unless he underwent a cleansing ceremony. In diplomatic circles in Rome there was a fear that the Navarene, being a prince of such high spirit, might regard this as humiliating and refuse to agree. Then someone, recalling the custom of the whipping boy, suggested that the whole matter could be carried off by proxy. It has been contended that Henry was kept in the dark until the ceremony had been performed.

Accordingly on September 16, 1595, the two ambassadors from France, D'Ossat and Du Perron, walked on foot to a church in Rome and knelt on the worn stone steps, in recognition of their unworthiness to go inside. Here they chanted together "Have Mercy, Lord" and on the closing line of each verse a switch was laid across their bent shoulders. It is said that the switch was a slender one and that orders had been given that the blows were to be light. Both of the ambassadors were later made cardinals, a more than fair exchange; a red hat for a somewhat less than pink shoulder blade.

EXERCISES AND SUGGESTIONS FOR THEMES

1. Give a brief definition, as strictly logical as you can make it, of *each* term in *one* of the following groups of terms:

    expedient, convenient, practical, politic
    skiff, shallop, canoe, kayak
    spark, coal, ember, brand
    battery (military), battery (electric), battery (in baseball),
        battery (as a legal term, connected with *assault*)
    civility, decorum, etiquette, protocol

2. Write a formal definition of one of the following terms: baccalaureate degree, civil marriage, in orbit (as in the sentence,

"The space capsule is in orbit"), chemistry major, Italian sonnet, archaism.

3. Write an informal definition of one of the following: a Broadway hit, margin of safety, dress rehearsal (for a wedding), dress rehearsal (for a play), panel discussion, traffic maintained, recreation center, country club, good sport, curfew.

4. Make a study of some term that has changed in meaning during recent times and write a definition in which you trace the successive changes. Use the general method employed by Mark Sullivan (page 225). Some suggestions:

missile	relief	jet
screen	stance	coach
retarded	purge	regiment
delinquent	satellite	security

5. Write an informal definition of one of the following pairs of terms. Use comparison and contrast.

conservative and liberal
prudence and timidity
a commercial advertisement and a "plug"
sophistication and maturity
frankness and vulgarity
elegance and fastidiousness

6. Does the use of figurative language in Brooks's definition of wit and humor (page 223) render the definition logically invalid? Test the validity of Brooks's definition by reducing it to a logical form in which you avoid figures of speech.

7. Use the "historical method" to define one of the following terms. That is, refer, as far as may be necessary, to remote origin, etymology, historical development.

college	deacon	fee simple
gerrymander	plain song	homestead
lynch	folio	viking
ostracize	lyric	university

2. ANALYSIS

Instead of defining the axe as a tool we may be called on to discuss axes in general and to declare how many kinds of axes there are and what they are like. Axes, we may discover, may be divided into groups according to the use to which they are put: wood-axes, meat-axes, battle-axes, and so on. Each of these three kinds of axes may, in turn, be subdivided, according to the material out of which they are made, or their weight, or the kind of handle or blade with which they are fitted. If we pursue the search to the end, until we have drawn up a scheme which includes all conceivable varieties of axes, we have then made an analysis of axes by the method of classification.

On the other hand, suppose that we consider the axe itself, any typical axe, and proceed to break it down into its essential parts. An axe consists of two main parts, a head and a handle (or helve). The head is wedge-shaped. Generally it has a blunt side which tapers to a cutting edge, but sometimes it has a cutting edge on each side. The head is pierced with a hole, oval in shape, in which the handle is fitted. It is generally made of tempered steel. The handle is made of wood. It is fitted to the head in such a way as to give a proper leverage for chopping and hewing. It is curved a little at the upper end and smoothed and narrowed so as to fit a chopper's hand. When we have carried such an examination of the parts of an axe down to the last essential detail, through all the necessary divisions and subdivisions, we have made an analysis of an axe by the method of partition.

Analysis is this process of logical division. The logical division of a group of individual objects or ideas is analysis by *classification*. The logical division of a single object or idea into its parts is analysis by *partition*. If the classification or partition is complete and consistent, so that all possible classes or all essential parts are identified and put in a systematic arrangement, then the analysis is a strict logical analysis.

Formal Analysis

Just as logical definition is the basis of formal definition, so logical analysis is the basis of formal analysis. Formal analysis must observe two absolutely rigid requirements: (1) the division must be complete; (2) the analysis must follow, throughout its process of division, one consistent principle of classification or partition.

Completeness of analysis means that everything must be accounted for. If you are classifying typewriters, your classification must include all kinds of typewriters without exception. Or if you are making an analysis, by partition, of an individual typewriter, you must not omit the tabular stop or the back-space key.

Consistency of principle is particularly important in analysis by classification. You must choose the principle of division which will bring the subject analyzed into the best logical order, and, having chosen that principle, you must adhere to it. You violate the rules of logical analysis and throw your explanation into confusion if, for example, you begin to classify trees according to the hardness of their wood and then, finding your analysis difficult to carry through, shift your base and classify trees according to leaf-shape, or bark, or size. Do not mix your principles of classification, but, if you find one basis of classification is not working out satisfactorily, discard it and try another.

The principles of logical analysis are the basis of scientific procedure. Scientific research is essentially analysis. Equipped with a working hypothesis, at which he has arrived by experiment and observation, the scientist proceeds to classify metals, or animals, or bacilli, or plants, according to their properties; and he is forever attempting, as he tests and examines object after object, to make his classification complete and correct. Or, making the process of division intensive rather than extensive, he analyzes a rock, a living tissue, a flower into its component parts.

Analysis is as pertinent and useful in other fields of knowledge as in physical science. Through analysis we bring our knowledge into order and make our reasoning powers work accurately. Analysis is most useful, of course, where knowledge must be treated on a large scale: as in the historian's study of social movements and their causes, the anthropologist's study of man's racial and cultural characteristics, the political scientist's examination of governmental institutions, the ecologist's consideration of the relationship between the forms of plant and animal life and the environment in which they are found. In its everyday practical use, it appears in the form of corporation reports, business surveys, architects' estimates, housing plans, government reports. For that matter, bookkeeping and accounting are systems of analysis. The weather report which you see in your newspaper is based upon careful scientific analysis.

The student will not have immediate occasion to engage in analysis on such a large scale, but there is hardly a task set for him in his college work which does not in some way or other call for an analytical procedure. His early work in chemistry is qualitative analysis. His mathematics problems, his course paper in history or political science, his study of poetry or drama or philosophy—all require him to make logical analysis the habit of his mind. Without this discipline his thinking will be weak and inaccurate, and his writing, on all serious subjects, will be shallow and impressionistic.

In the earlier stages of composition work, you were urged to look steadily at the subject, to break it up into its main divisions and subdivisions, to see the relation of the parts to the whole. You were required, perhaps, to make an outline showing such divisions. All this was analysis; and you should now see that the service performed by an outline is to compel you to analyze the subject. A good outline is an analytical scheme of a subject. That is its chief purpose and its only merit.

Practice in formal analysis is valuable in steadying your thinking and in making it accurate and conclusive. Like practice in definition, it is also valuable in so far as it demands scrupulous honesty and impersonality on the part of the writer. Your personal views of the subject which you are analyzing are of no immediate importance and must be set aside. Your object is to ascertain the truth and to set forth the truth, and your private opinions, strong and well-justified though they may be, must not be allowed to color your analysis. The biologist, when he studies the anatomy of the frog, is not permitted to have an opinion, good or bad, of frogs. The physician diagnosing his patient's ailments must not allow his good or bad opinion of his patient to interfere with his diagnosis. The purpose of formal analysis is to train you in this rational discipline and to make it carry over into your writing.

Certain principles should be emphasized.

First, *choose carefully the basis of division of the subject.* A two-part division (called a dichotomy) is the simplest, but the least trustworthy. Hats, for example, may be classified into hats that fit the wearer and hats that do not fit; but that classification does not tell us much about hats. A woman will probably classify hats according to the occasion for which the hat is to be worn, or according to the color schemes in the wardrobe she is planning. A man, possibly, will classify hats according to their durability. The hat-maker will have a series of classifications, according to material, price, and style. Whatever principle of division you choose, be sure that it can be carried through so as to reveal something important about hats—or whatever you are discussing.

Second, *follow through with utmost consistency your principle of division.* A division of literature into prose, poetry, history, detective stories, and propaganda would be absurd. The first two divisions would be made on the basis of literary form; the last three touch variously upon subject-matter and intention. In large-scale analyses, such as government reports or sociological surveys, the authors may use several different systems of classification, but they are then engaging in a series of analyses rather than in one analysis.

Third, *do not allow your divisions or subdivisions to overlap or repeat.* The main divisions must be mutually exclusive, and the subdivisions, taken within their groups, must be mutually exclusive.

Fourth, *be sure your analysis is complete.* In order to test for completeness, use the following check: the sum of the main divisions should equal the whole; and the sum of each group of subdivisions should equal the main division of which they are a part. Thus, the instruments of a symphony orchestra are divided into the following main groups: (1) strings; (2) brasses; (3) wood-winds; (4) percussion instruments. These four groups together add up to make the whole orchestra. And division 1, the strings, includes the following: violins, violas, cellos, bass viols, harp, piano (which add up to make the complete division).

Informal Analysis

Informal analysis, sometimes called "literary analysis," differs from formal analysis in being less complete in its division of the subject. It does not seek to give all the classes or parts into which the subject may be divided, but only those which are significant for purposes of discussion. It concentrates upon those aspects of the subject which will best illuminate and interpret it. Informal analysis often acknowledges its lack of completeness by some statement of the limits within which it works; but within those limits, generally, it proposes to be complete.

Since informal analysis is interpretative in its aims, it is naturally less severe in manner than formal analysis. It may therefore use freely the devices common in literary interpretation: figures of speech, analogies, a literary vocabulary. It may be humorous, sprightly, pugnacious. It may have an intimate, colloquial, personal flavor. But it must not take this direction at the expense of truth. It may not be logically complete, in the formal sense, but it must not be illogical. It must not do violence to facts; it cannot afford to be merely fanciful; it must not make a parade of jocularity, ill temper, prejudice, affectation.

A good newspaper editorial on the advisability of building a power dam at a certain site may be based upon the formal analysis of engineers and other experts, but from their reports it will select those points which are of the greatest interest and the greatest importance. The editorial is limited by requirements of space and by the necessity of appealing to a general, not an expert, audience; and it will therefore be an informal analysis. A geologist's report on the advisability of boring for oil must omit no relevant factor; it will be formal analysis. A student's paper on the oil industry, or on overproduction in the oil fields, or on the place of oil in American life will be an informal analysis because it will be selective, not exhaustive.

An informal analysis may indeed simplify its analysis so far as to concentrate upon one extremely significant aspect of the subject—one which is central in interpretation and can be taken as suggesting or symbolizing all that needs to be remembered for the specific purposes of the written piece. Thus Napoleon may be studied as the incarnation of the spirit of the French Revolution; or Tennyson as the voice of Victorian England; or the New Deal (in the phrase of one person who has discussed it) as "the first presidential administration with a social conscience." Such a centralization, of course, brings us once more to the old question of the guiding purpose in composition. The guiding purpose, for informal analysis, does exactly what the principle of division does for formal analysis: it gives the writer a standard for judging his own consistency and relative completeness in treating his subject.

Methods of Informal Analysis

The three methods most useful in informal analysis are (1) enumeration, (2) statement of root principle, and (3) statement of the problem. These three methods lead to the kind of division typical of analysis, but they make their approach in different ways.

1. Enumeration. Without trying to be all-inclusive as to facts, the writer sets forth, in order, the important points of his analysis. Thus the appeal of Sir Walter Scott's poetry to young people may be attributed to four qualities of that poetry: romantic subject-matter, simplicity of style, emphasis on action rather than motive, and Scott's own contagious enthusiasm. Scott's poetry may have other qualities that might be considered in another connection but that are excluded from this particular analysis. Similarly, William Henry Chamberlin, in discussing the advantages of the profit system, mentions two out of several possible advantages:

> Far from representing an expendable luxury or "surplus value," profits fulfill two indispensable functions in a free economy. The expectation of profit operates on millions of entrepreneurs, from the man who puts his savings into a restaurant, a service station, or a truck, to the big corporation that sets aside millions for a promising laboratory research project or an expedition into some rugged territory in search of some new source of needed mineral. This is the main force that sustains general employment at a high standard of living.
>
> Second in importance is the function of retained profits in making small businesses grow and big businesses become bigger. The link between profits and prosperity is clear and unbreakable. Only through profits can we hope to achieve that freedom of enterprise and risk-taking which will produce sustained economic growth of a magnitude to match that which has brought us the highest standard of living the world has ever known.—WILLIAM HENRY CHAMBERLIN, "Profits: Key to Prosperity."[1]

But an analysis by enumeration need not tabulate its points in one-two-three order. The following selection contains no numerical indicators, but nevertheless is an informal analysis by the enumerative method.

A COMPARISON OF THE GOVERNMENTS OF CANADA AND NEW ENGLAND[2]   *By Francis Parkman*

NOT INSTITUTIONS alone, but geographical position, climate, and many other conditions unite to form the educational influences that, acting through successive generations, shape the character of nations and communities.

[1] *The Freeman,* May, 1958.

[2] From *The Old Regime in Canada.*

It is easy to see the nature of education, past and present, which wrought on the Canadians and made them what they were. An ignorant population, sprung from a brave and active race, but trained to subjection and dependence through centuries of feudal and monarchical despotism, was planted in the wilderness by the hand of authority, and told to grow and flourish. Artificial stimulants were applied, but freedom was withheld. Perpetual intervention of government, regulations, restrictions, encouragements sometimes more mischievous than restrictions, a constant uncertainty what the authorities would do next, the fate of each man resting less with himself than with another, volition enfeebled, self-reliance paralyzed,—the condition, in short, of a child held always under the rule of a father, in the main well-meaning and kind, sometimes generous, sometimes neglectful, often capricious, and rarely very wise,—such were the influences under which Canada grew up. If she had prospered, it would have been sheer miracle. A man, to be a man, must feel that he holds his fate, in some good measure, in his own hands.

But this was not all. Against absolute authority there was a counter influence, rudely and wildly antagonistic. Canada was at the very portal of the great interior wilderness. The St. Lawrence and the Lakes were the highway to that domain of savage freedom; and thither the disfranchised, half-starved seignior, and the discouraged *habitant* who could find no market for his produce, naturally enough betook themselves. Their lesson of savagery was well learned, and for many a year a boundless license and a stiff-handed authority battled for the control of Canada. Nor, to the last, were church and state fairly masters of the field. The French rule was drawing towards its close when the intendant complained that though twenty-eight companies of regular troops were quartered in the colony, there were not soldiers enough to keep the people in order. One cannot but remember that in a neighboring colony, far more populous, perfect order prevailed, with no other guardians than a few constables chosen by the people themselves.

Whence arose this difference, and other differences equally striking, between the rival colonies? It is easy to ascribe them to a difference of political and religious institutions; but the explanation does not cover the ground. The institutions of New England were utterly inapplicable to the population of New France, and the attempt to apply them would have wrought nothing but mischief. There are no political panaceas, except in the imagination of political quacks. To each degree and each variety of public development there are corresponding institutions, best answering the public needs; and what is meat to one is poison to another. Freedom is for those who are fit for it. The rest will lose it, or turn it to corruption. Church and state were right in exercising authority over a people which had not learned the first rudiments of self-government. Their fault was not that they exercised authority, but that they exercised too much of it, and, instead of weaning the child to go alone, kept him in perpetual leading-strings, making him, if possible, more and more dependent, and less and less fit for freedom.

In the building up of colonies, England succeeded and France failed. The cause lies chiefly in the vast advantage drawn by England from the historical training of her people in habits of reflection, forecast, industry, and self-reliance,—a training which enabled them to adopt and maintain an invigorating system of self-rule, totally inapplicable to their rivals.

The New England colonists were far less fugitives from oppression than voluntary exiles seeking the realization of an idea. They were neither peasants nor soldiers, but a substantial Puritan yeomanry, led by Puritan gentlemen and divines in thorough sympathy with them. They were neither sent out by the king, governed by him, nor helped by him. They grew up in utter neglect, and continued neglect was the only boon they asked. Till their increasing strength roused the jealousy of the Crown, they were virtually independent; a republic, but by no means a democracy. They chose their governor and all their rulers from among themselves, made their own government and paid for it, supported their own clergy, defended themselves, and educated themselves. Under the hard and repellent surface of New England society lay the true foundations of a stable freedom,—conscience, reflection, faith, patience and public spirit. The cement of common interests, hopes, and duties compacted the whole people like a rock of conglomerate; while the people of New France remained in a state of political segregation, like a basket of pebbles held together by the enclosure that surrounds them.

It may be that the difference of historical antecedents would alone explain the difference of character between the rival colonies; but there are deeper causes, the influence of which went far to determine the antecedents themselves. The Germanic race, and especially the Anglo-Saxon branch of it, is peculiarly masculine, and, therefore, peculiarly fitted for self-government. It submits its action habitually to the guidance of reason, and has the judicial faculty of seeing both sides of a question. The French Celt is cast in a different mould. He sees the end distinctly, and reasons about it with an admirable clearness; but his own impulses and passions continually turn him away from it. Opposition excites him; he is impatient of delay, is impelled always to extremes, and does not readily sacrifice a present inclination to an ultimate good. He delights in abstractions and generalizations, cuts loose from unpleasing facts, and roams through an ocean of desires and theories.

While New England prospered and Canada did not prosper, the French system had at least one great advantage. It favored military efficiency. The Canadian population sprang in great part from soldiers, and was to the last systematically reinforced by disbanded soldiers. Its chief occupation was a continual training for the forest war; it had little or nothing to lose, and little to do but fight and range the woods. This was not all. The Canadian government was essentially military. At its head was a soldier nobleman, often an old and able commander, and those beneath him caught his spirit and emulated his example. In spite of its political nothingness, in spite of poverty and hardship, and in spite even of trade, the upper stratum of Canadian society was animated by the pride and fire of that gallant *noblesse* which held war as its only worthy calling, and prized honor more than life. As for the *habitant,* the forest, lake, and river were his true school; and here, at least, he was an apt scholar. A skilful woodsman, a bold and adroit canoe-man, a willing fighter in time of need, often serving without pay, and receiving from government only his provisions and his canoe, he was more than ready at any time for any hardy enterprise; and in the forest warfare of skirmish and surprise there were few to match him. An absolute government used him at will, and experienced leaders guided his rugged valor to the best account.

The New England man was precisely the material with which Cromwell formed his invincible "Ironsides"; but he had very little forest experience. His geographical position cut him off completely from the great wilderness of the interior. The sea was his field of action. Without the aid of government, and in spite of its restrictions, he built up a prosperous commerce, and enriched himself by distant fisheries, neglected by the rivals before whose doors they lay. He knew every ocean from Greenland to Cape Horn, and the whales of the north and of the south had no more dangerous foe. But he was too busy to fight without good cause, and when he turned his hand to soldiering it was only to meet some pressing need of the hour. The New England troops in the early wars were bands of raw fishermen and farmers, led by civilians decorated with military titles, and subject to the slow and uncertain action of legislative bodies. The officers had not learned to command, nor the men to obey. The remarkable exploit of the capture of Louisburg, the strongest fortress in America, was the result of mere audacity and hardihood, backed by the rarest good luck.

2. Statement of Root Principle.   In an analysis organized upon a statement of root principle, the writer attempts, before making any division, to express the meaning of his subject as a whole. He sums it up in a word. He concentrates his gaze upon the one feature of his subject that is the key to all the rest. In short, he gets at the root of the matter. After doing this, he may give the evidence that supports his centralized analysis, or, using his root principle as an aid to division, he proceeds by the method of partition or classification.

In "The Road of Rails," Robert Selph Henry reduces the principle of the railroad to one thing: "the track." He then proceeds, mainly by the method of partition, to apply this root principle.

THE ROAD OF RAILS[1]   *By Robert Selph Henry*

THE ESSENTIAL and unique thing about a railroad is the track. There were tracks long before there were locomotive steam engines, or even stationary steam engines, and no matter what may be the locomotive power of the future, still there will be tracks.

Rails joined together in track are, in effect, continuous girders of great strength and carrying capacity. Upon these girders, these two narrow strips of steel out of the whole width of the track structure, there is concentrated the load. By them, the load is distributed through the broader area of the timber ties and the still greater area of the ballast to the earth grade or the supporting structure beneath. That is the first job of track—to support the load.

Its second job is to furnish a smooth surface upon which a minimum of engine horsepower can do a maximum of transportation work. To drive a transport plane through the air requires, speaking in rough and general averages, about 100 engine horsepower for each ton of weight. Passenger automobiles have some sixty horsepower per ton, ordinarily, but passenger trains on rails are pulled at fast schedules by three or four horsepower per ton.

Speaking again in rough and general figures, the freight truck operating on the highway requires about fifteen horsepower per ton of weight. Maintaining similar speeds under ordinary operating conditions as to grades and curves, a freight train on tracks requires less than two horsepower per ton.

Even on the water the same sort of comparison as to expenditure of mechanical energy in doing transportation work holds good. Loads are moved in ships and barges with ease because the surface on which they are moved, water, is level. On level railroad track, the same amount of power moves the same loads at greater speed, just as a man can run faster and with less effort than he can swim.

Other surfaces can be, and are, built to perform the first two functions of track—furnishing a surface that is both smooth and supporting for the rolling wheel—but in its third job, guiding the wheels for whole trains of cars "tracking" behind an engine at speed, the road of rails is unique among all constructions on the surface of the earth.

3. Statement of a Problem.
The informal analysis which is based upon the statement of a problem—with its subsequent

[1] From *This Fascinating Railroad Business* by Robert Selph Henry, copyright © 1942, 1943, and 1946, used by special permission of the publishers, the Bobbs-Merrill Company, Inc.

solution worked out—is probably one of the most difficult of logical exercises, and it is also one of the most important of all the applications of logic. The statement of a problem calls for analysis because it requires the thinker or writer to separate relevant matters from irrelevant matters, important things from unimportant things, significant factors from insignificant or misleading factors. We may lay it down as an axiom, almost, that most of the problems put before us go unsolved, or are solved badly, because the nature of the problems themselves is not clearly perceived and is even less often clearly stated.

A judge's charge to a jury is a statement of the problem before the jury, considered in the light of the law. An architect who is employed to design a building of a certain type, meeting certain specifications as to cost and size, and located on a certain terrain, must state his problem and see it clearly before he can give an estimate of what the building will cost or draw the plans or sign a contract. A student who is asked to write a paper on the nature of the tragedy in Shakespeare's *Hamlet* must first ask himself what is the nature of the tragic conflict that involves the leading character—he must state the problem of the play, which is also the problem of Hamlet's character.

In the selection which follows, the author states the problem of the invasion of metropolitan centers into land space formerly occupied by a largely self-sustaining rural population or left in a wild or semi-wild state as a "forest reserve." In his lengthy article—of which "The Urban Sprawl" is but a small excerpt—Mr. Sears is concerned with the abuse of technology as applied to land-use. Earlier, he says: "If, as I believe, [technology] should be our servant and not our master, its advancement should be in the light of all scientific knowledge and not merely those facets which are of immediate use."

THE URBAN SPRAWL[1]   *By Paul B. Sears*

THE most obvious and acute pressure upon space is in our great cities and surrounding metropolitan areas, whose existence and expansion depend upon technology. They and the associated industries and highways that connect them are absorbing agricultural

[1] From "The Inexorable Problem of Space," by Paul B. Sears. *Science,* Vol. 127 (January 3, 1958), pp. 13–14. Reprinted by permission of *Science* and the author.

land in the United States at the rate of some million acres a year. This means fewer orange and walnut groves in California, dairy farms in Georgia, truck and tobacco land in Connecticut, and less of the proverbially fertile valley land along the Miami in Ohio. All of these instances I have seen, as I have seen 15,000-acre tracts of the best farm land condemned for military installations when less productive sites could have been chosen.

There are some 500 major cities of over 25,000 population in the United States. Assuming that they could be evenly distributed, and neglecting smaller towns and cities, each would be in the center of a rectangle roughly 80 miles square. I have seen a fair number of them in recent years and recall very few that were not sprawling out into suburbs with little heed to open space, recreation, agriculture, beauty, or even the protection of future values. An exception, as a taxi driver profanely informed me, was not growing because the local university had everything sewed up!

And between cities, across the land, highway departments are busily freezing the nation into a permanent interurban geometry. Often, in fact if not in theory, they are responsible to no one but themselves and their Euclidean rule that the shortest distance between points is a straight line. Only through leaders who will devise and citizens who will support better use of urban and highway space can growing blight be checked. Professional planners, who, by the way, are seldom summoned until it is too late for them to be of real use, now frankly regard the entire strip from Washington to Boston as one great metropolitan area. Any lingering doubts on this score should fade at the sight of a new throughway blasting its course among rocks and homes, across land and water.

At Washington, southern end of the megalopolitan strip, fateful decisions regarding the future allocation of American space are made. One of the cabinet members who has much to do with such decisions told a recent visitor, "For one individual who, like yourself, comes here to protest the exploitation of wilderness areas, parks, and other public lands, there are a dozen who come here to press the opposing view." No matter what the sympathies of such a public official, these are elementary facts of political life with which he must reckon.

There are, moreover, numerous agencies of government, not always in close harmony, that are charged to administer space and its resources. What happens is the resultant of many forces, including the pressure put upon Congress and the advice it receives from appropriate bureaus.

The late Colonel Greeley used to relate how much of our national forest space was reserved. Congress, alarmed at the rate at which Theodore Roosevelt was setting aside forest reserves, lowered the boom on him, but the law could not become effective until he signed it. During the few weeks of grace Roosevelt, Pinchot, and Greeley spent evenings sprawled on a White House floor with maps, for all the world like kids with a comic supplement, marking out forests while the President still had power to do so.

EXERCISES IN FORMAL AND INFORMAL ANALYSIS

1. Make a classification in skeleton form of any one of the following or of a similar group.
   a. Types of land found within the Great Plains region, the New England region, or other region of Canada or the United States
   b. Arrowheads used by North American Indians
   c. Show horses
   d. Customers in a supermarket
   e. Motorized boats for inland waterways
   f. Winter (or summer) resorts
   g. Types of immigration to America prior to (use a limiting date)

2. Write a formal or informal analysis in which you make use of the classification that you worked out for Exercise 1.

3. Write an analysis, by partition, of one of the following.
   a. A particular sonata, symphony, or other musical composition
   b. The attitude of the "average student" toward campus politics
   c. A modern service station
   d. The vote of a certain state or municipality in a particular election
   e. The attitude of a suburban homeowner in some particular election
   f. The role of the automobile in modern college life

4. What would be the most reasonable and useful basis for classifying one of the following groups?
   a. Week-end guests
   b. Popular song hits
   c. Motives for entering college
   d. Hunting dogs
   e. Modern magazines
   f. Types of guitar playing
   g. Folk ballads
   h. Tennis players
   i. Contemporary superstitions
   j. Informal clothing

After classifying one of the above groups (or some other group that may suggest itself), use your principle of classification to establish, in a logical way, the main divisions and subdivisions of a complete analytical scheme. Then write a theme for which this study is a guide.

5. Write a theme in which you use "root principle" as the basis of your discussion, after the fashion of Robert S. Henry's "The Road of Rails" (page 239).

6. Write a theme in which you state and discuss a problem related in some definite way to the problem discussed by Paul Sears in "The Urban Sprawl" (page 240).

7. Write a theme in which you define and analyze an abstract term after the method used by D. W. Brogan in the following paragraph:

> Culture can have two meanings. There is the meaning given to the world by the anthropologist, in which all social habits, techniques, religious practices, marriage customs, in fact everything—including the kitchen sink—is examined to throw light on how a particular society lives and moves, or just exists. Then there is "culture" in a narrower sense, in which we are concerned not with material techniques, not with the social organization that holds society together, but with the ideas, the aesthetic experiences and achievements, and the philosophical or religious ideas that affect and are affected by the aesthetic experiences and achievements of a given society. A special variant of the last sense of "culture" is the narrow identification of the word with the fine arts and the implicit relegation of the fine arts to the margin of life, to what is done in leisure or for leisure. —D. W. BROGAN, "The Character of American Culture," *America in the Modern World.*

CHAPTER 8

THE RESEARCH PAPER

THE research paper—sometimes called the investigative paper, the course paper, or the term paper—is a long expository essay or article which presents the results of systematic inquiry into facts. The term "research paper" may seem a little ambitious, since genuine research implies an original contribution to human knowledge in science or scholarship, and the average college student may feel himself far from ready to make such a contribution. Nevertheless, the tasks assigned in his various courses require from the very beginning an acquaintance with the *methods* of research. His instructors are certain to ask him to investigate a subject in the library and to write a paper on what he finds out.

This is research, or at least quasi-research, on a modest scale. Although a young writer's production may not at the moment seem to have much influence on the course of human events, the training in methods given by such assignments looks ultimately toward precisely that end. The methods of the research paper are the methods generally used in most of his assigned course papers, and later, if he undertakes graduate studies, the same methods will be in order.

Inevitably, the research paper employs the principles that have been emphasized throughout this book as of prime importance in expository writing. It must be clear, orderly, accurate, and substantial. The research paper is a real test of a student's power to gather material and organize it coherently. It is also a trial of mettle. Can he tackle a fairly complex subject, find out what the facts are, separate the relevant facts from the irrelevant facts, the up-to-date from the out-of-date, the true from the false, and then present his findings intelligently and effectively? If he can, then he may

244

have the satisfaction of knowing that his study of composition is really bearing fruit.

Because of the special character of the research paper, strong emphasis must be put on the words *accurate* and *substantial*. The research paper is an answer to two questions: (1) What are the facts? (2) What do the facts mean? These two questions, when properly understood, fuse into one question: What is the truth? For facts, rightly interpreted, are the truth. When not interpreted, they are merely facts, and may not even make sense. When badly interpreted, they are distortions of fact and may readily become falsehood. The writer of the research paper must therefore come to his work in an impartial frame of mind. He seeks only the truth. In the interest of truth he puts aside his own preconceptions and opinions. Until his investigation is complete, he has no right to an opinion and should forbear to make an interpretation. In short, he must be objective, non-partisan. The research paper demands, first, diligent and careful inquiry into the facts; second, accurate recording and reporting of the facts; third, winnowing of the important from the unimportant, the relevant from the irrelevant, until the orderly assemblage of selected material will permit a substantial discussion, reasonably complete within its limits; fourth, honesty and clarity in interpretation of the facts, with truth as the end in view.

CHOICE OF A SUBJECT

In choosing a subject for investigation, the student will do well to recall his earlier instruction (Chapter 2) on the advisability of electing a limited aspect of a subject rather than a vague field of discussion. He should focus the composition on a central idea and thereby narrow its scope, bring it under control, and achieve unity. For a research paper it would be unwise to attempt an investigation of feudalism; that subject is too large and unwieldly. But it would be entirely feasible and interesting to develop a paper entitled "Military Service As a Feudal Obligation." Similarly, it would be better to write on "Adaptation of the Plains Indians to Their Environment" than on "The Influence of the Great Plains Environment on the Western Movement of Population." "The Outlaw As Hero in Cowboy Ballads" is a far better subject than either "Cowboy Ballads" or "The Hero As Outlaw."

Below are listed certain "fields of investigation" in which

you may develop research paper projects by the process of limitation indicated above. The "fields" listed should suggest subjects into which, with the guidance of your instructor, you may make some preliminary inquiry before selecting your specific topic.

1. Literary and other artistic forms, their origin, growth, and character: epic, ballad, tall tale, sonata, madrigal, oratorio, spirituals, "schools" of painting, origins of specific art works (operas, poems, novels).

2. The origins of superstitions, customs, festivals, folkways.

3. Famous scientific discoveries or inventions.

4. Local history: the development of a town, village, city, county; or important events in local history.

5. What really happened? A study of some historical event: a decisive battle, a famous controversy, a notable trial, a shipwreck, a political victory or defeat, an important commerical enterprise, a feat of engineering.

6. Background studies of modern problems, such as labor relations, race relations, city slums, disease control, transportation, flood control. Do not enter into a partisan discussion. That is the province of argument. Instead, examine the conditions out of which social problems arise.

7. Traditions of place, region, or profession.

8. Studies in ancient or medieval history—such as the nature of the Greek city-state or the Holy Roman Empire.

9. Studies in the influence of climate or geography—such as the influence of the Japan Current on the Northwest, or of the Canadian winter on wheat farming.

10. The careers of important statesmen, kings, generals, artists, authors, religious leaders.

One important caution is appropriate here. In investigating matters of immediate contemporary interest, such as those listed under 6, you must realize that much of the material available to you is highly controversial and propagandistic. This may be true even when the material purports to be "scientific" and therefore "objective." The reliability of your "authorities" should be given careful consideration if you attempt such a topic.

In contrast, a subject from a noncontemporary field offers

the advantages of historical perspective and repeated research by competent investigators who will have no partisan interest. We know more about the Minoan culture of ancient Crete than was known even in the thoroughly scientific nineteenth century, more about Edgar Allan Poe and Mark Twain than the scholars of their times could know. A writer investigating such fields may shed new light on an old subject and will run little risk of getting mixed up with political or social crusades.

THE INVESTIGATION

Since the success of the research paper depends primarily upon the authenticity of the information it conveys, special attention must be given to the procedure by which such information is obtained.

When information is obtained at first hand, it is said to come from *primary sources*. It can be obtained at first hand if the subject permits direct investigation by the writer himself, and if he is skillful and experienced enough to do a good job of investigating.

A paper dealing with the study habits of college students could be prepared by anyone with proper facilities for observing students actually at work and with patience and intelligence enough to organize his findings. He could find out—by visiting, by getting answers to questionnaires, by personal interviews—what time of day or night they study; whether they work with the radio on or the radio off; whether they smoke, chew gum, eat candy, or gnaw pencils while engaged with their books; what positions they assume—sitting, prone, half-reclining, upright; whether they bite their lips, twirl their fingers, scratch their heads, drum on the table, whistle, sing, hum, or nervously pace the room at intervals.

Enough of such facts, when compiled and classified, would represent genuine research into first-hand material and might lead to interesting and valuable conclusions. Psychologists and sociologists, when they investigate human habits, go thus to the human subject itself, using, of course, the technique they have evolved to guide and check their investigations. The historian goes to his manuscripts, first-hand accounts, statistics—these are his primary sources. The geologist goes to his rocks, his fossils, his earth. The Shakespeare scholar goes to Elizabethan prompt books, the Quartos, the

First Folio. The chemist, physicist, and biologist go to the materials in their laboratories. Genuine research is based upon such primary sources.

During his college course a student may at times use the census reports or other compilations of statistical information. Or he may consult maps, original manuscripts, or facsimiles of manuscripts. Or, if he is making a literary study, he may go to the established text of Shakespeare or the letters and journals of Thoreau, as distinguished from the voluminous and sometimes misleading commentaries upon such authors. In all such instances he will be using primary sources.

But he will probably have more occasion to use *secondary sources*. The secondary sources are the literature of his chosen subject as set forth by accepted authorities. If he is writing about the theory of evolution, he will not be able to make first-hand scientific studies, as Darwin did; but he can read Darwin's *Origin of Species* and other books which explain and criticize Darwin's theories. These are his proper secondary sources. If his subject is "New Types of Motor Highways," he cannot make his study as a highway engineer would do it, but he can read what highway engineers have to say and what others who have studied that subject have written.

For his information, then, he must go to the library. The library is his laboratory, his testing-ground, his substitute for a field trip. If he is to go about his investigation properly, he must know how to find the information that the library has to offer and how to use it when he finds it. He must know what arrangements the modern library has made to serve him in his quest for information. And he must have an efficient and intelligent method of investigation. The following is the normal course of investigation for a research paper:

(1) Consult a general work of reference, such as a standard encyclopedia, and read the article or articles that bear on the subject. If the subject is not discussed in a separate article, search the index of the encyclopedia for references and follow up these references. The encyclopedia will give a condensed and authoritative survey of the subject and prepare you for later intensive study. At the end of an encyclopedia article there will generally be a list of important books

and articles that discuss the subject fully. Note these titles for future use.

For a historical subject it is a good plan to do preliminary reading in a standard history. For literary subjects consult the Cambridge histories of English and American literature or similar works. For biographical studies, consult the *Dictionary of National Biography* (English) and the *Dictionary of American Biography*. (A selected list of reference books is given on pages 250–253.)

(2) After you have acquired a background of general information, prepare a *working bibliography* of your subject. Make a tentative list of books and articles that deal with your subject. (See page 254 for a description of the method to be followed in preparing this list.) If you have secured a brief bibliography from an encyclopedia article, begin with that as your basis. Consult the card catalogue of the library (looking under subject-headings) to find other items and to see what titles are available in the library (see page 253). Consult the *Reader's Guide to Periodical Literature* for lists of articles in magazines. Early in your investigation it is advisable to scan the tables of contents and even the texts of some of the more promising books and articles, in order to see whether they offer what you want. Look also for the special bibliographies that generally appear in authoritative works. If your subject, for example, is "Cotton Culture," you will find that Rupert Vance's *Human Factors in Cotton Culture* contains an extensive bibliography of books and articles dealing with the subject. Such bibliographies will save time for you and give you authoritative guidance.

(3) When you have located your material and prepared a working bibliography, narrow your search to those books and articles which seem pertinent and up-to-date. You are now ready to begin your research proper.

(4) Read, and take notes on your reading. Keep a record, with complete bibliographical data, of all your reference sources. Use the form provided in *The MLA Style Sheet* (or other recommended manuals) and exemplified in this textbook.

(5) Organize your material and write your paper.

USE OF THE LIBRARY

Since your investigation depends in large measure upon your ability to use the library properly, you should lose no opportunity to familiarize yourself with its arrangements. Take this book to the library with you and use it as a guide. You cannot memorize the information given in the pages following, but by carrying out instructions as set forth here you will gradually become familiar with the ordinary sources of information and the right procedure in consulting them.

General Reference Books

Every library has a group of general reference books, called a *reference collection*. These books cannot be taken from the library, but they are generally placed upon open shelves in the reference room, where they can be easily consulted. Those listed below are some of the most important. They constitute, however, but a small part of the average reference collection.

Encyclopedias

Encyclopædia Britannica
The New International Encyclopedia. 1922–1930. (See Supplements for later years.)
Encyclopedia Americana

Dictionaries

1. Unabridged:
New English Dictionary on Historical Principles (known as the *Oxford English Dictionary*)
Webster's New International Dictionary of the English Language. Second Edition.[1]

Funk and Wagnalls New Standard Dictionary
New Century Dictionary
Craigie and Hulbert, *Dictionary of American English*

---

[1] The Third Edition of this dictionary is useful for definitions of new scientific terms and for certain other extensions of our vocabulary. Published in 1961, it reflects the influence of linguistics on lexicography.

2. Special Dictionaries:
Bergen and Cornelia Evans, *A Dictionary of Contemporary American Usage*
Roget's International Thesaurus
Webster's Dictionary of Synonyms

Biographical Dictionaries and Reference Books

Chambers's Biographical Dictionary
Dictionary of National Biography (English)
Dictionary of American Biography
Webster's Biographical Dictionary
Who's Who (English)
Who's Who in America

Yearbooks

New International Yearbook
Statesman's Yearbook
World Almanac

Reference Works Covering Special Fields

AGRICULTURE
    Bailey's Cyclopedia of American Agriculture
    U. S. Department of Agriculture Yearbook

BUSINESS AND ECONOMICS
    Clark, *Dictionary of Business and Finance*
    Munn, *Encyclopedia of Banking and Finance*

CLASSICS (Greek and Roman)
    Hadas, *Ancilla to Classical Reading*
    Harper's Dictionary of Classical Literature and Antiquities
    Oxford Classical Dictionary
    The Loeb Translations of Latin and Greek Classics

FINE ARTS
    American Art Annual
    Grove's Dictionary of Music and Musicians

Hamlin, *Architecture Through the Ages*
International Cyclopedia of Music and Musicians
Sturgis' Dictionary of Architecture and Building

HISTORY

Cambridge Histories (Ancient, Medieval, Modern)
Dictionary of American History
Yale Chronicle Series (American)

LITERATURE (English and American)

Cambridge History of English Literature
Cambridge History of American Literature
Hubbell, *The South in American Literature*
Oxford Companion to English Literature
Spiller *et al.*, *Literary History of the United States*
Twentieth Century Authors

POLITICAL AND SOCIAL SCIENCE

Encyclopedia of the Social Sciences
Encyclopedia of Modern World Politics
McLaughlin and Hart, *Cyclopedia of American Government*
Dictionary of Sociology

RELIGION

Catholic Encyclopedia
Strong, *Exhaustive Concordance of the Bible*
Hastings, *Encyclopedia of Religion and Ethics*
Universal Jewish Encyclopedia

SCIENCE

American Men of Science
Encyclopedia of Science and Technology

Atlases and Gazetteers

Rand McNally Commercial Atlas
Lippincott's Gazetteer
Shepherd's Historical Atlas

Indexes to Periodicals

Reader's Guide to Periodical Literature

Indexes the leading nontechnical periodicals from 1900 to the present. Note, however, that recently established magazines, some quarterlies, and lesser monthlies may not be indexed in the *Reader's Guide*.

Look up articles under subject-headings, unless you know the author's name. Subject-headings are standard classifications under which articles appearing in a current year are grouped: architecture, automobiles, housing, sports, and the like. Articles on prominent persons will be listed under the names of those persons.

Familiarize yourself with the list of abbreviations used in the *Reader's Guide*. Otherwise its system of references will be unintelligible.

Poole's Index

Indexes American and English periodicals from 1802 to 1907.

International Index: A Guide to Periodical Literature

Technical, scientific, and foreign periodicals—special emphasis on social sciences and the humanities since 1955.

New York Times Index

Useful not only as an index to the New York *Times*, but also as a guide to events, which, after the date has been determined from the *Times* index, can then be studied in other newspaper files.

(1) Applied Science and Technology Index (2) Business Index

Engineering, business, trade—formerly published singly as *Industrial Arts Index*.

Public Affairs Information Service Bulletin

A guide to government documents and to other information about public affairs and business.

Use of the Card Catalogue

The library card catalogue is a complete list, printed on cards, and arranged alphabetically, of all the books in the library. Most of the books are catalogued by author and title. Many are also catalogued by subject.

If you have already made up a working bibliography, your business with the card catalogue is simple and brief. Look up the titles of the books you want; make note of their call numbers, authors, and titles on the call slips furnished by the library; and secure at the library desk those books that are available.

If you wish to use the card catalogue to extend your bibliography, begin your search by looking for your subject. If your subject is "Mayan Pyramids," look for *Mayan*. In all likelihood some titles beginning with that word will be listed. Perhaps there will be a "subject card," and, after that card, a number of titles dealing with Mayan culture. But do not stop there. The Mayan pyramid and the culture that produced it will be discussed in books on American archæology and in books dealing with Mexico and Central America. Continue your search, then, under the headings: *Archæology, Mexico, Central America*. Use also the system of cross-reference (the "see cards") provided in the catalogue. If you do not find what you want, consult other subject headings.

The cards of the card catalogue have other uses. Each card contains the following information: (1) the call number, which shows the classification of the book and the place where the book is "shelved" in the stacks of the library; (2) the author's name; (3) the title and edition; (4) the place of publication, publisher, and date; (5) other technical information, such as the number of pages and the format; and (6) sometimes a condensed description of the contents of the book.

The *date of publication* may be of considerable importance to you. If you are looking up *Modern Housing*, you may be sure that books published from 1920 to 1962, say, are of special importance to you. The *condensed description* of the contents will help you by indicating whether or not a particular book touches your subject.

THE WORKING BIBLIOGRAPHY

As you make your investigation of available material, list every book and article that is pertinent to your subject. This list is your working bibliography. It is best to make the list on cards. Use a separate card for each individual item. (Do not take notes on bibliography cards.)

Every bibliography card should contain the following information—which is put down in the same form as that used in the final bibliography for the paper.

For a Book

1. Author's name. Put the last name first, and use the full name as printed on the title-page of the book. Record the editor's name in the same way if there is an editor rather than an author.
2. Title of the book—as given on the title-page. Volume number, if needed.
3. Place of publication, publisher, date of publication.[1] Other relevant information—such as edition, number of volumes, title of series (if the book is one of a series) and the like—should be entered.

SPECIMEN BIBLIOGRAPHY CARD—FOR A BOOK

> Blair, Walter, Theodore Hornberger, and Randall
>
> Stewart, eds. The Literature of the United States.
>
> Revised edition. 2 vols. Chicago: Scott, Foresman
>
> and Company, 1953.

For a Periodical

1. Author's name. Put the last name first, and use the full name as printed.
2. Title of the article.
3. Title of the periodical, volume number, date of issue, inclusive page numbers.

[1] Although *The MLA Style Sheet* does not use publishers' names, many scholars prefer to include them, especially for items still under copyright.

To the purely bibliographical matter illustrated below, you may wish to add, for your own convenience, some brief descriptive notation as to the character and usefulness of the item that you are recording. For example, if your subject is "The Primitive Background of the Maypole Dance," you may have entered on your card a reference to the 1951, one-volume, abridged edition of Sir James Frazer's *The Golden Bough.* Then you may also wish to note that this book is a condensation of the complete multi-volume edition and to add a reminder like this: "Compare with the text of the 12-volume edition, 1907–1915."

SPECIMEN BIBLIOGRAPHY CARD—FOR A PERIODICAL

> Carpenter, Frederic I. "Puritans Prefer Blondes,
>
> The Heroines of Melville and Hawthorne."
>
> New England Quarterly, IX (June, 1936),
>
> 253-272.

The working bibliography will serve you during the process of gathering material. Be careful to make *complete and accurate* bibliographical notations, since you will wish to avoid looking up the item a second time when you prepare your final bibliography. During the course of your study you should find other items to add to your working bibliography. These items, of course, should be entered exactly the same way. When you have written your paper, your final bibliography—which must be appended to your paper—will be made up from the working bibliography, *but it will consist only of the items from which you have actually drawn material.*

NOTE-TAKING

When you have found the sources of information, your next step is to read and to take notes on your reading.

Your notes must be accurate and discerning. Otherwise you will be confused and handicapped when you come to the actual writing of your paper. It is necessary to follow a carefully planned system of note-taking if you are to avoid loss of time and waste of energy.

For note-taking use cards of uniform size, preferably 3 by 5 inches or 4 by 6 inches. Note paper may of course be used, but cards are much more convenient because they can be more easily filed, grouped, arranged, and rearranged in any order you may wish. Use a separate card for each separate note. Limit the information recorded on each card to some important detail, point, or subtopic of your paper. Each note card should contain the following items:

(1) In the upper left-hand corner, a guide-word, key-phrase, or topic which identifies the material recorded on that card. When your notes are assembled, these key-phrases or guide-words will help you to organize your paper.

(2) Bibliographical identification. Do not repeat on the note card itself the *full* bibliographical information. Nevertheless you must enter identifying bibliographical references on the note cards—for example, the author's name and the title of his work: Prebble, *Culloden,* pp. 44–45.

Since you will depend on your note cards for the "documentation" of your paper, it is highly important to make an exact record *at the time when you take your notes.* Otherwise you will have to look up your sources a second time.

(3) The note itself. Do not make random jottings and hasty scribbles which you yourself may not be able to understand when you assemble your notes. Limit each note to a single important point. The content of the note may be either a summary of what the author consulted says or an exact quotation. If you use an exact quotation, preface it by a few words of summary or interpretation to indicate the bearing of the quotation upon your subject. You may of course wish to add comments of your own from time to time, which will serve to guide you in the construction of your paper.

If you use a direct quotation, record it *exactly* as it stands in the original—in the spelling and punctuation of the original—and enclose it in quotation marks. Only by such

SPECIMEN NOTE CARDS

Comparison of person-
alities. <u>Ideas in</u>
·<u>common</u>.

Blair, Hornberger, and Stewart,
<u>The Literature of the U.S</u>.

"Like Hawthorne, Melville was concerned with the darker
side of human fate." Both were compelled to dwell upon
the irrefutable reality of evil in human nature, to reject
the bland optimism of Emerson (who found only benevolence
in the Universe), and to portray mental and spiritual
tragedies. (Vol. II, ·p. 581.)

Misconceptions of relation-
ship. <u>Friendship</u> <u>a</u> <u>failure</u>.

Minnigerode, <u>Some</u> <u>Personal</u>
<u>Letters</u> <u>of</u> <u>Herman</u> <u>Melville</u>.

"One cannot rid oneself of the impression that Melville
was forever slapping Hawthorne on the back, to the unaccustomed surprise and private displeasure of the latter.
... In other words, one wonders, when all was said and
done, whether Melville did not take a mile of Hawthorne's
friendship for every inch vouchsafed."
(Pp. 54-55.)

---

care can you be accurate. You must later be able to distinguish your own ideas from the facts and opinions that you have gathered. Be especially careful to make accurate note of important dates and of the spelling of proper names. If you omit nonessential parts of a quoted sentence or passage, indicate the omission by ellipses. (Use three periods to indicate ellipses within a sentence; four, at the end of a sentence.)

Skill in note-taking can be gained only by practice. The following procedure will help you to acquire this skill.

Read through pertinent chapters of books (or other material) *before* taking notes. While reading, jot down on a card or a piece of paper the page numbers of passages to

TWO SPECIMEN NOTE CARDS

Student A's Note

The retinue of a Highland   Prebble, <u>Culloden</u>,
Chief, before 1745   pp. 44-45.

    At the head rode the Chief, described as "prickly proud." Next came his official bodyguard: a henchman or "foster-brother." Third: the Bard--the clan's singer, poet, historian, and genealogist. Fourth: the Piper--important in both peace and war. Fifth: The Bladier--the Chief's spokesman, legal counsel, and official toastmaster. Sixth: a group of "gillies" (boys or young men) carrying the Chief's sword and equipment.

Student B's Note

Pride as a characteristic   Prebble, <u>Culloden</u>,
of the Highland Scot   pp. 44-45.

    1. The clan chief set the example for physical behavior with "superior courage and superlative hardihood." (The comfort-loving chief who made himself a pillow of snow was disdained by his followers.)
    2. Edward Burt, an Englishman, commented early in the 18th century: Highlanders "have a pride in their family; almost everyone is a genealogist."
    3. The Bard's skill in rehearsing tales of valor from the past was a means of engendering pride.

which you will want to go back. Do *not* attempt to outline
everything you read, but look for information that is exactly
relevant to your subject. The preliminary reading will be useful in itself, as a means of building up general information.
When you have finished this reading, go back and take your
notes.

If you are compiling statistics, you have only the problem
of finding the figures you need and recording them accurately. But generally the problem is not so simple. In reading, you must constantly be on your guard to distinguish
between genuine fact and mere opinion. You may need to
compare different opinions and different interpretations
when authorities disagree. Be sure to note such disagreements
—in short, be alert to make comparisons.

What you finally put down should depend upon your
guiding purpose in the study that you are undertaking. Two
students consulting the same source will take different notes
if they have different subjects or different guiding purposes.
In the examples on page 259, Student A had as his subject
"The Social Structure of the Highland Clans." Student B's
subject was "Scottish Nationalism in the Early Eighteenth
Century." The two specimen note cards show how students
may differ in taking notes on the same material. For the
selection in question and the primary source material, see
pages 58–66.

DOCUMENTATION: FOOTNOTES

Every direct quotation used in your paper, every fact
derived from a source that you have consulted, every
opinion and interpretation not your own, whether quoted,
briefed, or paraphrased, must be properly credited to the
source from which it was derived.[1] Such crediting not only
gives your reader assurance of the substantial basis upon
which your discussion is founded and serves as a guarantee
of your good faith; it also enables your reader to consult, if
he wishes, the sources of information that you have used.

Footnotes are, of course, the authenticating references
which stand at the bottom of the page and bear numerals
corresponding to the numerals inserted in the text. (See
"Examples of Abbreviations, Citations, and Footnotes," page
262.)

[1] Exceptions may be made for common proverbs and familiar
quotations.

Footnotes are generally numbered in order from the beginning to the end of the paper. The reference numeral used in the text is placed *at the end* of the passage which it authenticates: that is, at the end of the sentence containing the subject-matter referred to, if the passage consists of only one sentence; at the end of the last sentence of the passage, if it covers several sentences. The reference numeral should stand slightly above and to the right of the closing word or terminal punctuation mark of the passage. Reference numerals may be inserted *within* a sentence when one or more items, within the same sentence, require supporting footnotes.

Footnotes should be separated from the text by a line ruled or typed across the paper, or at least two inches long. Leave at least one space above and below the line. Some writers prefer to place all annotations together at the end of a paper; they are then "notes," not "footnotes." This practice, although it is favored by some periodicals, is not generally followed in college papers.[1]

The Form of Footnotes

In the first footnote reference to a book you should give at least the author's name, title of book, and page reference. In *succeeding references* to the same item you should use the system of abbreviated reference customary in papers that require documentation. Under "Examples," page 262, suggested methods of abbreviated reference are given. The examples, if used as models, will give you more satisfactory guidance than generalized instructions.

Always remember that clarity and exactness, as well as compactness, are the qualities desired in footnotes. Avoid, therefore, any abbreviation or affectation that would cause confusion or inexactness. The author's surname and the page number will generally suffice for the reference if the first footnote reference is found in a recent note. If, however, an author with an identical surname is cited elsewhere in the paper, if several works by a given author are cited, or if the full reference is buried earlier in the text, your note should be enlarged accordingly. In such cases the full name

[1] For complete instruction as to preparation of manuscript see Marckwardt and Cassidy, *Scribner Handbook of English* (Chapter XIII), or similar material in other standard manuals. The "Specimen Research Paper" given below (pages 267–290) illustrates the correct form for typewritten material.

of the author should be given or the title of the book repeated.

For a newspaper or periodical, the method is the same as for a book. Your footnote reference may read as follows:

[5]Thornton Wilder, "Toward an American Language," *Atlantic Monthly*, CXC (July, 1952), 31.

For your succeeding references to this item you may use "*Ibid.*" (for a note identical in every respect to the immediately preceding one or different only as to page reference); "Wilder, *loc. cit.*" (other notes have intervened between this reference and the original one; reference is to the same passage); or "Wilder, p. 45" (intervening notes; page reference different).

Other Material Included in Footnotes

Observe that footnotes are not used *only* for purposes of authenticating source material. They may be used, and frequently are used (1) for brief comments or explanations which the writer does not wish to include in the text of his discussion and (2) for "see" or "compare" references in which the writer directs attention to parts of his own discussion or to items that have some relevance to his discussion but that are not specifically considered in his discussion.

Examples of Abbreviations, Citations, and Footnotes

anon. Anonymous.
 Anon. *The Women's Petition Against Coffee*. London: Jacob Thomason, 1674.

c. or *ca.* (*circa*). Used before dates which can be determined only approximately.
 Clark, George and William Aldis Wright, eds. *Shakespeare*. Stage Ed. 16 vols. Philadelphia: George Barrie and Son, *c.* 1899.

cf. (*confer*). Compare.
 [6] *Cf.* the versions of "The Daemon Lover" ballad from Virginia in the Appendix.

ed. or eds. Edited by, editor(s), or edition(s).
 Ross, Iain, ed. *The Gude and Godlie Ballatis*. Edinburgh: Oliver and Boyd, 1939.

 Faulkner, William. *The Sound and The Fury*. Modern Library Ed. New York: Random House, 1946.

et al.	(*et alii*). And others. Used when a book has several authors and only the first author is listed. Albert C. Baugh *et al., A Literary History of England,* p. 668.
f. or ff.	And the following page(s). [10] See also p. 106 f.
ibid.	(*ibidem*). In the same place. Used to avoid unnecessary repetition of author and title when a new page reference to the same author and title follows immediately. Used without a page number, it refers to the same author, title, *and page* as the footnote immediately preceding. [12] *Ibid.,* p. 217. [13] *Ibid.*
infra	Below. Used to refer to a later discussion. Since use of the Latin word saves no space, "below" may be used in its place and may be considered preferable by modernists. [2] See pp. 14–17 and footnote 16, *infra.*
l. or ll.	Line(s), as a line of verse. [18] *Cf.* "Ash Wednesday," ll. 17–26.
loc. cit.	(*loco citato*). In the place cited. Used to refer to the same passage referred to in a recent note. Never follow "*loc. cit.*" with a page number. [32] Williams, *loc. cit.*
MS or MSS	Manuscript(s). Used with a period when a catalogued manuscript is cited. [7] Harleian MS. 293, British Museum. Used without a period when the manuscript is not specifically catalogued. [8] Other MSS are housed in the National Archives.
N.B.	(*nota bene*). Take notice, mark well. [15] N.B. ll. 10–18, where the irony shifts to sarcasm.
n.d. and n.p.	No date and no place. Used when no date and/or no place of publication appear on the title page or copyright page of a book. Ashkirk, Angus. *Recollections of Bench and Bar.* N.p., n.d.
no. or nos.	Number(s). Used when listing the number of the issue of either a series or a periodical. Beaumont, Charles A. *Swift's Classical Rhetoric.* No. 8.

University of Georgia Monograph Series. Athens: U of Georgia Press, 1961.

McKelway, A. J. "The Scotch-Irish of North Carolina," *North Carolina Booklet,* IV, No. 11 (March, 1905), 3–24.

op. cit.   (*opere citato*). In the work cited. Used to refer to a passage on a different page of a work recently cited. In such cases, however, the author's name or his name and a shortened title are usually sufficient (see page 261).
19 Frierson, *op. cit.,* p. 67.

p. or pp.   Page(s). Used for books and "works." (This abbreviation is omitted in references to articles when a volume number is given.)
5 Constance Rourke, *American Humor,* p. 63.

passim   Here and there. Used to indicate citations scattered throughout a reference, or covering a number of pages.
10 Henry S. Lucas, *The Renaissance and the Reformation,* Chap. IV, *passim.*

pseud.   Pseudonym. Indicate the real name in brackets.
7 Mark Twain, pseud. [Samuel L. Clemens], *Life on the Mississippi,* p. 35.

q. v.   (*quod vide*). Which see.
13 "Harmony," *Encyclopedia Americana, q. v.*

sic   Thus. Used to signify that a given text is exactly reproduced. *Sic* may appear in quoted matter after a textual error in the original and should be enclosed in brackets.
"It never occurd [*sic*] to us that our northern dialect was inferior to that spoken in London."

supra   Above. Used to refer to a previous discussion. (See "*infra.*")
17 See James's opinion, *supra.*

s. v.   (*sub voce* or *verbo*). Under the heading or word. Used to refer to entries in dictionaries and encyclopedias—in which case page numbers are not necessary.
12 *Oxford Classical Dictionary, s.v.* "Libraries."

tr. or   Translator, translation, or translated by.
trans.   Pliny. *Letters,* trans. W. M. L. Hutchinson, 2 vols.

Loeb Classical Library. New York: G. P. Putnam's Sons, 1933.

vol. or vols. — Volume(s). See preceding entry. This abbreviation is usually omitted when volume numbers are designated by Roman numerals. (But it is properly used in the preceding example.) Note the following:
[9] Pliny, II, 48.
[10] Felix Reichman, "The Book Trade at the Time of the Roman Empire," *The Library Quarterly*, VIII (January, 1938), 40.

DOCUMENTATION: THE FINAL BIBLIOGRAPHY

The final bibliography should appear at the end of the research paper. (See page 288.) As has already been explained, it should contain only the items which have actually been used for reference in the paper. The bibliography should be arranged in alphabetical order, by authors, with last names first. The form of each entry follows the form prescribed for entries on the bibliography cards. (See page 255.) When a bibliography is extensive, and covers much periodical literature as well as books, it may be advisable to place books and articles in two separate lists. Scholarly dissertations frequently distinguish between primary and secondary sources or make other divisions, such as may be required by the nature of the material used in research.

THE COMPLETED PAPER

In the preceding sections, many technical details have been discussed. Do not allow this discussion, important though it may be for guidance, to give you an exaggerated notion of the intrinsic importance of footnotes, bibliography, methods of note-taking, and the like. All these things are only means to an end—the writing of a clear and well-authenticated exposition of your subject. Profusion of footnotes, however correct in form, and an extensive bibliography, no matter how impressive-looking, do not in themselves make a good research paper. The research paper must be, in itself, a good piece of writing, which embodies the results of your investigation and represents your own independent and mature interpretation of a subject.

The following specimen research paper, "The Friendship Between Hawthorne and Melville," has been prepared for this textbook by an experienced scholar and researchist to exemplify something of the content, organization, style, form of annotation, bibliography, and appearance of a manuscript. In these pages you will find examples of the most common footnote citations. You can refer to these as models if you are in doubt as to how to prepare any of your own footnotes.

Within the limits of a textbook of composition and rhetoric, which is devoted primarily to the larger problems of writing, it is not practicable or even possible to advise a student about all the *minutiae* and minor technicalities of annotation. The Modern Language Association has sponsored a standardized form of reference, in its *MLA Style Sheet*, in the hope of securing general uniformity. This and other manuals can be consulted for difficult problems of form.[1] No one manual or style sheet, however, can be completely authoritative in all fields of research. History, law, physical science, music, medicine, political science— all may have their peculiar refinements and needs in matters of documentation. The basic *principles* of annotation, nevertheless, have not changed since ancient times and are everywhere the same. The specimen paper that follows observes those principles and furthermore illustrates, as well as a single paper can, the accepted practice in our time. Notice also the form and contents of the complete bibliography at the end.

[1] Also in current use is Kate L. Turabian's *A Manual for Writers of Term Paper, Theses, and Dissertations,* published by the University of Chicago Press. Students of law and members of the legal profession frequently document their research in a manner suggested by *A Uniform System of Citation,* published by the Harvard Law Review Association.

The Friendship Between Hawthorne and Melville

By M. Thomas Inge

English 102, Section 12

Professor Davidson

June 23, 1963

The Friendship Between Hawthorne and Melville

The brief but influential friendship between Nathaniel Hawthorne and Herman Melville, two of the most powerful figures in
American letters, has been described as "one of the major events
in literary history."[1] When Hawthorne received a copy of Moby
Dick, which Melville had dedicated to him, he wrote in commen-
dation of the book a "joy-giving and exultation breeding" letter
to the author; in his reply, Melville commented, "when the big
hearts strike together, the concussion is a little stunning."[2]
And when a final evaluation is made of the total impact of these
two great hearts striking together, the concussion may well
prove to be a good deal more than stunning.

It was at a most crucial point in his life that the younger
Melville came in contact with Hawthorne, fifteen years his senior.
After his marriage in 1847, with two successful books already to
his credit (Typee and Omoo), Melville determined to support his
family entirely by means of his literary talents;[3] he turned out
in quick succession Mardi (March, 1849), Redburn (September,
1849), and White-Jacket (January, 1850). Seeking perhaps the

---

[1] Mark Van Doren, Nathaniel Hawthorne, p. 177.

[2] Merrell R. Davis and William H. Gilman, eds., The Letters
of Herman Melville, pp. 141, 143.

[3] F. O. Matthiessen, American Renaissance, p. 186.

appropriate atmosphere and solitude for the production of the
great work on the whale which was brewing within his mind, he
moved near Pittsfield, Massachusetts, in the summer of 1850.[4]
Late in May of the same year, Hawthorne had moved his family to
the Little Red House at nearby Lenox, seeking not only solitude
to write but also solitude from the political strife in Salem
following his removal from office at the Custom House, and from
the community strife offered by his neighbors as a result of the
publication of his "scandalous" novel, The Scarlet Letter.[5] Hawthorne, then, had already completed his most memorable success;
Melville was in the midst of his struggle with his most noble and
exhaustive effort. Their proximity and common literary interests
made their meeting inevitable.

But before a personal meeting occurred, both writers had been
aware of the other's work. Hawthorne had favorably reviewed
Typee for a Salem paper and had been reading Melville's later
novels with increasing enthusiasm. He praised the reality of
Redburn and White-Jacket and said that Mardi was "a rich book,
with depths here and there that compel a man to swim for his life."[6]
Before moving to Pittsfield, Melville had not granted himself the
time to read anything of Hawthorne's. Probably because of the

---

[4] Newton Arvin, Herman Melville, pp. 133-134.

[5] Randall Stewart, Nathaniel Hawthorne, pp. 86-100.

[6] Ibid., p. 107.

270

recent fame of The Scarlet Letter, as well as the nearness of its author,[7] Melville began to read Mosses from an Old Manse, already four years old, and he could not put it down. So intense was his excitement that he began a laudatory and appreciative review in the very midst of reading, an essay which remains one of the finest statements on Hawthorne.[8] Better than a criticism, it was, as Matthiessen designates it, the expression of "a creative mind disclosing its own ambitions and problems in response to the profound challenge that only a fellow artist can present."[9] No other contemporary American writer of note, Irving, Cooper or Dana, had so profoundly moved Melville before. In comparison with Hawthorne, he later concluded, "Irving is a grasshopper to him--putting the souls of the two men together, I mean."[10]

It was a few days before or after the writing of this essay that the two writers met in the flesh, but Melville concealed the fact that the piece was his by signing it "A Virginian Spending a July in Vermont." Hawthorne and his wife, of course, were quite delighted with the article. Hawthorne intuitively discerned that the reviewer was "no common man," and he wrote, "next to deserving

---

[7] Matthiessen, loc. cit.

[8] Reprinted in Willard Thorp, ed., Herman Melville, Representative Selections, pp. 327-335. It originally appeared in The Literary World for August 17 and 24, 1850.

[9] Matthiessen, pp. 186-187.

[10] Davis and Gilman, p. 121.

his praise, it is good to have beguiled or bewitched such a man into praising me more than I deserve."[11] Mrs. Hawthorne exultantly wrote to her mother, "At last some one speaks the right word of Mr. Hawthorne,"[12] and later she wrote of the unknown friend, "The freshness of primeval nature is in that man, & the true Promethean fire is in him."[13]

The meeting occurred on August 5, 1850, with this mutual appreciation already working as an influence towards a closer relationship. A party of literary people in the vicinity of Pittsfield had assembled to climb Monument Mountain and explore the Ice Glen. Randall Stewart describes the event in this manner:

> It was a jolly occasion. Dr. [Oliver Wendell] Holmes served champagne in a silver mug. Melville astonished the group by his agile and bold mountain climbing. In the darkness of the Ice Glen Hawthorne called out ominous warnings--in fact, according to James T. Fields' report, he was "among the most enterprising of the merry-makers." During a thunder-shower Hawthorne and Melville took shelter under a great rock and so had a special opportunity of getting acquainted.[14]

Only two days later, Hawthorne wrote to a friend, "I liked Melville so much that I have asked him to spend a few days with me."[15] The acquaintanceship had an auspicious beginning.

---

[11] Stewart, p. 108.

[12] Ibid.

[13] Eleanor Melville Metcalf, Herman Melville, Cycle and Epicycle, p. 90.

[14] Stewart, p. 107.

[15] Ibid.

A four-day visit in early September was followed by more than a year of frequent trips and walks, private conversational meetings, and exchanges of letters.[16] Hawthorne reported that in their conversations, they touched upon "time and eternity, things of this world and the next, and books, and publishers, and all possible and impossible matters," their sessions lasting deep into the night.[17] Something of the exhilaration Melville experienced in these conversations is reflected in the lyrical and fanciful description he wrote of the celestial talks to be carried on between the two in the next world:

> If ever, my dear Hawthorne, in the eternal times that are to come, you and I shall sit down in Paradise, in some little shady corner by ourselves; and if we shall by any means be able to smuggle a basket of champagne there (I won't believe in a Temperance Heaven), and if we shall then cross our celestial legs in the celestial grass that is forever tropical, and strike our glasses and our heads together, till both musically ring in concert,--then O my dear fellow-mortal, how shall we pleasantly discourse of all the things manifold which now so distress us,--when all the earth shall be but a reminiscence, yea, its final dissolution an antiquity.[18]

[16]Ibid., pp. 107-121.

[17]Randall Stewart, ed., The American Notebooks by Nathaniel Hawthorne, p. 220. One critic, in a persuasive article, has suggested another topic which may have entered their conversations: "Hawthorne's own experience with matters of the sea may have been among the subjects they canvassed in these sessions, or...it may have contributed largely to his pleasure in the younger man's company. Hawthorne, of course, was no sailor, and we rarely think of him in connection with the sea; nevertheless, he was linked to it by his family, by his own interest, by his reading, and even by a number of his own writings." Harrison Hayford, "Hawthorne, Melville, and the Sea," New England Quarterly, XIX (December, 1946), 435-436.

[18]Davis and Gilman, p. 128.

Today we cannot view this encounter of supernal minds in its full light, as none of Hawthorne's letters to Melville have survived.[19] But Hawthorne's letters must have been as frank and congenial as Melville's, if not as rhapsodic or immoderate; Melville referred to one of them as an "easy-flowing long letter . . . which flowed through me and refreshed all my meadows."[20]

To Hawthorne's family, Melville was a strangely fascinating man. Mrs. Hawthorne was remarkably perceptive in understanding his inner qualities; she wrote of him as "A man with a true, warm heart, and a soul and an intellect,--with life to his finger-tips; earnest, sincere, and reverent; very tender and modest. And I am not sure that he is not a very great man."[21] The following nostalgic lines, written by Julian, Hawthorne's son, in recalling the days of Melville's visits, reflect a peculiar enthrallment:

> But Melville himself made up for everything by the tremendous stories he used to tell about the South Sea Islands and the whale fishery. Normally he was not a man of noticeable appearance; but when the narrative inspiration was on him; he looked like all the things he was describing--savages, sea-captains, the lovely Fayaway in her canoe, or the terrible Moby Dick himself. There was vivid genius in this man, and he was the strangest being that ever came into our circle.[22]

---

[19] Julian Hawthorne, Nathaniel Hawthorne and His Wife, I, 398.

[20] Davis and Gilman, p. 135.

[21] Stewart, Nathaniel Hawthorne, pp. 108-109.

[22] Julian Hawthorne, Hawthorne and His Circle, p. 32.

The close relationship which their proximity had fostered was necessarily interrupted when in November of 1851, Hawthorne moved to West Newton,[23] but by no means did this end their friendship. Melville continued to read and admire Hawthorne's writings, and in September of 1852, after Melville had finished Pierre, he so admired Hawthorne's methods that he turned over to him for his own use the outline of a story about a woman named Agatha, whose husband had deserted her, the details of which were furnished by a New Bedford lawyer. The subject reminded Melville of Hawthorne's story "Wakefield"[24] and made the material appear especially suited to Hawthorne. But Hawthorne hesitated to accept the task, and Melville later requested the return of the material. The story remained unwritten by either author.[25] This is the nearest the two ever came to any sort of collaboration.

Hawthorne's actual regard for Melville is clear in his attempts to aid him at a period of great despair in his life. Despite the masterful artistry displayed in Moby Dick, the novel was unpopular, and publication expenses only increased Melville's debt. The sharply censorious reception of Pierre nearly finished off his ability to support himself as a writer, in a world seemingly unmindful of superior talent. To add to his difficulties,

---

[23] Stewart, Nathaniel Hawthorne, pp. 120-121.

[24] Davis and Gilman, p. 155.

[25] Stewart, Nathaniel Hawthorne, pp. 135-136.

Harper's stock of his books was lost when the publishing house burned in 1853.[26] When Franklin Pierce was elected President, Hawthorne found himself in a most advantageous position, as Pierce's friend and biographer. He immediately sought to obtain for Melville a consulate, perhaps at Honolulu. Despite the support of several other friends, the effort accomplished nothing. Hawthorne received his award from Pierce of the consulship at Liverpool, and he crossed the sea, leaving his friend Melville behind to turn to the lecture hall as a way of alleviating his financial burdens.[27]

We are not to imagine that Hawthorne was unaffected by his inability to assist his friend. Three years later, in 1856, the two friends met once again for some final talks at Liverpool. Hawthorne's thoughts upon first seeing him reveal the deep affection with which he still regarded his friend; he wrote quite frankly of the encounter: "I felt rather awkward at first; because this is the first time I have met him since my ineffectual attempt to get him a consular appointment from General Pierce. However, I failed only from real lack of power to serve him; so there was no reason to be ashamed, and we soon found ourselves on pretty much our former terms of sociability and confidence."[28]

---

[26]Arvin, pp. 197-198.

[27]Ibid., pp. 198-199; and Stewart, Nathaniel Hawthorne, pp. 139-140.

[28]Randall Stewart, ed., The English Notebooks by Nathaniel Hawthorne, p. 432.

Melville arrived at Liverpool on the first leg of a trip to
Palestine, and he spent a few days rekindling the conviviality
once common between the two writers. After a walk together on
one of those days, Hawthorne set down in his journal some of the
most revealing lines ever written on Melville:

> Melville, as he always does, began to reason of
> Providence and futurity, and of everything that lies
> beyond human ken, and informed me that he had "pretty
> much made up his mind to be annihilated"; and, I think,
> will never rest until he gets hold of a definite be-
> lief . . . He can neither believe, nor be comfortable
> in his unbelief; and he is too honest and courageous
> not to try to do one or the other. If he were a
> religious man, he would be one of the most truly reli-
> gious and reverential; he has a very high and noble
> nature, and better worth immortality than most of us.[29]

Hawthorne could only offer encouragement to Melville, and send
him on his way in a better frame of mind. And here the mere
chronicle of their intimate association may well end. But the
manifestations of their influences upon each other must be
considered.

Not until recent years has the actual success of this friendship been understood in its proper perspective. A serious misconception of Hawthorne's role in the relationship originated
with Melville's early biographers, Raymond Weaver and Lewis
Mumford. A typical comment by one critic of their school reads:
"One cannot rid oneself of the impression that Melville was forever slapping Hawthorne on the back, to the unaccustomed surprise

---

[29] Ibid., pp. 432-433.

and private displeasure of the latter."[30] This view results from an attempt to over-dramatize Melville as a lone and unrecognized genius among his contemporaries, and no doubt owes something to the older critical view of Hawthorne as austere, moody and unapproachable. Hawthorne was a naturally aloof person,[31] admittedly; but that the elder, more reserved friend could not return the exuberant affection of the younger with a commensurate fervor gives us no reason to believe that Melville's offered comradeship met with cool and utter rejection on Hawthorne's part.

Weaver characteristically writes that when Melville came to know Hawthorne, "his eager soul rushed to embrace Hawthorne's as that of a brother in despair. Exultant was his worship . . . absolute his desire for surrender."[32] And he goes on to explain how Hawthorne allowed him to languish there like a rejected lover. Mumford subsequently writes, "Melville's relation with Hawthorne counts as one of the tragedies of his life . . . . Friendship itself must have seemed a mockery, when he found that the dearest friend and closest intellectual companion he had yet encountered

---

[30]Meade Minnigerode, Some Personal Letters of Herman Melville and a Bibliography, pp. 54-55. See also the comments of Henry Seidel Canby, "Hawthorne and Melville," in Classic Americans, pp. 248-250; Lawrance Thompson, Melville's Quarrel with God, p. 127; and Arvin, pp. 205-206.

[31]Julian Hawthorne, Nathaniel Hawthorne and His Wife, I, 88-89.

[32]Raymond Weaver, Herman Melville, Mariner and Mystic, p. 337. Note also his theory that Hawthorne viewed Moby Dick as "grossly shocking," p. 329.

was bound tight in the arctic ice, and many leagues away."[33] Without Hawthorne's actual letters by which to judge his reaction to Melville, such conclusions must forever remain one-sided. And there is no other evidence to support such theories.

Mumford carries the misconception even further, to what proved to be a ridiculous extreme, by making Hawthorne out a villain in stating that he mocked Melville's spiritual quandary by creating the character Ethan Brand, in the short story of the same name, in his likeness.[34] This may well stand as one of the more notable faux pas in American literary interpretation. The first to correct it was Randall Stewart, upon publication of Mumford's book in 1929. Stewart proved that Hawthorne wrote the story six months before he met Melville and that it had also been outlined in his journal two years before Melville published his first book.[35] Later critics have pointed out Hawthorne's humanity and the sympathetic, gregarious side of his personality, which would have allowed him to respond fully to Melville's friendship.

---

[33] Lewis Mumford, Herman Melville, p. 145.

[34] Ibid. Actually this theory originated with Edward J. O'Brien in an article published before Mumford's biography, "The Fifteen Finest Short Stories," Forum, LXXIX (June, 1928), 909. See also Newton Arvin, Hawthorne, p. 169 (who no longer mentioned the theory when he later wrote his volume on Melville); Thompson, p. 141; and (surprisingly enough, within the past few years) Harry Levin, The Power of Blackness, p. 65.

[35] Randall Stewart, "Ethan Brand," Saturday Review of Literature, V (April 27, 1929), 967.

Insofar as their fundamental dispositions were concerned,
Hawthorne and Melville were of two different breeds. There is a
reflection of this in the contrast of their styles: Hawthorne's
is entirely uneccentric and fastidiously neat; Melville's is
extravagant and undisciplined.[36] In temperament, Melville was
highly emotional and impulsive, but Hawthorne was more reserved
and prudent in expression of feelings; such, at least, is deducible
from all that has been written and said of them both. What one
critic observes, however, should be noted:

> Melville, at the time of their intimacy, was thirty-one,
> a young man bursting with a glorious impatience to explore
> within himself the regions of soul and heart that his
> previous work had only touched; Hawthorne, the man who had
> contributed so much to this impatience, had already, in
> middle age, written his masterpiece. Youthful ardor,
> if it ever had been his, had given way to a more comfort-
> able civility.[37]

But they both held a great many impulses and ideas in common.

The darker side of human fate compelled them both to dwell
upon the irrefutable reality of evil in human nature, to portray
mental and spiritual tragedies, and to reject the bland optimism
of Emerson, who found only benevolence in the Universe.[38] Like
Milton, perhaps, they wished to assert, if possible, the justice

---

[36] Weaver, p. 330.

[37] Edward G. Lueders, "The Melville-Hawthorne Relationship
in Pierre and The Blithedale Romance," Western Humanities Review,
IV (Autumn, 1950), 325.

[38] Walter Blair, Theodore Hornberger, and Randall Stewart,
eds., The Literature of the United States, revised edition,
II, 581.

of God's ways to man.[39] Perhaps no other writers of their age,
certainly not Emerson, Thoreau, Longfellow, Whittier or Whitman,
felt so acutely "the pain of suffering humanity."[40] At least
Hawthorne could resign himself to accepting the scheme of things,
however unreasonable, while Melville persisted in defying it.[41]
The two possessed, in common, "an intellectual honesty and disinterestedness, a skepticism, a distrust of fashionable panaceas, a
sense of the humor as well as the tragedy of life, and an appreciation also of life's good things."[42] Without the last two
mentioned, all the rest might have been insufferable.

At that late point in his life, Hawthorne would hardly have
been influenced by Melville in matters of mind or style.[43] But
the influence of Hawthorne upon Melville may prove to be of greater
consequence than many have suspected. Melville discovered Shakespeare and Hawthorne at the same time and felt that the latter
did not suffer by comparison; indeed, he was convinced of the
increasing greatness of American writers. The realization that
other mortal men were disturbed by grave thoughts inspired him
to a great artistic awakening.[44] Melville remarked significantly

---

[39]Henry F. Pommer, Milton and Melville, p. 16.

[40]William Braswell, "Herman Melville and Christianity" (unpublished Ph. D. dissertation, University of Chicago, 1934), p. 211.

[41]Blair et al., loc. cit.

[42]Stewart, Nathaniel Hawthorne, p. 111.

[43]Matthiessen, p. 188.

[44]Thorp, pp. xxxvi-xxxvii, 333 ff.

upon first reading him, "already I feel that this Hawthorne has
dropped germinous seeds into my soul. He . . . shoots his strong
New England roots in the hot soil of my Southern soul."[45] Five
determining influences on Melville's career have been pointed out:
the religious orthodoxy of his home, from which he rebelled; his
brutal experiences as a sailor, especially among savage cultures
where he saw the corrupting influences of western society; his
reading in literature and philosophy; his literary and artistic
friends in New York; and Hawthorne's sympathy, "which more than
any other factor contributed to the fruition of his genius."[46]

There have been numerous suggestions as to the results of
this influence. Randall Stewart has denoted two of the general
lines it followed. "One is allegory: the allegorical development in Melville may very well have been stimulated by his reading
of Hawthorne . . . . A second . . . is suggested by what Melville
called the 'blackness' in Hawthorne. . . . Melville, like Hawthorne, studied the deep mystery of sin."[47] Both authors came
to value the theme of a piece of fiction, the deeper meaning
beneath the surface action, above plot, characterization, or
imagery.[48] This is the basic theory which underlies the use of

---

[45] Ibid., p. 341.

[46] Ibid., pp. xxxix-xl.

[47] Randall Stewart, "Melville and Hawthorne," South Atlantic
Quarterly, LI (July, 1952), 442.

[48] Blair et al., II, 591.

allegory. The "power of blackness" in Hawthorne, which fascinated Melville, he recognized as deriving its force from "its
appeals to that Calvinistic sense of Innate Depravity and Original
Sin, from whose visitations, in some shape or other, no deeply
thinking mind is always and wholly free."[49] Melville knew there
was a similar "blackness" within himself, and this justified his
own intent to give it open expression in his writing.

Another critic has made much of the fact that in Mardi,
Pierre, The Blithedale Romance, and The Marble Faun, Melville
and Hawthorne both portray blonde heroines as being virtuous and
pure, and brunettes as being women of passion and sinful
experience.[50] But since this convention had become common among
mid-nineteenth century writers, and Melville had used it in
Mardi before meeting Hawthorne, this is less an influence, probably, than the unconscious use of the same tradition.

Because Moby Dick was completed during the high point of the
friendship, that work should show a wide degree of Hawthorne's
influence. It is a logical argument that the entire complexion
of the novel, originally planned as a romantic narrative of the
whale fishery, changed under the influence of the new intellectual
stimulation his friend offered; "and in his state of excited stimulation Melville was not content merely to feed new raw material

---

[49] Thorp, p. 333.

[50] Frederic I. Carpenter, "Puritans Prefer Blondes, The
Heroines of Melville and Hawthorne," New England Quarterly, IX
(June, 1936), 253-272.

into his story. . . . He was emotionally obliged to put into it
some of the force of his new philosophical convictions, and he
could hardly have avoided thinking of it, in the secret recesses
of his mind, as a possible medium through which these convictions
could reach Shakespearian heights of expression."[51] Moby Dick.
contains distinct variations from the pattern Melville's fiction
had followed previously: "In this novel Melville's unseen world
is supernatural rather than metaphysical, revenge is a stronger
motive than envy in demonic action, the blond image is superseded
by the image of fire." One critic suggests that these variations
originated in his reading of Mosses from an Old Manse and examines
in detail how imagery, character, and theme reflect a similar
influence.[52]

Many of the discussions of influence rest upon the now
unaccepted theory that a breach occurred in the friendship between
Hawthorne and Melville. Melville's sense of being rejected is
supposed to have found vent in the narrative poem Clarel, in which
Vine, an older, reticent man rejects an ultimate bond of sympathy
with the young American Clarel, travelling in the Holy Land.[53]
The little poem "Monody," two lines of which read, "To have known

---

[51] Leon Howard, Herman Melville, p. 169.

[52] Nathalia Wright, "Mosses from an Old Manse and Moby Dick:
the Shock of Discovery, "Modern Language Notes, LXVII (June,
1952), 387-392.

[53] Arvin, Herman Melville, pp. 206-209.

him, to have loved him . . .; And then to be estranged in life,"
is supposed to allude to Hawthorne.[54] Most of the theories of
this type center upon the controversial novel Pierre.

Willard Thorp was the first to point out the close correspondence between Pierre and Hawthorne's Blithedale Romance,
both of which appeared in 1852. The heroes of both books are
perfectionists who fail because of their excessive idealism. The
moral to be drawn from the character and errors of Hollingsworth
also is suitable for Pierre's tragedy, which is as Hawthorne states
it, "an exemplification of the most awful truth in Bunyan's book
of such; from the very gate of heaven there is a by-way to the
pit!" And both works are critical of reformers, Transcendental
optimists, and "new-light Apostles."[55]

Accepting these suggestions, Henry A. Murray in his more
psychiatric than scholarly introduction to his edition of Pierre,
at first sensibly suggests that among the numerous roots of the
section "Chronometricals and Horologicals" are the conversations
with and the writings of Hawthorne (especially "The Birthmark"
and The Blithedale Romance). But his next theory is hard to
accept: "Strip Plinlimmon of the disguising title of Grand
Master . . . and snatch off his false beard, and you have a
striking physical and psychological likeness of Hawthorne, the

---

[54] Ibid., p. 205.

[55] Thorp, pp. xxxviii - xxxix.

inscrutable Paul Pry of the guilty human heart. " And Hollingsworth, the philosophic villain of The Blithedale Romance, is con-
versely a portrayal of Melville. This points toward the unlikely
theory that an estrangement took place, "so mutually traumatic
that each of them felt compelled to write an interpretation, an
apologia, a vindication, of his position," the novels being the
result.[56]   Edward G. Lueders has subsequently modified Murray's
theory and more thoroughly investigated points of comparison and
contrast in the two novels, both of which undoubtedly owe something to the relationship.[57]

Of most importance to Melville was the sympathetic understanding Hawthorne offered; Melville received so little of it in
his lifetime. After he read Hawthorne's enthusiastic letter concerning Moby Dick, now lost to us, he replied, "A sense of un-
speakable security is in me this moment, on account of your having
understood the book. "[58] If we can accept Melville's statement as
literal, Hawthorne could do more at that moment than the one
hundred or more subsequent years of literary criticism and
explication have been able satisfactorily to accomplish with
Moby Dick. How few writers of genius ever find one such all-
comprehending reader during their lives! And how worthwhile that
must have made the effort!

---

[56] Henry A. Murray, ed., Pierre, by Herman Melville, pp.
lxxvii-lxxix.

[57] Lueders, pp. 323-334

[58] Davis and Gilman, p. 142.

When he dedicated the work to Hawthorne, Melville was doing much more than expressing his affection and respect for a friend. He was telling us exactly who was responsible for the book. If Melville had not encountered Hawthorne at a crucial moment, Moby Dick might well have been just one more romantic narrative of the sea in a long line of such. In pre-Hawthorne days, those were precisely the terms Melville used to describe the work in progress.[59] But under the profound influence of Hawthorne's accomplishment in fiction, the embodiment of the great philosophic truth of the evil inherent in the universe, within the framework of allegorical narrative, Melville did his friend one better. He produced a mammoth allegory which flung a challenge in the face of God Himself to explain the presence of that evil. It is significant that Melville never again wrote anything as intellectually shallow as those early romantic novels. It is possibly no exaggeration to say that Melville's accomplishment as a great American writer is largely attributable to that "stunning concussion" of his mind and Hawthorne's.

---

[59] In a letter to the publisher describing the novel, as he was writing the first draft, he said, "The book is a romance of adventure, founded upon certain wild legends in the Southern Sperm Whale Fisheries, and illustrated by the author's own personal experience, of two years & more, as a harpooner." Ibid., p. 109.

Bibliography

Arvin, Newton. Hawthorne. Boston: Little, Brown, and Company, 1929.

_____. Herman Melville. The American Men of Letters Series. N. p.: William Sloane Associates, 1950.

Blair, Walter, Theodore Hornberger, and Randall Stewart, eds. The Literature of the United States. Revised edition. 2 vols. Chicago: Scott, Foresman and Company, 1953.

Braswell, William. "Herman Melville and Christianity." Unpublished Ph. D. dissertation, University of Chicago, 1934.

Canby, Henry Seidel. Classic Americans. New York: Russell & Russell, Inc., 1959.

Carpenter, Frederic I. "Puritans Prefer Blondes, The Heroines of Melville and Hawthorne." New England Quarterly, IX (June, 1936), 253-272.

Davis, Merrell R., and William H. Gilman, eds. The Letters of Herman Melville. New Haven: Yale University Press, 1960.

Hawthorne, Julian. Hawthorne and His Circle. New York: Harper & Brothers, 1903.

_____. Nathaniel Hawthorne and His Wife. Fourth edition. 2 vols. Boston: James R. Osgood and Company, 1885.

Hayford, Harrison. "Hawthorne, Melville, and the Sea." New England Quarterly, XIX (December, 1946), 435-452.

Howard, Leon. Herman Melville. Berkeley: University of California Press, 1951.

Levin, Harry. The Power of Blackness. New York: Vintage Books, 1960.

Lueders, Edward G. "The Melville-Hawthorne Relationship in Pierre and The Blithedale Romance." Western Humanities Review, IV (Autumn, 1950), 323-334.

Matthiessen, F. O. American Renaissance, Art and Expression in the
      Age of Emerson and Whitman. New York: Oxford University
      Press, 1941.

Metcalf, Eleanor Melville. Herman Melville, Cycle and Epicycle.
      Cambridge: Harvard University Press, 1953.

Minnigerode, Meade. Some Personal Letters of Herman Melville and
      A Bibliography. New York: Edmond Byrne Hackett, The Brick
      Row Book Shop, 1922.

Mumford, Lewis. Herman Melville. New York: Harcourt, Brace &
      Company, 1929.

Murray, Henry A., ed. Pierre, by Herman Melville. New York:
      Farrar, Straus, 1949.

O'Brien, Edward J. "The Fifteen Finest Short Stories." Forum,
      LXXIX (June, 1928), 908-914.

Pommer, Henry F. Milton and Melville. Pittsburgh: University
      of Pittsburgh Press, 1950.

Stewart, Randall. "Ethan Brand." Saturday Review of Literature,
      V (April 27, 1929), 967.

_____. "Melville and Hawthorne." South Atlantic Quarterly,
      LI (July, 1952), 436-446.

_____. Nathaniel Hawthorne. New Haven: Yale University
      Press, 1948.

_____, ed. The American Notebooks by Nathaniel Hawthorne.
      New Haven: Yale University Press, 1932.

_____, ed. The English Notebooks by Nathaniel Hawthorne.
      New York: Modern Language Association of America, 1941.

Thompson, Lawrance. Melville's Quarrel with God. Princeton:
      Princeton University Press, 1952.

Thorp, Willard, ed. Herman Melville, Representative Selections.
      American Writers Series. New York: American Book Company,
      1938.

Van Doren, Mark. Nathaniel Hawthorne. The American Men of
      Letter Series. N. p.: William Sloane Associates, 1949.

Weaver, Raymond M. *Herman Melville, Mariner and Mystic.* New York: George H. Doran Company, 1921.

Wright, Nathalia. "*Mosses from an Old Manse* and *Moby Dick*: The Shock of Discovery." *Modern Language Notes*, LXVII (June, 1952), 387-392.

CHAPTER 9

ARGUMENTATIVE WRITING

DESPITE the great popularity in our time of forums, panel discussions, symposiums, and subsidized tours of college and high school debating teams, we actually have little formal argument, of the classic type, that our forefathers for many centuries practiced and apparently relished, or at least demanded as proper. A political debate of the scale and quality of the Lincoln-Douglas debates of the past century is all but inconceivable today. William Jennings Bryan of Nebraska was probably the last great American orator who could hold an audience for as long as he chose to speak. Bryan's speeches, though they might indulge in "flights of rhetoric," nevertheless generally were systematic arguments conforming to the classic pattern that can be traced from Demosthenes and Cicero, through Pitt and Burke, Patrick Henry, Webster, Calhoun, and Lincoln, almost to the present day.

Now, in contrast, we commonly have the informal "speech" rather than the formal "address." The "speech" is likely to be too brief for elaborate logical development. It is cut to fit the inexorable stop-watch limit of 15 to 30 minutes radio or television time. In any case, it puts a premium on informality —the unbuttoned ease of the "fireside chat," the joking luncheon talk, the lounging "panel" with cigarettes and ashtray set conveniently near the nervous hands of the "discussants."

Similar tendencies appear in our argumentative writing. Instead of such formal arguments as Madison and Hamilton wrote for *The Federalist* or the lengthy, solidly composed essays that our quarterly, monthly, and even weekly periodicals published, as recently as the nineteen-thirties, we have the brisk, short, newspaper editorial, the popular commenta-

291

tor's "column," and the type of magazine article that, for
want of a better name, we may call the article of opinion.

THE ARTICLE OF OPINION

If it appears in a newspaper or a weekly periodical, the
article of opinion may be no longer than a thousand words.
It reaches greater length in the monthly magazine, and there
may display some of the characteristics of the formal essay,
in so far as it deals with a serious subject and makes some
show of conclusiveness. But only in the quarterlies, for the
most part, is an author encouraged to write with a degree of
thoroughness and formality. Generally, the article of opinion,
even when it uses a polished literary style, keeps an informal
tone and has some air of novelty or freshness.

That is to say, it is journalistic—or more journalistic than
literary. It is in the midstream of current events—is "newsy"
and topical. In presenting "facts," the article of opinion is
likely to become somewhat reportorial; it takes on some of the
characteristics of narrative. But the report of the facts
always carries with it some interpretation of the facts, and
an alert reader soon realizes that the interpretation is as
much intended to convince as to inform. The article of
opinion, in short, hopes to *persuade* the reader to accept, or
at least to entertain, a particular interpretation of the facts
presented. The "proposition" concerning which the author
wishes to convince the reader may not be explicitly stated.
It is embedded in the interpretation, and that interpretation,
in turn, rests upon a *judgment* of the right or wrong, the
truth or falsehood of a given situation, or the advisability or
inadvisability of a certain course of action.

Despite its informal and sometimes dramatic manner, the
article of opinion is, then, *argument,* however subtly it may
be disguised as "fact." In its reasoning it is, or should be,,
subject to the laws of thought that for centuries have
governed sound thinking and that form the basis of sound
argument. If it cannot meet such tests, it is deceiving us by a
display of mere rhetoric or by a misuse of rhetoric.

But we should not discard rhetoric because it is being
misused or is capable of misuse. We can readily see that in
our argumentative writing today, as in our speech-making,
"rhetoric," as the *art of persuasion,* is being favored over
"dialectic," which may be defined as *the method of distinguishing true propositions from false ones.* We can also note

that rhetoric is no less rhetoric when it tries to pass itself off as non-rhetoric—that is, as "objective" science, sociological analysis, "expert" testimony, "on the scene" reporting, or the like; this, indeed, can be the most seductive and misleading kind of rhetoric.

Yet the use of rhetoric to persuade is legitimate, if rightly understood and applied. Indeed, we could hardly get along without rhetoric, since people will not necessarily be led to act properly through a dry, dialectical presentation of true and false, good and bad, practical and impractical. At the same time, it is clear that a powerful rhetoric may be exceedingly dangerous, even disastrous, if it persuades people to favor the false rather than the true, the bad rather than the good, the impractical rather than the practical. Modern argument, which often conceals its process of argument—as in advertising appeals, sales talks, propaganda—needs to be carefully examined to discover the dialectic (reasoning process) for which the rhetoric serves as vehicle and motor. In the composition of argument, of whatever kind, the student must constantly remind himself that sound reasoning is the basis of sound argument. Without sound reasoning, he may deceive himself first, and then, through rhetoric misapplied, may deceive others; or else, if the unsoundness of his argument is detected by others, he may meet with rejection and incur blame.

DEFINITION AND ANALYSIS

A brief article of opinion cannot hope to define its terms, develop its distinctions, and analyze and organize its evidence in the elaborate and leisurely manner of the formal essay. But no piece of argumentative writing—whether brief editorial or long essay—can be considered valid unless, within the scale permitted by its limits, it observes the principles of argumentation. Definition and Analysis (see Chapter 7) are essential parts of argumentation, since a reasoned conclusion cannot be attained, and when attained cannot be supported, without the use of these instruments of logic. Definition and analysis are also valuable for their effect upon the "tone" of an argument because they are a guarantee of a writer's honesty of purpose with regard to the facts. By approaching the facts in an inquiring spirit rather than in a cocksure, assertive manner, a writer sets his readers' minds to work in a similar spirit of inquiry. It is far better thus to invite the reader to think than to arouse his emotions and, in so doing, perhaps create antagonism. We are influenced by a fair and calm statement of reasoned opinions, whether or not we accept them completely.

SOUNDNESS OF ARGUMENT

When is an argument sound? What is a good presentation? The two questions are really inseparable, but for purposes of explanation it is best to consider them in order.

1. *Soundness of argument consists first in a clear and definite statement of what is to be proved.* In formal argumentation this statement is called the *proposition* or *question.* There is no satisfaction in arguing about "woman's place," "intercollegiate football," "examinations," "the Supreme Court," if the argument is not centered upon a specific statement which permits a reasoned affirmative and negative. The matter to be argued can be put in the form of a question: "Shall married women be employed as teachers?" Or "Is intercollegiate football advantageous to higher education?" Or it may be put in the form of a statement: "Industry-wide bargaining in labor disputes should be abolished by law."

If the statement contains any terms that may be misunderstood, they should be defined. No argument can proceed intelligently unless people know what they are arguing about. Suppose the proposition is as follows: "The standard of living in the backward areas of the world ought to be raised." In that statement are three terms which need defining. What is a "standard of living"? What are "backward areas"? What do you mean by "raised"? If you attempt to argue the proposition as stated, without defining the terms, you may find the premises of your argument attacked by your opponents or critics. Or you may find that the argument is getting nowhere because one side means by "standard of living" ability to purchase manufactured goods, but the other side is thinking of "standard of living" as referring to moral and intellectual conditions, or even physical vigor.

Definiteness of statement means also precision in discerning and stating the issues which are to be argued. The issues are the essential points which have to be proved if the question as a whole is to be upheld. It requires some skill to distinguish true issues from false issues. To discover the issues involved in the question of whether or not moving pictures should be censored, let us first set down a number of possible issues, just as they come to mind. The issues are best stated in the form of specific questions.

1. Do the movies need reform?
2. Has censorship succeeded or failed in the past?
3. Will censorship injure the artistic quality of the movies?
4. Will censorship hurt their entertainment value?
5. Will it decrease movie admissions and therefore injure business?
6. Who will do the censoring?
7. What will Hollywood think?
8. Why do not the movies censor their own pictures?
9. Do not the public prefer uncensored pictures?
10. Is censorship practicable?
11. Does censorship violate constitutional rights?
12. Will it result in social good to the people as a whole?
13. Why not wait and see what will happen?
14. Will it increase taxes?

Reviewing this list of possible issues, we realize at once that some selection must be made. Some of the questions (like number 7) are irrelevant; others (like number 13) are absurd; others may be combined. Probably the argument rests on five main issues.

1. Do the movies need reform?
2. Is censorship a practicable kind of reform?
3. Is it constitutional and legal?
4. Will censorship injure the movies artistically?
5. Will censorship result in social good?

If we prove that the movies need reform; that censorship is a legal and practicable kind of reform; that it will not injure the art of the movies; and that it will result in social good—then we win the argument. But if the opposition can show that these issues cannot be sustained, then we lose the argument.

2. *Sound argument must rest upon evidence.* Evidence consists of solid and established facts. Loud assertions and violent approval or disapproval may *express* opinion, but do not make opinion acceptable to others. Rather, they bring the opposite—antagonism, denial, angry retort. To get at the solid facts that compose evidence (and that carry conviction) we must eliminate emotional reactions, sentimental

notions, hearsay, propaganda. We must know that the facts we use are really facts. Evidence must therefore meet three requirements:

(a) It must bear directly upon the issues. Loose talk, funny stories, personal reminiscences, though they may be pleasant, prove nothing whatever. You may convince people of your amiability by telling them funny stories, but unless the funny stories illustrate a point (and hence make possible an argument by analogy) they are not evidence.

(b) The evidence must be authoritative, unbiased, and up to date. In some instances, personal experience may furnish reliable evidence, but it should be considered carefully to see whether it offers grounds for making a generalization. If it comes from wide observation, done close at hand, it may be valuable. If it comes from a narrow or isolated experience, or an experience colored by strong personal feeling, it may not be trustworthy. A resident of Minnesota who goes to Florida in the winter is not, for that reason, an authority on agriculture in the South. On the other hand, a man who has lived on a large cotton plantation in the Mississippi Delta may know much about raising cotton, and yet his view may not take in the varying conditions of the cotton culture in the Carolina Piedmont and Texas. We laugh at the foreign visitor who, after looking at New York and living for two weeks on a dude ranch in Wyoming, goes home and writes a book about America; but our own opinions often have an equally shallow basis of personal experience.

Is a newspaper story authoritative evidence? A magazine article? A book? A lecture by a college professor? If the newspaper story is written by a trained and experienced reporter, and if the newspaper has no partisan reason for coloring or editing the report, it may be good evidence. Since newspapers deal with the changing aspect of affairs from day to day and have, at any moment, policies, formulas, and interests that may be hidden from the reader, we may do well to regard newspaper accounts with a certain amount of skepticism. A magazine article represents a more mature interpretation, and often a more competent one; but again we are justified in looking for marks of prejudice or narrowness of any sort. If the lecturer is really an authority, he may be able to give solid help, within the field of his special knowledge. Books are the most reliable guide of all, for only in books are we likely to find the mature and serious studies of the great authorities. Yet here again we must be watchful. It is better to consult several authorities rather than one, and, when they disagree, to examine the methods by which they have arrived at their interpretations, to study their points of view and special interests, and even to note the sources from which they may have derived their opinions. Last, it is of course necessary to use up-to-date information. A book on American government written in 1875 may contain valuable theories and be historically interesting; but many of its *facts* will be out of date.

(c) Enough evidence must be presented to support the argument effectively. How much, will be a matter of judgment and proportion. Remember that it is better to have a few good pieces of evidence than a mass of weak evidence. Concentrate upon what will be convincing and let the rest go.

It is also necessary to deal with evidence which may seem to support another view than your own. In formal argumentation, this part of the general process of argument is called refutation. If you can show that evidence which seems to support another view is not good evidence or does not prove what it seems to prove, you strengthen your own argument. If you neglect to consider evidence contrary to your own argument, you weaken your cause.

3. *Sound argument must be logical argument.* It is impossible to discuss here, with any real completeness, the laws of thought. These lie in the province of formal logic and are a separate study. We can, however, emphasize the necessity of sound logic by reviewing briefly the operation of inductive and deductive methods of reasoning and by showing where errors may arise.

We use the *inductive method* when we reason from the particular to the general. We use the *deductive method* when we reason from the general to the particular.

When a large number of particulars are accepted as pointing toward a generalization as being true or probably true, an induction has been made. We *infer* that the particulars produce the generalization. Sound thinking consists in making a justifiable, or logical, inference and in avoiding false inference.

Newton's statement of the law of gravitation is an example of a generalization based upon particulars. He made an induction. Induction, as has been pointed out (see page 222), is the method of science. Walter Reed was able to infer the cause of yellow fever by reasoning that since all persons bitten by a certain kind of mosquito caught the disease and other persons, not bitten, did not catch it, therefore the mosquito carried the disease. This generalization, however, was first set up as a working hypothesis; it had to be verified by prolonged experiment and observation. Science always begins with a working hypothesis, which it either accepts as a true generalization, or abandons, or modifies, according to what may be shown by its long and careful examination of particulars.

Whenever we use inductive reasoning, we should emulate the thoroughness and dispassionateness of science, though of course we cannot often observe and test on the same scale. The use of statistics in argument—though it may be tricky and unreliable—is an approximation of the inductive method of science. We use induction, on a small scale, if we infer from much observation of college life that large-scale education is wasteful because many students are lazy or indifferent or more attentive to social activities than to studies. The more particulars we can find that point the same way, the more likely the generalization is to be true.

Argument by example or analogy is an easier and more attractive use of induction. An example, in inductive reasoning, is really a parallel, from which a generalization applicable to a particular instance is inferred. If you argue that the development of many political parties in the United States is undesirable, and point, as an example, to some European country where multiple parties persist, apparently to the detriment of good government, you are arguing inductively, by example. In argument by analogy, the particular is chosen from some sphere remote or different from the one under consideration, but one that has enough likeness to render the generalization convincing. If you argue that it is vicious to pay athletes for performing, and give as your reason that such payment corrupts the morals both of athletes and of public, and if you then cite, as analogy, the gladiatorial combats of ancient Rome, you are reasoning by analogy.

But reasoning by example or analogy has obvious dangers. To be logically acceptable, the example or analogy must be a true parallel. If the differences between French politics and American politics, or between the French situation and the

American situation, are greater than the resemblances, then it will not necessarily be true that multiplicity of parties will cause the same injury to our government as in France. The gladiatorial combats of ancient Rome may not be a good analogy to subsidized athletics in America, and if so, the generalization falls down. A striking example or an analogy may *seem* so persuasive that it may influence thinking even though it is not logically sound. Lincoln's famous "House Divided" speech is an example of an argument by analogy that was extremely influential; yet the studies of some historians seem to indicate that the figure of the house divided against itself had a great deal more poetry than logic in it. When an example or an analogy is not logically sound, it is open to easy attack by an opponent. Probably argument by example or analogy is as much exposition as argument. The example or analogy explains or illustrates, even when it is not strictly logical. But be careful to choose an example that is really typical or an analogy that is really plausible, if you do not wish to have your argument questioned.

The deductive method of reasoning from general to particular appears in all argument in which a principle is set up and then applied to a group of particulars. The principle may be a generalization that has been reached by a process of induction; or it may be some general truth which is assumed as a matter of course to be acceptable to all concerned in the argument.

The Syllogism

A true statement may be derived as the result of the application of the inductive process to experience. To apply the result of inductive thinking to new particulars is deductive thinking. Back of all deductive thinking is the scheme of thought which logicians call a *syllogism*. If the syllogism is properly applied to the scheme of thought which is being undertaken, it serves as a test of the validity of the assertion which is being made. Only by such a means can we be assured that the assertion is consistent with itself and the bases upon which it is founded. The bases are called "premises," and the resulting assertion is called the "conclusion."

A syllogism therefore consists of two premises and a conclusion drawn from those premises. The *major premise* states a generalization assumed to be true or already proved as true. The *minor premise* is a specific statement which

asserts that some item is included in this generalization. The
conclusion infers a logical connection as apparent between
the premises. For illustration, we may now state a common
argument in the form of a syllogism:

> MAJOR PREMISE: *Athletic exercise is beneficial to young men.*
> MINOR PREMISE: *Football is a form of athletic exercise.*
> CONCLUSION: *Therefore, football is beneficial to young men.*

The logical validity of this syllogism, as of every syllogism,
depends upon the correctness of major and minor premise.
If each of these is necessarily and invariably true, as stated,
then the conclusion must necessarily be true. The syllogism
given above contains certain debatable parts, especially in
its major premise, and therefore the conclusion is not a
perfectly logical conclusion.

In order to insure exactness and complete validity of
thinking, logicians long ago developed laws of logic and
syllogistic exercises which illustrate those laws.[1] In logic we
are offered perfect syllogisms like the following:

> MAJOR PREMISE: *All men are mortal.*
> MINOR PREMISE: *Socrates is a man.*
> CONCLUSION: *Therefore Socrates is mortal.*

One premise may be stated in the negative form as in the
following syllogism:

> MAJOR PREMISE: *No kettles are made of wax.*
> MINOR PREMISE: *This object is made of wax.*
> CONCLUSION: *Therefore this object is not a kettle.*

Other perfect syllogisms will appear in mathematics, since
in mathematics thinking can be abstract and perfect. In
plane geometry, for example, a syllogism would take a form
like this:

> MAJOR PREMISE: *A straight line is the shortest distance be-*
> *tween two points.*
> MINOR PREMISE: *The line XY, between the points X and Y,*
> *is a straight line.*
> CONCLUSION: *Therefore the line XY is the shortest distance*
> *between the points X and Y.*

In general, if one premise is negative, the conclusion will

---

[1] For a complete discussion of the syllogism see Bennett and
Baylis, *Formal Logic* (Chapter VI); Hepp, *Thinking Things
Through* (Chapter 19); or similar works.

be negative. If both premises are positive, the conclusion will be positive. If both premises are negative, there will not be any valid conclusion. The following is an example of the third situation:

MAJOR PREMISE: *No lazy person is a good student.*
MINOR PREMISE: *No good student will ever fail.*
CONCLUSION: *Therefore . . .*

We cannot complete any assertion because, so far as we are instructed by our premises, the lazy person may or may not fail. If the minor premise had read, "Good students are the only ones that pass," we should have had only one negative premise and thus could have concluded, "No lazy person will pass."

In the type of disjunctive syllogism known as the *dilemma,* the major premise states an alternative between two choices; the minor premise denies one choice; the conclusion is the remaining choice. For the conclusion to be valid, however, it is necessary that the two choices exhaust all possibilities.

MAJOR PREMISE: *This cloth is either linen or cotton.*
MINOR PREMISE: *It is not cotton.*
CONCLUSION: *Therefore it is linen.*

It should be evident that the validity of the chain of reasoning represented in any syllogism depends upon the soundness of the premises. If the premises are not true, or if either premise is not true or is doubtful, the conclusion is inevitably untrustworthy.

The following statements have the *form* of a syllogism:

MAJOR PREMISE: *All men are two-headed creatures.*
MINOR PREMISE: *John is a man.*
CONCLUSION: *Therefore John is a two-headed creature.*

But the conclusion is false, and indeed absurd, because the major premise is false.

In practice, of course, we rarely encounter a chain of thought expressed with the precise formality of a syllogism. Commonly we encounter the abbreviated form of the syllogism which is known as the *enthymeme* (from the Greek *en,* "in," and *thumos,* "mind"). In the enthymeme one of the three parts of the syllogism is implied but not expressed; the reader is left to supply the missing part. Thus we may read, "Since Socrates is a man, he is mortal." In this enthymeme or incomplete syllogism, the major premise exists only by inference. We assume that all men are mortal; our experience upholds this premise; and hence we do not question the conclusion.

On the other hand, it may be said, "Everyone who does not study will not pass; and you are not studying." Here the conclusion, "You will not pass," is omitted. The minor premise is omitted in a statement of the following kind: "All cheating is dishonest, and this paper is dishonest." The omitted premise is, "This paper is cheating."

Most often, however, the major premise is omitted. Statements which involve such a causal connection as is indicated by the use of words like *since, because, therefore,* and *thus* almost always involve omission of the major premise. For example, we may say, "Since I am tired, I shall not go to the movie." The conclusion is, "I shall not go to the movie." The minor premise is, "I am tired." To reach such a conclusion the major premise must have been, "Whenever I am tired I do not go to the movie."

Common Fallacies

A fallacy is an error, or failure, of logic. Fallacies can be detected by submitting the sequence of thought in any given instance to the test of the syllogism. If the sequence of thought can be expressed in the form of a correct syllogism, the thought is logical. If no correct syllogism can be thus constructed, the thought is illogical. Misapplications of the syllogism are common in our thinking and writing, as, indeed, they have been throughout human history. Most commonly such misapplications, which lead to errors of logic, occur in connection with the enthymeme or abridged form of the syllogism.

The following list includes some of the most common types of fallacies, but it by no means exhausts all the possible fallacies. In the preceding discussion you have been warned against other fundamental errors—for example, errors of fact and errors of vague, weak, or incorrect definition. Here are listed only those errors which are directly related to the deductive process. All have one characteristic in common: either they cannot be set up into any intelligible syllogism or they involve a premise which can hardly be assumed if it is explicitly stated.

1. *Begging the question.* Begging the question is the fallacy of assuming as true something that is not proved. This

fault may occur either in the major premise or in the minor premise of a syllogism.

A farmer argues: "I do not see why my son should waste his time studying Latin. He is only going to be a farmer." The question is begged in the word *waste.* The unproved assumption is that it is a waste of time for farmers' sons to study Latin.

A woman says to her friend: "I recommend that you read *Triple Towers,* because it reveals an interesting mind. You might know that a man with the author's mind would write a book like that." The unproved assumption is in the second sentence.

Arguments for depriving the United States Supreme Court of the power to declare laws unconstitutional may run like this: "The Supreme Court ought not to have the power to declare Federal laws unconstitutional because the justices are not competent to pass on the wisdom of social legislation." The fallacy here is in wrongly assuming that the Supreme Court can legally pass on the *wisdom* of social legislation; and there is also an implied false definition or conception of *Federal laws, unconstitutional,* and *pass on.*

The fallacy of begging the question sometimes takes the form called "reasoning in a circle," as in the following sentences: "If we fully develop the resources of the country, people will have a higher standard of living. If they have a higher standard of living, they will become more ambitious and will fully develop the resources of the country."

2. *Non sequitur.* (It does not follow.) The fallacy of *non sequitur* consists in drawing a wrong conclusion from given premises. The commonest type of *non sequitur* is the fallacy known as the *post hoc* fallacy (from the Latin sentence, *post hoc ergo propter hoc:* "after this, therefore on account of it"). A man sees a black cat cross the road. Soon afterwards he is involved in an automobile accident. If he infers that, since the accident came *after* his encounter with the black cat, therefore the cat caused the accident, he is guilty of the *post hoc* fallacy. Superstitions and popular beliefs lead, of course, to a great many such fallacies. It was formerly a popular belief that malaria was caused by damp night air, which brought miasmatic vapors. The chain of logic was as follows: people sat in damp night air; they then caught malaria; therefore damp night air caused malaria. Actually it was a malaria-bearing mosquito (winging its way through

damp night air) which caused the disease. But *non sequitur*'s
are just as common among the highly educated as among
the uneducated, and just as common in our supposedly en-
lightened age as in the supposedly backward days. People
"jump to conclusions." Somehow they seem to prefer to go
wrong. It is hard to follow a strict logical discipline.

3. *Ignoring the question.* The question is ignored when
the ground of argument is shifted in some way from real
issues to false issues. In popular parlance, this is "to drag a
red herring across the trail." A candidate for public office
asks to be elected because he is a war veteran, because he
holds seniority privileges which will be lost if he is not
elected, or (by implication if not by direct utterance) because his father was a distinguished man. All such claims
ignore the real question—the candidate's suitability for office.

In another form, ignoring the question is *argumentum ad
hominem* ("argument against an opponent rather than
against his thesis"—Bennett and Baylis, *Formal Logic*).
People may argue that X's opinions on politics should not be
considered or respected because he is a college professor—
or college student. During Andrew Jackson's campaign for
the Presidency his opponents circulated slanders against the
general and his wife—a vicious example of *argumentum ad
hominem.* This fallacy, of course, is the commonest of all
fallacies, but it is one of the most dangerous to sound thinking. It is the last resource of the shallow and unscrupulous
thinker.

Any appeal to prejudice or emotion, *when offered as a
substitute for logical argument,* is a form of ignoring the
question.

4. *False dilemma.* A false dilemma is created if we are
asked to choose between two courses of action or two interpretations of a situation when more than two choices are
possible. The student who argues against intellectual interests on the ground that, at college, it is better to be a good
fellow than a grind, is setting up a false dilemma. The "two
horns" of a dilemma of this kind do not present all the possible choices.

EXERCISES

1. Test the validity of the conclusions in the following syllogistic
groups.

a. Everybody can understand plain language; poets are often misunderstood; therefore poets should learn to write plain language.
b. Prehistoric monsters are extinct; alligators are not extinct; therefore alligators are not prehistoric monsters.
c. Rational creatures are accountable for their actions; dogs are not rational creatures; therefore dogs are not accountable for their actions.
d. This flower that I found in a New England meadow is either a wildflower or a garden escape; I cannot find it in my *Guide to New England Wildflowers;* then it must be a garden escape.
e. Most fat men are good-humored; Mr. Pickwick is a fat man; therefore Mr. Pickwick is good-humored.

2. Test and discuss the validity of the following incomplete syllogisms.

a. Since the thirteen American colonies were able to agree peacefully on a Federal constitution, it is obvious that we should work toward world peace through a world constitution.
b. Because eighteenth century England drew its best leaders from the landed aristocracy, this class should be encouraged in the United States.
c. Travel by airplane is the best because it is the quickest.
d. Man is, by nature, the most social and gregarious, and, therefore, the least selfish of animals.

3. Identify and discuss the fallacies of logic involved in the following statements.

a. If everybody goes to college, everybody will earn higher wages; then our higher standard of living will naturally produce better colleges.
b. I refuse to employ Smith; he comes from a family of opportunists and status-seekers.
c. A vote for Mr. Goodboy is a vote for Progress because all the Goodboys are progressive in their thinking.
d. I left my umbrella on the bus; so it is certain to rain before I go home.
e. Try Hornswoggle's Syrup; it's better because it tastes better.
f. Eighteen-year-old boys were subject to draft for the armed services. Therefore the voting age should be lowered.
g. There should be no laws regulating marriage because marriage is entirely the private affair of the two individuals concerned.

PRESENTATION

Good organization, clear and effective language, all of the rhetorical devices that make writing effective—these must be used as a matter of course in the article of opinion. Yet there still remain certain matters of strategy, peculiar to argument, which must be pointed out.

The writer of an article of opinion assumes that his readers are to be convinced by his arguments. He does not "carry coals to Newcastle," or seek to convert those who are already of his own way of thinking. Nor can he convince people against their will. It is impossible to browbeat people into accepting opinions different from their own. To be really persuasive, sound argument is a first essential, but there must be something more than sound argument. People are likely to be repelled, at first, or even antagonized, by the expression of an opinion contrary to what they hold. Everybody's first impulse, upon encountering a contrary opinion, is to express his own opinion, perhaps even more strongly than before. The great problem of the article of opinion is to overcome this entirely natural antagonism.

A temperate and conciliatory manner is one of the best ways of overcoming antagonism. A belligerent approach stirs up belligerence in others. It is true that certain writers of the iconoclastic school (George Bernard Shaw, H. L. Mencken, Bernard DeVoto, Dwight MacDonald) have used the belligerent approach with some success. In order to get the reader's attention, these writers have chosen to shock him by violent or paradoxical assertions, even at the risk of antagonizing him completely. But it is doubtful whether this method succeeds in the long run. The conciliatory approach is best for most purposes. It is good ethics as well as good strategy to be completely fair to other points of view. It is good strategy to make concessions to the other side in those respects where concessions can be made. If then, despite such concessions, the arguer can still make a good case, his position becomes all the stronger. Above all, if the writer can begin his discussion on some point about which everybody can be expected to agree and then proceed, with this as his premise, to build his argument, he has made the best possible beginning. His reader's attention—and possibly momentary sympathy—is gained. The way is open to carry the reader along, step by step. Mark Antony's famous speech in

Shakespeare's *Julius Cæsar* makes exactly this approach. "I come to bury Cæsar, not to praise him," says Antony, addressing a mob which might as easily hiss him as applaud him. Then, after a recitation of Cæsar's philanthropies and personal excellencies, he prepares the way for his denunciation of the conspirators.

AN ARGUMENT AGAINST PAYMENT OF SALARIES TO EXECUTIVE OFFICERS OF THE FEDERAL GOVERNMENT[1] *By Benjamin Franklin*

SIR, IT is with reluctance that I rise to express a disapprobation of any one article of the plan, for which we are so much obliged to the honorable gentleman who laid it before us. From its first reading, I have borne a good will to it, and, in general, wished it success. In this particular of salaries to the executive branch, I happen to differ; and, as my opinion may appear new and chimerical, it is only from a persuasion that it is right, and from a sense of duty, that I hazard it. The Committee will judge of my reasons when they have heard them, and their judgment may possibly change mine. I think I see inconveniences in the appointment of salaries; I see none in refusing them, but on the contrary great advantages.

Sir, there are two passions which have a powerful influence in the affairs of men. These are *ambition* and *avarice:* the love of power and the love of money. Separately, each of these has great force in prompting men to action; but when united in view of the same object, they have in many minds the most violent effects. Place before the eyes of such men a post of *honor,* that shall at the same time be a place of *profit,* and they will move heaven and earth to obtain it. The vast number of such places it is that renders the British government so tempestuous. The struggles for them are the true source of all those factions which are perpetually dividing the nation, distracting its councils, hurrying it sometimes into fruitless and mischievous wars, and often compelling a submission to dishonorable terms of peace.

And of what kind are the men that will strive for this profitable pre-eminence, through all the bustle of cabal, the heat of contention, the infinite mutual abuse of parties, tearing to pieces the best of characters? It will not be the wise and moderate, the lovers of peace and good order, the men fittest for the trust. It will be the bold and violent, the men of strong passions and indefatigable activity in their selfish pursuits. These will thrust themselves into your government, and be your rulers. And these, too, will be mistaken in the expected happiness of their situation; for their van-

[1] Speech in the Constitutional Convention, June 2, 1787.

quished competitors, of the same spirit, and from the same motives, will perpetually be endeavoring to distress their administration, thwart their measures, and render them odious to the people.

Besides these evils, sir, though we may set out in the beginning with moderate salaries, we shall find that such will not be of long continuance. Reasons will never be wanting for proposed augmentations, and there will always be a party for giving more to the rulers, that the rulers may be able in return to give more to them. Hence, as all history informs us, there has been in every state and kingdom a constant kind of warfare between the governing and the governed; the one striving to obtain more for its support, and the other to pay less. And this alone has occasioned great convulsions, actual civil wars, ending either in dethroning of the princes or enslaving of the people.

Generally, indeed, the ruling power carries its point, and we see the revenues of princes constantly increasing, and we see that they are never satisfied, but always in want of more. The more the people are discontented with the oppression of taxes, the greater need the prince has of money to distribute among his partisans, and pay the troops that are to suppress all resistance and enable him to plunder at pleasure. There is scarce a king in a hundred, who would not, if he could, follow the example of Pharaoh—get first all the people's money, then all their lands, and then make them and their children servants forever.

It will be said that we do not propose to establish kings. I know it. But there is a natural inclination in mankind to kingly government. It sometimes relieves them from aristocratic domination. They had rather have one tyrant than five hundred. It gives more of the appearance of equality among citizens; and that they like. I am apprehensive, therefore—perhaps too apprehensive—that the government of these States may in future times end in a monarchy. But this catastrophe, I think, may be long delayed, if in our proposed system we do not sow the seeds of contention, faction, and tumult, by making our posts of honor places of profit. If we do, I fear that, though we employ at first a number and not a single person, the number will in time be set aside; it will only nourish the foetus of a king (as the honorable gentleman from Virginia very aptly expressed it), and a king will the sooner be set over us.

It may be imagined by some that this is an utopian idea, and that we can never find men to serve us in the executive department, without paying them well for their services. I conceive this to be a mistake. Some existing facts present themselves to me, which incline me to a contrary opinion. The High Sheriff of a county in England is an honorable office, but it is not a profitable one. It is rather expensive, and therefore not sought for. But yet it is executed, and well executed, and usually by some of the principal gentlemen of the county. In France, the office of Counsellor, or member of their judiciary parliaments, is more honorable. It is therefore purchased at a high price; there are indeed fees on the law proceedings, which are divided among them, but these fees do not amount to more than three per cent on the sum paid for the place. Therefore, as legal interest is there at five per cent, they in fact pay two per cent for being allowed to do the judiciary business of the nation, which is at the same time entirely exempt from the burden of paying them any salaries for their services. I do not, however, mean to recommend this as an eligible mode for our judiciary department. I only bring the instance to show that the pleasure of doing good and serving their country, and the respect such conduct entitles them to, are sufficient motives with some minds to give up a great portion of their time to the public, without the mean inducement of pecuniary satisfaction.

Another instance is that of a respectable society, who have made the experiment, and practiced it with success, now more than a hundred years. I mean the Quakers. It is an established rule with them that they are not to go to law, but in their controversies they must apply to their monthly, quarterly, and yearly meetings. Committees of these sit with patience to hear the parties, and spend much time in composing their differences. In doing this they are supported by a sense of duty and the respect paid to usefulness. It is honorable to be so employed, but it was never made profitable by salaries, fees, or perquisites. And indeed, in all cases of public service, the less the profit the greater the honor.

To bring the matter nearer home, have we not seen the greatest and most important of our offices, that of General of our Armies, executed for eight years together, without the smallest salary, by a patriot whom I will not now offend by any other praise; and this, through fatigues and distresses, in common with the other brave men, his military friends and companions, and the constant anxieties peculiar to his station? And shall we doubt finding three or four men in all the United States, with public spirit enough to bear sitting in peaceful council, for perhaps an equal term, merely to preside over our civil concerns, and see that our laws are duly executed? Sir, I have a better opinion of our country. I think we shall never be without a sufficient number of wise and good men to undertake, and execute well and faithfully, the office in question.

Sir, the saving of the salaries, that may at first be proposed, is not an object with me. The subsequent mischiefs of proposing them are what I apprehend. And therefore it is that I move the amendment. If it is not seconded or accepted, I must be contented with the satisfaction of having delivered my opinion frankly, and done my duty.

EXERCISE

Benjamin Franklin's speech is an excellent example of a brief formal argument of the classical type. In the first paragraph, after some courteous preliminaries, Franklin states the proposition: "I see inconvenience in the appointment of salaries. . . ." Next he sets forth the premises on which his argument is grounded—the influence of "ambition and avarice" in the affairs of men. In the development of his main argument against salaries for the executive department, Franklin seeks to show how the influence of "ambition and avarice" have operated in past governments; he draws the inference that they may operate similarly in the new Republic of the United States. He refutes the probable charge that his view is "utopian," and in this portion of his argument relies upon two analogies (the "High Sheriff of a county in England"; the society of the Quakers); further strengthens his argument by the example of George Washington; and, in conclusion, rejects the idea that "the saving of salaries" is an object with him.

The following questions may assist your study:

1. Are the premises of Franklin's argument sound?

2. Did they apply to the American situation at the time?

3. What are the issues involved? Are they directly stated or merely implied?

4. How valid and applicable is the historical argument offered in paragraph 4?

5. How valid and how effective are the analogies advanced by Franklin in paragraphs 5 and 6?

6. Why does Franklin reserve "the General of the Armies" for a climactic point?

7. Franklin's proposition was not accepted by the convention. Viewing it in the perspective of nearly two centuries, do you find in it any points that a student of government would still have to take into serious account?

LET'S NOT GET OUT THE VOTE[1]   *By Robert E. Coulson*

THREE years ago anyone who failed to vote had to face the combined scorn of both political parties, the school-teachers, boy scouts, war veterans, chambers of commerce, and leagues of women voters. Last year bar associations, girl scouts, tavern keepers, President Eisenhower, radio and TV stations, and junior chambers of commerce joined the crusade. There is every prospect that in future elections, nonvoters will face jail sentences or fines, or be called to testify before investigating committees.

Before this happens, someone should come to their defense. Nonvoters are often more intelligent, more fair-minded, and just as loyal as voters. The right not to vote is as basic as the right to. If voting is made a duty, it ceases to be a privilege.

Let's look at the voting behavior of Mr. and Mrs. Whipcord and Mrs. Whipcord's brother Harold, on the day of the local school-

[1] From *Harper's Magazine,* Vol. 211 (Nov., 1955). Reprinted by permission of the author.

board election. Mrs. Whipcord says, "I have studied the candidates and have made up my mind. I will vote for Jones." Mr. Whipcord says, "I know nothing about the candidates or the issues. I will stay home, and allow the election to be decided by the votes of those who have made a study and formed an opinion." Harold says, "I don't know anything about the candidates or the problems, but by golly, I'm going to vote. It's my duty. I'll pick the fellows with the shortest names."

If there is a bad citizen among these three, which one is it? Whose procedure is least likely to bring good government to the school district?

Non-voting, multiplied by the thousands, is said to mean voter apathy, and this is supposed to be a sin. Have we lost our sacred American right to be apathetic? Suppose Mr. Whipcord studied the candidates carefully and concluded that Candidate Jones was a boob and Candidate Smith a thief. Is it un-American to refuse to choose between them? Or suppose he is satisfied that Jones and Smith are equally qualified, equally able, and that the school's problems are in good hands no matter which man wins. He is not apathetic; he is satisfied. Why should he be forced to choose between candidates on some esoteric basis?

The notion that "getting out the vote" makes for better election results is neither non-partisan, patriotic, nor logical. It is a device to favor the machines of both parties. It handicaps independent candidates, unfairly burdens the party in power, makes elections more expensive to conduct, greatly slows the tallying and—worst of all—places the emphasis on the ritual of voting rather than the thought behind the vote.

If you fill in all the blank spaces on the ballot, the political machines will steal three-fourths of your vote. Let's see how this works, in a typical primary election.

Here are seven offices to be filled by nomination, with two or three candidates for each office. Citizen Stringfellow is interested in seeing Jones win for Auditor. He has no information about the candidates for Attorney General, Treasurer, Superintendent of Schools, or the others. He votes for Jones and then looks on down the list. He has been persuaded that it is his duty to vote for somebody for each office. So for six of the seven offices, he marks an X opposite the name best known to him, or the name on top, or the name suggested by his committeeman. These are machine candidates, and Citizen Stringfellow has given away six-sevenths of his vote.

After him, comes Citizen Stalwart, who knows the candidates for two of the seven offices. He also fills in all the blanks, letting the machine steal five-sevenths of his vote. One of his blind votes cancels out the intelligent vote cast by Citizen Stringfellow. At this rate, during a day's balloting, the candidates backed by the strongest machines with the biggest publicity budgets will win, even though not a single voter had an intelligent preference for them.

Is this what Thomas Jefferson had in mind?

"Getting out the vote" is always partisan. A calm and dignified effort benefits the party in power. An excited or hysterical effort benefits the party out of power. The Republicans were very happy to use the pressure of "neutral" groups in the 1952 elections. But they had better learn that this is a two-edged sword. Next time, the girl scouts, veterans' groups, radio stations, newspapers, and community funds may be out needling the Republicans with propaganda.

"Vote this time or your vote may be gone forever." "This may be your last chance." "Vote now or never." Anyone who is led to the polls by such arguments is going to vote against whoever brought us to the edge of this crevasse. As the pressure on the public increases, the party out of power is most likely to benefit in direct proportion to it.

All public-opinion surveys show that a certain proportion of the electorate has no opinion about many vital issues, does not know who is running for office, and does not care. A gentle campaign to bring a submissive one-third of the apathetic sheep to the polls gets out a voting majority for the candidates who have had the greatest amount of publicity—who usually belong to the party in power. A rip-snorting effort to get out all the ignoramuses tends to turn them into the rebel column, and thus benefits the outs.

In either event, the girl scouts should wash their hands of it. The job of getting out the vote is a partisan effort which belongs to the professionals.

The silliest idea of all is the notion that it is un-American or unpatriotic not to vote. "A plague on both your houses" is a fair American attitude—all too often a logical one. Stupidity does not become wisdom by being multiplied.

In every election not more than one-third of the people care very much how it comes out. A certain percentage may have some sort of belief or opinion without feeling very strongly about it; another percentage may have studied the matter a little without forming an opinion; another percentage may not even have studied it; and so on, until we come to the people who are not even aware that an election is being held. The more we urge these people to clutter up the polling place, the more delay there is in voting, the more the cost of ballots and clerks, and the slower the returns.

If Candidate Jones would normally have won by 3,000 votes to 1,000, and we corral 10,000 more people into the polling places, won't Candidate Jones still win, by 8,000 to 6,000? Mathematically the last-minute coin flippers may make the election look close, but what patriotic purpose is accomplished?

And if the coin-flippers should happen to defeat the will of the informed majority, the cause of good government would emphatically not have been served.

Our city had a referendum recently in which the people voted for a tax increase to build an incinerator and against a tax increase to operate it. Every one of your communities has probably known referendums where the voters approved the bonds for a school but disapproved the sites, or voted for the site and against the bonds. All those voters who marked in opposite directions on the same afternoon were unwisely pressured into voting.

You have also seen primary elections where the boob with the catchy name ran away from the able man whose publicity was colorless. You have seen final elections where the straight party voters and the blank fillers smothered any discriminating choices which the thoughtful voters had made. You may have noticed with distress some of the undignified didos, cruel epithets, pompous verbosities, and Shakespearean gestures with which even good men became burdened early in their campaigns. All of these are caused in large measure by "get out the vote" efforts which emphasize putting a cross in half the squares.

Instead of urging people to vote, we ought to be urging them to study and form opinions. If thought and inspection of the candidates do not create a real desire to vote, then the citizen should be encouraged to stay at home on election day. A low vote is part of the public record and itself a significant voter reaction which ought to be preserved. Maybe neither of the candidates was worth voting for.

Certainly the right to vote is important and should not be curtailed. A fool who is willing to walk all the way to the polling place should be given every freedom to record every stupid impulse he feels, for these will tend to cancel each other out. But no one should pretend that marking X in a square is any proof of patriotism or even intelligence. It is not your duty to vote, but, if you choose to, then it should be your duty to be intelligent about it.

EXERCISE

This is an article of opinion of the informal, journalistic type. But it has a serious purpose, for Mr. Coulson exposes one absurdity by setting up counterabsurdities in quasi-logical parallel, somewhat after the fashion of Jonathan Swift in "A Modest Proposal." In essence, this is a form of parody. Mr. Coulson's assertion of "the right *not* to vote" is a parody of the do-gooder's platitudinous exhortations about "the right to vote." Of the same nature is his rhetorical question: "Have we lost our sacred American right to be apathetic?"

1. What other instances of parody do you find?

2. Is Mr. Coulson cynical about the right to vote, or does he wish, through his use of mockery and irony, to direct our attention

to some evil far greater than the failure of voters to go to the polls—
an evil of which this failure is but a symptom?

3. How would you justify the term "journalistic" as applied to
this article? Point out all specifically journalistic features.

4. What are the principal rhetorical features of the article?

5. Does the article, despite its light and bantering tone, have a
valid logical framework? How would you state Mr. Coulson's argument in plain logical terms? Do the same for the opposing argument.

THE TRUE ORIGIN OF ACADEMIC FREEDOM[1]

By Russell Kirk

THE present, when we come to seek for truth in it, is found to be
no more than a thin film—sometimes a scum—upon the deep well
of the ages; and perhaps no one does more mischief than the
visionary who endeavors to guide us by *a priori* assumptions about
the unknowable future. It is only by reference to the past that we
can obtain some grip upon the meaning of an idea disputed in
modern society.

"Academic freedom is a specific kind of freedom," Mr. Sidney
Hook writes. "It is the freedom of professionally qualified persons
to inquire, discover, publish and teach the truth as they see it in
their field of competence, without any control or authority except
the control or authority of the rational methods by which truth is
established. Insofar as it acknowledges intellectual discipline or
restraint from a community, it is only from the community of
qualified scholars which accepts the authority of rational inquiry."
Now the trouble with this definition is that no such degree of
liberty for scholars and teachers has long prevailed anywhere. Mr.
Hook really is writing of his ideal, rather than describing a tradition or defining the phrase as it has acquired meaning from the
experience of civilized society. Mr. Hook goes on to say that academic freedom is not an absolute, but that society finds it expedient
to extend this freedom to the Academy because society at large
benefits from the consequences of unhampered inquiry. If, then, the
Academy either fails to accomplish its educational goals, or if it
violates other moral values more weighty than academic freedom,
the community does right to abridge academic freedom.* Mr. Hook,
believing that such checks upon the general principle ought to be
employed only very seldom, nevertheless remarks that "the *justification* of academic freedom must lie in its fruits."

[1] From *Academic Freedom* by Russell Kirk, Copyright 1955,
Henry Regnery Company, Chicago. Reprinted by permission of
Henry Regnery Company.

* Sidney Hook, *Heresy, Yes—Conspiracy, No*, pp. 154–61. [Kirk's
note.]

Here I begin to part company with Mr. Hook. He goes on to argue that the Academy, or university, is "a semi-public institution," a part of the community, subject in theory to the will of the community. I think he goes too far. Although rights may have a justification in their fruits, they may also have a justification in prescriptions; and although the Academy exists in part for the sake of the community, it exists also for its own sake, and more especially for the sake of private wisdom and private needs. "Its ultimate fruits are to be found not in the private, professional delight of the connoisseur of ideas, although this has merit, too, but in the public good which includes, let us hope, the multiplied private delights of others besides professors." I find in this sentence of Professor Hook's an ominous fondness for intellectual collectivism. And I believe that here Mr. Hook is unhistorical.

The first regular Academy of which we have much knowledge was the school of Plato. Now Plato's Academy did not exist in any immediate way for the benefit of the community; indeed, Plato and his pupils commonly were at odds with their community, in a political sense. The allegiance of the Academy was to something grander even than Athens: to Truth. For Truth, and in defiance of the people of Athens, Plato's master Socrates had died. Plato and his disciples were not public servants. They taught and studied for their "private, professional delight," and for the conservation and enlargement of Truth. It is true, of course, that Athens and all the civilized world benefited, in time, from their labors; but that is not the primary justification for the freedom of mind enjoyed and defended by the philosophers in the groves of the Academy. The community, indeed, often hampered them a great deal, and put the first of its great thinkers to death, and forced the second to flee to Megara and Syracuse, and compelled the third, on occasion, to take refuge in Asia. All political communities, even wisdom-loving Athens, tend to dread or despise their academies, so that to lay down the dogma of academic responsibility to the community, in Professor Hook's definition, is to run the risk of subjecting the liberties of the academy to the prejudices of the multitude, and to run the risk of subjecting the free human person to an abstract state. I do not mean to imply that philosophers have no responsibilities toward their fellow-men; indeed, the pursuit of Truth puts upon them very grave responsibilities; but they need always to remember that it is Truth they worship, not humanity, and that it is by Truth they must be judged, not Demos. If philosophers are treated as servants, even as the servants of a faceless Community, presently they will acquire the proverbial vices of servants, with few of the redeeming virtues of simple loyalty to persons.

Plato's Academy, for twenty-three centuries, has been to scholars the grand model of freedom to pursue the Truth. Although continuity of institutions is one principal evidence of prescriptive

rights, it is not the only evidence. Our modern universities and
colleges are not descended in a direct line, of course, from the
Academy of Athens; but when, nine centuries after Plato began
to teach, Justinian closed the schools of Athens, the idea of academic freedom was not extinguished. A memory may have as much
power as a living thing, or more. And already the first of the great
Christian universities, that of Constantinople, was nearly a century
old when the end came to the Athenian philosophers. But my principal concern, just now, is this: the Academy of Athens, like the
other great schools of antiquity, was not founded by the community, nor did it owe its primary allegiance to the community. It was
instituted by private persons for their "private, professional delight"
—or, to speak more accurately than Professor Hook does, to enable
them to pursue the Truth without being servants of an evanescent
community. And this idea of intellectual freedom, the freedom of
the Academy, has ever since been the model for all men trained in
the classical disciplines.

But modern learning owes even more to medieval institutions
than it does to its classical strain; and besides, there subsists a
direct historical continuity between the medieval universities and
much modern education, even in America. We ought, then, to pay
close attention to academic freedom as it existed in the medieval
university. Mr. Hook, no friend to the Schoolmen, nevertheless
confesses that "within the framework of certain key assumptions
of Christian doctrine, a considerable degree of academic freedom
was enjoyed by the medieval university at a time when civil freedom for the citizens of the community was hardly an embryonic
concept.* Although Mr. Hook intends to be fair here, I think he has
missed the point, which is this: there was freedom in the medieval
universities *because* they existed within a framework of "certain
key assumptions of Christian doctrine," not in despite of their
Christian origin. Just as the Platonic Academy was free *because*
its primary allegiance was to the Truth, and not to the community,
so the medieval universities were free *because* their allegiance was
to the Truth, as it was given to them to perceive it, and not to the
community. Their framework of assumptions did not restrain
them; it protected them. The Schoolmen, like the philosophers of
the Academy, were dedicated men—dedicated to the service of
Truth. The philosopher, in Greece, was a man apart, superior to
many human frailties, especially to the varieties of concupiscence;

* This generalization also verges on the unhistorical: a very
  considerable degree of civic freedom was enjoyed by the
  burghers of most of the towns in which universities came to
  be established. But at least Professor Hook recognizes that the
  freedom of the universities was not *derived* from the freedom
  of the general community. [Kirk's note.]

and he was revered accordingly. The Schoolman was a cleric, usually vowed to celibacy, and expected to lay aside, so far as he could, the vanities of the world; therefore he was privileged accordingly. These men were not servants but masters; not the agents of the community, but seekers after divine love and wisdom. They undertook their work with a high consecration. And the Academy, or the university, was a place consecrated to the apprehension of an order more than human, and a duty more than mundane. . . .

* * * * *

We ought not to endeavor to revise history according to our latter-day notions of what things *ought* to have been, or upon the theory that the past is simply a reflection of the present. The medieval universities did indeed enjoy academic freedom, in a larger measure, probably, than any academies before or since. But they enjoyed that freedom *because* of their status as religious institutions, not in despite of it. They did not obtain that freedom from the "community," nor as bands of enterprising secularists. Their prerogatives rarely were challenged, because everyone assumed that the universities were a natural part of the order of things here below, and because no one had presumption sufficient to sit in judgment upon the universities. When, during and after the Reformation, the universities lost their status as so many autonomous parts of a universal church, they lost their independence correspondingly. In Protestant Europe, they came under the jurisdiction of the national churches and of the rapacious national monarchies; in Catholic Europe—although to a lesser extent—they came under the jurisdiction of the re-invigorated and consolidated Papacy, and of the sovereigns who, as in Spain and in France, made royal influence over the church establishment within their realms a condition of their support for the Roman cause. In fine, the dissolution of medieval universalism meant that learning, like nearly everything else, was forced to submit to new and more rigid dominations. With the complete or partial secularization of society which followed upon the French Revolutionary era, in nearly every country except Britain the universities were stripped of what remained of their old rights, and became little better than state corporations.

My point is this: in the Middle Ages, as in classical times, the academy possessed freedom unknown to other bodies and persons because the philosopher, the scholar, and the student were looked upon as men consecrated to the service of Truth; and that Truth was not simply a purposeless groping after miscellaneous information, but a wisdom to be obtained, however imperfectly, from a teleological research. The community did not create these privileges of the Academy, any more than the community created wisdom;

rather, the community simply recognized the justice of the Academy's claim to privilege. The community did not expect to be served, except in the sense that it might be so fortunate as to gather some crumbs that fell from the academic table. Like Socrates and like Aquinas, the learned man, the teacher, was a servant of God wholly, and of God only. His freedom was sanctioned by an authority more than human. Now and then that freedom was violated, just as anointed kings were murdered or reverend priests were robbed, on occasion; yet it scarcely occurred to anyone to attempt to regulate or to suppress the freedom of the Academy; it was regarded almost as a part of the natural and unalterable order of things. Masters and scholars, moreover, were so jealous of their rights, and so ready to band together against any infringement upon their prescriptive prerogatives, that very great power and very great boldness were required for an invasion of the universities. This unity and this spirited defiance of the vulgar came, in considerable part, from the Schoolmen's conviction that they were Guardians of the Word, fulfilling a sacred function, and so secure in the right. In medieval times, it was precisely their "framework of certain key assumptions of Christian doctrine" that gave masters and students this high confidence. Far from repressing free discussion, this framework encouraged disputation of a heat and intensity almost unknown in universities nowadays—except possibly, among us, on certain political questions. Every medieval university had its colleges and parties and factions armed cap-a-pie —sometimes literally at sword's-point, or fife and drum ecclesiastic —against one another. They were free, these Schoolmen, free from external interference and free from a stifling internal conformity, because the whole purpose of the universities was the search after an enduring truth, beside which worldly aggrandizement was as nothing. They were free because they agreed on this one thing, if on nothing else, that the fear of God is the beginning of wisdom.

FREEDOM OF SPEECH:
TWO SUPREME COURT OPINIONS

I. Abrams v. United States, 250 U. S. 616 (1919)

Delivered by Oliver Wendell Holmes

Persecution for the expression of opinions seems to me perfectly logical. If you have no doubt of your premises or your power and want a certain result with all your heart you naturally express your wishes in law and sweep away all opposition. To allow opposition by speech seems to indicate that you think the speech unimportant, as when a man says that he has squared the circle, or that you do not care wholeheartedly for the result, or that you doubt either your power or your premises. But when men have realized that time has upset many fighting faiths, they may come to believe even more than they believe the very foundations of their own conduct that the ultimate good desired is better reached by free trade in ideas—that the best test of truth is the power of the thought to get itself accepted in the competition of the market, and that truth is the only ground upon which their wishes safely can be carried out. That at any rate is the theory of our Constitution. It is an experiment, as all life is an experiment. Every year if not every day we have to wager our salvation upon some prophecy based upon imperfect knowledge. While the experiment is part of our system I think we should be eternally vigilant against attempts to check the expression of opinions that we loathe and believe to be fraught with death, unless they so imminently threaten immediate interference with the lawful and pressing purposes of the law that an immediate check is required to save the country. I wholly disagree with the argument of the Government that the First Amendment left the common law as to seditious libel in force. History seems to me against the notion. I had conceived that the United States through many years had shown its repentance for the Sedition Act of 1798 by repaying fines that it imposed. Only the emergency that makes it immediately dangerous to leave the correction of evil counsels to time warrants making any exception to the sweeping command, "Congress shall make no law . . . abridging the freedom of speech." Of course I am speaking only of expressions of opinion and exhortations which were all that were offered here, but I regret that I cannot put into more impressive words my belief that in their conviction upon this indictment the defendants were deprived of their rights under the Constitution of the United States.

Mr. Justice Brandeis concurs with the foregoing opinion.

II. Gitlow v. People of New York, 268 U. S. 652 (1925)

Delivered by Edward Terry Sanford

1. It is a fundamental principle, long established, that the freedom of speech and of the press which is secured by the Constitution, does not confer an absolute right to speak or publish, without responsibility, whatever one may choose, or an unrestricted and unbridled license that gives immunity for every possible use of language, and prevents the punishment of those who abuse this freedom. . . .

2. That a State in the exercise of its police power may punish those who abuse this freedom by utterances inimical to the public welfare, tending to corrupt public morals, incite to crime, or disturb the public peace, is not open to question. . . .

3. And for yet more imperative reasons, a State may punish utterances endangering the foundations of organized government and threatening its overthrow by unlawful means. These imperil its own existence as a constitutional State. Freedom of speech and press, said Story, does not protect disturbances of the public peace

or the attempt to subvert the government. It does not protect publications or teachings which tend to subvert or imperil the government or to impede or hinder it in the performance of its governmental duties. It does not protect publications prompting the overthrow of government by force; the punishment of those who publish articles which tend to destroy organized society being essential to the security of freedom and the stability of the State. And a State may penalize utterances which openly advocate the overthrow of the representative and constitutional form of government of the United States and the several States, by violence or other unlawful means. In short, this freedom does not deprive a State of the primary and essential right of self-preservation; which, so long as human governments endure, they cannot be denied. . . .

4. By enacting the present statute the State has determined, through its legislative body, that utterances advocating the overthrow of organized government by force, violence, and unlawful means, are so inimical to the general welfare and involve such danger of substantive evil that they may be penalized in the exercise of its police power. That determination must be given great weight. Every presumption is to be indulged in favor of the validity of the statute. . . . That utterances inciting to the overthrow of organized government by unlawful means, present a sufficient danger of substantive evil to bring their punishment within the range of legislative discretion, is clear. Such utterances, by their very nature, involve danger to the public peace and to the security of the State. They threaten breaches of the peace and ultimate revolution. And the immediate danger is none the less real and substantial, because the effect of a given utterance cannot be accurately foreseen. The State cannot reasonably be required to measure the danger of every such utterance in the nice balance of a jeweler's scale. A single revolutionary spark may kindle a fire that, smouldering for a time, may burst into a sweeping and destructive conflagration. It cannot be said that the State is acting arbitrarily or unreasonably when in the exercise of its judgment as to the measures necessary to protect the public peace and safety, it seeks to extinguish the spark without waiting until it has enkindled the flame or blazed into the conflagration. It cannot reasonably be required to defer the adoption of measures for its own peace and safety until the revolutionary utterances lead to actual disturbances of the public peace or imminent danger of its own destruction, but it may, in the exercise of its judgment, suppress the threatened danger in its incipiency. . . .

5. We cannot hold that the present statute is an arbitrary or unreasonable exercise of the police power of the State, unwarrantably infringing the freedom of speech or press; and we must and do sustain its constitutionality.

EXERCISES AND SUGGESTIONS FOR THEMES

1. Use the selection by Russell Kirk, "The True Origin of Academic Freedom," and the two Supreme Court opinions as sources for developing themes on subjects like the following: The True Function of a College Newspaper; Responsibilities of an Editor; Some Popular Fallacies about Freedom of Speech; Should Students Be the Mr. Fix-It's of the Nation? Student Participation in Politics; Is Censorship Inevitable?

2. Bearing in mind Franklin's argument against salaries for certain officials, what arguments would you develop *for* or *against* the following propositions?

   a. Adequate pay for school-teachers will improve the quality of teachers and of public education.

   b. The Federal government should pay the campaign expenses of candidates for the office of President.

   c. Officers in the armed services of the United States should receive salaries equal to those they would receive for comparable work in private life.

3. Read the editorial page of a newspaper over a period of some days. Study the logic of the editorials and of the signed columns written by commentators. List and classify the methods of argument most often used. Also list and classify any errors of logic that you discover.

4. Study two or three articles of opinion in current magazines recommended by your instructor. Classify the evidence presented by the authors to support their views. Use the following scheme of classification.

   a. Statistical evidence.

   b. Quotations, summaries, or references from expert and authoritative sources.

   c. Evidence originating in first-hand observation by the author.

   d. Unauthenticated evidence of any sort—hearsay, rumor, unverified reports, unidentified or questionable sources of information.

   e. Opinions or unwarranted assumptions used as evidence.

Reclassify your findings to see whether the evidence presented is, as a whole: (1) partial or impartial; (2) representative or not representative. Note any obvious distortions of fact, propaganda, prejudice, emotionalism.

Write a theme in which you embody the results of your survey.

5. Write an "editorial" on some question of public importance. Remember that an editorial is, in principle, a brief article of opinion—that is, if it is an argumentative editorial; and that, while it must meet the special requirements of the editorial page, it must also conform to the requirements of logic and good taste.

6. In what form should the following topics be put if they are to be argued about with satisfaction? Frame the proposition involved in at least three of the topics, and state the issues that will have to be proved if the proposition is to be argued successfully.

a. We hold that whoever has the right to hang has the right to educate.—THOMAS BABINGTON MACAULAY.

b. Colleges ought to get out of the entertainment business and give up big-time football.

c. If we forget all about good manners and proper dress, how can we claim to be civilized?

d. How can we ever develop community feeling in a big "consolidated" county high school?

e. Freight trucks on the highways are a menace to passenger traffic and have an unfair advantage over the railroads.

f. "Drum majorettes" symbolize perfectly the vulgarity of modern American society.

7. Test the reasoning of the following statements.

a. Enjoyment is less an end in science than it is in literature.
—JOHN BURROUGHS, "Science and Literature."

b. Only the wise man is free, and every man unwise is a slave.
—CICERO.

c. My countrymen, know one another and you will love one another.—SENATOR L. Q. C. LAMAR, Mississippi.

d. Men who eat the same kinds of food or wear the same styles of clothing or live in the same kinds of climate understand one another better than men who do not. But those who understand one another most fully are those who have read the same books.—MOSES HADAS, *Old Wine, New Bottles.*

e. For symbol and allegory, the shadow-world is a far better realm than the hard, false "realism" of science fiction. A return to the ghostly and Gothick might be one rewarding means of escape from the exhausted latitude and inhumanity of the typical novel or short story of the Sixties. Unlike the True Narration, the fictional ghostly tale can possess plot, theme, and purpose. It can piece together in some pattern the hints which seem thrown out by this or that vision or haunting or case of second-sight. It can touch keenly upon the old reality of evil—and upon injustice and retribution. It can reveal aspects of human conduct and longing to which the positivistic psychologist has blinded himself. And it still can be a first-rate yarn.
—RUSSELL KIRK, "A Cautionary Note on the Ghostly Tale," *The Surly Sullen Bell.*

f. The authority of government, even such as I am willing to submit to,—for I will cheerfully obey those who know and can do better than I, and in many things even those who neither know nor can do so well,—is still an impure one; to be strictly just, it must have the sanction and consent of the governed. It can have no pure right over my person and my property but what I concede to it. The progress from an absolute to a limited monarchy, to a democracy, is a progress toward a true respect for the individual.
—HENRY D. THOREAU, "Civil Disobedience."

CHAPTER 10

DESCRIPTIVE AND NARRATIVE WRITING

THE aim of expository writing is to inform and explain. It appeals to the understanding first of all. The aim of descriptive and narrative writing is not to explain but to evoke reality by calling up an image of what has been seen, heard, felt, enacted. Description and narration are therefore rightly called imaginative or creative. As literary forms, they must be distinguished from the matter-of-fact description and narration that may be found in catalogues, textbooks, advertisements, court records, and the like. The United States post office puts on its bulletin boards "descriptions" of criminals who are wanted by Federal officers; but these descriptions are informative and technical; they identify, but do not, in the artistic sense, "create" an image. On the other hand, Victor Hugo's description, in *Les Misérables,* of the escaped convict Jean Valjean, creates an image; we see, we imagine the ex-galley-slave as he asks lodging at the home of the Bishop. A sociologist, working up a "case history," may plot the time-sequence of what a woman department-store employee does in her off-hours, from the time when she leaves the counter until she reports for work again next morning. This is perhaps a kind of "narration" of happenings, but a rather lifeless kind. O. Henry, dealing with the same situation, gives the "feeling" of the employee's experience as she hurries toward her lonely "flat":

> Dulcie hurried homeward. Her eyes were shining, her cheeks showed the delicate pink of life's—real life's—approaching dawn. It was Friday; and she had fifty cents left of her last week's wages.
>
> The streets were filled with the rush-hour floods of people.

> The electric lights of Broadway were glowing—calling moths from miles, from leagues, from hundreds of leagues out of darkness around to come in and attend the singing school. Men in accurate clothes, with faces like those carved on cherry stone by the old salts in sailors' homes, turned and stared at Dulcie as she sped, unheeding, past them. Manhattan, the night-blooming cereus, was beginning to unfold its dead-white, heavy-odored petals.—O. HENRY, "An Unfinished Story," *The Four Million.*

As forms of creative writing, description and narration are closely allied. One is an accessory of the other, and the two often blend indistinguishably. Is a lively account of a football game description or narration? The progress of events is told, but it cannot be told effectively except in terms of the setting: the color and noise of the crowd, the music of the band, the look of the sky overhead and of the turf underneath, with its white lines across which the players move rapidly. Yet this picture is of an event, not of a setting; and it lives as the story of the game, with its series of strokes and counter-strokes, is set forth in proper order. Informal essays and reminiscences of people and places are likely to emphasize the descriptive element. Anecdotes, incidents, accounts of historical events and of course all fiction, whether within the brief limits of the tale or short story or within the wider bounds of the novel—all these emphasize the narrative element. It is best therefore to use the compound term *descriptive and narrative writing* rather than the separate terms *description* and *narration*. We isolate one from the other at this point only for purposes of study and practice.

1. DESCRIPTIVE WRITING

A description is likely to be a portion of a composition rather than a separate and fully rounded composition in itself. In a narrative the descriptive element may amount to no more than phrases and sentences interspersed here and there to bring out character, setting, or emotion, as in the following passage from a novel by William Faulkner:

> The boy's diction was slow now, recapitulant, each word as though chosen simply and carefully and spoken slowly and clearly for the ear of a foreigner: "Listen, cap'm. When I turn off here, it's just a short cut. A short cutoff to a better road. I am going to take the cutoff. When I come to the short cut. To the better road. So we can get there, quicker. See?"

"All right," Christmas said. The car bounced and rushed on, swaying on the curves and up the hills and fleeing down again as if the earth had dropped from under them. Mail boxes on posts beside the road rushed into the lights and flicked past. Now and then they passed a dark house.
—WILLIAM FAULKNER, *Light in August.*[1]

But we speak here of larger descriptive passages, such as the student will have occasion to write—extended descriptions. Such passages occur frequently in narrative writing and even in some kinds of expository writing. When studied, these descriptive passages reveal an organization, a selection of details, and a selection of language that make, or tend to make, a unity of effect. A description, thus considered, is a complete picture and may be treated as a unified, partially independent composition.

What are the principles and methods that secure this unity of effect in descriptive writing? The landscape painter follows certain principles of design and perspective. He has a procedure for handling colors and masses. He works with brush and oils, or with water colors or pastels. The result, his complete picture, comes instantaneously before the physical eye. The writer's medium is words. He builds up his picture, bit by bit, and has only words with which to suggest to his reader the object that he is trying to describe. He paints slowly, for the mind's eye. He cannot produce an instantaneous view of the whole picture. His problem is to find the literary parallel to the instantaneous view. He must organize his description so that it will convey, when it has been read, something of the completeness and finality that the painter secures.

Point of View in Description

Point of view is a device for organizing the description by directing the reader's attention to a consistent order, a definite underlying structure, in the object or scene which is being described. The point of view is the literary equivalent of perspective in painting.

The point of view may be either physical or mental, or both in combination. In each instance it must be definitely indicated or clearly implied. It must be consistent through-

[1] From *Light in August* by William Faulkner. Copyright 1932 by William Faulkner. Reprinted by permission of Random House, Inc.

out the description; or, if good reason arises to shift the point of view (as may happen in an extended description), the change must be noted. When the time element enters into the point of view, as when a writer is describing the passage of a boat across a lake or the changes of light between sunset and dark, a similar indication must appear.

The point of view also establishes the scale of the description, and this scale, once established, must not be violated. If you are describing a house as seen from a cliff a mile away from the house, you must describe it as it looks at that distance. You destroy the scale and make the description ridiculous if, at the distance of a mile, you seem to represent yourself as identifying the color of the window curtains or the pattern made by moss on the chimney.

In the following description, the physical point of view is established in the first sentence. The two girls, Constance and Sophia, are looking down into the Square from the showroom window of the Baines shop. Gradually we realize, too, that we are "seeing" the progress of Maggie not only with their eyes but with their minds, their adolescent "attitudes." But back of this immediate focus is also the generally controlling "omniscient point of view" of the author, who to some extent "intrudes" descriptive details and explanatory matter (e.g., "another proof of the architect's incompetence") of which the girls could have no precise knowledge. Such an intrusion would seem objectionable to those who prefer the strict Hemingway technique (see "The Lieutenant Escapes," page 362); but it can hardly be denied that Bennett's procedure is fully successful.

OVERLOOKING MAGGIE[1]   *By Arnold Bennett*

THEY pressed their noses against the window of the show-room and gazed down into the Square as perpendicularly as the projecting front of the shop would allow. The show-room was over the millinery and silken half of the shop. Over the woollen and shirting half were the drawing-room and the chief bedroom. When in quest of articles of coquetry, you mounted from the shop by a curving stair, and your head rose level with a large apartment having a mahogany counter in front of the window and along one side, yellow linoleum on the floor, many cardboard boxes, a magnificent hinged cheval glass, and two chairs. The window-sill being lower

---

[1] From *The Old Wives' Tale* by Arnold Bennett. Reprinted by permission of Doubleday & Co., Inc. and by permission of The Owners of the Copyright.

than the counter, there was a gulf between the panes and the back
of the counter, into which important articles such as scissors, pencils, chalk, and artificial flowers were continually disappearing:
another proof of the architect's incompetence.

The girls could only press their noses against the window by
kneeling on the counter, and this they were doing. Constance's
nose was snub, but agreeably so. Sophia had a fine Roman nose;
she was a beautiful creature, beautiful and handsome at the same
time. They were both of them rather like racehorses, quivering
with delicate, sensitive, and luxuriant life; exquisite, enchanting
proof of the circulation of the blood; innocent, artful, roguish, prim,
gushing, ignorant, and miraculously wise. Their ages were sixteen
and fifteen; it is an epoch when, if one is frank, one must admit
that one has nothing to learn; one has learnt simply everything in
the previous six months.

"There she goes!" exclaimed Sophia.

Up the Square, from the corner of King Street, passed a woman
in a new bonnet with pink strings, and a new blue dress that sloped
at the shoulders and grew to a vast circumference at the hem.
Through the silent sunlit solitude of the Square (for it was Thursday afternoon, and all the shops shut except the confectioner's and
one chemist's) this bonnet and this dress floated northwards in
search of romance, under the relentless eyes of Constance and
Sophia. Within them, somewhere, was the soul of Maggie, domestic
servant at Baines's. Maggie had been at the shop since before the
creation of Constance and Sophia. She lived seventeen hours of
each day in an underground kitchen and larder, and the other
seven in an attic, never going out except to chapel on Sunday evenings, and once a month on Thursday afternoons. "Followers" were
mostly strictly forbidden to her; but on rare occasions an aunt from
Longshaw was permitted as a tremendous favor to see her in
the subterranean den. Everybody, including herself, considered that
she had a good "place," and was well treated. It was undeniable,
for instance, that she was allowed to fall in love exactly as she
chose, provided she did not "carry on" in the kitchen or the yard.
And as a fact, Maggie had fallen in love. In seventeen years she had
been engaged eleven times. No one could conceive how that ugly
and powerful organism could softly languish to the undoing of
even a buttycollier, nor why, having caught a man in her sweet
toils, she could ever be imbecile enough to set him free. There are,
however, mysteries in the souls of Maggies. The drudge had probably been affianced oftener than any woman in Bursley. Her em-
ployers were so accustomed to an interesting announcement that
for years they had taken to saying naught in reply but "Really,
Maggie!" Engagements and tragic partings were Maggie's pastime.
Fixed otherwise, she might have studied the piano instead.

"No gloves, of course!" Sophia criticized.

"Well, you can't expect her to have gloves," said Constance.

Then a pause, as the bonnet and dress neared the top of the Square.

"Supposing she turns round and sees us?" Constance suggested.

"I don't care if she does," said Sophia with a haughtiness almost impassioned; and her head trembled slightly.

There were, as usual, several loafers at the top of the Square, in the corner between the bank and the "Marquis of Granby." And one of these loafers stepped forward and shook hands with an obviously willing Maggie. Clearly it was a rendezvous, open, unashamed. The twelfth victim had been selected by the virgin of forty, whose kiss would not have melted lard! The couple disappeared together down Oldcastle Street.

"*Well!*" cried Constance. "Did you ever see such a thing?"

While Sophie, short of adequate words, flushed and bit her lip.

In "Manhattan from the Bay," the point of view is that of an observer on a sailboat returning to New York from "the wide bay southeast of Staten Island." The description proceeds in order of space—the city and its surroundings as seen in relation to certain landmarks: "to the left the North river," "to the right the East river," "and rising out of the midst . . . V-shaped Manhattan."

MANHATTAN FROM THE BAY[1] *By Walt Whitman*

June 25.—RETURNED to New York last night. Out to-day on the waters for a sail in the wide bay, southeast of Staten Island—a rough, tossing tide, and a free sight—the long stretch of Sandy Hook, the highlands of Navesink, and the many vessels outward and inward bound. We came up through the midst of all, in the full sun. I especially enjoy'd the last hour or two. A moderate seabreeze had set in; yet over the city, and the water adjacent, was a thin haze, concealing nothing, only adding to the beauty. From my point of view, as I write amid the soft breeze, with a sea-temperature, surely nothing on earth of its kind can go beyond this show. To the left the North river with its far vista—nearer, three or four warships, anchor'd peacefully—the Jersey side, the banks of Weehawken, the Palisades, and the gradually receding blue, lost in the distance—to the right of the East river—the mast-hemm'd shores—the grand obelisk-like towers of the bridge, one on either side, in haze, yet plainly defin'd, giant brothers twain, throwing free graceful inter-linking loops high across the tumbled tumultous current below—(the tide is just changing to its ebb)—the broad water-

[1] From *Specimen Days in America.*

spread everywhere crowded—no, not crowded, but thick as stars in the sky—with all sorts and sizes of sail and steam vessels, plying ferryboats, arriving and departing coasters, great ocean Dons, iron-black, modern, magnificent in size and power, fill'd with their incalculable value of human life and precious merchandise—with here and there, above all, those daring, careening things of grace and wonder, those white and shaded swift-darting fish birds, (I wonder if shore or sea elsewhere can outvie them,) ever with their slanting spars, and fierce, pure, hawk-like beauty and motion—first-class New York sloop or schooner yachts, sailing, this fine day, the free sea in a good wind. And rising out of the midst, tall-topt, ship-hemm'd, modern, American, yet strangely oriental, V-shaped Manhattan, with its compact mass, its spires, its cloud-touching edifices, group'd at the centre—the green of the trees, and all the white, brown and gray of the architecture well blended, as I see it, under a miracle of limpid sky, delicious light of heaven above, and June haze on the surface below.

In the following selection, the physical point of view is that of Tess Durbeyfield as she walks down the slopes and over the level valley toward the dairy. But Hardy uses the privilege of the "omniscient" author to enrich and interpret a scene that, if described strictly in Tess's own language, would be far simpler and less interesting.[1]

THE VALLEY OF THE GREAT DAIRIES[2]

By Thomas Hardy

TESS DURBEYFIELD, then, in good heart, and full of zest for life, descended the Egdon slopes lower and lower towards the dairy of her pilgrimage.

The marked difference, in the final particular, between the rival vales now showed itself. The secret of Blackmoor was best discovered from the heights around; to read aright the valley before her it was necessary to descend into its midst. When Tess had accomplished this feat she found herself to be standing on a carpeted level, which stretched to the east and west as far as the eye could reach.

The river had stolen from the higher tracts and brought in particles to the vale all this horizontal land; and now, exhausted,

---

[1] Percy Lubbock, in *The Craft of Fiction* (Chapter VI), explains how Flaubert, in *Madame Bovary,* exercises this privilege to advantage.

[2] From *Tess of the D'Urbervilles.* Reprinted by permission of the Trustees of the Hardy Estate, The Macmillan Company of Canada Limited, and Macmillan & Co. Ltd., London.

aged, and attenuated, lay serpentining along through the midst of its former spoils.

Not quite sure of her direction Tess stood still upon the hemmed expanse of verdant flatness, like a fly on a billiard-table of indefinite length, and of no more consequence to the surroundings than that fly. The sole effect of her presence upon the placid valley so far had been to excite the mind of a solitary heron, which, after descending to the ground not far from her path, stood with neck erect, looking at her.

Suddenly there arose from all parts of the lowland a prolonged and repeated call—

"Waow! waow! waow!"

From the furthest east to the furthest west the cries spread as if by contagion, accompanied in some cases by the barking of a dog. It was not the expression of the valley's consciousness that beautiful Tess had arrived, but the ordinary announcement of milking-time —half-past four o'clock, when the dairymen set about getting in the cows.

The red and white herd nearest at hand, which had been phlegmatically waiting for the call, now trooped towards the steading in the background, their great bags of milk swinging under them as they walked. Tess followed slowly in their rear, and entered the barton by the open gate through which they had entered before her. Long thatched sheds stretched around the enclosure, their slopes encrusted with vivid green moss, and their eaves supported by wooden posts rubbed to a glossy smoothness by the flanks of infinite cows and calves of bygone years, now passed to an oblivion almost inconceivable in its profundity. Between the posts were ranged the milchers, each exhibiting herself to a whimsical eye in the rear as a circle on two stalks, down the center of which a switch moved pendulum-wise; while the sun, lowering itself behind this patient row, threw their shadows accurately inwards upon the wall. Thus it threw shadows of these obscure and homely figures every evening with as much care over each contour as if it had been the profile of a Court beauty on a palace wall; copied them as diligently as it had copied Olympian shapes on marble *facades* long ago, or the outline of Alexander, Cæsar, or the Pharaohs.

Charles Dickens, following a method different from Hardy's, gives us a description of Peggotty's house as it looked to the boy, David Copperfield. In all consistency, Dickens must do this, since David is the narrator. To an adult the queer place would seem a poor makeshift, no better than a shanty. To the boy's view it is wholly romantic and charming.

PEGGOTTY'S HOUSE[1]   *By Charles Dickens*

HAM carrying me on his back and a small box of ours under his arm, and Peggotty carrying another small box of ours, we turned down lanes bestrewn with bits of chips and little hillocks of sand, and went past gas-works, rope-walks, boat-builders' yards, shipwrights' yards, ship-breakers' yards, caulkers' yards, riggers' lofts, smiths' forges, and a great litter of such places, until we came out upon the dull waste I had already seen at a distance; when Ham said:

"Yon's our house, Mas'r Davy!"

I looked in all directions, as far as I could stare over the wilderness, and away at the sea, and away at the river, but no house could *I* make out. There was a black barge, or some other kind of superannuated boat, not far off, high and dry on the ground, with an iron funnel sticking out of it for a chimney and smoking very cosily; but nothing in the way of a habitation that was visible to *me.*

"That's not it?" said I. "That ship-looking thing?"

"That's it, Mas'r Davy," returned Ham.

If it had been Aladdin's palace, roc's egg and all, I suppose I could not have been more charmed with the romantic idea of living in it. There was a delightful door cut in the side, and it was roofed in, and there were little windows in it; but the wonderful charm of it was, that it was a real boat which had no doubt been upon the water hundreds of times, and which had never intended to be lived in, on dry land. That was the captivation of it to me. If it had ever been meant to be lived in, I might have thought it small, or inconvenient, or lonely; but never having been designed for any such use, it became a perfect abode.

In the following excerpt from James Joyce's story, "The Dead," we have an example of a modern artist's treatment of an interior scene. The point of view is that of Gabriel Conroy, the frustrated husband of Gretta. Although the description seems very matter-of-fact, even dry, in its cold presentation of details, careful examination will reveal that all is "filtered" through the consciousness of Gabriel. Throughout, he is observant with eye and ear, yet he is also reflective to the point of being painfully reminiscent in the middle portion. Note that the description (which is never far from being "narration") conveys the sensation of being isolated and "trapped" in the midst of a festive gathering. Gabriel cannot casually "escape" as do the "four young men" who leave when Mary Jane begins her Academy piece and return just in time to join the applause.

[1] From *David Copperfield.*

IN THE MISSES MORKAN'S DRAWING-ROOM[1]

By James Joyce

GABRIEL could not listen while Mary Jane was playing her Academy piece, full of runs and difficult passages, to the hushed drawing-room. He liked music but the piece she was playing had no melody for him and he doubted whether it had any melody for the other listeners, though they had begged Mary Jane to play something. Four young men, who had come from the refreshment-room to stand in the doorway at the sound of the piano, had gone away quietly in couples after a few minutes. The only persons who seemed to follow the music were Mary Jane herself, her hands racing along the key-board or lifted from it at the pauses like those of a priestess in momentary imprecation, and Aunt Kate standing at her elbow to turn the page.

Gabriel's eyes, irritated by the floor, which glittered with beeswax under the heavy chandelier, wandered to the wall above the piano. A picture of the balcony scene in *Romeo and Juliet* hung there and beside it was a picture of the two murdered princes in the Tower which Aunt Julia had worked in red, blue and brown wools when she was a girl. Probably in the school they had gone to as girls that kind of work had been taught for one year. His mother had worked for him as a birthday present a waistcoat of purple tabinet, with little foxes' heads upon it, lined with brown satin and having round mulberry buttons. It was strange that his mother had had no musical talent though Aunt Kate used to call her the brains carrier of the Morkan family. Both she and Julia had always seemed a little proud of their serious and matronly sister. Her photograph stood before the pierglass. She held an open book on her knees and was pointing out something in it to Constantine who, dressed in a man-o'-war suit, lay at her feet. It was she who had chosen the names of her sons, for she was very sensible of the dignity of family life. Thanks to her, Constantine was now senior curate in Balbriggan and, thanks to her, Gabriel himself had taken his degree in the Royal University. A shadow passed over his face as he remembered her sullen opposition to his marriage. Some slighting phrases she had used still rankled in his memory; she had once spoken of Gretta as being country cute and that was not true of Gretta at all. It was Gretta who had nursed her during all her last long illness in their house at Monkstown.

He knew that Mary Jane must be near the end of her piece for she was playing again the opening melody with runs of scales

[1] From *Dubliners* by James Joyce. Originally published by B. W. Huebsch in 1916. Reprinted by permission of The Viking Press, Inc. and by The Society of Authors as the literary representative of the Estate of the late James Joyce.

after every bar, and while he waited for the end the resentment died down in his heart. The piece ended with a trill of octaves in the treble and a final deep octave in the bass. Great applause greeted Mary Jane as, blushing and rolling up her music nervously, she escaped from the room. The most vigorous clapping came from the four young men in the doorway who had gone away to the refreshment-room at the beginning of the piece but had come back when the piano had stopped.

Dominant Impression

Dominant impression is a means of centralizing a description around some feature or quality of the object described. The impression thus emphasized may be a striking characteristic of the object itself, notable enough to impress any observer; or it may be an interpretation made by the writer— he tells how the object impresses itself upon his own mind or selects and arranges details so as to secure the effect that he wants.

Thus Edgar Allan Poe, in "The Fall of the House of Usher," emphasizes the somberness of the autumn day and of the old mansion which his traveler is approaching. His purpose, of course, is to create a mood or atmosphere for the events of the story.

THE HOUSE OF USHER　　　　　　*By Edgar Allan Poe*

DURING the whole of a dull, dark, and soundless day in the autumn of the year, when the clouds hung oppressively low in the heavens, I had been passing alone, on horseback, through a singularly dreary tract of country; and at length found myself, as the shades of evening drew on, within view of the melancholy House of Usher. I know not how it was—but, with the first glimpse of the building, a sense of insufferable gloom pervaded my spirit. . . . I looked upon the scene before me—upon the mere house, and the simple landscape features of the domain—upon the bleak walls—upon the vacant eye-like windows—upon a few rank sedges —and upon a few white trunks of decaying trees—with an utter depression of soul which I can compare to no earthly sensation more properly than to the after-dream of the reveller upon opium —the bitter lapse into everyday life—the hideous dropping off of the veil. There was an iciness, a sinking, a sickening of the heart—an unredeemed dreariness of thought which no goading of the imagination could torture into aught of the sublime.

Poe in part suggests the appearance of the landscape and the house by describing the emotions of the traveler who "looks upon the scene." Robert Penn Warren in his description of the army breaking camp, is less concerned with the emotions of the observer, Adam Rosenzweig, than with the stir and seeming confusion of the military operation. The dominant impression—indicated in the unusual word "formication" and summed up in the final sentence—is of a busy anthill.

ARMY BREAKING CAMP[1] *By Robert Penn Warren*

IT WAS full light, and past, by the time he got out beyond the camp to the main road. Progress through the camp had been slow enough. Now, company by company, troops were falling in. Men rushed about, seemingly with no purpose. Here and there an officer with the gold of his rank gleaming in the fresh light, sat a restive horse, watching sleepily, uttering no sound. But from those points where the formations were accreting, the yelped orders of sergeants and lieutenants broke, rising and falling, filling the bright air with hysteria and outrage.

In company street after company street now, the formations had assumed solidity, like blocks of hewn stone set in swirling water.

The road itself, Adam realized as soon as he had broken past the hutment of the Ninth Vermont, was packed. The traffic, he noticed, with surprise, was moving on the left—a system which, for some reason of their own, the soldiers must have set up for the occasion.

Thus the inbound traffic was on the side of the road away from him—an interminable line of supply wagons, ammunition trains, new ambulances with paint bright, untried, and canvas white as snow. Beyond that movement he could see field after field of parked wagons mathematically disposed, waiting to be sucked into that movement southeastward. Meanwhile in the interstices of that as yet unbroken mathematical pattern, there was the same swirl and angry formication as in the camp behind him. Men were putting mules into harness. From these fields rose a nervous ululation, no word distinguishable in that confused distance. Above that area some last blue wisps of smoke from newly abandoned cork fires yet hung, raveling slowly into the brightness of air.

Reluctantly, sadly, he brought his gaze to rest on the flow of traffic nearer him, the outbound traffic, that movement which he would soon join—all the nondescript traffic of the hangers-on moving northwestward; the hooded wagons of sutlers; carts, light four-wheelers; here and there a local peddler with a pushcart;

[1] From *Wilderness, A Tale of the Civil War*, by Robert Penn Warren. © Copyright 1961 by Robert Penn Warren. Reprinted by permission of Random House, Inc.

washer-women with bundle on head—not somebody's laundry now
but their own miserable possessions; small adventurers with, no
doubt, a pack of greasy cards in pocket and a dilapidated valise
in hand; the blank, undefinable, faceless ones whose purposes
must have always been indecipherable and who now moved with
the great mass, empty-handed as at birth or carrying some gro-
tesquerie like a painted chamber-pot, a carved clock, a large
simpering portrait in oil of a child that could never have sprung
from the loins of the carrier, or the Holy Bible in a size large
enough for the pulpit.

A great boot had, as it were, kicked over the winter camp like
an ant hill, and the life was seething desperately forth.

When the dominant impression is both greatly simplified
and greatly exaggerated, the result is generally caricature.
The cartoonist gets his effects by making a naturally long
chin immensely long, or a large paunch exceedingly large.
In *David Copperfield*, Dickens accents heavily the unctuous
humility of Uriah Heep, who is always "umble," has an oily
smile, and is forever bowing and rubbing his hands together. James Thurber's satirical sketch of his fictional friend
Vereker applies the same principle:

> Vereker had a way of flinging himself at a sofa, kicking
> one end out of it; or he would drop into a fragile chair like
> a tired bird dog and something would crack. He never
> seemed to notice. You would invite him to dinner, or, what
> happened oftener, he would drop in for dinner uninvited,
> and while you were shaking up a cocktail in the kitchen he
> would disappear. He might go upstairs to wrench the bathtub
> away from the wall. ("Breaking lead pipe is one of the truly
> enchanting adventures in life," he said once), or he might
> simply leave for good in one of those inexplicable huffs of
> his which were a sign of his peculiar genius. —JAMES
> THURBER, "Something to Say," *The Thurber Carnival*.

The following passage from Herman Melville's *Moby Dick*
has in it a considerable element of exaggeration, but Melville's purpose is to produce a heroic effect, not, as in Thurber's description, a comic one. Captain Ahab, after suffering
an all but mortal injury from the White Whale, has sworn
to wage a feud to the death upon his adversary. The description is centralized by Melville's emphasis of Ahab's scar,
which on the realistic plane represents an actual physical
wound or blemish; in a symbolic way it represents a scar
upon his very soul.

CAPTAIN AHAB *By Herman Melville*

THERE seemed no sign of common bodily illness about him nor of the recovery from any. He looked like a man cut away from the stake, when the fire has overrunningly wasted all the limbs without consuming them, or taking away one particle from their compacted aged robustness. His whole high, broad form seemed made of solid bronze, and shaped in an unalterable mould, like Cellini's cast Perseus. Threading its way out from among his gray hairs, and continuing right down one side of his tawny scorched face and neck till it disappeared in his clothing, you saw a slender rod-like mark, lividly whitish. It resembled that perpendicular seam sometimes made in the straight, lofty trunk of a great tree, when the upper lightning tearingly darts down it, and without wrenching a single twig, peels and grooves out the bark from top to bottom, ere running off into the soil, leaving the tree still greenly alive, but branded. Whether that mark was born with him, or whether it was the scar left by some desperate wound, no one could certainly say. By some tacit consent, throughout the voyage little or no allusion was made to it, especially by the mates. But once Tashtego's senior, an old Gay-Head Indian among the crew, superstitiously asserted that not till he was full forty years old did Ahab become that way branded, and then it came upon him, not in the fury of any mortal fray, but in an elemental strife at sea. Yet, this wild hint seemed inferentially negatived by what a gray Manxman insinuated, an old sepulchral man, who, having never before sailed out of Nantucket, had never ere this laid eye upon wild Ahab. Nevertheless, the old sea-traditions, the immemorial credulities, popularly invested this old Manxman with preternatural powers of discernment. So that no white sailor seriously contradicted him when he said that if ever Captain Ahab should be tranquilly laid out—which might hardly come to pass, he muttered —then, whoever should do that last office for the dead would find a birth-mark on him from crown to sole.

So powerfully did the whole grim aspect of Ahab affect me, and the livid brand which streaked it, that for the first few moments I hardly noted that not a little of this overbearing grimness was owing to the barbaric white leg upon which he partly stood. It had previously come to me that this ivory leg had at sea been fashioned from the polished bone of the sperm whale's jaw. "Aye, he was dismasted off Japan," said the old Gay-Head Indian once; "but like his dismasted craft, he shipped another mast without coming home for it. He has a quiver of 'em."

Selection of Details

In the descriptions given above, the student will notice that the authors do not attempt to give *all* the details visible in a scene or apparent in some individual. A clear and total picture could never be established by a mere list of details. Instead, the picture would be overcrowded, blurred, out of focus. The artist who paints a tree does not reproduce in line and color every leaf and twig, but selects the details which, *in the medium of line and color,* compose the image of a tree. Similarly, in literary description, the writer selects details which, *in the medium of language,* evoke his subject.

Whitman, with New York harbor before him, accents relatively few objects: the warships anchored in the North river; the obelisklike towers of the bridge; the ferryboats; and V-shaped Manhattan with its piled towers. In Hardy's description of Blackmoor Vale, we notice the serpentining river, the solitary heron, the "Waow!" of the cow-callers, the milch cows viewed as circles on two stalks, with the tails as pendulums.

In these and other instances the point of view or the dominant impression provides some design or motif of description. The details amplify this design or motif, which corresponds to the topic in exposition. If a physical point of view governs, the arrangement of details will be spatial and may use some especially significant detail (like "V-shaped Manhattan") as a kind of climax. Or the description may begin with a general impression, supported by concrete details arranged in some consistent order. David Copperfield's general impression of the ship-hulk is immediately supported by references to the "delightful door," the roof, the little windows.

One does not expect in literary description the logical order of expository writing. The progress of a description is the order of artistic design, as is the pattern of a vase or of a piece of music. But since descriptive writing deals with nature and humanity, and since words after all have a content of idea, and are not merely sounds, the pattern of description will rarely if ever be a *mere design,* as the design of a carpet is a mere design. The "image" conveyed by a good description is an arrangement determined partly by the material observed and partly by what the writer wishes to make of it, but it is a communication between writer and reader and must make sense. The following brief selection will suggest how a skilful writer in a comparatively few strokes can create a scene, with contrasts and shadings, as well as the persons in it and their "encounter."

AT THE AMERICAN CONSULATE[1]   *By Elizabeth Spencer*

WHETHER she sought advice or whether her need was for somebody to talk things over with, she had gone one day directly after lunch to the American consulate, where she found, on the second floor of a palazzo whose marble halls echoed the click and clack of typing, one of those perpetually young American faces topped by a crew cut. The owner of it was sitting in a seersucker coat behind a standard American office desk in a richly panelled room cut to the noble proportions of the Florentine Renaissance. Memos, documents, and correspondence were arranged in stacks before him, and he looked toward the window while twisting a rubber band repeatedly around his wrist. Mrs. Johnson had no sooner got her first statement out—she was concerned about a courtship between her daughter and a young Italian—than he had cut her off. The consulate could give no advice in personal matters. A priest, perhaps, or a minister or doctor. There was a list of such as spoke English. "Gabriella!" An untidy Italian girl wearing glasses and a green crepe blouse came in from her typewriter in the outer office. "There's a services list in the top of that file cabinet. If you'll just find us a copy." All the while he continued looking out of the window and twisting and snapping the rubber band around his wrist. Mrs. Johnson got the distinct impression that but for this activity he would have dozed right off to sleep.

Selection of Language

The choice of words in descriptive writing is governed by the same considerations as those discussed above. The language at every point must shape in the reader's mind the image that the writer seeks to convey. General and abstract words are of little use; they convey no image. Description is a process of visualization, and the writer of description must make his language concrete and specific. His aim is, as Joseph Conrad said, "to make you hear, to make you feel, . . . to make you see." General and abstract words cannot possibly make the necessary appeal to the senses. In the passage quoted above (page 325), Faulkner does not say that the automobile moved rapidly over the rough road, but that it

[1] From *The Light in the Piazza*, by Elizabeth Spencer. Copyright ©, 1960, by Elizabeth Spencer. Reprinted by permission of the McGraw-Hill Book Company, Inc.

bounced, swayed, and fled up and down hill "as if the earth had dropped from under them."

The diction of descriptive writing is thus in a very different category from the diction of matter-of-fact writing. Matter-of-fact writing uses words for their denotative and logical content. In a scientific treatise words must mean exactly what they say, and no more; they must never have overtones of meaning; they must never mean more than they say. In descriptive writing, the author seeks exactness of *connotation*. Overtone of meaning is what he is seeking, because he wants his words, while denoting certain objects and features of objects, also to *suggest* something over and above mere logical meaning. The vocabulary of descriptive writing always means more than it says, in so far as it sets the imagination to working and surrounds the object with an aura of associations.

For these reasons, the language of descriptive writing is more concrete and specific than the language of expository writing; and, besides, it makes greater and freer use of all the rhetorical devices that help to make an image vivid. Among these devices, figures of speech are of first importance.

The matter-of-fact writer will say of a certain person: he is small in size, and thin, but he is active in his movements. Conrad, writing of such a person, uses a simile: "a little man, dry as a chip and agile as a monkey." The root of a tree, in Conrad's "The Lagoon," shows "writhing and motionless, like an arrested snake." Lafcadio Hearn describes the dew-fall in a tropic night as follows: "Under the roof of our hotel I hear a continuous dripping sound; the drops fall heavily, like the bodies of clumsy insects."

The following passages illustrate the uses of figures of speech in descriptive writing:

> Through the falling dusk, the machine boomed steadily with a new sound, a solemn roar, rising at intervals to a rattling impatient yell as the cylinder ran momentarily empty.—HAMLIN GARLAND, *A Son of the Middle Border.*

> It was a fast train and it did not always stop at Jefferson. It halted only long enough to disgorge the two dogs: a thousand costly tons of intricate and curious metal glaring and crashing up and into an almost shocking silence filled with

puny sounds of men, to vomit two gaunt and cringing phantoms whose droop-eared and mild faces gazed with sad abjectness about at the weary pale faces of men who had not slept very much since night before last, ringing them about with something terrible and eager and impotent.—WILLIAM FAULKNER, *Light in August*.[1]

Although the diction of descriptive writing tends to be richly connotative and metaphorical, certain cautions must be observed. An excess of metaphor is cloying and artificial; it is like cake that has been too heavily spiced. It is better to have a plain descriptive style than a style that seems forced, affected, ornate. The metaphors must come at the place where they really contribute to the effect; they must not get in one another's way. A study of the examples given in this chapter will show that most good writers observe a principle of balance: they are neither excessively plain nor excessively "literary." The ideal descriptive style is a style that directs the reader to the subject described rather than to the verbal means by which the subject is evoked or suggested.

Another caution needs to be made against the use of adjectives, catch-phrases, figures of speech that have become trite or conventional. "Eyes like stars," "the blanket of the snow," "the carpet of the grass," "the cottage nestling in the valley," and the like, have long since lost any effectiveness that they may once have possessed.

Furthermore, the work of conveying impressions must be distributed among the various parts of speech. It would be unwise to issue a prohibition against the use of adjectives and adverbs; but it is a common error to attempt to make them do all the work of description. They cannot effectively do all that work. Nouns and verbs must do their part. The phrase is an important element in descriptive writing. The principles explained in the two chapters on sentences and words are of the greatest importance in descriptive writing and may be studied and applied with good result because, in descriptive writing, the work is done within narrow limits, and technical details can be analyzed and controlled with greater satisfaction than in extensive compositions.

---

[1] From *Light in August* by William Faulkner. Copyright 1932 by William Faulkner. Reprinted by permission of Random House, Inc.

HURRICANE[1]   *By Frances Woodward*

THREE O'CLOCK. Three-thirty. . . . The wind began to confuse
you. You knew if it would just stop for a few minutes there would
be things to do, things to say, before it began again. . . . You
could do things like getting your awnings down, like shoring a
plank or so against a tree which, leaning too far, too long, drenched
in the salt rain, might break. . . . You could even talk to people
sensibly instead of shouting at them, three feet away as they
might be, and seeing by their faces that they hadn't heard you
at that. . . . You could decide what to do about the boats, if only
this damned wind would just stop. . . . But, more all the time,
the wind seemed to wrap itself around you, engulf you, make you
a part of itself, so that you were alone in it, deafened in it, blinded
by its wetness. It wasn't a wind—it was a state of being. It was
breaking windows now and tossing bricks off chimneys. Things
were moving that could not move, that must not move. And you
were alone in it, in spite of all the people who were in it with you.

Saint Peter Lemos, leaning against the storm, carrying two
anchors out of his house door, was angry—angry because he
was worried, angry because he was mixed up, because wind
didn't blow this way, because a man couldn't be sure his boat
would hold . . . even with these extra anchors . . . even with
every man in the fish fleet working on the docks to steady the
boats. "Lena!" he shouted. "Keep those children in the house.
Can't you see the water already breaking on our wall? Can't you
see. . . . You get them in!" He left for the dock at a dogtrot.

Mrs. Saint Peter heard him . . . and didn't hear him . . . and
snatched dish towels to cover the windmill. . . . You couldn't get
it down . . . this wind. . . . She pulled the grandchildren into the
house with her, roughly, away from the sight of the sea. . . .
"You, Manny! You, Adelina! You stay outa the wet. You help
me put towels here where the rain comes under the door. You
heard your grandpa?"

Four o'clock. Four-fifteen. The wind possessed the port, and all
the people in it, and all the things in it. The wind and the rain
—the warm, driving, salt-tasting rain. . . . The rain began to
come through tight window-sashes, to overflow deep eaves gutters,
to be a brackish brook in the streets. . . . And the wind began
to take things. Two elms on High Street leaned at an angle six
impossible feet farther than trees can lean—recovered—leaned
again, from the very roots, pushed up the roots themselves, heaved
the roots against the bricks, against the curbing, against the
asphalt. And, roots and all, they fell—not fast, inexorably. The

[1] From "Wind and Fury," by Frances Woodward. *The Atlantic
Monthly*, December, 1938. Reprinted by permission of *The
Atlantic Monthly.*

first one lay square across the street and the second one crashed down on Miss Malvina Parton's house, through the roof, shearing, all groaning branch and odor of bruised leaves, through the dining room, through the clutter which was furniture and porcelain and crystal chandelier. . . .

Four-thirty. Quarter to five. There was nothing in the world but wind and salt rain. Nothing else in your mind, nothing else to occupy you. The whole universe was just a loud whirling. People struggled over the unfamiliar clutter of their own yards, careless of the falling trees, on errands of enormous and evasive importance, seeing other people moving, but seeing them as isolated strangers. Deaf, unable to make the other deaf hear you, whirled and soaked outdoors, impotent and shaken inside houses. . . .

Expository Description

At the beginning of this chapter a distinction was made between expository writing—which appeals first of all to the "understanding"—and descriptive and narrative writing—which strive "to evoke reality by calling up an image."

It is proper to note that expository writing sometimes borrows the methods of literary description to such an extent that, except in its emphasis upon matter-of-fact, it becomes almost indistinguishable from description. For this borderline kind of writing the name *expository description* may be appropriately used. The following description of Lake Erie is of this type. Although it is heavily weighted with matter-of-fact detail, it is so organized as to emphasize a dominant image ("Lake Erie is intimate and wayward"), and it ascribes to the lake characteristics that imply individuality and even "personality." In such devices the author follows the method of the literary naturalists (Thoreau, Burroughs, Muir) rather than of the man of science or commerce. It is not at all the description that a geologist would write; nor is it, on the other hand, the kind of "blurb" that an advertising agency would compose for a pamphlet intended for tourists.

LAKE ERIE[1]   *By Harlan Hatcher*

LAKE ERIE is intimate and wayward. Of the five Great Lakes, Erie is fourth in size, for only Ontario is smaller. Cool, deep Lake Superior is the Amazonian one; Lake Huron, wild and island-studded, is next; and Lake Michigan with her gates of gold at

[1] From *Lake Erie* by Harlan Hatcher, copyright © 1945, used by special permission of the publishers, the Bobbs-Merrill Company, Inc.

Mackinac and the silver finger of Green Bay to break her regular coast line is third. Lake Erie is less than half the size of Lake Michigan—9,940 square miles in area, or a little larger than the state of Vermont.

The long grain ships, loaded to the Plimsoll line with wheat from the elevators at Duluth, ease down the Livingstone Channel past Grosse Isle and out into the western corner of Lake Erie. They swing round at the Detroit River Lighthouse and head east-southeast through Canadian waters and keep between the buoys north of Ontario's Pelee Island. They usually have the wind behind them as they clear Point Pelee and Southeast Shoal Light and steer straight for Buffalo, about 200 miles away at the eastern corner. They are never far from land. At the widest point the Erie shores are only fifty-eight miles apart; at the narrowest they are separated by only twenty-eight miles. In her present state Erie is shallow. Her thirty-foot-depth contour is regularly about a mile offshore. Her harbors were filled with sand which has had to be dredged out. Her deepest soundings are but 210 feet, 1,000 feet less than Superior's, and 660 feet less than Michigan's; and her mean depth is only ninety feet. That is one reason why Erie is vagrant and temperamental rather than brooding.

Erie's waters stir in this shallow bowl. Perhaps saucer is more accurate than bowl. Or, if we think of its shape as well as it shallowness, it is more like a trencher of the era of Hawkins and Drake. The water from Lake Huron pours hurriedly under the International Bridge at Sarnia and Port Huron. It flows down the St. Clair River, widens lazily out into a lake in the St. Clair Flats, then gathers itself together again at Windmill Point to become the Detroit River. It moves on down the twenty-eight-mile-long channel past Detroit and Windsor, flows around the islands in the river, and spreads imperceptibly into the long narrow basin that confines Lake Erie. At the Buffalo end it is channeled once more and funneled out through the Niagara River under the Peace Bridge past Squaw Island at the rate of 215,000 cubic feet each second. Then it runs rapidly down to spill over the Niagara Falls into Lake Ontario, about 330 feet below the level of Lake Erie.

The northern half of Lake Erie belongs to Canada, the southern half to the United States. The province of Ontario borders its entire north shore—all the way from Fort Erie at the entrance to the Niagara, and Port Colborne where the ships enter the Welland Canal, to Amherstburg and Windsor on the Detroit River. The province is shaped exactly like a big Indian arrowhead with its point aimed straight at Detroit. The Erie shore forms one edge of the point, the Huron shore the other; the Niagara escarpment is its southern barb, the Saugeen Peninsula the northern. Its neck is the narrow strip of land between Georgia Bay and the Hamilton wedge of Lake Ontario. Only a few small creeks and one fairly large river—the Grand—flow down from the north into Lake Erie. The Thames River is only a few miles away, but it runs parallel to the Lake Erie shore and empties into Lake St. Clair. The regular shore line is broken only by the jutting peninsulas of Point Pelee and Rondeau in the west and Long Point in the east.

The big port cities of the province are on Georgia Bay and Lake Ontario at the neck of the arrowhead. The Erie shore line on Canada's side is a bit lonely. There are no great cities, few roaring mills, no giant elevators, fine harbors, long wharves or railroad yards on the north coast. The smokestacks of the International Nickel Company's plants loom up against the sky at Port Colborne where they are clearly visible from the steamship lanes on Lake Erie. The stacks and brick walls of the mills at Amherstburg rise high above the texas houses of freighters going up the Amherstburg Channel in the Detroit River. Between them are beaches and summer resorts, quiet towns and fishing villages, marshes, forestry stations, and provincial parks.

The proud cities with crowded harbors and teeming lake commerce are on the United States side. The recital of their names sounds like a Walt Whitman chant to the muscular new world whose sons and daughters have erected monuments fit for these states: Detroit, Toledo, Sandusky, Huron, Vermilion, Lorain, Cleveland, Fairport, Ashtabula, Conneaut, Erie, Dunkirk, and Buffalo. These are the harbors where the great ships come and go. These cities receive the stupendous tonnage of ore and grain that flows in an ever-increasing river of red and gold from Duluth and Superior, Ashland and Marquette, Chicago and Milwaukee. And from seven of these cities flows back an equally stupendous tonnage in the unending black river of coal for the thriving cities of the Upper Lakes.

EXERCISES AND SUGGESTIONS FOR THEMES

In selecting subjects for descriptive themes, prefer objects, persons, scenes with which you are familiar. Avoid the grander aspects of nature—mountains, canyons, the ocean—unless you can contrive to visualize your subject as a whole in some striking way (as Thoreau, for example, views Cape Cod as the bared and bended arm of Massachusetts) and relate it to human activity. If you choose a historical subject either for matter-of-fact or imaginative description, you must do enough research to give your description authenticity.

1. In the preceding selections from Arnold Bennett and James

Joyce, how does the point of view used by each author influence the choice of details and the language? Develop, by careful analysis, the suggestions given on pages 327 and 332.

2. Make a study of the use of figurative language—both brief and extended figures of speech—in the selections from Whitman, Hardy, and Warren. To what extent does the effect of these descriptions depend upon figurative rather than matter-of-fact language?

3. In the selection "At the American Consulate," what contrasts and shadings does Elizabeth Spencer use to obtain her effect? Does she make use of "dominant impression"?

4. By what means does Frances Woodward in "Hurricane" intensify and maintain the dominant impression? What differences of mood, pace, and diction do you find in the selections from Hardy, Warren, Woodward, and Spencer?

5. Taking material from your own experience or from recent direct observation, write a description of an interior in which you follow the method of James Joyce in "The Misses Morkan's Drawing-Room"; of an exterior scene in which you use the method of Hardy in "The Valley of the Great Dairies"; or of Warren in "Army Breaking Camp."

6. Write a description in which you make use of dominant impression and appeal to the senses through verbal imagery. Some suggestions: Cabin Among Live Oaks; Canyon Picnic; Milking Time in a Modern Dairy; Tree Experts at Work; Fog at Twilight; Motel at 6 P. M.; Blonde Fashion Model; Old Man on Snowshoes; Pumping Station on the Pipe Line; Ice Ballet; Jet Liner Taking Off; Suburban Family at Early Breakfast; Girl on Water Skis.

7. Write a description in which you use some physical or mental characteristic of an individual in a symbolic way (as in Melville's "Captain Ahab").

2. NARRATIVE WRITING

Technically, a narrative is a sequence of connected actions, so told or written as to make a complete and satisfying whole. The action related is generally physical: it represents what happens during some significant portion of human experience, and there can be no experience that is not in some way or other physical experience. Nevertheless, mental experience is also significant. The external acts of human beings are often less important than their mental states, and the true meaning of men's deeds can often best be told by relating what goes on in their heads. The action of a narrative can therefore be mental in part. In some modern narratives the action is almost wholly mental.

The other basic features of narrative are a character or

characters, the person or persons whose experience is being related; a place or "scene," since the events related must have a particular location; and a time-sequence, for events take place in a definite order of time. Last, the narrative must have a meaningful organization—a form. To use Aristotle's terms, it must have a beginning, a middle, and an end. The parts of the general action must be so connected, and the circumstantial details so chosen, as to make a complete whole.

Accounts of happenings in nature—the eruption of a volcano, the action of a storm—may seem to be narratives that lack a character. But such events acquire significance only as they are seen in relation to human experience. A volcanic eruption, if it is to be reported, must be witnessed by a human observer. It acts upon people and institutions as do hurricanes, forest fires, floods. In order to state in narrative form the meaning of purely natural events, we tend to ascribe human traits to natural phenomena. In Homer's *Iliad* the hero Achilles fights the angry river-god, Scamander. Modern writers avoid this ancient type of mythologizing and personification. But in the short novel *Typhoon,* Joseph Conrad, by oblique dramatic means, builds the typhoon into a "character" that displays an almost personal animus towards ship and crew. In stories of animals, from Aesop's fables to Kipling's *Jungle Books,* wild animals are endowed with human speech, human virtues, human frailties.

But the true nature of narrative is better revealed when we compare it with other types of writing. An explanation of a process is in some respects like a narrative, since it represents events in sequence and refers to human experience. But it is likely to be impersonal and nondramatic, as in the following selection from a very practical handbook of sailing:

> The inexperienced should stay ashore when sailing gets hard. For others, a stiff breeze can be fun—and safe, too—provided a few precautions are taken. If the wind is very strong and the boat is being overpowered, the sail area should be reduced by reefing. To put in a reef, the mainsail must be dropped and, if feasible, an anchor put out. The loose sail is then furled neatly along the foot and secured by reef points, which are short strings sewn into the canvas at intervals. Reef points should be tied under the sail, above the sail track; at tack and clew the sail is lashed directly to the boom. Once the reef has been taken, the shortened mainsail is raised

again. Many small sailboats have roller reefing gear, which
is a godsend. Simply turning a crank rotates the boom and
wraps the sail like a paper towel on a roll. When the breeze
pipes up, it is also wise to secure all loose objects below, such
as dishes, coolers, anchors, instruments, and whisker or spinnaker poles. All unnecessary gear in the cockpit—cushions,
cameras, binoculars—should also go below. On deck every
movable object should be lashed down. Halyards must be
cleared so that sails can be lowered immediately, should conditions warrant. The crew is going to get wet; so it should don
foul-weather gear and sit on the high side of the boat to
counteract the heel of the hull. But not so far out as to inspire
that chilling call, "Man overboard."—BILL WALLACE, *Sailing.*[1]

Here a series of actions is set forth—in a somewhat lively
and interesting manner. But the purpose of the quasi-narrative is expository. Dramatic interest is subordinated to the
overwhelming necessity of giving clear and accurate information. The persons of the quasi-narrative are taken for
granted; they are merely an impersonal "crew." The only
suggestion of dramatic conflict between men and sea comes
in the last sentence.

In the following passage from Conrad's story of a fine ship
caught in a severe storm, the focus of interest is on the actions of men responding to the tremendous onslaught of the
sea. Even the ship becomes an animate "character."

The thirty-second day out of Bombay began inauspiciously.
In the morning a sea smashed one of the galley doors. We
dashed in through lots of steam and found the cook very wet
and indignant with the ship: "She's getting worse every day.
She's trying to drown me in front of my own stove!" He was
very angry. We pacified him, and the carpenter, though
washed away twice from there, managed to repair the door.
Through that accident our dinner was not ready till late, but
it didn't matter in the end because Knowles, who went to
fetch it, got knocked down by a sea and the dinner went over
the side. Captain Allistoun, looking more hard and thin-
lipped than ever, hung on to full topsails and foresail, and
would not notice that the ship, asked to do too much, appeared to lose heart altogether for the first time since we
knew her. She refused to rise, and bored her way sullenly
through the seas. Twice running, as though she had been

[1] Reprinted by permission of Golden Press, Inc., and The Ridge
Press from *Sailing: A Golden Handbook.* Copyright 1961 by
Golden Press, Inc.

blind or weary of life, she put her nose deliberately into a big wave and swept the decks from end to end. As the boatswain observed with marked annoyance, while we were splashing about in a body to try and save a worthless washtub: "Every blooming thing in the ship is going overboard this afternoon."—JOSEPH CONRAD, *The Nigger of the Narcissus.*[1]

True narrative, whatever its subject matter or course of development, will center on individuals in a particular situation, involved in a series of definite occasions that take shape in a unified dramatic pattern. If the narrative deals with *actual* persons, it will then be "matter-of-fact" narrative and adhere faithfully—as in history, autobiography, and reminiscence—to actual events. If it deals with imagined characters and situations, it will be fiction, and the author will shape events to fit his theme and purpose.

The point is that, even though the basic materials of exposition and narrative may often be the same, the treatment is not at all the same. The governing principle of narrative differs from the governing principle of fiction.

The Illusion of Reality

A narrative seeks to convey, as expository writing does not, the *illusion of reality*. By special means, used only in the various forms of narrative, a narrative "re-creates" an actual experience or "creates" an imaginary one in such a way that the reader is persuaded to conceive himself as present at the scene of the action, watching, in his mind's eye, the progress of events, and drawn into them as a sympathetic participant. He shares in the emotions of the characters. He identifies himself with their life. He "lives over" the happenings of the narrative. In the technical phrase, he has a vicarious experience.

The composition of a narrative is determined by the author's desire to establish the illusion of reality for the events which he is recounting. Before we consider the means by which the narrative writer accomplishes his end, it is necessary to comment on the nature of the illusion which he is creating. It is not a deception, a trick, a lie. It is an illusion (that is, in the dictionary phrase, "an unreal image, a deceptive appearance") only in the sense that the events being related are not actually occurring at the time of the reading

[1] Reprinted by permission of J. M. Dent & Sons Ltd., London.

of the narrative. A narrative of events is not the same thing as the events themselves any more than a portrait of a beautiful woman is the flesh-and-blood person. When the ghost of Hamlet's father speaks to Hamlet in Shakespeare's play, we know that it is not an actual ghost but an actor, who is speaking lines written centuries ago. When Hamlet dies at the end of the drama, we know that the actor is not dying but is acting a death. A historical narrative of some battle is not the actual battle. What we get from a narrative, as from a play, is a significant representation of something that has happened or that may be imagined as happening. If the author is skillful, we become absorbed in his representation, as we do in the play on the stage. The illusion thus created may well be a high and noble form of reality and thus an aspect of truth. It has this difference from actual experience: that—although actual experience is fleeting, and cannot be recovered once it has gone, and furthermore is rarely intense in character, and may be confusing rather than clear—a narrative of experience gives experience a lasting form, permits it to be recovered and re-experienced in that form by any reader, establishes it forever in a certain degree of intensity, and makes it stand forth clear and precise.

The actual experience of fighting the battle of Thermopylæ was possible only once, to the Greeks and Persians who took part in it. But for centuries readers have relived that battle in the famous account of it given by Herodotus. The events of Poe's story "The Gold Bug" never happened at all; but many readers have had the imagined experience which Poe the story writer contrived that they should have—and always in the exact form in which Poe intended the experience to be imagined.

The Method of Narrative

By what method does the writer of narrative achieve this powerful illusion? The method develops from the narrative writer's differentiation of his subject-matter and from the necessity of dramatizing that subject-matter.

The subject-matter of a narrative is a *situation* affecting one or more characters in such a way that a conflict arises between opposing forces which can be followed to its inevitable or reasonable conclusion. Perhaps it would do equally well to say that the subject-matter is the experience of a character or characters involved in a situation which brings

about an interplay of opposing forces. But it is well to emphasize situation, because the statement of the situation puts the
narrative on its way. The situation also implies the limits of
the action which is to be related, for when the conflict inherent in the situation has been worked out, the end of the
narrative will have been reached. The situation, the characters, the conflict of forces, the development of the conflict
to its logical end—these are the indispensable elements of a
narrative.

What is a narrative situation? Much labor might be ex-
pended without achieving a completely satisfactory definition. It might be defined as a difficulty of some sort that
somehow must be faced by the characters of the narrative.
It is an intrusion of matters incalculable or strange or dis-
concerting into normal human relationships.

Two people eating breakfast in a commonplace way do not
make a situation. If a writer says, "The average American
husband eats breakfast with his wife at some time between
seven and eight o'clock in the morning," that is not a statement of a situation; it is a sociological observation. But if
the writer says, "Not until John had drunk his second cup of
coffee and read the comic strips did he realize that neither
of them had spoken a word since they started on the orange
juice; and now Anne was softly crying into her napkin,"
then we have a situation. We know that trouble is brewing
and that the story of that trouble is about to be told.

How will it be "told"? It will not be told but written. In
a stage drama it will be acted. That is, persons taking the
"parts" of the characters will simulate the action to be related, principally through spoken dialogue, but with some
help, too, from gestures, facial expression, and stage "business." A written—or literary—narrative also simulates an
action, but through the medium of written or printed words.
It "tells" or "describes" or "relates" the action conceived as
taking place.

Literary narrative is much less dependent on dialogue
than the play. In fact, it can dispense with dialogue entirely.
The stage play is limited to the stage and to actually visible
and audible means of representation, but narrative is un-
limited in its range. It can enter the thoughts of the characters while they are speaking, can give the reaction of the
characters to one another and to events, can represent both
their sensations and their ideas. It can shift the time and

place of action at will. It can summon up past action at any relevant point. In one way or another it can interpret the action for the reader.

To convey the significant details of action in this way, so that the struggle of opposing forces is developed and the attention of the reader is directed to the important and meaningful aspects of the action, is a kind of dramatization no less valid than the dramatization of a play. The physical immediacy of the play, which works upon the eyes and ears of an audience, makes it very attractive and absorbing, but that same physical immediacy also limits the play severely. Many of the stage devices for indicating place and interpreting action are very awkward. The "scenery" is all too obviously a painted contrivance. The soliloquy used in a Shakespearean play is a rather clumsy, artificial device for commenting on the action and rendering the thoughts of a character. The literary narrative lacks the immediate physical appeal of the play, but its range is infinitely wider. It can dramatize anything that is relevant to the action. The resources of narrative are so varied that, even though it be read silently, without a speaking voice to give it emphasis, it works powerfully upon the reader's mind. In Sir Philip Sidney's phrase, the narrative writer "holdeth children from play, and old men from the chimney corner."

Other Features of Narrative

A successful narrative must establish *tension* and maintain that tension until a satisfying conclusion is reached. It must be *circumstantial* in its account of events: that is, it must provide enough details to dramatize the action effectively. And it must have a *focus*: that is, the narrative interest must be organized around the fortunes or desires of a single character.

Tension

The tension of narrative is one of its chief distinguishing features. In expository and argumentative writing there is comparatively little tension. Whatever curiosity may be aroused is intellectual curiosity. The reader is informed or persuaded, and the appeal to the emotions, if it is made at all, is a side issue. In narrative the reader's curiosity is emotional. He identifies himself with the characters of the narrative and is impelled to follow the progress of events to their outcome. The opening situation centers his attention upon some conflict of forces. The Green Mountain Boys are preparing to attack Ticonderoga. How will they attack it and will the attack succeed? Daniel Boone has been captured by Indians. Will he escape the torture stake and, if so, when, where, how? Cinderella is sitting alone while her sisters go off to the ball. She would like to go, too, but how can she when she has no gown and no coach? What will happen when, after the fairy godmother has provided these essentials, she arrives at the ballroom, even more gorgeously clad than her sisters?

These are small illustrations of how tension is established. It is maintained by "keeping the reader in suspense," as is commonly said. Technically, this means that the action is developed by a series of incidents or episodes, each of which leads to the one that follows it, and in each of which the struggle of opposing forces shifts into a new phase. These incidents or episodes correspond to the scenes of a play. The narrative writer could not and should not present the whole body of events available to him. He selects from the whole body of events only those which he can represent significantly in a single, unified series. The incident, episode, or "scene" which carries the greatest amount of tension deals, of course, with the decisive event of the series. It will always be near the end of the series and will constitute the "turning point" or "climax" of the action. But each incident will also have its own point of chief tension, which constitutes a minor climax; and each will have, until the decisive moment is reached, its portion of unsolved complication which will lead the reader on to the next incident.

Narratives differ in degree of tension. In some amusing or instructive bit of autobiographical narrative, such as any of us can relate, the struggle between contending forces may not be very grim. The tension will be correspondingly slight. But it must be there if the account is a true narrative. In historical narrative the tension varies with the subject-matter. An account of Pickett's charge at Gettysburg is inherently more exciting than an account of the quarrels in Washington's cabinet. Narratives of fact, which must take their material as they find it, may strive through dramatic means to create a tension sufficient to hold the reader; but if they are mere chronicles, they will have no tension. Narratives of fiction, such as stories and novels, use the device known as plot. Plot is a highly developed means of presenting the struggle of opposing forces and thus of maintaining a high degree of tension.

Circumstantiality

Tension cannot be achieved, and the struggle of opposing forces cannot be presented convincingly, unless the narrative is richly circumstantial. It must explore and set forth in narrative form the particulars which compose the real substance of the action. A narrative without abundant particulars is but a summary, a mere statement of generalities. It is impossible to secure the illusion of reality unless the narrative presents, bit by bit, the significant details of the experience which is being related. Without these, the reader cannot create in his own mind the image of events. In expository and argumentative writing, a generalization will be made and then will be followed by the particulars that illustrate it or validate it—only enough particulars to do that. In narrative, the particulars carry the burden of the narrative. The reader *infers* from the particulars just what is going on and what its "meaning" is. The generalization—if any is intended—is left unstated, for it is the purpose of a narrative to "evoke" the experience, not to explain it or argue about it.

Generalized and Circumstantial Narrative

A distinction must therefore be made between *generalized* narrative and *circumstantial* narrative. A newspaper report of an event (though called a "story" in newspaper parlance) uses generalized narrative. It is in summary form, with relatively few particulars, and these broadly indicated: names, places, times, numbers, and circumstances that can be "featured." The newspaper reporter writes: "Fire, starting at an early morning hour, destroyed an entire block in the business section of North Main Street today." He makes no attempt to "evoke" the experience of the fire. His purpose is to convey authentic information in a condensed form. Accordingly, after some mention of any interesting or tragic features of the occurrence, he names the business houses affected, estimates the financial loss, and of course outlines the efforts of the fire department. History textbooks, because they must compress their accounts of events into relatively small space, resort to generalized narrative. The older British and American novelists—Fielding, Scott, Thackeray,

Cooper—use a considerable amount of generalized narrative, and modern critics sometimes find fault with them on this account. Yet they usually return to circumstantial narrative in time to save the story, and it must be admitted that they, like their contemporaries among the great historians—Gibbon, Macaulay, Prescott—can sometimes make an art of generalized narrative itself.

Indeed, generalized narrative is both legitimate and necessary in transitional passages, in cutbacks and recapitulations, in certain types of matter-of-fact narrative. In fictional narrative it is to be avoided, for only a circumstantial narrative can be truly dramatic.

The principle applies even to short passages. Unless the particulars are set forth vividly, in concrete and specific terms, the texture of the prose will become loose, characterization vague and slack, and the narrative will "talk about" events rather than present them. The good writer does not say: "Then, by the exercise of great ingenuity and tact, our friend persuaded the hotel to cash a check." Instead, he goes at the problem in somewhat this fashion:

> The elevator boy leered insolently, or seemed to, as he flung open the door. Henry ignored him and strode grandly past. He hoped he didn't look as scared as he felt. As he stepped along the thick carpet to the desk, he debated with himself. What was the right technique? Should he throw himself on the mercy of the management? Or just open his checkbook on the marble counter and begin to write, as if cashing a check were something he did anywhere, as a matter of course. Then an idea came to him. . . .

Focus of Narrative

A narrative is not unified as exposition is unified, by close adherence to a topic. Its unity is "dramatic unity," which in part derives from concentration on a limited action, isolated from the confused general welter of events. Equally important in securing dramatic unity is the *focus of the narrative,* sometimes called "angle of narration" or "point of view."

The focus of the narrative is the particular aspect of events toward which the author directs the reader's attention, in order to bring the action into meaningful perspective. Generally it will be the particular character or characters to whom the events are of central importance and through whom, accordingly, a point of reference is established.

In historical narrative and some other kinds of matter-of-fact narrative the action may have such a pattern that, in its very nature, it is centralized. In an account of a battle, attention necessarily centers on the struggle of contending armies, but is likely to focus more narrowly on "our army" rather than that of "the enemy," whose actions are related only with reference to "our army."

Narrowing the focus still further, the author may concentrate on the personality and strategy of the commanding general, who becomes the symbol of the army that he commands. Thus Bruce Catton, in *A Stillness at Appomattox,* frequently uses Grant as his focus in his account of the 1864 and 1865 campaigns of the Army of the Potomac. In Douglas Southall Freeman's massive four-volume *R. E. Lee,* the focus is, even more strictly, the mind of General Lee. Freeman excludes general historical issues and develops his complex account in terms of what Lee knew, thought, guessed, or planned at the time of the events themselves.

In autobiographical narrative the focus is, naturally, the person who is relating his own experience. Historical and biographical narratives require third-person narration. In these the focus will be on the person who is "making history." In fictional narrative the focus becomes involved in the very complex problem of "point of view," which will be discussed in connection with the short story (see pages 365–383).

Types of Narrative

If considered according to their use, narratives may be divided into two classes: dependent and independent. If classified according to content and essential character, they are either narratives of fact or narratives of fiction. A dependent narrative is a narrative inserted into exposition or argument, usually to illustrate or emphasize some point under discussion. Anecdote and incident are the most familiar forms of dependent narrative. An independent narrative is a narrative written to stand alone. Autobiography, biography, history, reminiscent narrative, the folk tale, the short story, the novel—all these are independent narratives.

Here we are concerned with the much more important distinction between narrative of fact and narrative of fiction. Although each of these broad types borrows methods from the other, the types are set apart by differences of subject matter, purpose, and technique. Narratives of fact are concerned with the world of actual happenings. They present real persons and events, and their purpose is above all to give a true and authentic report, with whatever "interpretation" is needed for the sake of clarity. In general they are more straightforward in method than narratives of fiction; but since most authors prefer to interest the reader rather than repel him, we will find that the greatest writers of history, biography, and reminiscence are far from disdaining the arts of narrative when they wish to "recreate" the past. Narratives of fiction, of course, deal with imagined happenings. If they deal with actual happenings, they are more concerned with establishing the "illusion of reality" than with a documentary kind of authenticity or mere historical sequence as such. They practice the art of narrative in its full richness, are often indirect and even symbolical in method rather than straightforward, and are fundamentally dramatic. The tale, the short story, the novel are the principal prose forms of fictional narrative.

Autobiographical and Reminiscent Narrative

Practice in simple and relatively brief narratives of fact is advisable before going on to the more complex and difficult tasks of fictional narrative. In autobiographical and reminiscent narratives the material is ready at hand and the writer can devote his entire attention to narrative technique. In Marquis James's "The Run on the Cherokee Strip," the narrative is retold as the author heard it from his mother and father. James therefore assumes the character of a reporter who, in reminiscent mood, is reproducing, as faithfully as he can, what the original narrators said. The narrative affords opportunities for studying narrative focus; combination of expository, descriptive, and narrative elements; diction; and other aspects of narrative technique.

THE RUN ON THE CHEROKEE STRIP[1] *By Marquis James*

FROM my mother I learned of Papa's own part in the race. It was the kind of story that Mama, with her love of horses, would tell with relish.

Especially for the Run, Papa had bought a race horse in El Reno.

[1] From *The Cherokee Strip* by Marquis James. Copyright 1945 by Marquis James. Reprinted by permission of The Viking Press, Inc.

It was wind-broken but otherwise a sound and strong animal, capable of carrying my father's more than two hundred pounds.

"In his young days your father was a real fancy rider," Mama would say. "And for a man of his size very easy on a horse."

This was no small tribute. My mother was about as accomplished a judge of riding as any woman in our part of the country.

The Run was a young man's undertaking. My father was crowding forty-nine, a good twenty years older than the average man who entered the race on horseback with serious intentions of reaching Enid in time to stake anything. A year and a half of law practice in Old Oklahoma and the Indian nations had made him fairly used to the saddle again. Nevertheless, he took three weeks to condition himself and to find out what he and his horse could do. He knew the ropes well enough to get himself the best possible place on the starting line—smack on the Chisholm Trail, just north of Hennessey, in Old Oklahoma.

You could begin your race anywhere you could get to on one of the four borders of the Strip, which was about a hundred and sixty-five miles east and west by fifty-eight miles north and south. Papa picked the Hennessey section because it lay closest to Enid, which he figured would be *the* town of the Strip. There was also the Trail to follow. It made for easier riding and led straight to the desired townsite. On a prairie, experience is necessary to preserve a sense of direction.

Mama's understanding was that Papa spent about three days and nights on the line, holding his place. The wonder is the wait wasn't longer, considering the premium on places in the neighborhood of the Trail. I have heard men tell of spending three weeks on the line. Probably they were with covered-wagon outfits, but, unless close to water, they must have got pretty tired of it. The sheets of some of the wagons were scrawled with notices of intention such as "Oklahoma or Bust." Substituting "Texas" or "Oregon," the phrase had been western usage for a good fifty years.

The line was patrolled by soldiers to prevent anyone from crossing over before the opening gun. The country had been evacuated by the cattle outfits which formerly leased it from the Indians. Excepting land-office and post-office staffs and soldiers on the site of each county seat, the Strip was depopulated. That was the theory, and it came tolerably close to being the fact. Nobody knows how many sooners did manage to hide out in the promised land before the opening gun was fired, but probably not more than you would find trying to obtain their ends by illegal means in any collection of a hundred thousand persons. . . .

After a man had staked a claim he had to "file" at the nearest land office. In order to file he was required to exhibit an evidence of registration permitting him to make the Run in the first place. Registration slips were issued from booths along the line. It was in no way difficult for a prospective sooner who knew the country to register a week before the Run and sneak up a draw through the thinly patrolled line. He could camp in the blackjacks west of Enid, for instance, and ride out with the first honest comers—as Mr. Wilcox suspected the man in light blue overalls had done. A cavalry troop encamped on the Enid site had reconnoitered the surrounding country for three weeks. Though the lieutenant in command was sure a number of sooners had eluded him they must have formed a minute proportion of the whole body of settlers.

The Hennessey stretch of the line broke five minutes before the official gun. Somebody may have discharged a firearm by accident. My father was in the saddle and ready. Waiting only to see that there was no turning back the tide, he, too, set off, keeping to the Chisholm Trail and reining his horse to a pace it could maintain for fifteen or sixteen miles and have a spurt left for an emergency.

The Chisholm Trail was the name cowmen gave to the Oklahoma section of the Abilene Trail, greatest of the southwestern cattle thoroughfares. It ran from San Antonio, Texas, to the railway terminus at Abilene, Kansas, a distance of eighteen hundred miles. Though little used for cattle drives since the completion of the Rock Island Railroad through the Cherokee Strip in 1889, the famous prairie road was still distinct. Like a carelessly laid ribbon, which your eye would lose in the dips and pick up in the rises of the undulating plain, the Oklahoma part stretched almost due north. On level places it was like several ribbons side by side. These markings were the Trail's core, made by the wheels of chuck wagons, calf wagons, freighters and stages. When wheels and hoofs wore through the sod, creating a "high center," teamsters would start a new road alongside the old. For two or three hundred yards on either side of these ruts the grass had been beaten down by the feet of the cattle. This on level stretches. To ford a stream or cross a draw the Trail narrowed.

The race was going well for my father. At first many riders and some drivers passed him; but this he had counted on. In the fullness of time, without increasing the pace of his horse, he began to pass them. When Papa calculated that he had gone about fifteen miles he was feeling the strain, and his horse was feeling it. Ahead of him were perhaps fifty riders in sight whom he doubted his ability to pass. (Fifty out of fifteen thousand starters from Hennessey.)

Glancing to the east my father saw the top of a distant string of trees. That meant a stream, an asset of great value to a claim: also an asset of great value to my father, who liked trees. They were the thing he missed most on the plains. Turning his horse from the Trail, he crossed the Rock Island track and the bed of a dry creek. He urged his tiring mount up the rise. On the other side he saw only a shallow draw, its naked sides exposing coarse sandy soil tinted from red to orange. Was this a wild-goose chase? Holding a northeast course he made for the next rise. He was traveling over short-grass prairie, knobby-surfaced and with washes of bare red soil: a good place for a horse, especially a tired, wind-broken horse, its breath coming in rasps, to stumble; and no good to grow anything. The crest of this second rise brought a welcome sight into view: the trees he had seen from the Trail; and beyond them more trees.

Watering the roots of the first trees was a disappointing stream, hardly more than a yard wide. (This was the driest season of the year.) But better trees were beyond; indeed, what seemed a veritable forest, in terms of the plains, with a noble green mass—surely the granddaddy of all the trees in the Cherokee Strip—dominating the whole. The first of these trees were soon reached. The creek was wider there: ten or twelve feet across. The illusion of a grove had been caused by the way the creek curved in the shape of an S. Papa followed the course of the stream in the direction of the Big Tree. He crossed the creek once and found that, to reach the Big Tree, he must cross again or double a loop. He started to double the loop and came upon a steep ravine. The ravine wouldn't have been much to head, but Papa didn't take the time. Precious minutes had been lost feeling his way toward the trees. On the next fold of the prairie to the south other riders were in sight. Unseen riders might be coming up the draws. Papa wanted that creek, flowing in the shape of an S with good bottom land in the loops; and he wanted the Big Tree. His horse barely made the steep yonder side of the ravine. A few rods farther, at the high point on our pasture, luxuriant in red top, Papa dismounted and set his stake on what proved to be the Southeast Quarter of Section 17, Township 22, Range 6 West of the Indian Meridian.

It was 12:53 P.M., September 16, 1893. As the Hennessey line had broken at 11:55, my father had ridden seventeen miles in fifty-eight minutes without injuring his horse. A note of pride would touch Mama's tone as she spoke the last four words. Walter Cook covered eighteen miles in fifty to fifty-five minutes—he carried no watch and no one seems to have timed him exactly. . . .

Having driven his stake, Papa set up a pup tent to which he affixed an American flag. I would like to know who gave him that flag, which was the last thing my father would ever have thought of taking along. From the tent he could see almost the entire claim, barring the East Draw and where the bluff hid the creek. He removed his saddle and, leading his horse so it would cool off gradually, began a tour of his estimated boundaries—probably looking for the markers. In the East Bottom he found a man preparing to set his stake. Cases of lead poisoning developed from a number of such meetings that day. But this man was no sooner or intentional claim-jumper. He rode with Papa to higher ground and took a look at the tent and the flag.

"You beat me out, stranger," said the man. "I'll strike eastward a piece."

Papa wished him luck, and never saw the man again.

EXERCISES

1. What is the focus of narrative in "The Run on the Cherokee Strip"? Does it shift at any point?

2. What parts of the selection are expository rather than narrative?

3. At what point does the narrative become dramatic? What elements of conflict constitute the dramatic action?

4. Identify instances of generalized narrative; of sharply circumstantial detail.

5. Look up the word *sooner* in the dictionary. What are its original and its derived meanings? What words in the narrative may be thought to have such a local or special historical meaning as not to be familiar to the average reader? Is Marquis James open to criticism for using them without giving the reader a definition? Or has he a right to assume that the reader knows the words or can readily discover their meanings and historical associations?

Narratives of Fiction: Imagined Action and Historical Background

A familiar type of fictional narrative is found in novels and stories that have a definite *locus* as to time and place, but that deal with wholly imaginary characters taking part in imagined actions. Ernest Hemingway's *A Farewell to Arms* deals with events and scenes of World War I in Italy; but though, to this extent, it has a "historical background," it is not a "historical novel." No historical personages appear in the novel. The hero, Lieutenant Frederick Henry, an American officer serving with an ambulance unit on the Italian front, is an imaginary character; and although he is represented as being present during certain actual events—such as the retreat from Caporetto—the story of his participation in those events is fictional, not "real" in a matter-of-fact sense. The "historical background" itself—the significant physical details of war on the Italian front—may seem "authentic," and doubtless Hemingway took pains to render them accurately. But his real interest is in presenting the significant aspects of one tragic human experience—the truth of art, rather than the truth of history. In the following selection, which is well worth study as a closely organized and subtly presented narrative unit, we see Lieutenant

Henry at a critical moment, when he is mistaken for a
German agent in Italian uniform and is in danger of being
summarily shot by the Italian battle police who are striving
to check the retreat. Note that the action is related from the
Lieutenant's point of view, both in terms of his physical
sensations and of his mental reactions to the crisis. Suspense is maintained, great tension is created, and the
extreme isolation of the Lieutenant is emphasized by his
being depicted as one of a group of officers who, in turn, are
harshly examined and inexorably sentenced to be shot.

THE LIEUTENANT ESCAPES[1]   *By Ernest Hemingway*

BEFORE daylight we reached the bank of the Tagliamento and followed down along the flooded river to the bridge where all the
traffic was crossing.

"They ought to be able to hold at this river," Piani said. In the
dark the flood looked high. The water swirled and it was wide.
The wooden bridge was nearly three-quarters of a mile across, and
the river, that usually ran in narrow channels in the wide stony
bed far below the bridge, was close under the wooden planking.
We went along the bank and then worked our way into the crowd
that were crossing the bridge. Crossing slowly in the rain a few
feet above the flood, pressed tight in the crowd, the box of an
artillery caisson just ahead, I looked over the side and watched
the river. Now that we could not go our own pace I felt very tired.
There was no exhilaration in crossing the bridge. I wondered what
it would be like if a plane bombed it in the daytime.

"Piani," I said.

"Here I am, Tenente." He was a little ahead in the jam. No one
was talking. They were all trying to get across as soon as they
could: thinking only of that. We were almost across. At the far
end of the bridge there were officers and carabinieri standing on
both sides flashing lights. I saw them silhouetted against the sky-
line. As we came close to them I saw one of the officers point to a
man in the column. A carabiniere went in after him and came out
holding the man by the arm. He took him away from the road. We
came almost opposite them. The officers were scrutinizing every
one in the column, sometimes speaking to each other, going forward to flash a light in some one's face. They took some one else
out just before we came opposite. I saw the man. He was a lieutenant-colonel. I saw the stars in the box on his sleeve as they
flashed a light on him. His hair was gray and he was short and fat.

[1] Reprinted with the permission of Charles Scribner's Sons from
A Farewell to Arms by Ernest Hemingway. Copyright 1929
Charles Scribner's Sons; renewal copyright © 1957 Ernest
Hemingway.

The carabiniere pulled him in behind the line of officers. As we came opposite I saw one or two of them look at me. Then one pointed at me and spoke to a carabiniere. I saw the carabiniere start for me, come through the edge of the column toward me, then felt him take me by the collar.

"What's the matter with you?" I said and hit him in the face. I saw his face under the hat, upturned mustaches and blood coming down his cheek. Another one dove in toward us.

"What's the matter with you?" I said. He did not answer. He was watching a chance to grab me. I put my arm behind me to loosen my pistol.

"Don't you know you can't touch an officer?"

The other one grabbed me from behind and pulled my arm up so that it twisted in the socket. I turned with him and the other one grabbed me around the neck. I kicked his shins and got my left knee into his groin.

"Shoot him if he resists," I heard some one say.

"What's the meaning of this?" I tried to shout but my voice was not very loud. They had me at the side of the road now.

"Shoot him if he resists," an officer said. "Take him over back."

"Who are you?"

"You'll find out."

"Who are you?"

"Battle police," another officer said.

"Why don't you ask me to step over instead of having one of these airplanes grab me?"

They did not answer. They did not have to answer. They were battle police.

"Take him back there with the others," the first officer said. "You see. He speaks Italian with an accent."

"So do you, you——," I said.

"Take him back with the others," the first officer said. They took me down behind the line of officers below the road toward a group of people in a field by the river bank. As we walked toward them shots were fired. I saw flashes of the rifles and heard the reports. We came up to the group. There were four officers standing together, with a man in front of them with a carabiniere on each side of him. A group of men were standing guarded by carabinieri. Four other carabinieri stood near the questioning officers, leaning on their carbines. They were wide-hatted carabinieri. The two who had me shoved me in with the group waiting to be questioned. I looked at the man the officers were questioning. He was the fat gray-haired little lieutenant-colonel they had taken out of the column. The questioners had all the efficiency, coldness and command of themselves of Italians who are firing and are not being fired on.

"Your brigade?"

He told them.

"Regiment?"

He told them.

"Why are you not with your regiment?"

He told them.

"Do you not know that an officer should be with his troops?"

He did.

That was all. Another officer spoke.

"It is you and such as you that have let the barbarians onto the sacred soil of the fatherland."

"I beg your pardon," said the lieutenant-colonel.

"It is because of treachery such as yours that we have lost the fruits of victory."

"Have you ever been in a retreat?" the lieutenant-colonel asked.

"Italy should never retreat."

We stood there in the rain and listened to this. We were facing the officers and the prisoner stood in front and a little to one side of us.

"If you are going to shoot me," the lieutenant-colonel said, "please shoot me at once without further questioning. The questioning is stupid." He made the sign of the cross. The officers spoke together. One wrote something on a pad of paper.

"Abandoned his troops, ordered to be shot," he said.

Two carabinieri took the lieutenant-colonel to the river bank. He walked in the rain, an old man with his hat off, a carabiniere on either side. I did not watch them shoot him but I heard the shots. They were questioning some one else. This officer too was separated from his troops. He was not allowed to make an explanation. He cried when they read the sentence from the pad of paper, and they were questioning another when they shot him. They made a point of being intent on questioning the next man while the man who had been questioned before was being shot. In this way there was obviously nothing they could do about it. I did not know whether I should wait to be questioned or make a break now. I was obviously a German in Italian uniform. I saw how their minds worked; if they had minds and if they worked. They were all young men and they were saving their country. The second army was being reformed beyond the Tagliamento. They were executing officers of the rank of major and above who were separated from their troops. They were also dealing summarily with German agitators in Italian uniform. They wore steel helmets. Only two of us had steel helmets. Some of the carabinieri had them. The other carabinieri wore the wide hat. Airplanes we called them. We stood in the rain and were taken out one at a time to be questioned and shot. So far they had shot every one they had questioned. The questioners had that beautiful detachment and devotion to stern justice of men dealing in death without being in any danger of it. They were questioning a full colonel of a line regiment. Three more officers had just been put in with us.

"Where was his regiment?"

I looked at the carabinieri. They were looking at the new-comers. The others were looking at the colonel. I ducked down, pushed between two men, and ran for the river, my head down. I tripped at the edge and went in with a splash. The water was very cold and I stayed under as long as I could. I could feel the current swirl me and I stayed under until I thought I could never come up. The minute I came up I took a breath and went down again. It was easy to stay under with so much clothing and my boots. When I came up the second time I saw a piece of timber ahead of me and reached it and held on with one hand. I kept my head behind it and did not even look over it. I did not want to see the bank. There were shots when I ran and shots when I came up the first time. I heard them when I was almost above water. There were no shots now. The piece of timber swung in the current and I held it with one hand. I looked at the bank. It seemed to be going by very fast. There was much wood in the stream. The water was very cold. We passed the brush of an island above the water. I held onto the timber with both hands and let it take me along. The shore was out of sight now.

THE SHORT STORY

A universally acceptable definition of a short story probably cannot be devised. It is one of the most variable forms in our literature and is continually escaping from the bounds to which critics would confine it. Nevertheless, like other literary forms, it has its principles of composition. These principles can be defined and illustrated. They are not rules, to be memorized and applied mechanically, but true principles—guiding principles—derived from the successes and failures of experienced writers.

The range of the short story, both in subject matter and form, is best realized from close study of numerous good examples. But some characteristic features of the short story can be described. These mark the approximate limits of the *genre*.

The Oral Tale and the Short Story

The short story as we know it developed out of the traditional oral tale. For centuries a tale was *told*—and is still often told today—to a listening audience, generally by a practiced teller of tales. Its medium was the spoken word.

It was carried in memory and transmitted from person to person, and from generation to generation, through the remembered spoken words only. Very largely because of these conditions, the folk tale as it survives to us follows highly conventional patterns. Its subject-matter is nearly always either marvelous or humorous. It is never "realistic" or "psychological" as our written stories are. The folk tale delights in queer or unusual events, beyond the pale of ordinary life. But its characters are not developed as individuals; they are stereotypes. A folk tale that treats ordinary life is likely to be a humorous story or one that illustrates some homely truth. Its plot is nearly always sharply defined and involves physical action. The characters are symmetrically arranged. The development of the plot is likely to be symmetrical also. The folk tale delights in—and needs—a great deal of repetition, an obvious balance, easy and conventional formulas of description and narration. It is prone to indulge in generalized narrative. Since its medium is the spoken word, its idiom is colloquial. It speaks with the tongue of the people, not in the refined and self-conscious language of the educated classes.

The short story first appears in literary history as a conscious and somewhat refined imitation of the folk tale. The next historical stage is a deliberate exploitation and extension of the narrative effects of the folk tale. As soon as artists realize that their medium is the written or printed word and no longer the spoken word, they explore the literary possibilities of the form. The tale then becomes the short story, a completely literary type, adapted to reception by readers rather than by listeners. This process of historical development is analogous in many respects to the development of the so-called literary ballad from the true folk ballad. An old story like Irving's "Rip Van Winkle" is a literary imitation of a folk tale. It stands in about the same relationship to the folk tale as Walter Scott's "Proud Maisie" would stand to a true ballad. But a story by William Faulkner or Ernest Hemingway is at as great a distance from the folk tale as Keats's "La Belle Dame Sans Merci" and Coleridge's "The Ancient Mariner" are from an old ballad like "Sir Patrick Spens."

The oral tradition, however, is very powerful. In the United States, where it has remained a part of our culture, the popularity of the oral tale has been so great that even to this day it strongly influences the practice of many very sophisti-

cated writers of short stories. These "borrow" some of the
effects of the folk tale, especially its racy colloquial idiom.
But they borrow and exploit only those effects which can be
used successfully in a *written* story. If they are skillful in
so doing, the story is a success. On the other hand, *a naïve
or unconscious echoing* of the method of the folk tale—as
in the use of a rigid plot, generalized narrative, stereotyped
characters, forced ending—is a certain mark of the novice,
and is sure to bring failure. Such practice does violence to
the medium of the short story—the written word.

The first limitation upon the short story is, therefore, its
medium. It can achieve only those effects which can
be achieved by written or printed words. Although it may
be read aloud—and should be—it does not depend, for its
survival, upon recital from memory by tale tellers. It cannot
rely upon voice, gestures, rhythmic repetition to supply a
meaning that is not in the written words themselves. Its
arrangement is a literary arrangement, not an oral arrangement.

The second important limitation upon the short story is
its shortness. This term has no valid reference to "length"—
that is, mere number of words. It refers to dramatic concentration. In his choice of subject the story writer elects
to deal with a situation that can be explored dramatically
within brief limits—brief as compared with the limits of a
novel or a novelette. The story will then be sufficiently "long"
to round out the conflict in the narrative, yet not so short
as to leave it insufficiently dramatized. At the upper limit of
"length" are stories like Conrad's "Heart of Darkness" or
Henry James's "Daisy Miller." At the lower limit are some
of the stories of Chekhov, O. Henry, Hemingway, which
occupy but a few pages of print.

All the devices of narrative appear in the short story, but
as conditioned by the dramatic concentration of its form. It
has only the kind of plot, the degree of characterization, the
thematic emphasis, the amount of setting that can be
adapted to its brief limits. A highly complicated plot is not
practicable in a short story. The interest of the story is
generally concentrated in one or two characters, not divided
among many. Elaborate symbolic treatment, though possible,
should ordinarily be avoided. Leisurely description is out of
order except in stories of "atmosphere" in which setting
becomes a dominant element.

Point of View in the Short Story

The point of view from which a story is related must be clearly evident throughout. In modern times it has become an important technical device which has undergone much development and refinement in the hands of various masters of prose fiction.

In a strictly technical sense, there are only two basic types of point of view: (1) the *omniscient* or impersonal point of view; (2) the *limited* or personal point of view. In a story written from the omniscient point of view the author assumes the role of an all-seeing, all-knowing observer who, without declaring his identity or speaking in the first person, relates in objective fashion all the events of the story. In a story written from a limited point of view, the author presents the story as if it were being told from the point of view of someone who has observed the action or is either an important or minor participant in the action. Balzac's "Christ in Flanders," Stephen Crane's "The Open Boat," Stephen Vincent Benét's "The Devil and Daniel Webster" are examples of stories that use the omniscient point of view. Poe's "The Fall of the House of Usher" and Sherwood Anderson's "I'm a Fool" are examples of the limited or personal point of view.

In practice there are various refinements in the use of these two main types. An author may focus his omniscience mainly upon one principal character as the center of the action, but not without an occasional shift to some other character's point of view. Such shifting, however, would hardly be practicable in any but rather long stories and is frowned upon by modern story writers. In stories with a limited point of view, a first person narrator may be handled in at least two ways. The narrator of the story may be (1) either a mere observer of the action, not a participant, or (2) a character who is both a participant and an observer. Furthermore, third person narration may be used in a story with a limited point of view when the focus is consistently and exclusively upon a character who is, in Henry James's term, the "central intelligence"—that is, the participant-observer through whose experience the reader is made to realize the action of the story. But such a character is not the narrator of events. This method combines the sharp focus of the limited point of view with the freedom of the omniscient method. In Poe's "The Fall of the House of Usher" a minor character is narrator; in "The Telltale Heart" the narrator is the principal character. In Henry James's "Daisy Miller" a Europeanized American, Winterbourne, is both witness and, in a real sense, an indirect cause of tragedy.

The omniscient point of view offers by far the widest range of possibilities, since it permits a great variety of persons and events and a broad perspective on the human scene. But the freedom it allows may create difficulties. The author may be tempted to wander too far. The story may become diffuse or prolix. Or, still worse, he may fall into the vice so much deplored by modern critics, of intruding his own personality and prejudice into what is supposed to be an impersonal account. He becomes, in short, the Visible Author of the older British and American novels and stories, butting into his story with preachments and comments, or perhaps with a more disguised intrusion.[1]

The Visible Author belongs to the days of Scott, Dickens, and Thackeray. In those days it was fashionable to address the "dear reader," and to begin an incident with some such flourish as this: "Let us now follow the bewitching Miss X—— into her boudoir and discover the effect of Mr. Y——'s cruel trifling with her affections." Such things are not done in stories of the twentieth century—not seriously. The author of today must be an Invisible Author. If he intrudes and becomes a Visible Author, even for a moment, the dramatic effect is spoiled, just as if, in a play, the author were to enter upon the stage and instruct the audience about what the actors are doing and saying.

Modern writers of fiction take care to remain "invisible"— that is, not to intrude or seem to intrude an obviously biased interpretation into the narrative. Sometimes they are so anxious to prune away any semblance of an imposed interpretation that their narratives become exceedingly spare and noncommittal. In Hemingway's "The Killers" we are given only the most simple particulars of action and dialogue. The reader must give very shrewd attention to the particulars if he is to discover what the story is about.

When the limited point of view is used, the author automatically becomes invisible, because he is bound to represent the course of events strictly from the point of view of the character chosen as narrator-participant or narrator-observer. A consistent form of dramatization is thus obtained by

[1] See Joseph Warren Beach, *The Twentieth Century Novel,* and Percy Lubbock, *The Craft of Fiction.*

natural means. The author will represent the action and setting only in terms of the narrator's—or leading character's—awareness of them. The words and actions of other characters, the interpretation of events, the interplay of motives, the clash of forces will be rendered exclusively from one point of view.

The limited point of view thus affords a principle of selection which makes the composition of the story relatively easy as compared with the composition of a story from an omniscient point of view. It is as if the author need not take full responsibility for deciding what to say, or how much to say. His narrator-participant or narrator-observer takes that responsibility. The story then, in a fashion, "tells itself."

If the narrator's or principal character's view of events is fumbling and imperfect, that is not the author's fault. The narrator's imperfections may even be used to the advantage of the story, for he may unconsciously reveal, or may be made to reveal, more than he seemingly intends. The reader, quick to seize such unconscious revelation, will take pleasure in his superiority over the narrator. He will then exercise independent judgment upon the events related by the narrator; and thus the author, although bound to the limited point of view, will have some of the advantages of the omniscient point of view, without its handicaps. In the first sentence of Poe's "The Telltale Heart" the narrator says: "True!—nervous,—very, very dreadfully nervous I have been and am! but why *will* you say that I am mad?" The reader knows or suspects that this narrator, who is also the principal character, is indeed mad. With this superior knowledge he is able to exert objective judgment upon the extraordinary recital of events that follows.

The limited point of view also has its disadvantages. The limitation upon what can be seen and heard narrows the range of the story. Only one person's thoughts can be revealed. One person's motives, judgments, desires, prejudices are always in the foreground, and we get a "firsthand" account of events only within those limits. All the rest is "second hand": it must be inferred or comes to the reader with the coloring of the narrator's views. Most modern writers are ready to accept these possible losses because the limited point of view affords them a device for obtaining clear, sharp dramatization, for bringing the entire story into focus, and for organizing its action and establishing its tone.

Point of View: A Summary

The following outline indicates the principal ways in which point of view is used in prose fiction.

1. *Omniscient Point of View.* Third person narration.
   a. No identifiable narrator. All-knowing, all-seeing author moves at will from character to character, mind to mind. Objective and impersonal passages of description or interpretation; but earlier authors may become "visible" in intrusive commentary.
   b. No identifiable narrator. Focus on one principal character as center of action, but not exclusively from his point of view.
2. *Limited Point of View.*
   a. First person narration, in which narrator is observer of action rather than participant.
   b. First person narration in which narrator is participant in action as either a principal character or a minor figure.
   c. Third person narration. Focus on one person as "central intelligence" with exclusive use of his point of view. Invisible author.

Other Features of the Short Story

The major difficulties involved in the composition of a short story center in two questions: (1) *What is the story about?* (2) *Whose story is it?* Only when the author is able to answer those questions will he be able to shape his story— that is, to answer such related questions as: Where ought I to begin? How shall I end the story? What point of view shall I use? What arrangement of events is best? What special technical means shall I use?

The question, *What is the story about?* directs attention to the central meaning, or theme, of the story. Stated in an another form, it is: What aspect of human experience is revealed by the struggle between contending forces that is depicted in this story? The answer to this question gives the "theme" of the story—the "idea" it contains, the possible "generalization" or "truth" to which all the elements of the story contribute. Poe had in mind such a thematic, unifying organization when he wrote, in his criticism of Hawthorne's *Twice-Told Tales*, his famous statement of what he believed to be the great main principle of story-writing:

A skilful literary artist has constructed a tale. If wise, he has not fashioned his thoughts to accommodate his incidents; but having conceived, with deliberate care, a certain unique or single *effect* to be wrought out, he then invents such incidents—he then combines such events as may best aid him in establishing this preconceived effect. If his very initial sentence tend not to the outbringing of this effect, then he has failed in his first step. In the whole composition there should be no word written, of which the tendency, direct or indirect, is not to the one pre-established design.

Kipling's story "The Man Who Was" is not "about" a polo game, or a Russian officer's love of strong drink, or the conflict between Russian and British imperialism on the Indian frontier, although all those matters are a part of the scheme of the story. It is about the power of regimental tradition in the British army—tradition which developed a loyalty so strong that it could survive the extremest trials. This habit of loyalty also meant loyalty to Great Britain, and the survival of loyalty in that poor wreck, "the man who was," suggests to us, indirectly and symbolically, something very important about human nature itself. Every part of the story contributes to this theme.

The second question—*Whose story is it?*—relates to what has been called "the focus of character."[1] The answer to this question determines who is to be the *protagonist,* or main character, of the story—that is, the person to whom the events related are of crucial importance. The selection of the protagonist may also influence, or even determine, the point of view of the story. Naturally the question *Whose story is it?* also identifies the characters and forces that are either "for" or "against" the main character. The principal force or character that is "against" the main character is the *antagonist.*

Once an author has answered these two fundamental questions, he is in a position to control the direction of his story and to shape it so that every detail will fall into its right place and will bear its right relationship to every other detail. Writing the story should then become a process of exploring a human situation in such a way that its meaning will be revealed dramatically. It should *not* be a process of imposing upon events a forced schematic arrangement (an artificial "plot") which is not inherent in the events themselves. Good

[1] As in Brooks and Warren, *Understanding Fiction,* pp. 586–588.

stories are not "made up." Rather they are discovered or apprehended by those who have the capacity for seeing events in a dramatic form. To write a story is to unfold its dramatic nature and to disentangle it from all that is irrelevant.

The *beginning* of a story is extremely important, not merely because it must be so devised as to engage the reader's attention, but also because it fixes the point in time at which a situation is already sufficiently developed to be capable of being dramatized within relatively brief limits. The end must be implied in the beginning—must be latent in it. The point at which to take hold of a story must therefore be a significant point, relatively near the end of the series of events to be set forth. The beginning will necessarily involve a certain amount of "exposition"—that is, the place, the time, the characters must somehow be identified, and the reader must be put in possession of enough information to enable him to answer for himself the questions, *Who? When? Where?* In a skilful dramatic rendition much of this information will be conveyed by inference. It is not necessary for the author to indulge in direct explanation. No definite rule can be laid down, however. The student will do well to consider and analyze the methods of beginning a story that are used by good writers. Generally, he will find, they launch the reader, in the classic phrase, *in medias res.*

The story should then proceed, as if by its own motive power and not by artificial contrivance, through the stages of the action. These, as has been said, will be incidents linked one to another like scenes in a play. They should develop and steadily heighten the tension created through the dramatic revelation of the opening events. The story must move step by step as the struggle of contending forces is dramatized. What the story writer is rendering by such means may be called, in technical terms, the *complication.* It proceeds until the narrative reaches a decisive moment—the *climax* of the story. Generally the climax will be fairly near the end of the story and will be followed by a scene or two which will constitute the *denouement,* or dramatic conclusion, of the story. In some stories climax and denouement coincide.

According to its dominant tendency, a story may be either a plot story, a character story, or, less often, a story of setting or "atmosphere." But such terms indicate emphasis only. There can be no plot without characters and setting; and no character can be dramatized without at least the vestiges of a narrative design. The basic elements appear in combination. Each is supported by the others.

The prose idiom of a short story is a narrative idiom, which does not resemble the idiom of exposition and argumentation. What it is like can best be learned from close examination of good stories. Again, no general rules can be laid down. The idiom of narrative prose, like the idiom of poetry, achieves its results more through suggestion than through explicit statement. It may seem very matter-of-fact and simple, but it is likely to imply much more than it explicitly says. The story writer, obliged to seek dramatic concentration, must weight his prose with meaning, even when he chooses to speak, as he often does, in the vocabulary of an unlettered person. For him no less than for the poet every word must count, and every word must ring with overtones. He must use not one word too many and yet must have exactly enough. He must catch the inflection of the voice he would render. He must be avid to discover how in sheer words the movement of life may be represented. He must watch the "pace," or rhythm, of his prose. He must deal in images, not in abstractions and generalities. He should avoid needless elaboration and fear undue complexity of construction. The sentences of narrative prose are likely to be straightforward and uncomplicated. They are not clogged with the subordinations and reservations found in expository prose.

The most important thing of all in story writing is to have a story to tell. If you have a story, it is possible to write that story. Yet you may not discover what that story really is or how it ought to be written until you have not only written it but rewritten it—perhaps several times.

THE LAST DAY IN THE FIELD[1] *By Caroline Gordon*

THAT was the fall when the leaves stayed green so long. We had a drouth in August and the ponds everywhere were dry and the water courses shrunken. Then in September heavy rains came. Things greened up. It looked like winter was never coming.

"You aren't going to hunt this year, Aleck?" Molly said. "Remem-

---

[1] "The Last Day in the Field" is reprinted with permission of Charles Scribner's Sons from *The Forest of the South* by Caroline Gordon. Copyright 1935 Charles Scribner's Sons.

ber how you stayed awake nights last fall with that pain in your leg."

In October light frosts came. In the afternoons when I sat on the back porch going over my fishing tackle I marked their progress on the elderberry bushes that were left standing against the stable fence. The lower, spreading branches had turned yellow and were already sinking to the ground but the leaves in the top clusters still stood up stiff and straight.

"Ah-ha, it'll get you yet!" I said, thinking how frost creeps higher and higher out of the ground each night of fall.

The dogs next door felt it and would thrust their noses through the wire fence scenting the wind from the north. When I walked in the back yard they would bound twice their height and whine, for meat scraps Molly said, but it was because they smelt blood on my old hunting coat.

They were almost matched liver-and-white pointers. The big dog had a beautiful, square muzzle and was deep-chested and rangy. The bitch, Judy, had a smaller head and not so good a muzzle but she was springy-loined too and had one of the merriest tails I've ever watched.

When Joe Thomas, the boy that owned them, came home from the hardware store he would change his clothes and then come down the back way and we would stand there watching the dogs and wondering how they would work. They had just been with a trainer up in Kentucky for three months. Joe said they were keen as mustard. He was going to take them out the first good Saturday and he wanted me to come along.

"I can't make it," I said. "My leg's worse this fall than it was last."

The fifteenth of November was clear and so warm that we sat out on the porch till nine o'clock. It was still warm when we went to bed towards eleven. The change must have come in the middle of the night. I woke once, hearing the clock strike two and felt the air cold on my face and thought before I went back to sleep that the weather had broken at last. When I woke again towards dawn the cold air slapped my face hard. I came wide awake, turned over in bed and looked out of the window. The sun was just coming up behind a wall of purple clouds streaked with amber. As I watched, it burned through and the light everywhere got bright.

There was a scaly bark hickory tree growing on the east side of the house. You could see its upper branches from the bedroom window. The leaves had turned yellow a week ago. But yesterday evening when I walked out there in the yard they had still been flat, with green streaks showing in them. Now they were curled up tight and a lot of leaves had fallen to the ground.

I got out of bed quietly so as not to wake Molly, dressed and went down the back way over to the Thomas house. There was no one stirring but I knew which room Joe's was. The window was open and I could hear him snoring. I went up and stuck my head in.

"Hey," I said, "killing frost!"

He opened his eyes and looked at me and then his eyes went shut. I reached my arm through the window and shook him. "Get up," I said. "We got to start right away."

He was awake now and out on the floor, stretching. I told him to dress and be over at the house as quick as he could. I'd have breakfast ready for us both.

Aunt Martha had a way of leaving fire in the kitchen stove at night. There were red embers there now. I poked the ashes out and piled kindling on top of them. When the flame came up I put some heavier wood on, filled the coffeepot and put some grease on in a skillet. By the time Joe got there I had coffee ready and had stirred up some hot cakes to go with our fried eggs. Joe had brought a thermos bottle. We put the rest of the coffee in it and I found a ham in the pantry and made some sandwiches.

While I was fixing the lunch Joe went down to the lot to hitch up. He was just driving the buggy out of the stable when I came down the back steps. The dogs knew what was up, all right. They were whining and surging against the fence, and Bob, the big dog, thrust his paw through and into the pocket of my hunting coat as I passed. While Joe was snapping on the leashes I got a few handfuls of straw from the rack and put it in the foot of the buggy. It was twelve miles where we were going; the dogs would need to ride warm coming back.

Joe said he would drive. We got in the buggy and started out, up Seventh street, on over to College and out through Scufftown. When we got into the nigger section we could see what a killing frost it had been. A light shimmer over all the ground still and the weeds around all the cabins dark and matted the way they are when the frost hits them hard and twists them.

We drove on over the Red River bridge and out into the open country. At Jim Gill's place the cows had come up and were standing there waiting to be milked but nobody was stirring yet from the house. I looked back from the top of the hill and saw that the frost mists still hung heavy in the bottom and thought it was a good sign. A day like this when the earth is warmer than the air currents is good for the hunter. Scent particles are borne on the warm air; and birds will forage far on such a day.

It took us over an hour to get from Gloversville to Spring Creek. Joe wanted to get out as soon as we hit the big bottom there but I held him down and we drove on through and up Rollow's hill to the top of the ridge. We got out there, unhitched Old Dick and turned him into one of Rob Fayerlee's pastures—I thought how surprised Rob would be when he looked out and saw him grazing there—

put our guns together and started out, with the dogs still on leash.

It was rough, broken ground, scrub oak with a few gum trees and lots of buckberry bushes. One place a patch of corn ran clear up to the top of the ridge. As we passed along between the rows, I could see the frost glistening on the north side of every stalk. I knew it was going to be a good day.

I walked over to the brow of the hill. From there you could see off over the whole valley—I've hunted over every foot of it in my time—tobacco land, mostly. One or two patches of cowpeas there on the side of the ridge. I thought we might start there and then I knew that wouldn't do. Quail will linger on the roost a cold day and feed in shelter during the morning. It is only in the afternoon that they will work out well into the open.

The dogs' whining made me turn around. Joe had bent down and was about to slip the leashes. "Hey, boy," I said, "wait a minute."

I turned around and looked down the other side of the hill. It looked better that way. The corn land of the bottoms ran high up on to the ridge in several places there and where the corn stopped there were big patches of ironweed and buckberry. I stooped and knocked my pipe out on a stump.

"Let's go that way," I said.

Joe was looking at my old buckhorn whistle that I had slung around my neck. "I forgot to bring mine," he said.

"All right," I said, "I'll handle 'em."

He unfastened their collars and cast off. They broke away, racing for the first hundred yards and barking, then suddenly swerved. The big dog took off to the right along the hillside. The bitch, Judy, skirted a belt of corn along the upper bottomlands. I kept my eye on the big dog. A dog that has bird sense knows cover when he sees it. This big Bob was an independent hunter. I could see him moving fast through the scrub oaks, working his way towards a patch of ironweed. He caught the first scent traces just on the edge of the weed patch and froze. Judy, meanwhile, had been following the line of the corn field. A hundred yards away she caught sight of Bob's point and backed him.

We went up and flushed the birds. They got up in two bunches. I heard Joe's shot while I was in the act of raising my gun and I saw his bird fall not thirty paces from where I stood. I had covered a middle bird of the larger bunch—that's the one led by the boss cock—the way I usually do. He fell, whirling head over heels, driven a little forward by the impact. A well-centered shot. I could tell by the way the feathers fluffed as he tumbled.

The dogs were off through the grass. They had retrieved both birds. Joe stuck his in his pocket. He laughed. "I thought there for a minute you were going to let him get away."

I looked at him but I didn't say anything. It's a wonderful thing
to be twenty years old.

The majority of the singles had flown straight ahead to settle
in the rank grass that jutted out from the bottom land. Judy got
down to work at once but the big dog broke off to the left, wanting
to get footloose to find another covey. I thought of how Gyges, the
best dog I ever had—the best dog any man ever had—used always
to want to do the same thing, and I laughed.

"Naw, you won't," I said. "Come back here, you scoundrel, and
hunt these singles."

He stopped on the edge of a briar patch, looked at me and
heeled up promptly. I clucked him out again. He gave me another
look. I thought we were beginning to understand each other better. We got some nice points among those singles and I found him
reasonably steady to both wing and shot, needing only a little control.

We followed that valley along the creek bed through two or
three more corn fields without finding another covey. Joe was
disappointed but I wasn't worrying yet; you always make your
bag in the afternoon.

It was twelve o'clock by this time. We turned up the ravine towards Buck Springs. They had cleared out some of the big trees
on the sides of the ravine but the spring itself was just the same:
the tall sycamore tree and the water pouring in a thin stream over
the slick rocks. I unwrapped the sandwiches and the pieces of cake
and laid them on a stump. Joe had got the thermos bottle out of his
pocket. Something had gone wrong with it and the coffee was stone
cold. We were about to drink it that way when Joe saw a good tin
can flung down beside the spring. He made a trash fire and we
put the coffee in the can and heated it to boiling.

Joe finished his last sandwich and reached for the cake. "Good
ham," he said.

"It's John Ferguson's," I said. I was watching the dogs. They
were tired, all right. Judy had scooped out a soft place between
the roots of the sycamore but the big dog, Bob, lay there with his
forepaws stretched out before him, never taking his eyes off our
faces. I looked at him and thought how different he was from
his mate and like some dogs I had known—and men, too—who
lived only for hunting and could never get enough no matter how
long the day was. There was something about his head and his
markings that reminded me of another dog I used to hunt with
a long time ago and I asked the boy who had trained him. He said
the old fellow he bought the dogs from had been killed last spring,
over in Trigg: Charley Morrison.

Charley Morrison. I remembered how he died. Out hunting by
himself and the gun had gone off, accidentally, they said. Charley

had called the dog to him, got blood all over him and sent him home. The dog went, all right, but when they got there Charley was dead. Two years ago that was and now I was hunting the last dogs he'd ever trained. . . .

Joe lifted the thermos bottle. "Another cup?"

I held my cup out and he filled it. The coffee was still good and hot. I lit my pipe and ran my eye over the country in front of us. I always enjoy figuring out which way they'll go. This afternoon with the hot coffee in me and the ache gone from my leg I felt like I could do it. It's not as hard as it looks. A well-organized covey has a range, like chickens. I knew what they'd be doing this time of day: in a thicket, dusting—sometimes they'll get up in grapevine swings. Then after they've fed and rested they'll start out again, working always towards the open.

Joe was stamping out his cigarette. "Let's go."

The dogs were already out of sight but I could see the sedge grass ahead moving and I knew they'd be making for the same thing that took my eye: a spearhead of thicket that ran far out into this open field. We came up over a little rise. There they were. Bob on a point and Judy, the staunch little devil, backing him, not fifty feet from the thicket. I saw it was going to be tough shooting. No way to tell whether the birds were between the dog and the thicket or in the thicket itself. Then I saw that the cover was more open along the side of the thicket and I thought that that was the way they'd go if they were in the thicket. But Joe had already broken away to the left. He got too far to the side. The birds flushed to the right and left him standing, flat-footed, without a shot.

He looked sort of foolish and grinned.

I thought I wouldn't say anything and then found myself speaking:

"Trouble with you, you try to out think the dog."

There was nothing to do about it now, though, and the chances were that the singles had pitched through the trees below. We went down there. It was hard hunting. The woods were open, the ground heavily carpeted everywhere with leaves. Dead leaves make a tremendous rustle when the dogs surge through them; it takes a good nose to cut scent keenly in such dry, noisy cover. I kept my eye on Bob. He never faltered, getting over the ground in big, springy strides but combing every inch of it. We came to an open place in the woods. Nothing but big hickory trees and bramble thickets overhung with trailing vines. Bob passed the first thicket and came to a beautiful point. We went up. He stood perfectly steady but the bird flushed out fifteen or twenty steps ahead of him. I saw it swing to the right, gaining altitude very quickly, and it came to me how it would be.

I called to Joe: "Don't shoot yet."

He nodded and raised his gun, following the bird with the barrel. It was directly over the treetops when I gave the word and he shot, scoring a clean kill.

He laughed excitedly as he stuck the bird in his pocket. "*Man!* I didn't know you could take that much time!*"

We went on through the open woods. I was thinking about a day I'd had years ago, in the woods at Grassdale, with my uncle, James Morris, and his son Julian. Uncle James had given Julian and me hell for missing just such a shot. I can see him now, standing up against a big pine tree, his face red from liquor and his gray hair ruffling in the wind: "*Let him alone. Let him alone!* And establish your lead as he *climbs!*"

Joe was still talking about the shot he'd made. "Lord, I wish I could get another one like that."

"You won't," I said. "We're getting out of the woods now."

We struck a path that led through the woods. My leg was stiff from the hip down and every time I brought it over the pain would start in my knee, zing, and travel up and settle in the small of my back. I walked with my head down, watching the light catch on the ridges of Joe's brown corduroy trousers and then shift and catch again as he moved forwards. Sometimes he would get on ahead and then there would be nothing but the black tree trunks coming up out of the dead leaves that were all over the ground.

Joe was talking about that wild land up on the Cumberland. We could get up there some Saturday on an early train. Have a good day. Might even spend the night. When I didn't answer he turned around. "Man, you're sweating!"

I pulled my handkerchief out and wiped my face. "Hot work," I said.

He had stopped and was looking about him. "Used to be a spring somewhere around here."

He had found the path and was off. I sat down on a stump and mopped my face some more. The sun was halfway down through the trees, the whole west woods ablaze with light. I sat there and thought that in another hour it would be good dark and I wished that the day could go on and not end so soon and yet I didn't see how I could make it much farther with my leg the way it was.

Joe was coming up the path with his folding cup full of water. I hadn't thought I was thirsty but the cold water tasted good. We sat there awhile and smoked. It was Joe said we ought to be starting back, that we must be a good piece from the rig by this time.

We set out, working north through the edge of the woods. It was rough going and I was thinking that it would be all I could do to make it back to the rig when we climbed a fence and came out at one end of a long field. It sloped down to a wooded ravine, broken ground badly gullied and covered with sedge everywhere except where sumac thickets had sprung up—as birdy a place as ever I saw. I looked it over and I knew I'd have to hunt it, leg or no leg, but it would be close work, for me and the dogs too.

I blew them in a bit and we stood there watching them cut up the cover. The sun was down now; there was just enough light left to see the dogs work. The big dog circled the far wall of the basin and came upwind just off the drain, then stiffened to a point. We walked down to it. The birds had obviously run a bit, into the scraggly sumac stalks that bordered the ditch. My mind was so much on the dogs that I forgot Joe. He took one step too many and the fullest blown bevy of the day roared up through the tangle. It had to be fast work. I raised my gun and scored with the only barrel I had time to peg. Joe shouted: I knew he had got one too.

We stood awhile trying to figure out which way the singles had gone. But they had fanned out too quick for us and after beating around the thicket for fifteen minutes or so we gave up and went on.

We came to the rim of the swale, eased over it, crossed the dry creek bed that was drifted thick with leaves and started up the other side. I had blown in the dogs, thinking there was no use for them to run their heads off now we'd started home, but they didn't come. I walked a little way, then I looked back and saw Bob's white shoulders through a tangle of cinnamon vines.

Joe had turned around too. "Look a yonder! They've pinned a single out of that last covey."

"Your shot," I told him.

He shook his head. "No, you take it."

I went back and flushed the bird. It went skimming along the buckberry bushes that covered that side of the swale. In the fading light I could hardly make it out and I shot too quick. It swerved over the thicket and I let go with the second barrel. It staggered, then zoomed up. Up, up, up, over the rim of the hill and above the tallest hickories. I saw it there for a second, its wings black against the gold light, before, wings still spread, it came whirling down, like an autumn leaf, like the leaves that were everywhere about us, all over the ground.

COMMENTARY

The old hunter of this story, whom Molly addresses as "Aleck," is the principal character in Caroline Gordon's novel, *Aleck Maury, Sportsman,* and in her famous story, "Old Red." The theme is suggested in the unobtrusive, yet quietly powerful title, "The *Last* Day in the Field." Aleck is narrator, and the story is told strictly from his point of view, with no interpretative comment by an omniscient author. Although the story is personal and subjective so far as it follows Aleck's mind, gives his judgments, and renders his sensations, it is "objective" in presentation. All that happens is given in dramatic terms. Here, as in life, the reader must exert his independent judgment to determine the "meaning" of what goes on. What looks like a simple account of an autumn quail-hunt by Aleck and his young friend turns out to be a subtle story of a tragic, though rich and tender, moment when Aleck knows beyond debate that he will hunt quail no more.

Outdoor life, or here more specifically the life of the hunter, is Aleck's master passion. Nowhere does Caroline Gordon say that this is Aleck's dominant characteristic, but he reveals himself as a man who thinks of the weather as a hunter, not a farmer, would. He feels the turn of the season as the dogs do. Against his own better judgment and his wife's objections, he ignores his injured knee and goes on one more hunt. His every act—whether a minor act like preparing early breakfast or a major act like figuring the direction of a quail's flight—is a part of the ordered and sacred ritual of the hunt, which is to him the supreme, the most intense joy of life. He has more of the traditional wisdom of the hunter than he can impart to young Joe Thomas, in whom he sees a replica of himself at an earlier stage of the hunter's career. We realize all this as, bit by bit, Aleck involuntarily discloses the overmastering desire of his being.

But as a man he is subject to the common fate—mortality, the inevitable approach of old age. The immediate obstacle he must overcome is the injured knee, which to a young man might be only a temporary annoyance. To Aleck it brings fatigue, pain, and despair in the midst of the surroundings and actions that have always given him keenest joy. The tragedy is deepened by the contrast between Aleck and his young friend, who has the strength that Aleck lacks. But it is not unbearable tragedy, for we are led to perceive that Joe Thomas is on the way to becoming such a hunter as Aleck has been. When Joe says at the end, as the last quail of the day is about to be flushed, "No, you take it," this act is a chivalrous acknowledgment of Aleck's preeminence—of his triumph as the bird whirls down "like an autumn leaf."

The prose of the story observes an ancient principle: *Ars celare artem* ("The art is to conceal art")—that is, never to permit the technique of the writing to obscure the purpose for which the writing is done. We seem to look "through" the words at the object. Caroline Gordon seems to make no particular effort to "describe" or "characterize," yet we are constantly *there*, in the scene, aware of all its physical aspects and of the movements of the characters. Probably it is an enormous help to the art of the story that we receive it in terms of one man's consciousness. The hunter's view of the "last day" limits the experience that is being rendered, but it affords a practical principle of selection. The details are rich, accurate, sharp, convincing.

With these suggestions in mind, make your own analysis of the story. Give particular attention to the following points.

1. The beginning of the story. Why is this particular "beginning point" chosen? How much "exposition" is given? How are the theme and tone suggested?

2. The division into "scenes" (comparable to the scenes of a play). What are the several scenes or divisions of the story? How are they linked? How is tension created and maintained?

3. What is the decisive moment of the story?

4. Is paragraph four, beginning "Ah-ha, it'll get you yet!" intended to have a slightly symbolic, anticipatory meaning? Point out all passages in the story that have symbolic overtones.

5. As an exercise, write one of the episodes of the story from Joe Thomas' point of view or from an omniscient point of view. Would it be possible to tell the story from the point of view of Molly, Aleck's wife?

INDEX